G000297566

STREE

Northamptonshire

First published in 1999 by

Philip's, a division of
Octopus Publishing Group Ltd
2-4 Heron Quays, London E14 4JP

Second edition 2003
Third impression with revisions 2006
NHPBD

ISBN-10 0-540-08288-0 (pocket)
ISBN-13 978-0-540-08288-9 (pocket)

© Philip's 2006

Contents

III **Key to map symbols**

IV **Key to map pages**

VI **Route planning**

VIII **Administrative and Postcode boundaries**

1 **Street maps** at 2½ inches to 1 mile

240 **Town maps** of Banbury, Buckingham, Rugby and Stamford

242 **Index** of towns and villages

243 **Index** of streets, hospitals, industrial estates, railway stations, schools, shopping centres, universities and places of interest

Digital Data

The exceptionally high-quality mapping found in this atlas is available as digital data in TIFF format, which is easily convertible to other bitmapped (raster) image formats.

The index is also available in digital form as a standard database table. It contains all the details found in the printed index together with the National Grid reference for the map square in which each entry is named.

For further information and to discuss your requirements, please contact Philip's on 020 7644 6932 or james.mann@philips-maps.co.uk

Key to map symbols

III

	Motorway with junction number (22a)
	Primary route – dual/single carriageway
	A road – dual/single carriageway
	B road – dual/single carriageway
	Minor road – dual/single carriageway
	Other minor road – dual/single carriageway
	Road under construction
	Tunnel, covered road
	Rural track, private road or narrow road in urban area
	Gate or obstruction to traffic (restrictions may not apply at all times or to all vehicles)
	Path, bridleway, byway open to all traffic, road used as a public path
	Pedestrianised area
DY7	**Postcode boundaries**
	County and unitary authority boundaries
	Railway, tunnel, railway under construction
	Tramway, tramway under construction
	Miniature railway
Walsall	**Railway station**
	Private railway station
South Shields	**Metro station**
	Tram stop, tram stop under construction
	Bus, coach station

◆	**Ambulance station**
◆	**Coastguard station**
◆	**Fire station**
◆	**Police station**
✚	**Accident and Emergency entrance to hospital**
H	**Hospital**
✛	**Place of worship**
𝒊	**Information Centre** (open all year)
P	**Parking**
P&R	**Park and Ride**
PO	**Post Office**
⋏	**Camping site**
⟱	**Caravan site**
►	**Golf course**
⤬	**Picnic site**
Prim Sch	**Important buildings, schools, colleges, universities and hospitals**
River Medway	**Water name**
	River, weir, stream
	Canal, lock, tunnel
	Water
	Tidal water
	Woods
	Built up area
Church	**Non-Roman antiquity**
ROMAN FORT	**Roman antiquity**
87 / 58	**Adjoining page indicators**

Acad	Academy	Inst	Institute	Recn Gd	Recreation Ground
Allot Gdns	Allotments	Ct	Law Court		
Cemy	Cemetery	L Ctr	Leisure Centre	Resr	Reservoir
C Ctr	Civic Centre	LC	Level Crossing	Ret Pk	Retail Park
CH	Club House	Liby	Library	Sch	School
Coll	College	Mkt	Market	Sh Ctr	Shopping Centre
Crem	Crematorium	Meml	Memorial	TH	Town Hall/House
Ent	Enterprise	Mon	Monument	Trad Est	Trading Estate
Ex H	Exhibition Hall	Mus	Museum	Univ	University
Ind Est	Industrial Estate	Obsy	Observatory	Wks	Works
IRB Sta	Inshore Rescue Boat Station	Pal	Royal Palace	YH	Youth Hostel
		PH	Public House		

■ The small numbers around the edges of the maps identify the 1 kilometre National Grid lines

■ The dark grey border on the inside edge of some pages indicates that the mapping does not continue onto the adjacent page

The scale of the maps on the pages numbered in blue is 3.92 cm to 1 km • 2½ inches to 1 mile • 1: 25344

0	¼	½	¾	1 mile
0	250m	500m	750m	1 kilometre

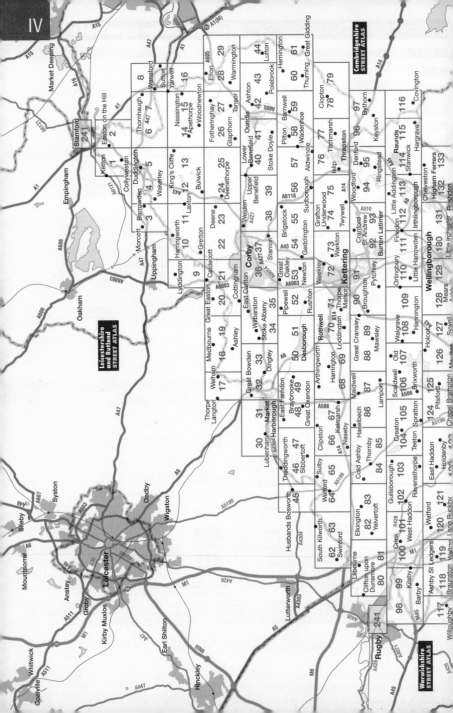

Key to map pages

Map pages at 2½ inches to 1 mile

| 122 |

Scale

0 5 10 15 km

0 5 10 miles

V

Newton Bromswold

Wymington **148 149** Knotting Green

Irchester **146 147** Podington Wollaston

Strixton Hinwick **164 165** Bozeat

Warrington **180**

Great Doddington **144 145** Earls Barton

Castle Ashby **162 163** Grendon Yardley Hastings

Denton **178 179** Olney

Ravenstone **194 195**

Clapham

Bedford

Kempston

Cranfield

Luton

Dunstable

Leighton Buzzard

Bletchley

Milton Keynes

Newport Pagnell

Wolverton

Winslow

Buckingham **240**

Bicester

Banbury **240**

Boothville **142 143** Ecton

Cogenhoe **160 161** Great Houghton

Quinton **176 177** Horton

Hartwell **192 193**

Long Street **206 207** Hanslope

Castlethorpe **218** Cosgrove

Calverton **229**

Church Brampton **140 141** Kingsthorpe

Northampton

Far Cotton **158 159**

Rothersthorpe **174 175** Collingtree

Blisworth **190 191** Roade

Stoke Bruerne **204 205** Alderton

Paulerspury **216 217** Potterspury

Lillingstone Lovell **226 227** Lillingstone Dayrell

Old Stratford **228** Wicken

Thornton **235**

Great Brington **138 139** Harlestone

Harpole **156 157** Kislingbury Nether Heyford

Bugbrooke **172 173** Gayton Pattishall

Astcote **174 175** Tiffield

Greens Norton **202 203** Towcester

Pury End **214 215** Silverstone

Bradford **225**

Whiltton **136 137** Norton Brockhall

Dodford **154 155** Weedon

Everdon **170 171** Farthingstone

Maidford **186 187** Blakesley

Woodend **200 201** Weston Abthorpe

Wappenham **212 213**

Syresham **224** Turweston

Evenley **234**

Daventry **135**

Staverton **152 153** Badby Newnham

Charwelton **168 169**

Hinton **184 185** Eydon Canons Ashby

Moreton Pinkney **198 199** Culworth

Sulgrave **210 211** Greatworth Helmdon

Halse **222 223** Whitfield

Brackley

Hinton-in-the-Hedges **232 233** Croughton

150 151 Helidon

134

Priors Marston **166 167** Priors Hardwick

Byfield **182 183** Aston le Walls

Chipping Warden **196 197** Wardington

Williamscott **208 209** Chacombe Middleton Cheney

Warkworth **219**

Thenford **220 221** Farthinghoe

Kings Sutton **230 231** Charlton Adderbury

Aynho **236 237** Clifton Souldern

Cottisford **239**

238

Wormleighton **181**

Claydon

Southam

Bedfordshire STREET ATLAS

Buckinghamshire STREET ATLAS

Oxfordshire STREET ATLAS

Route planning

Scale

0 1 2 3 4 5 6 7 8km

0 1 2 3 4 5miles

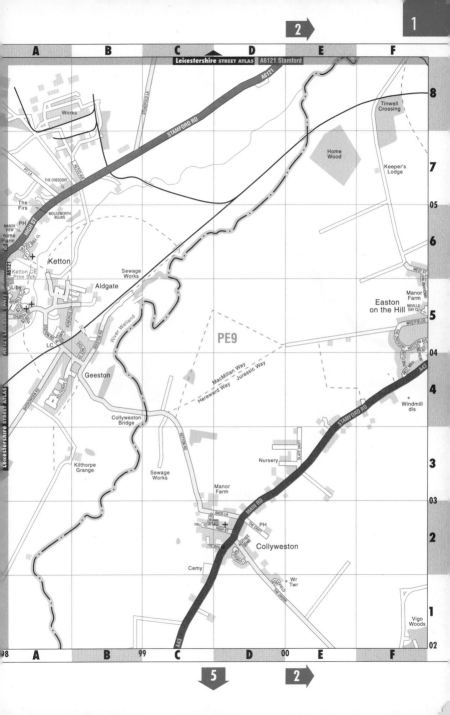

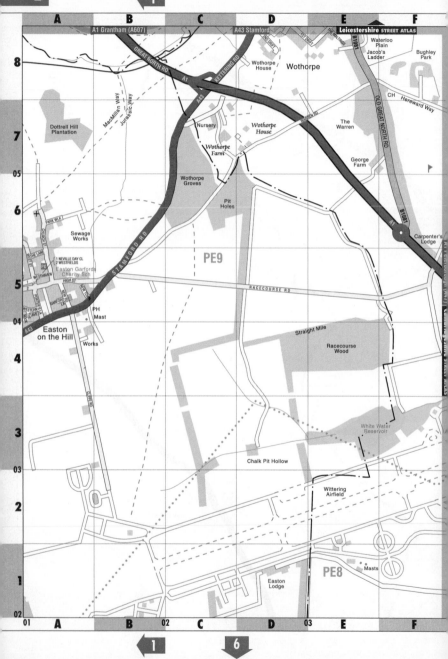

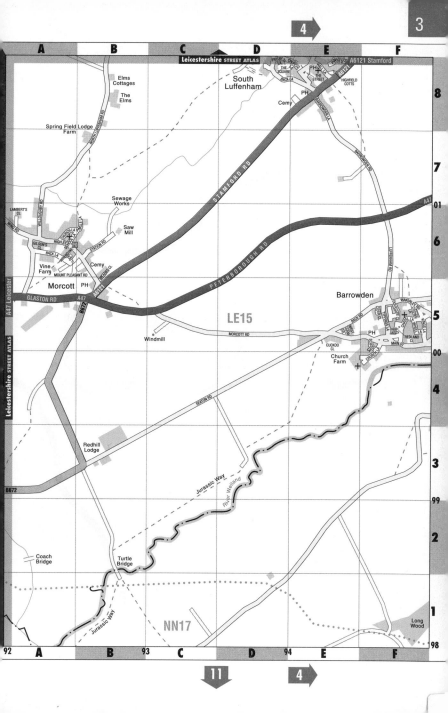

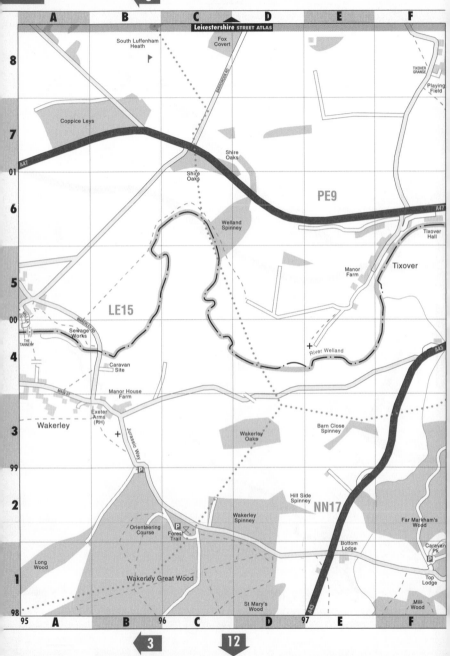

3

Leicestershire STREET ATLAS

8

South Luffenham
Heath

Fox
Covert

TIXOVER
GRANGE

Playing
Field

7

Coppice Leys

Shire
Oaks

01

Shire
Oaks

PE9

6

Welland
Spinney

Tixover
Hall

5

LE15

Manor
Farm

Tixover

00

Sewage
Works

THE
TANNERY

River Welland

4

Caravan
Site

Manor House
Farm

A43

MAIN ST

Exeter
Arms
(RH)

Wakerley

Jurassic Way

Wakerley
Oaks

Barn Close
Spinney

3

99

P

2

Hill Side
Spinney

NN17

Far Markham's
Wood

Orienteering
Course

P
Forest
Trail

Wakerley
Spinney

Caravan
Pk

P

Long
Wood

Bottom
Lodge

Top
Lodge

1

Wakerley Great Wood

St Mary's
Wood

Mill
Wood

98

95   A   96   B   C   97   D   E   F

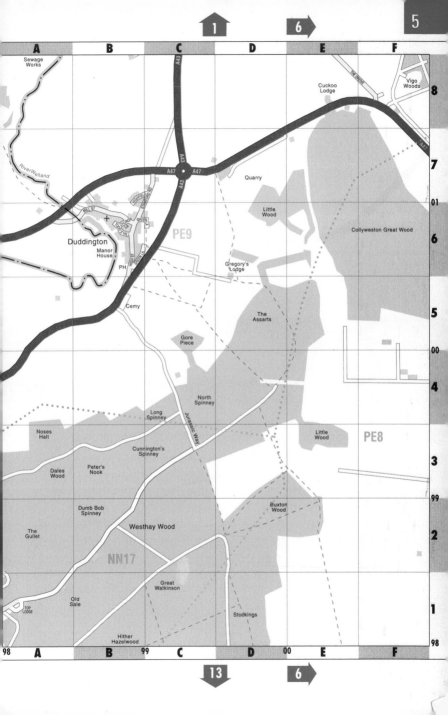

	A	B	C	D	E	F

Sewage Works

River Welland

A43

A47   A47

A47

Cuckoo Lodge

Vigo Woods

THE DROVE

8

Quarry

Little Wood

Collyweston Great Wood

01

7

6

Duddington

CHURCHILL RD

EXPRESS RD

HULL ST

CHURCH HILL

GREEN

HIGH ST

PE9

Manor House

PH

Gregory's Lodge

Cemy

The Assarts

5

Gore Piece

00

North Spinney

4

Long Spinney

Jurassic Way

Noses Halt

Little Wood

PE8

Cunnington's Spinney

Dales Wood

Peter's Nook

3

Dumb Bob Spinney

Buxton Wood

99

The Gullet

Westhay Wood

2

NN17

Old Sale

Great Watkinson

TOP LODGE

Stockings

1

Hither Hazelwood

98

PE9

A47

8

7

01

Rogue
Sale

COLLYWESTON
CROSS ROADS

6

Wittering
Lodge

A4

Easton Hornstocks

Wittering
Coppice

5

Westhay
Cottages

00

PE8

Westhay
Farm

Cross Leys
Farm

4

Upper
Moiseys

Upper
Forty Acre

Cromwell
Sink Sale

Westhay
Lodge

3

Pebblegate
Sale

99

Law's
Lawn

St John's Wood
Farm

2

Rose
Lodge

1

Memorial

98

8

7

01

6

5

00

4

3

99

2

1

98

Nature
Reserve

Deardon
Wood

Lady
Wood

Gazley
Lodge

Beech
Spinney

PE9

Southorpe
Bottom

Wall
Spinney

Crow
Spinney

Sutton
Wood

Research
Centre

PE6

Sacrewell
Lodge

Jubilee
Spinney

WINDGATE WAY

RUSSELL HILL

OLD NORTH RD

Thornhaugh

Sacrewell Farm &
Country Centre

Hereward Way

Top Field
Spinney

Hell
Corner

Mill
House

PE8

Black Swan
Hill

A6118

A47

Heath
House

PE5

BLACK SWAN
SPINNEY

OLD NORTH RD

SWAN LA

PETERBOROUGH RD

PH

NEW CL

Wansford

Nene Way

Mast

River Nene

Deep
Springs

THE DRIFT

RISE WAY

KIRKWOOD

ROBINS FIELD

THE STABLES

OLD LEICESTER RD

WANSFORD RD

YARWELL RD

BRIDGE END

Wansford
Bridge

Hotel

LONDON RD

A6118

GREAT NORTH RD

The
Bungalow

Stibbington
Hall

Sutton

Manor
Farm

MANOR RD

The
Grange

GAZELEY RD

VICARS CL

CHURCH LA

Manor
Farm

Bunkers
Hill

Field Studies
Centre

OLD GREAT NORTH RD

Stibbington

SCHOOL RD

Stibbington
House

ELTON RD

Nene Way

Ship End
Pits

B671

Depot

Sewage
Farm

OLD GREAT NORTH RD

Toll Bar
Spinney

A1

Nene Valley Railway

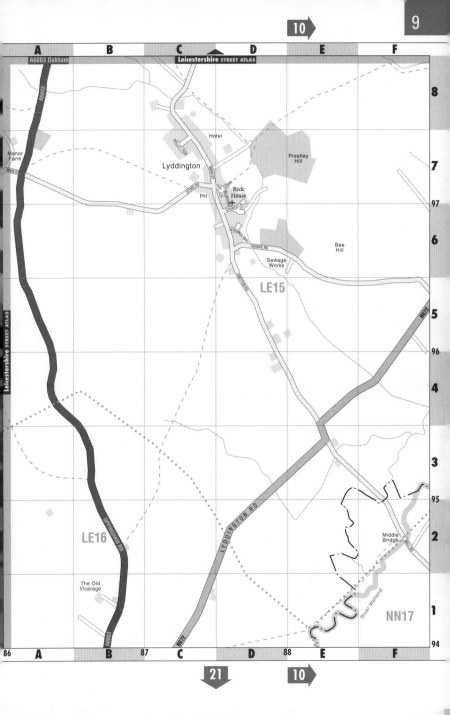

9

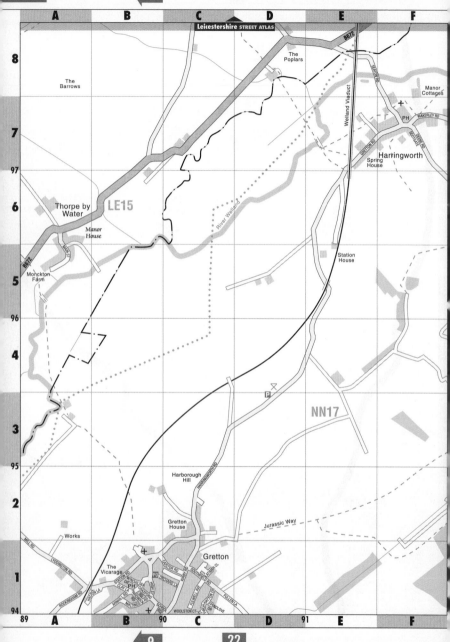

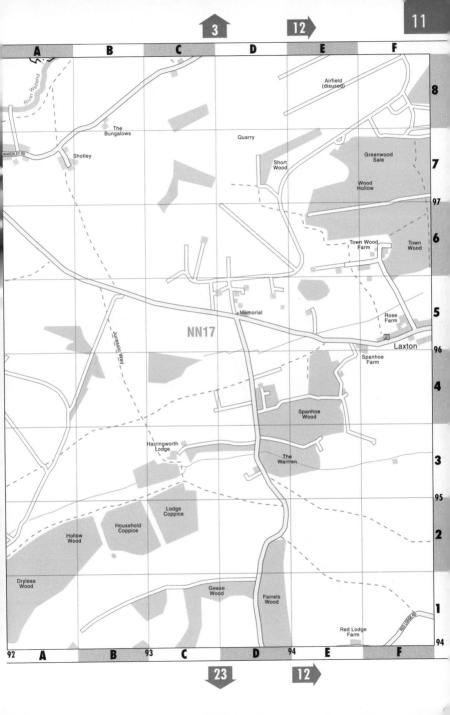

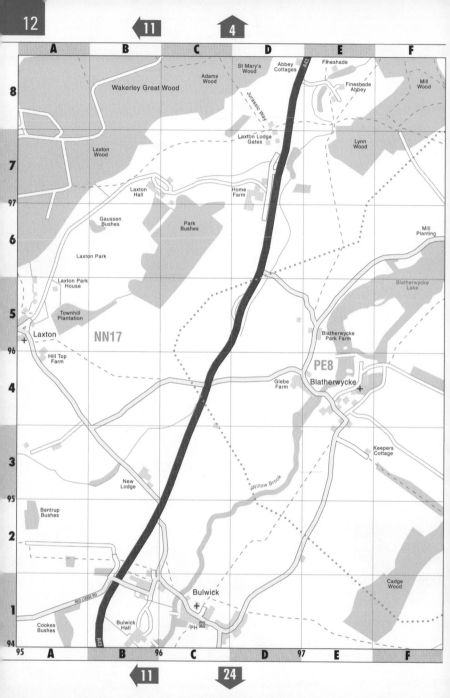

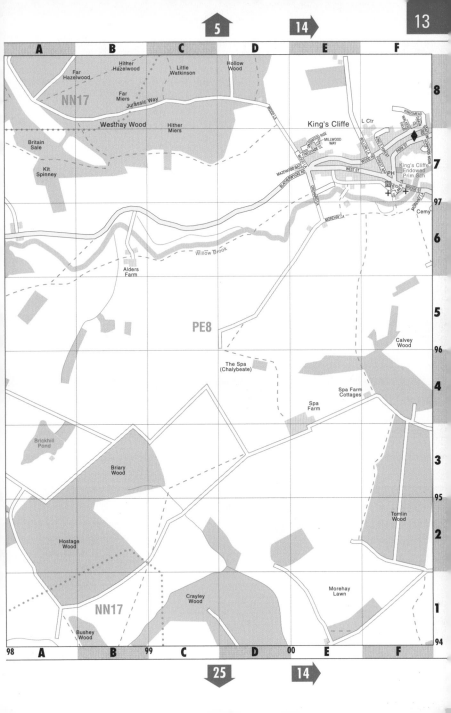

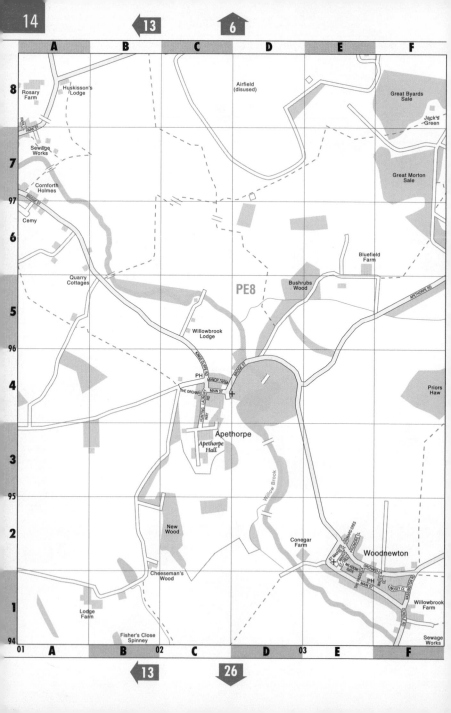

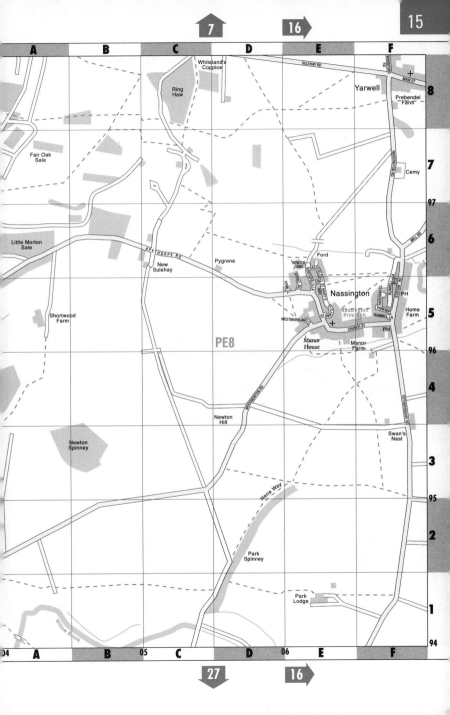

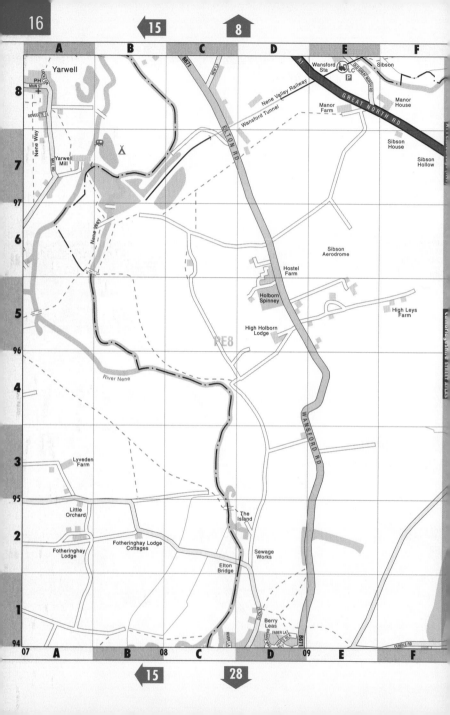

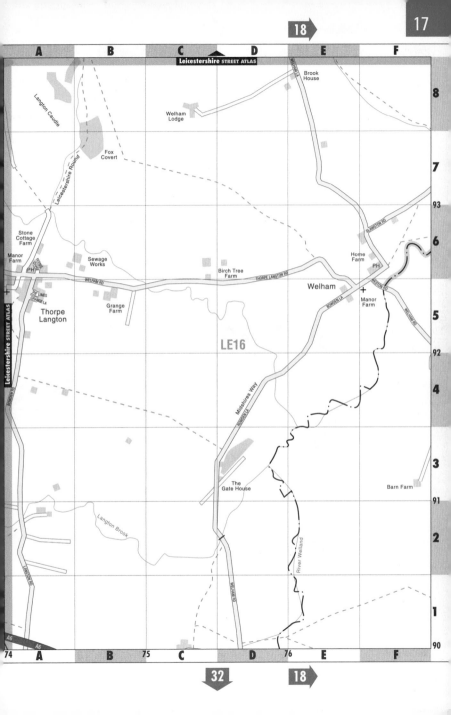

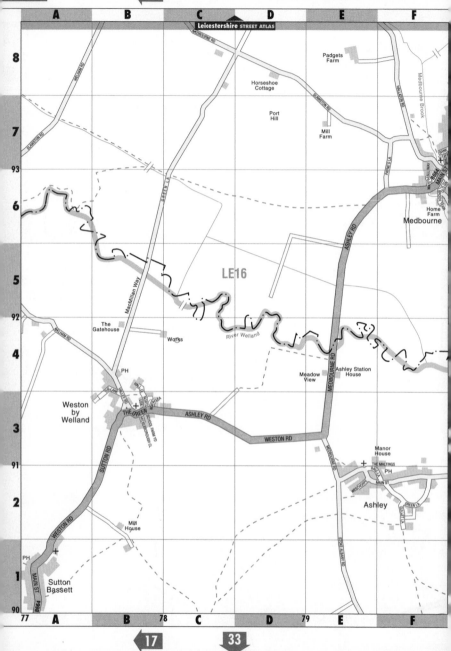

LE16

Medbourne

Padgets
Farm

Horseshoe
Cottage

Port
Hill

Mill
Farm

Home
Farm

Macmillan Way

The
Gatehouse

Works

River Welland

Weston
by
Welland

Meadow
View

Ashley Station
House

PH

THE GREEN

ASHLEY RD

WESTON RD

Manor
House

THE MALTINGS

PH

Ashley

Mill
House

PH

Sutton
Bassett

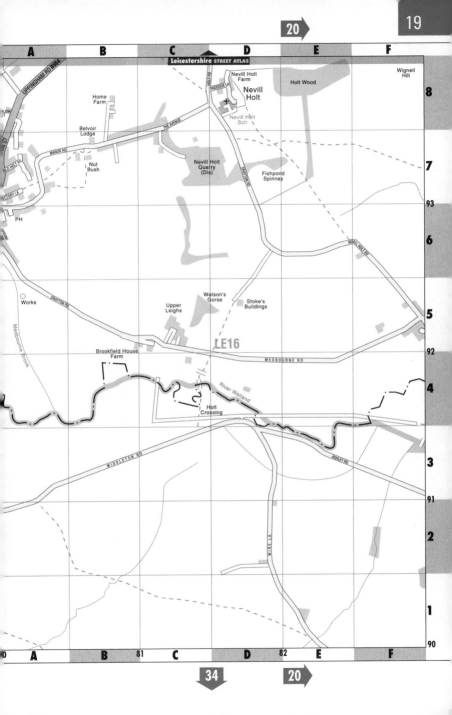

19

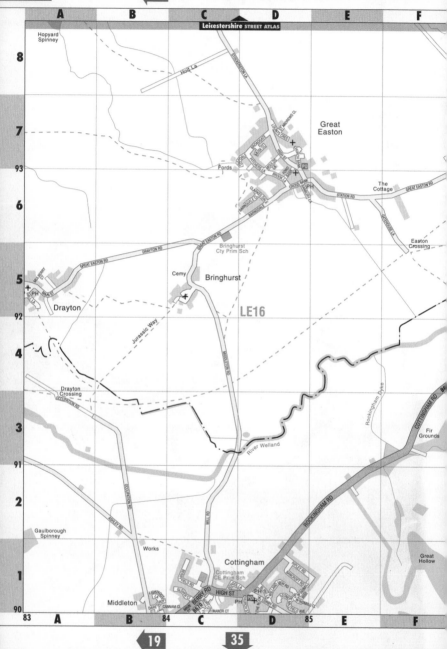

19 35

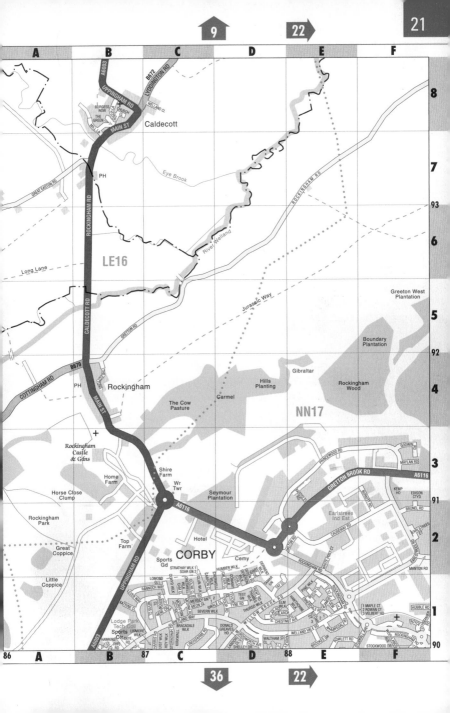

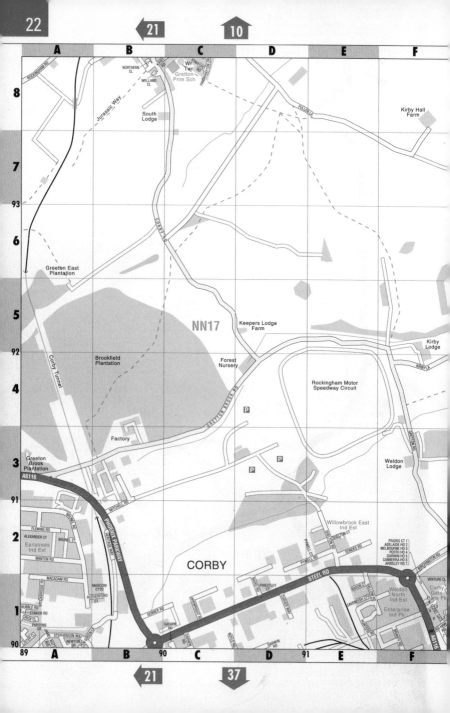

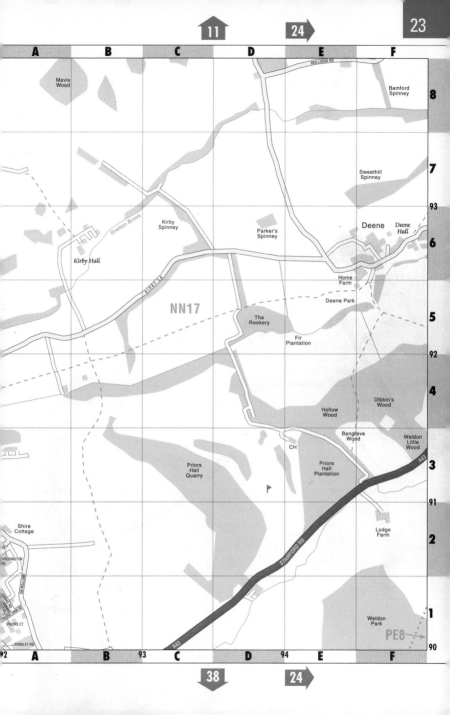

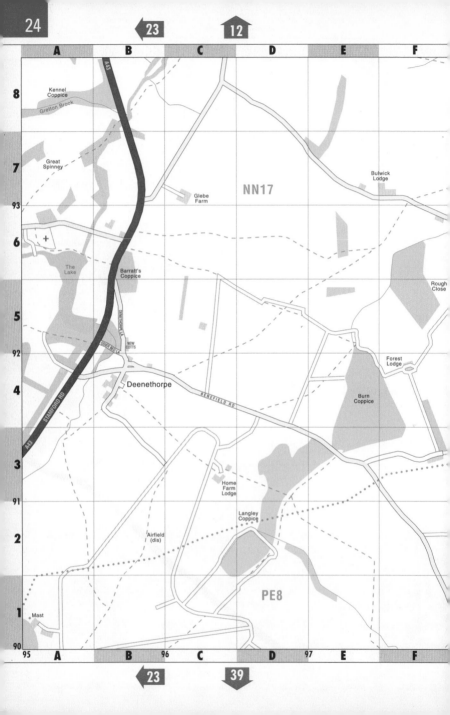

23
12

Kennel
Coppice

Gretton Brook

Great
Spinney

Glebe
Farm

NN17

Bulwick
Lodge

The
Lake

Barratt's
Coppice

Rough
Close

DEENTHORPE LA

NEW
COTTS

Forest
Lodge

Deenethorpe

BENEFIELD RD

Burn
Coppice

STAMFORD RD

A43

Home Farm
Lodge

Langley
Coppice

Airfield
(dis)

PE8

Mast

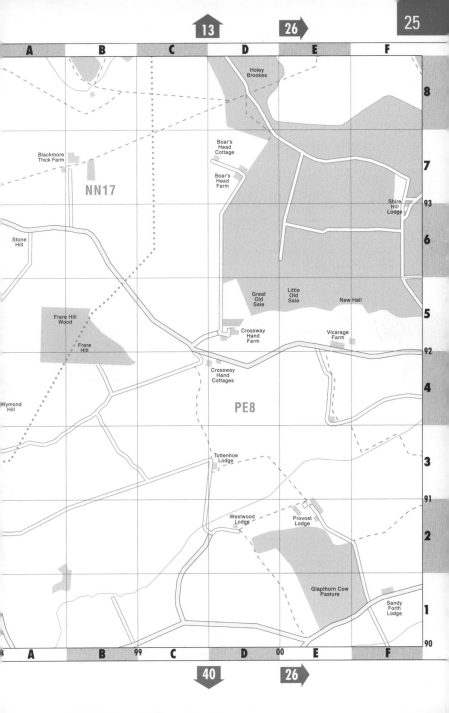

A   B   C   D   E   F

8

Holey
Brookes

Boar's
Head
Cottage

7

Blackmore
Thick Farm

Boar's
Head
Farm

NN17

Shire
Hill
Lodge   93

Stone
Hill

6

Frere Hill
Wood

Great
Old
Sale

Little
Old
Sale

New Hall   5

Frere
Hill

Crossway
Hand
Farm

Vicarage
Farm   92

Crossway
Hand
Cottages

Wymond
Hill

PE8

4

Tottenhoe
Lodge

3

Westwood
Lodge

Provost
Lodge   91

Glapthorn Cow
Pasture

2

Sandy
Forth
Lodge   1

90

A   B   99   C   D   00   E   F

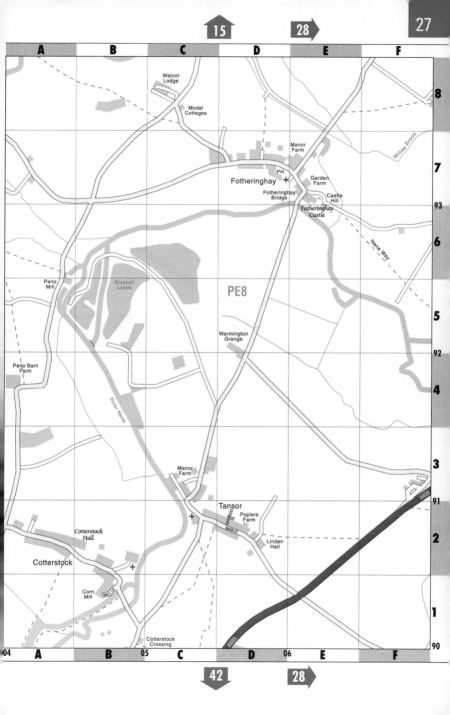

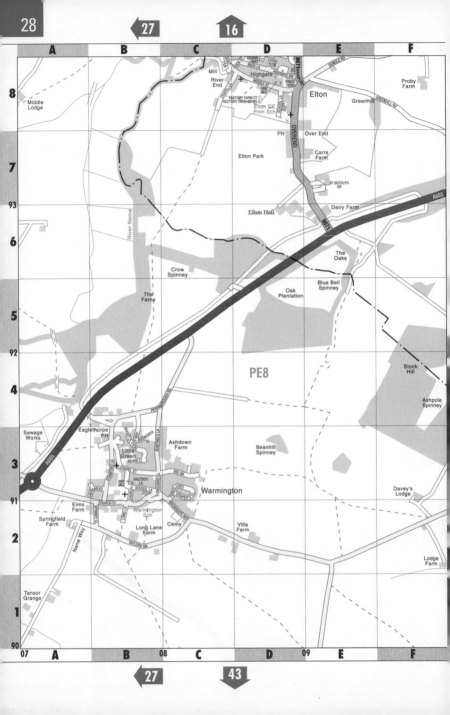

A B C D E F

PE8

Lodge
Farm

CH

Elton
Furze

Furze
Farm

Rectory
Farm

Elton Lodge
Farm

GREENHILL RD

A605

A605 Peterborough (A1139)

8

7

93

Greenhill
Lodge

GREENHILL RD

Bate's
Lodge

6

Lawrence's
Lodge

PE7

5

92

Cambridgeshire STREET ATLAS

Stockhill
Lodge

Bonser's
Lodge

BULLOCK RD

Tookey
Farm

Billing Brook

4

PE8

Field End
Close

Morborne
Hill

Mast

Mast

Radio
Station

3

91

Long Spinney

Papley
Gorse

America
Farm

Horse Close
Hovel

2

Morborne
Hill Top

1

90

10 A B 11 C D 12 E F

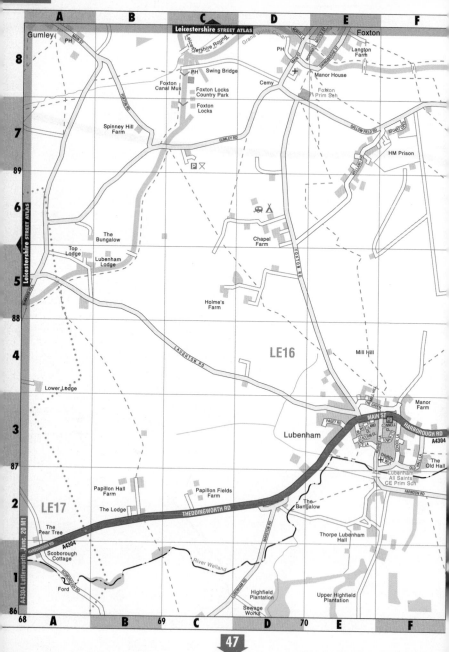

Gumley

Foxton

Langton Farm

PH

Swing Bridge

Foxton Canal Mus

Foxton Locks Country Park

Foxton Locks

Spinney Hill Farm

Cemy

Manor House

Foxton Prim Sch

HM Prison

The Bungalow

Top Lodge

Lubenham Lodge

Chapel Farm

Holme's Farm

LE16

Mill Hill

Lower Lodge

Manor Farm

PAGET RD

MAIN ST

HARBOROUGH RD

A4304

Lubenham

Papillon Hall Farm

Papillon Fields Farm

The Lodge

THEDDINGWORTH RD

The Bungalow

The Old Hall

Lubenham All Saints CE Prim Sch

LE17

The Pear Tree

A4304

Scoborough Cottage

Thorpe Lubenham Hall

Ford

River Welland

Highfield Plantation

Upper Highfield Plantation

Sewage Works

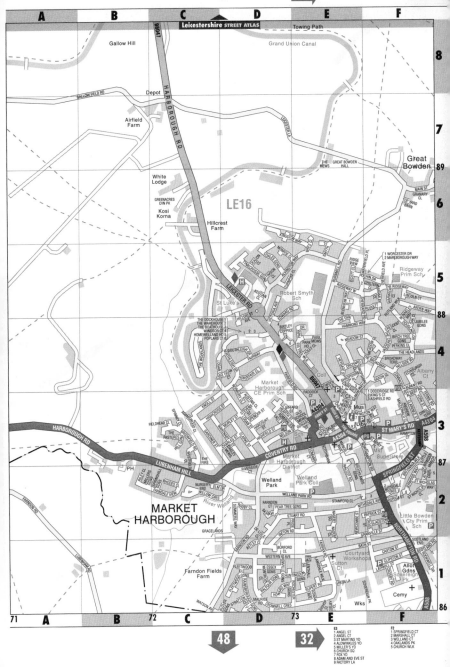

Leicestershire STREET ATLAS

Towing Path

Gallow Hill

Grand Union Canal

B6047

HARBOROUGH RD

GALLON FIELD RD

Depot

Airfield
Farm

White
Lodge

GREENACRES
CVN PK

Kosi
Korna

Hillcrest
Farm

LE16

Great
Bowden

GREAT BOWDEN
HALL

THE
MEWS

MAIN ST

GRANARY
CL

OF YARD
BARN

1 WORCESTER DR
2 MARLBOROUGH WAY

Ridgeway
Prim Sch

RIDGE
VIEW

KINGSTON WAY

COALS RD

MILL GORSE CL WAY

COATES RD

POCHIN DR

LINCOLN CT

ARDEN WAY

JUBILEE
GDNS

BIRCH TREE
GDNS

PERKINS CL

THE HEADLANDS

BROADWAY
TERR

Robert Smyth
Sch

MEADOW ST

HAMMOND WAY

Albany
Ct

ORCHARD ST

St Luke's

KESTIAN CL

LEICESTER RD

H

BURTLEY DR

COPPICE

PARK
PARK MEWS
RD CT

THE DOCKHOUSE 1
THE WAREHOUSE 2
THE BOATHOUSE 3
WINDSOR CT 4
HOMEWELL RD 4
POPLARS CT 6

HOMESTEAD

SOUTHLEY CL

FAIRWAY

B6047

PADDOCK
CT

Coll

Market
Harborough
CE Prim Sch

GIFFARD

1 DODDRIDGE RD
2 KING'S CT
3 ASHFIELD RD

Mus

P

P

A4304

THE FIRS

FIELDHEAD CL

KNOLL ST

SPRINGFIELD ST

HARBOROUGH RD

LUBENHAM HILL

PH

RILEY CL

MILLERS
END

RHODES CL

NURSERY
END

ELM DR

WILLOW CRES

FARNDALE VIEW

Coventry Rd

H

Market
Harborough
District

RIVERSIDE

River Welland

Welland
Park

Welland
Park Coll

WELLAND PARK RD

STAMFORD CL

A4304

St Mary's Rd

HAMPTON CL

A508

P

Superstore

P

Little Bowden
Cty Prim
Sch

NORTHAMPTON RD

A508

SPRINGFIELD ST

ST NICHOLAS
WAY

MARKET
HARBOROUGH

FARNDON

PEAR TREE GDNS

CROSBY CL

STUART RD

BORFORD CL

WESTERN GROVE

HUNTINGDON
GDNS

ESSEX GDNS

SUTTON

COURTYARD
WORKSHOPS

GREEN LA

Wks

Allot
Gdns

SOVEREIGN
PK

Cemy

Farndon Fields
Farm

FLEETWOOD
CL

WATSON AVE

CROMWELL CRES

E3
1 ANGEL ST
2 ANGEL CT
3 ST MARTINS YD
4 ALDWINKLES YD
5 MILLER'S YD
6 CHURCH SQ
7 FOX YD
8 ADAM AND EVE ST
9 FACTORY LA

F2
1 SPRINGFIELD CT
2 MARSHALL CT
3 WELLAND CT
4 OAKLANDS PK
5 CHURCH WLK

8

7

89

6

5

88

4

3

87

2

1

86

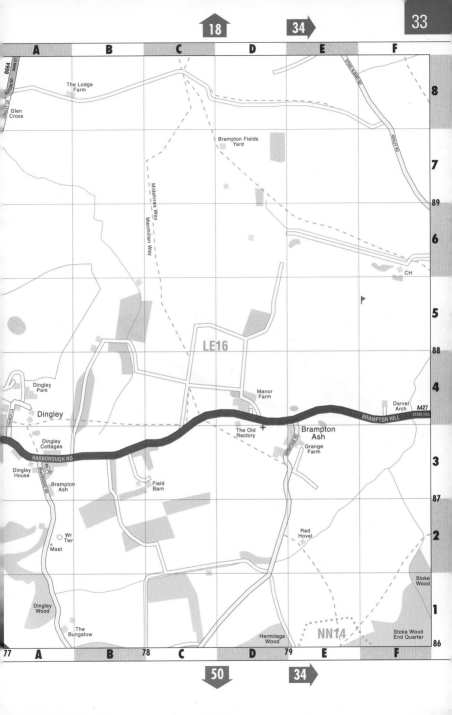

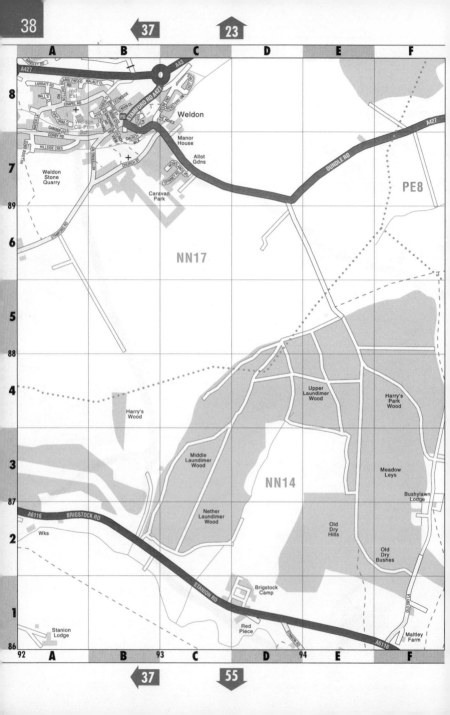

A B C D E F

8

Yoke
Hill

OUNDLE RD

Meml

The
Grange

Middle
Farm

TOWNSEND CT

GROVE DR

A427

Lammas
Farm

Upper
Benefield

7

89

PE8

6

Yokehill
Farm

Sheepwalk
Spinney

5

88

Blackthorns

Spring
Wood

CAUSIN WAY

4

Cockendale
Wood

Blackthorn
Lodge

Springwood
House

ocase
Farm

The
Cottages

Fermyn
Woods
Hall

Lodge
Cottages

Springwood
Lodge

3

87

Deer
Park

NN14

2

Stubby
Stiles

Samby
Skyes

Luscote's
Lodge

Tresham
Lodge

1

BENEFIELD RD

HARLEY WAY

86

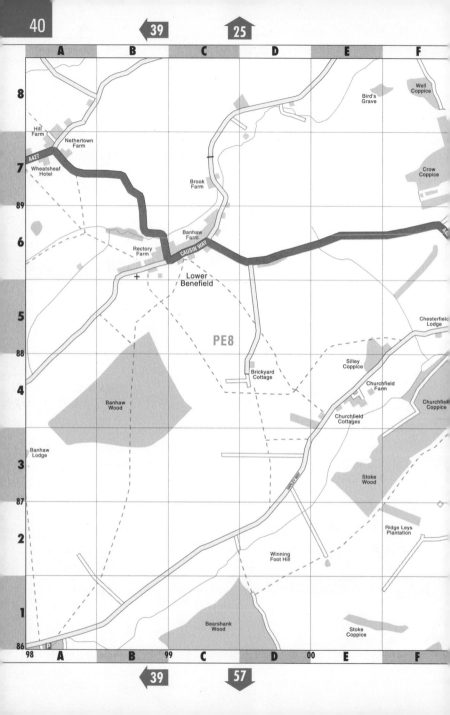

A B C D E F

8

7

89

6

5

88

4

3

87

2

1

86

Rectory Farm

Tansor Wold Farm

Tansor Wold

Miriam's Cover

Stamford Hovels

Stamford Cover

Toll Bar Gate

The Gorse

Warmington Spinney Plantation

PE8

Ashton Wold Farm

West Lodge

Ashton Wold House

Greenhouse Corner

Ashton Wold

The Common

Lutton Hovels

Water Gap Field

Allard's Home

Polebrook

Lake Fields

Bluestone Covert

Lutton Road Cottages

MAIN ST

MORTARD

HALL

Polebrook CE Prim Sch

LUTTON RD

Polebrook Airfield Nature Reserve

Polebrook Lodge

Rectory Farm

Airfield (disused)

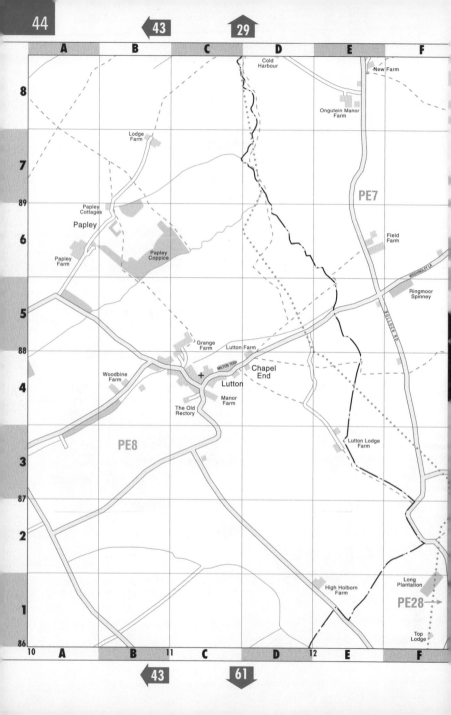

Cold Harbour

New Farm

Ongutein Manor Farm

PE7

Lodge Farm

Papley Cottages

Papley

Field Farm

Papley Coppice

WASHINGLEY LA.

Papley Farm

Ringmoor Spinney

Grange Farm

Lutton Farm

Woodbine Farm

Chapel End

Lutton

MILTON TERR.

Manor Farm

The Old Rectory

BULLOCK RD

PE8

Lutton Lodge Farm

High Holborn Farm

Long Plantation

PE28

Top Lodge

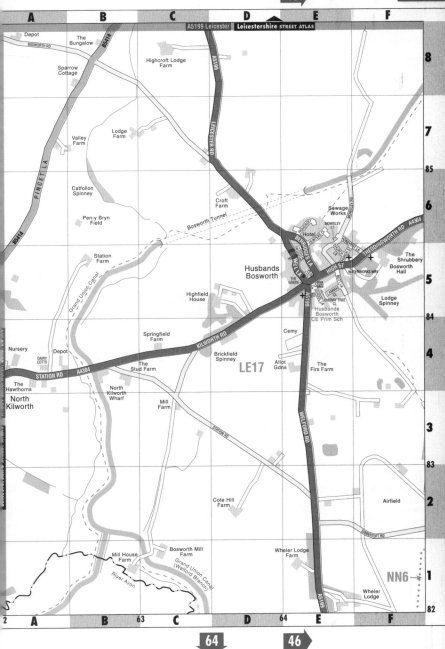

Leicestershire STREET ATLAS   A4304 Market Harborough

8

The Crown (PH)

Cemy

MAIN ST

THE BUNGALOWS

Works

Theddingworth

BARN QUITS

7

HARBOROUGH RD

Dene Lodge

Damside Spinney

Old Folly

Quiet Fields

Home Farm

BOSWORTH RD

Pebble Hall

85

Woodside Farm

Hothorpe Hall

THEDDINGWORTH RD

6

A4304

LE17

River Welland

Broxhill Buildings

5

Spring Hollow

Gravel Pit Spinney

84

Nichol's Hill Spinney

Long Spinney

Barn-hill Spinney

Hothorpe Hills

4

Coombe-hill Spinney

LE16

3

Carland Spinney

83

The Wrongs

The Roserie

Coombe Farm

2

WELFORD RD

Airfield

SIBBERTOFT RD

PH

Sibbertoft

WELFORD RD

KENNELS

CHURCH ST

1

NN6

Depot

Jurassic Way

Sulby Lodge

The Kennels

82

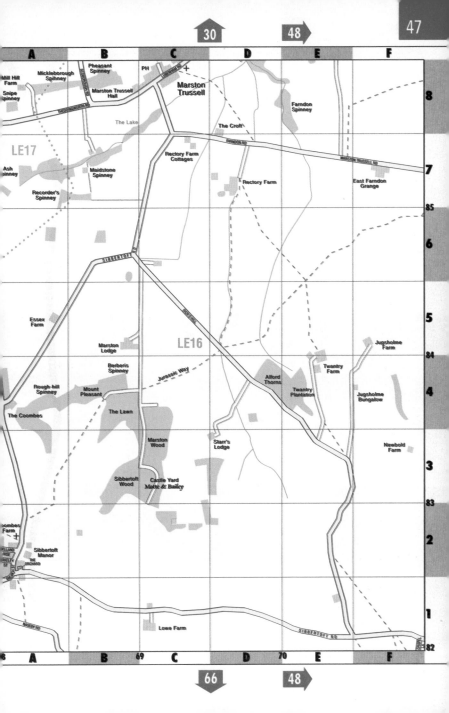

30
48

A   B   C   D   E   F

8

PH
Mill Hill Farm
Mickleborough Spinney
Pheasant Spinney
Marston Trussell Hall
Marston Trussell
Farndon Spinney
Snipe Spinney

The Lake
The Croft

LE17

FARNDON RD
MARSTON TRUSSELL RD

Rectory Farm Cottages

7

Ash Spinney
Maidstone Spinney
Rectory Farm
East Farndon Grange

Recorder's Spinney

85

6

SIBBERTOFT

Essex Farm

5

LE16

Marston Lodge
Jugsholme Farm

84

Berberis Spinney
Jurassic Way
Twantry Farm

4

Rough-hill Spinney
Mount Pleasant
Alford Thorns
Twantry Plantation
Jugsholme Bungalow

The Coombes
The Lawn

Marston Wood
Starr's Lodge
Newbold Farm

3

Sibbertoft Wood
Castle Yard Motte & Bailey

83

Coombes Farm

2

Sibbertoft Manor
THE ORCHARD
WELLAND RISE
STANLEY ST

1

MARKET RD
Lowe Farm
SIBBERTOFT RD

82

A   B   C   D   E   F
68   69   70

66
48

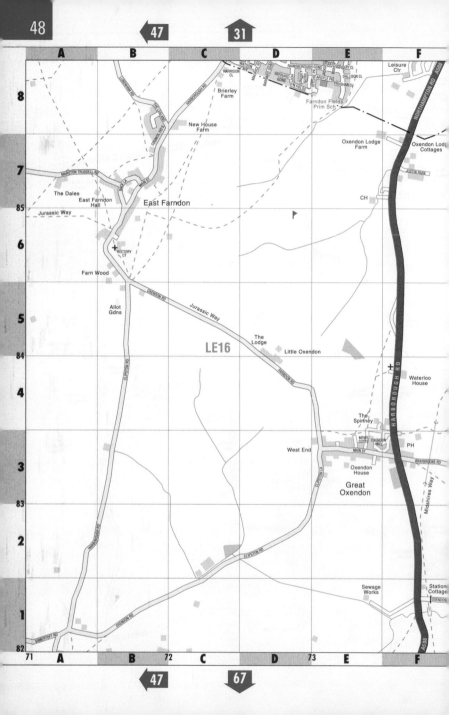

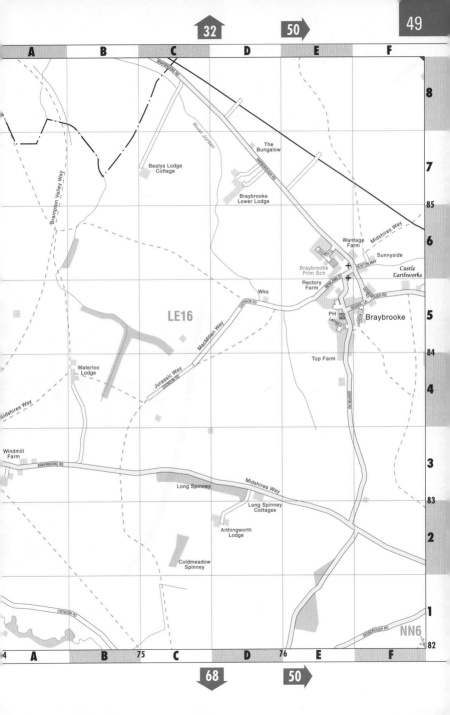

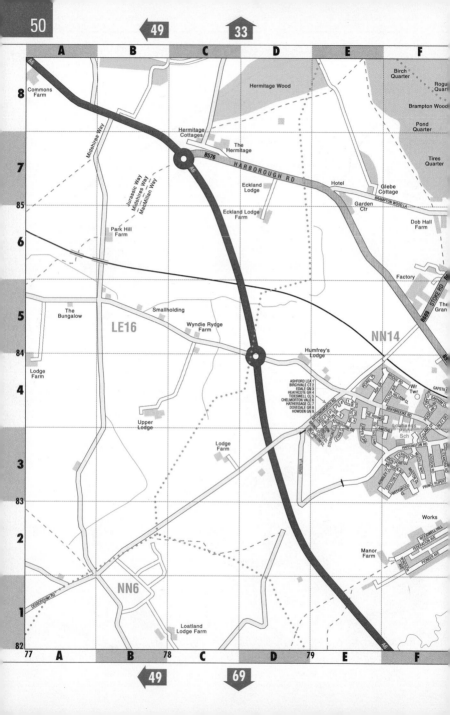

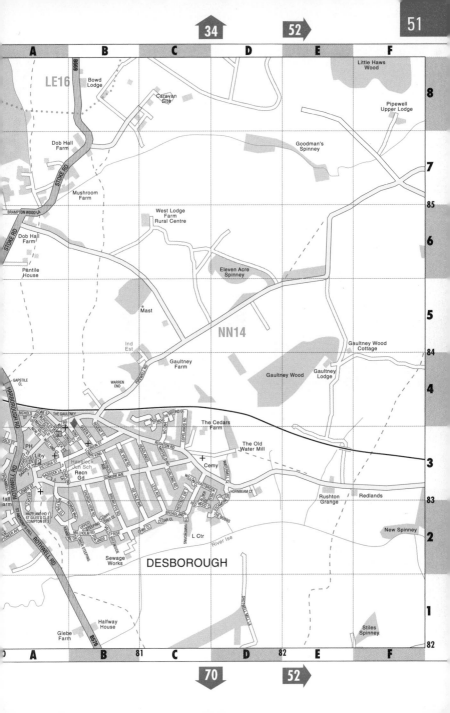

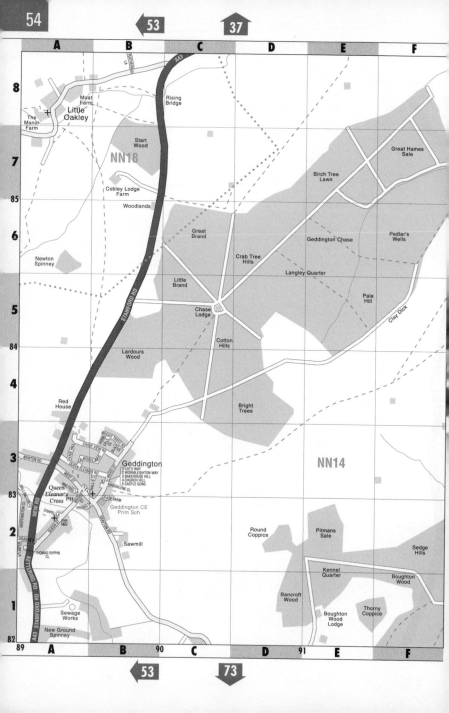

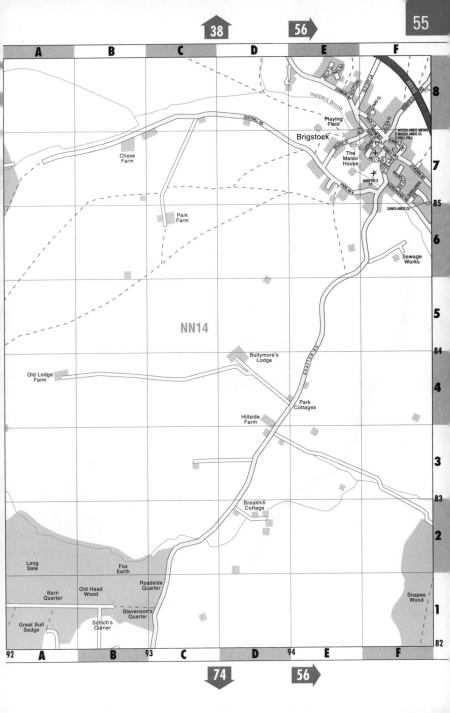

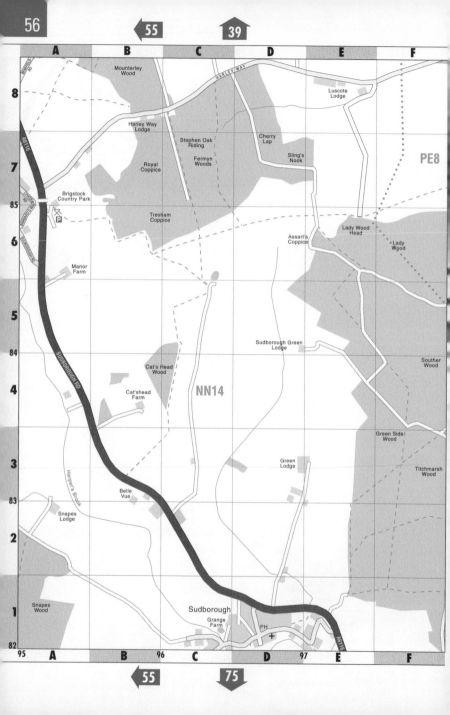

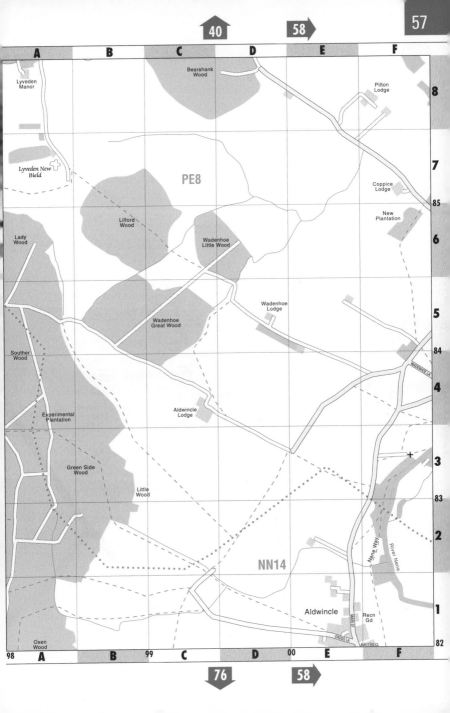

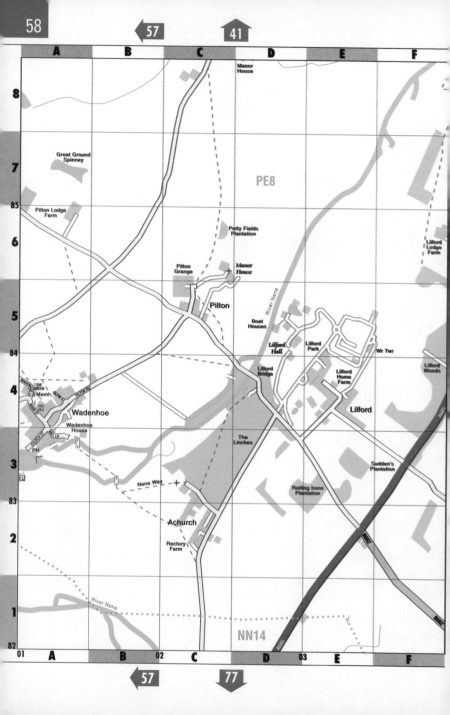

57
41

A B C D E F

8

Manor
House

Great Ground
Spinney

7

PE8

85

Pilton Lodge
Farm

Petty Fields
Plantation

6

Lilford
Lodge
Farm

Pilton
Grange

Manor
House

River Nene

Pilton

5

Boat
Houses

84

Lilford
Park

Lilford
Hall

Wr Twr

Lilford
Woods

Lilford
Bridge

THE GREEN
Meml

Lilford
Home
Farm

4

Wadenhoe

Lilford

CHURCH ST

Wadenhoe
House

PH

The
Linches

Sudden's
Plantation

3

P

Nene Way

Ratling Irons
Plantation

83

A605

Achurch

2

Rectory
Farm

River Nene

1

A605

NN14

82

01 A B 02 C D 03 E F

57
77

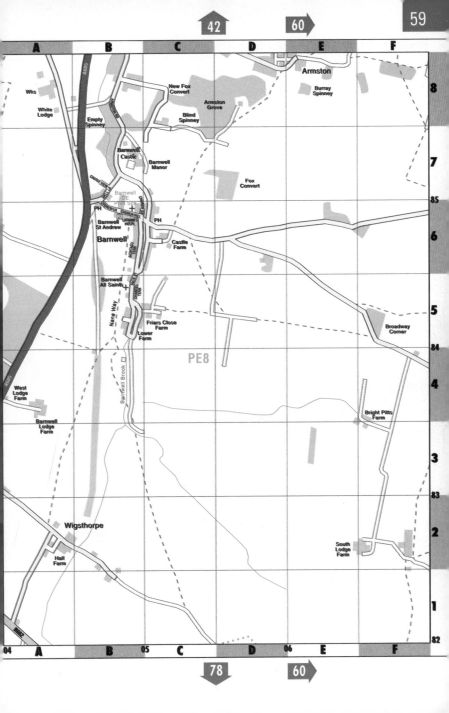

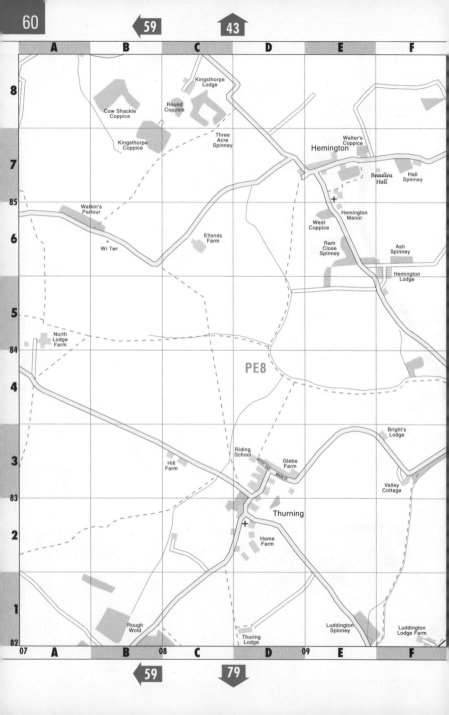

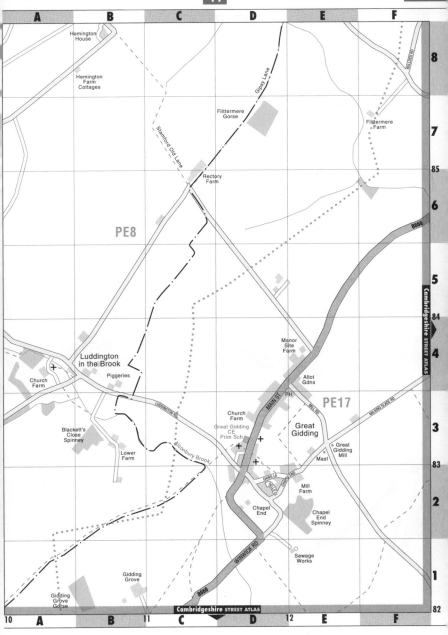

A B C D E F

8

Hemington
House

Hemington
Farm
Cottages

Gipsy Lane

7

Flittermere
Gorse

Flittermere
Farm

85

Stamford Old Lane

Rectory
Farm

6

PE8

B660

5

84

Manor
Site
Farm

4

Luddington
in the Brook

Piggeries

Church
Farm

Allot
Gdns

PH

MAIN ST

MILL RD

MILKING STILE RD

PE17

3

Blackett's
Close
Spinney

LUDDINGTON RD

Church
Farm

Great Gidding
CE
Prim Sch

Great
Gidding

Great
Gidding
Mill

Lower
Farm

Alconbury Brook

SAINTS LA

CHAPEL END

Mast

83

Chapel
End

Mill
Farm

2

Chapel
End
Spinney

WINWICK RD

Sewage
Works

Gidding Grove

1

Gidding
Grove
Gorse

B660

82

10 A B 11 C D 12 E F

Cambridgeshire STREET ATLAS

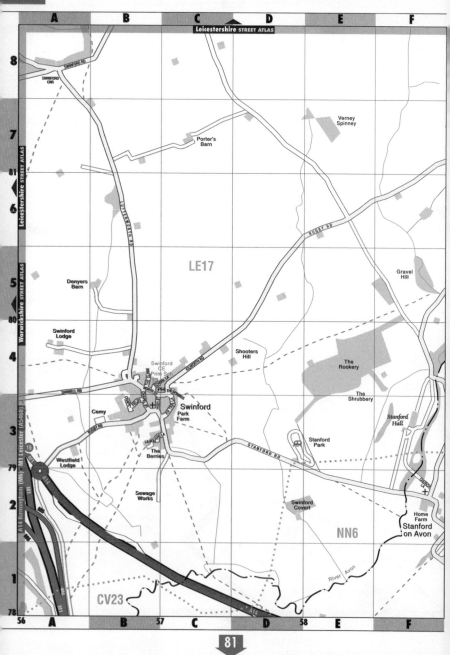

Verney
Spinney

Porter's
Barn

Leicestershire STREET ATLAS

RUGBY RD

LE17

Gravel
Hill

Denyers
Barn

Swinford
Lodge

Warwickshire STREET ATLAS

Shooters
Hill

The
Rookery

Swinford
CE
Prim Sch

The
Shrubbery

Stanford
Hall

Cemy

Swinford
Park Farm

Stanford
Park

STANFORD RD

The
Berries

Westfield
Lodge

Sewage
Works

Swinford
Covert

NN6

Home
Farm
Stanford
on Avon

River Avon

CV23

A14

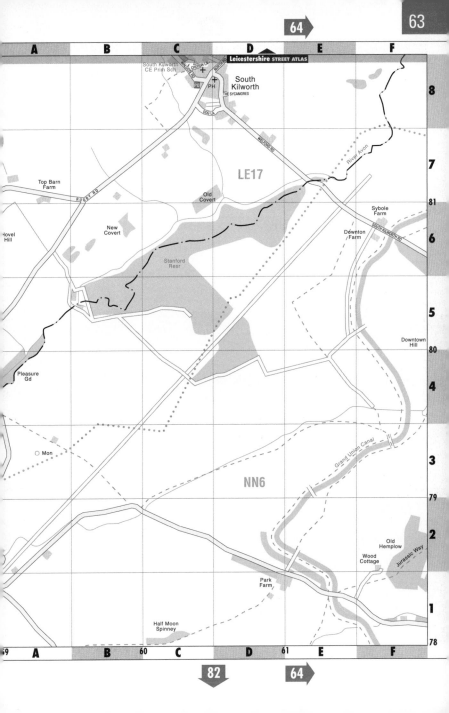

A B C D E F

South Kilworth
CE Prim Sch

South
Kilworth

PH

THE SYCAMORES

River Avon

LE17

Top Barn
Farm

RUGBY RD

Old
Covert

Sybole
Farm

Dewnton
Farm

SOUTH KILWORTH RD

8

7

81

Hovel
Hill

New
Covert

Stanford
Resr

Downtown
Hill

6

5

80

Pleasure
Gd

4

Mon

Grand Union Canal

NN6

3

79

Old
Hemplow

Wood
Cottage

Jurassic Way

2

Park
Farm

1

Half Moon
Spinney

78

A B C D E F

8

Grand Union Canal (Welford Branch)

Glebe Farm

LE17

Grand Union Canal

Lodge Farm

River Avon

7

Sybolds Spinney

81

Marina

Hill House

Welford Resr

Welford Lodge

Welford Grange Farm

NASEBY RD

Hotel
Sewage Works

THE SQUARE

6

Allot Gdns

Sulby Lodge Farm

PH

Hallfield Cottage

FIELD CLOSE

Welford Sibbertoft & Sulby Endowed Sch

ORCHARD TERR

HIGH ST

PH

Welford

SOUTH KILWORTH RD

PO

5

CHAPEL LA

WOODFORD GLEBE

80

THE LYS

WEST RD

NEWLANDS RD

4

Jurassic Way

Court Lane Farm

COURT LA

NORTHAMPTON RD

A5199

3

Fish Pond Covert

79

The Glebe

Hemplow Hills

West Hill Farm

HEMPLOW DR

Hemploe Lodge Farm

NN6

2

Dark Spinney

Prince of Wales Spinney

Watts Lodge Farm

Welford Lodge Farm

1

78

62 A B 63 C D 64 E A14 F

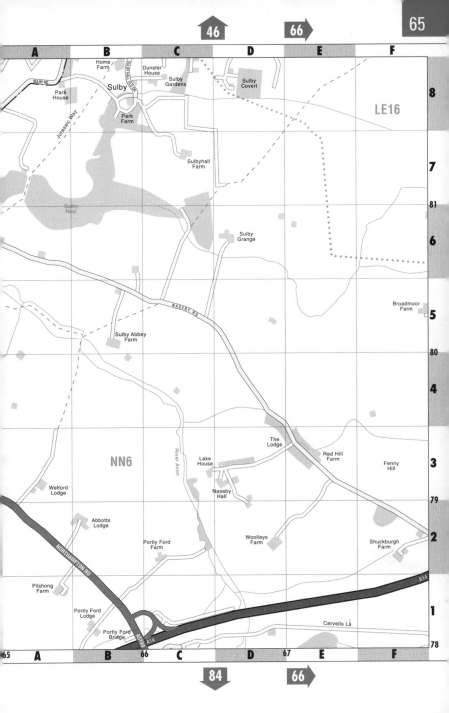

NN14

8

Weekley Hall
Wood

Cid
Wood

NN14

7

Glendon
Lodge

Weekley Hall
Farm

Burdyke

Upper
Farm

81

NN16

Weekley

6

Dalby
Cl.

Allot
Gdns

Well
Cottage

Prim
Sch

5

Montagu
Sch

One Acre
House

Kettering
Town
FC

Recn
Gd

80

North Field

Superstore

Avondale
Jun & Inf
Schs

Avondale
Mews

4

Grange Pk

Ruth Gdns

Allot
Gdns

River Ise

3

KETTERING

Avenue Terr

Wellington

Allot
Gdns

Northall St   Eskdale

79

A4300 Lower St   A4300 Montagu St

Windmill Ave

NN15

2

Prim
Sch

Cerny

Mus
Liby

Ise
Com Coll

St Mary's Rd

Henry Gotch
Sch

Cerny

A6018
Northampton   Rd

A6000

Windmill
Wlk

St Bernards
Sch

1

Rech
Gd
Kettering

St
Mary's

Inst

Rossley
Sch

78

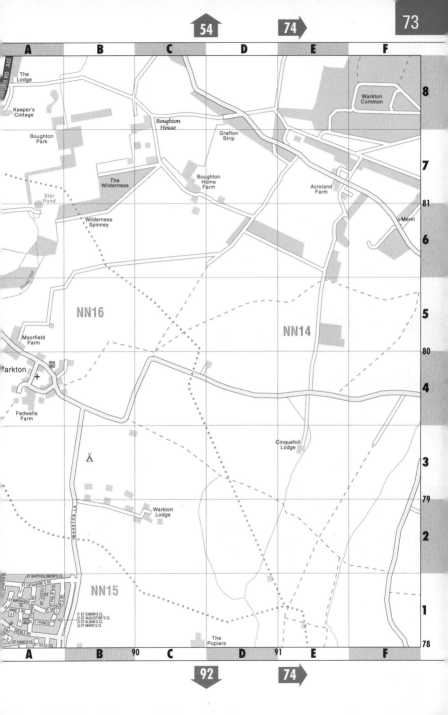

A   B   C   D   E   F

8

The Lodge

Keeper's Cottage

Warkton Common

Boughton House

Boughton Park

Grafton Strip

7

The Wilderness

Boughton Home Farm

Acreland Farm

81

Star Pond

Meml

Wilderness Spinney

6

River Ise

NN16

5

Moorfield Farm

NN14

80

arkton

PO

4

Fedwells Farm

3

Cinquefoil Lodge

WARKTON LA

79

Warkton Lodge

2

ST BARTHOLOMEW'S CL
ST CATHARINE'S RD
ST BARNABAS
ST PHILIP'S CL
ANNE'S RD
DEEBLE RD
ST FRANCIS
ST CHAD'S CL
ST GILES CL

NN15

1 ST SIMON'S CL
2 ST AUGUSTINE'S CL
3 ST ALBAN'S CL
4 ST MARK'S CL

1

The Poplars

78

A   B   90   C   D   91   E   F

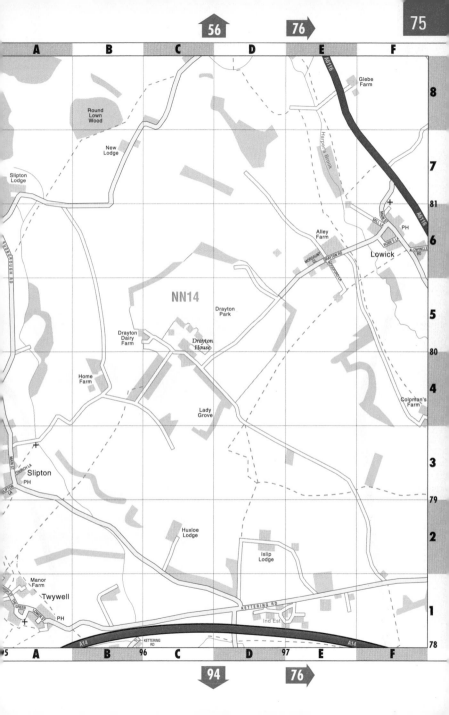

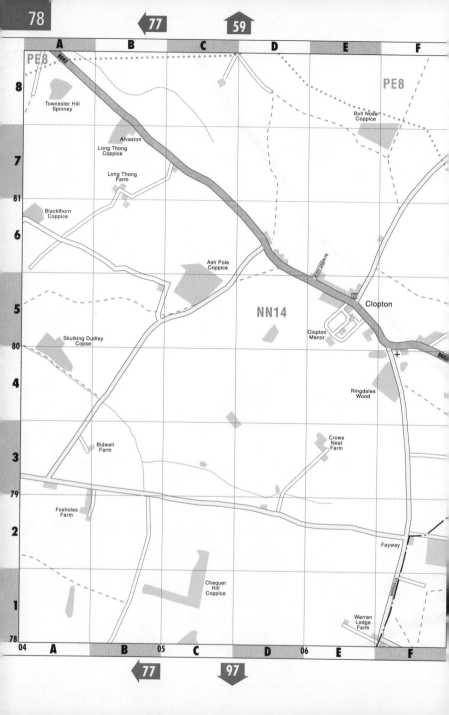

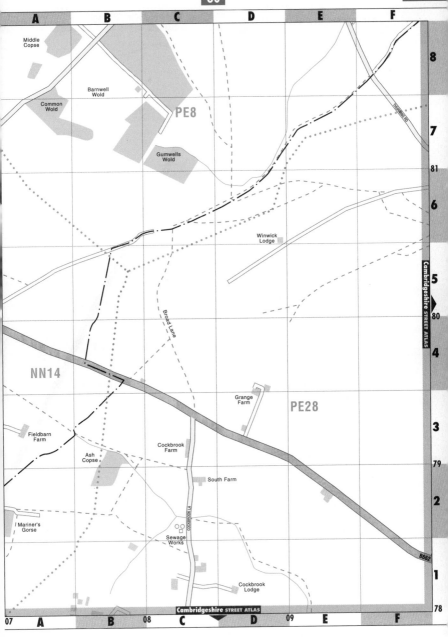

60

A B C D E F

8

7

81

6

Middle
Copse

Barnwell
Wold

Common
Wold

PE8

Gumwells
Wold

Winwick
Lodge

5

80

Broad Lane

4

NN14

Grange
Farm

PE28

3

79

Fieldbarn
Farm

Cockbrook
Farm

Ash
Copse

South Farm

2

Mariner's
Gorse

Sewage
Works

1

Cockbrook
Lodge

B662

78

07 A B 08 C D 09 E F

Cambridgeshire STREET ATLAS

LE17

Mill Farm

St Thomas Cross (PH)

NEWTON RD

Dow Bridge

River Avon

Lilbourne Furze

Lilbourne Gorse

Dunsmore Farm

Cemy

Clifton upon Dunsmore

Almond Bank

Manor Farm

Dunsmore

Magpie Lodge Farm

NORTH RD

PH

MAIN RD

Clifton Hall Farm

SOUTH RD

LILBOURNE RD

Dunsmore House

CV23

Masts

Dunsmore Home Farm

Hotel

Clifton Hall

HILLMORTON LA

The Meadows

Warwickshire STREET ATLAS

Grange Farm House

Masts

Home Farm

Clifton Brook

Oxford Canal

CV21

A1
1 BROMWICH RD
2 PETTIVER CRES
3 WIGSTON RD
4 THE MEWS
5 LOWER HILLMORTON RD

Oxford Canal Walk

RUGBY

THE LOCKS

Hillmorton Locks

Normandy Farm

Rugby Radio Station

Masts

1 BONNINGTON CL
2 LANDSEER CL

Masts

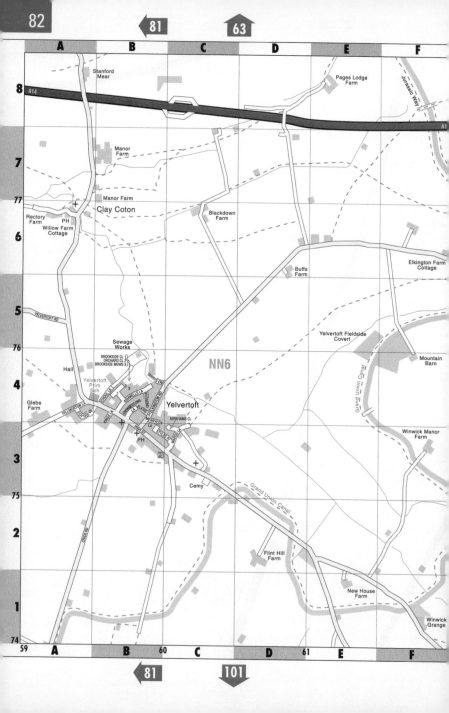

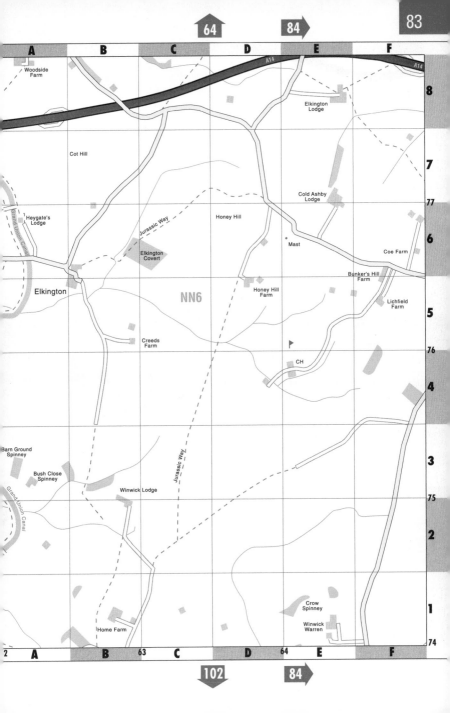

A   B   C   D   E   F

A14

Woodside
Farm

Elkington
Lodge

8

Cot Hill

7

Cold Ashby
Lodge

77

Heygate's
Lodge

Honey Hill

Jurassic Way

* Mast

6

Coe Farm

Elkington
Covert

Bunker's Hill
Farm

Elkington

NN6

Honey Hill
Farm

Lichfield
Farm

5

Creeds
Farm

76

CH

4

Barn Ground
Spinney

Bush Close
Spinney

Jurassic Way

3

Winwick Lodge

75

Grand Union Canal

2

Crow
Spinney

1

Home Farm

Winwick
Warren

74

A B C D E F

8

Reservoir
Farm

SCHOOL LA
KNIGHTS HILL
BARWELL ST
BAKERS/RISE

PH

Naseby

Cromwell
Farm

Brankley
Farm

Hospital
Farm

DUTTON CL

Naseby
Battle & Farm
Mus

Oak
Farm

7

77

The Grange
Farm

6

NN6

Purser's
Hills

Vale
Farm

5

New
Covert

76

Old
Covert

4

Stubb
Purlieu

3

75

Calender
Farm

Cott Hill
Spinney

2

Cottesbrooke
Park

Hanwell
Spinney

1

A5199

Foalfoot
Spinney

74

68 A B 69 C D 70 E F

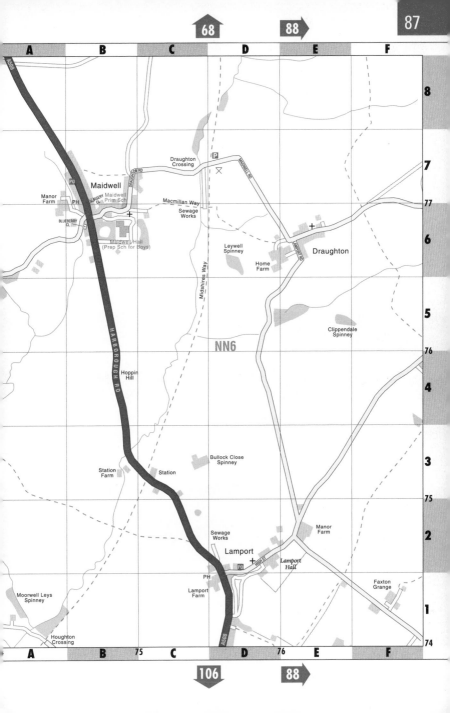

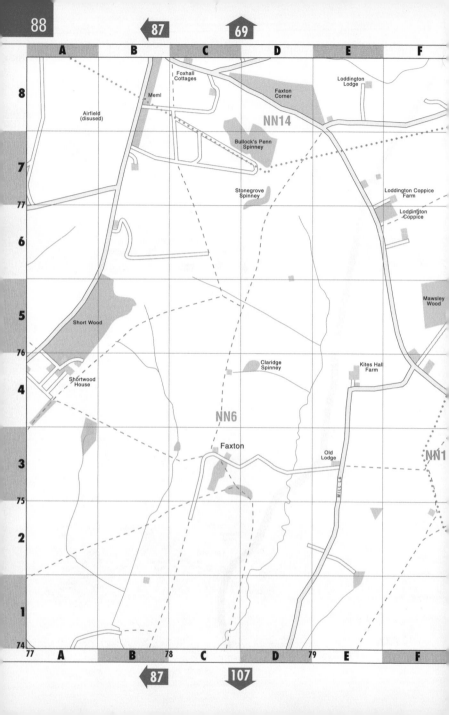

A **B** **C** **D** **E** **F**

Ashpole
Spinney

Springlong

Loddington
Grange

Cransley
Resr

8

Mawsley
Furze

Hall
Farm

7

Mill
Farm

NN14

77

NN6

Mawsley
Lodge

Great
Cransley

6

Cransley
Wood

Cransley
Hall

Birch
Spinney

Cransley
Lodge

Cemy

New
Lodge

5

Old
Lodge

76

Mawsley
Village

FOX COVERT

4

THE
JITTY

Mast

Old Poor's
Gorse

3

75

Red
Lodge

NN6

2

Hockley
Lodge

1

White
Lodge

Highcroft
Farm

74

A **B** 81 **C** **D** 82 **E** **F**

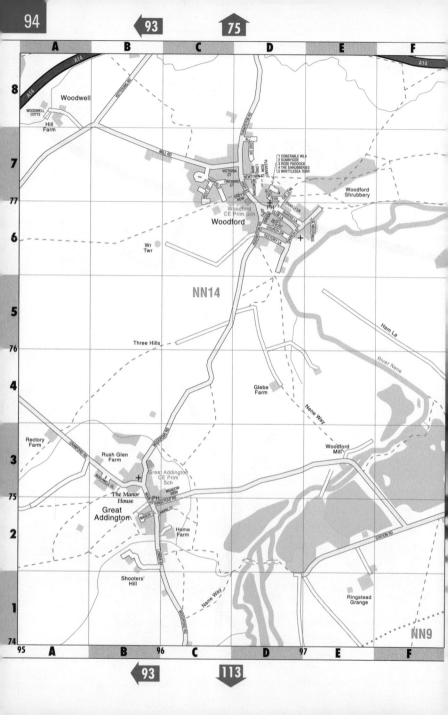

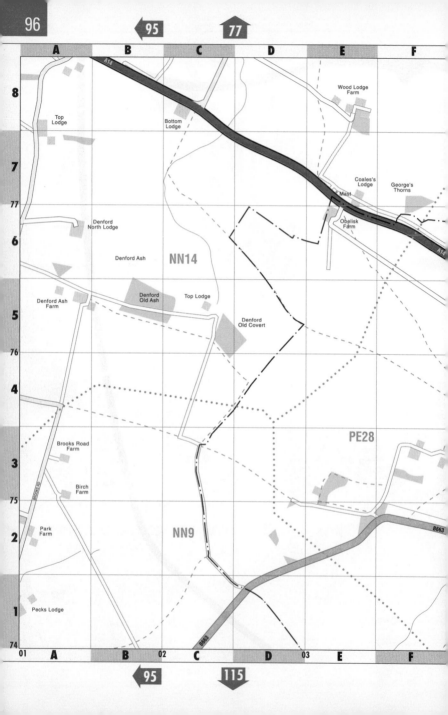

NN14

Firing
Range

PE28

Slipe
Cotts

TOLL BAR LA

B663

Smith's
Farm

Scott's
Farm

CHURCH
LA

Bythorn

MANOR LA

SCHOOL LA

MAIN ST

Bythorn
House

PH

Keyston

Manor
Farm

HILLSIDE
COTTS

TOLL BAR LA

The
Acres

OLD CROFT

THE
PARK

PH

A14 Huntingdon

A14

CHAINBRIDGE LA

Clack La

SWINEBROOK LA

Crow's Nest Hill

A428 Rugby, Coventry

CV2

CV22

CV23

Onley

Crick

NN6

Crick Tunnel

Jurassic Way

Grand Union Canal

WEST HADDON RD

A428 CRICK RD

WATFORD RD

Crackshill Farm
Crack's Hill
The Bungalow
Flinthill
Heygates Farm
Glebe Farm
Mount Pleasant
Wold Farm
Nursery
Wold Farm
1 COLEMAN CL
2 THORNTON CL
3 ASHWORTH CL
4 WOLSEY CL
Crick Wharf
Cottage Farm
West Lodge
Montrose Farm
Silsworth Lodge
Flavell's Lodge
Limes Farm
The Old Lodge
Watford Covert
Heygate Farm
Home Farm
Poole's Lodge
Northingworth Lodge

8
7
73
6
5
72
4
3
71
2
1
70

A B 60 C D 61 E F

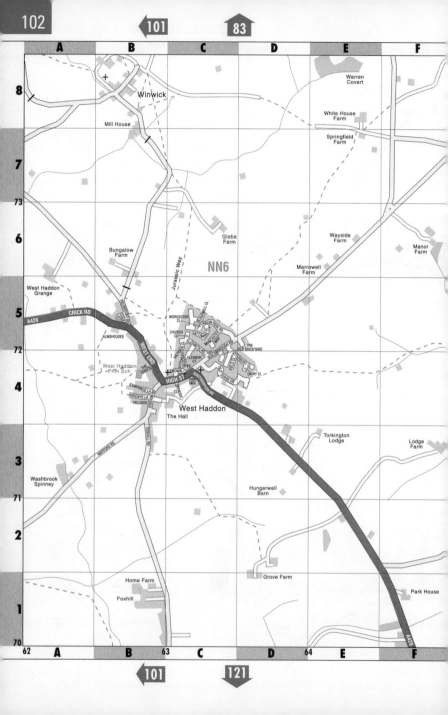

Winwick

Warren Covert

White House Farm

Mill House

Springfield Farm

Wayside Farm

Manor Farm

Glebe Farm

Jurassic Way

NN6

Marrowell Farm

Bungalow Farm

West Haddon Grange

THE OLD BRICKYARD

A428 CRICK RD

WORCESTER CL

CHURCH CL

ALMSHOUSES

WEST END

West Haddon Prim Sch

ELEANOR CT

DAIRY CL

HIGH ST

STAFFORD LA

HARDAYS LA

HILLSIDE

PO

West Haddon

The Hall

WATFORD RD

FOXHILL RD

Torkington Lodge

Lodge Farm

Hungerwell Barn

Washbrook Spinney

Home Farm

Foxhill

Grove Farm

Park House

A428

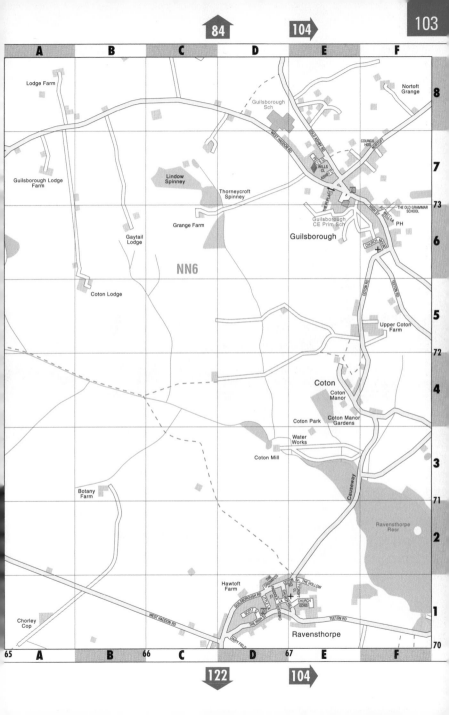

Blackpits Spinney

Square Hedge Spinney

Cottesbrooke

The Old Rectory

Lodges Spinney

Oak Spinney

Cottage Farm

The Green Lane

Hollowell Resr

Hollowell Grange

Great Creaton Lodge

NN6

Neaton Cottage

Hollowell Lodge

Hollowell

Home Farm

HONEYPOT CL

LANGHAM CL

BRIXWORTH RD

WELFORD RD

Great Creaton Prim Sch

GUILSBOROUGH HILL

ORCHARD CL

THE GREEN

CREATON RD

HOLLOWELL RD

CHURCH HILL

PIDGEON PK

Sewage Works

Creaton

PH

Blackberry Hill Farm

TEETON LA

JUDGES CT

Highgate House

Pastures Farm

Macmillan Way

A5199

Ravensthorpe Lodge

Ladymoors Farm

Ravensthorpe Resr

Water Works

Teeton Lodge

Hall

Teeton

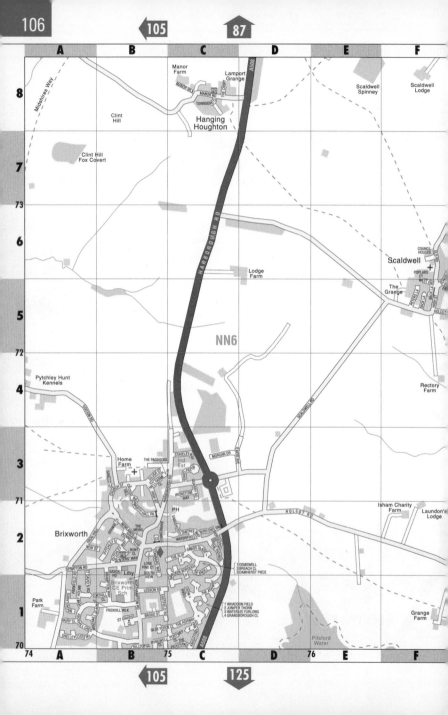

A B C D E F

8

Oak
Spinney

BROUGHTON RD

7

SCALDWELL RD

CROSS ST

TOWNSON CL

MANSEY CL

WHYTES CL

CHESTERS LA

FAXTON
END

HARRINGTON RD

MILL LA

Old

Grange
Farm

PH

BRIDLE ST

73

WALGRAVE RD

6

CHERRY HILL

ESP

HOLCOT LA

OLD RD

TOWNSEND RD

SPRINGFIELD RD

5

NN6

Ford

Mill
Farm

HOLCOT RD

72

Rectory
Farm

Cemy

4

Works

Brixworth
Fox Covert

3

71

Pitsford Water

2

Grange Farm
Cottages

HOLCOT RD

HILLSIDE RD

New Grange
Farm

P

Causeway

BRIXWORTH RD

The
Lodge

1

70

A B C D E F

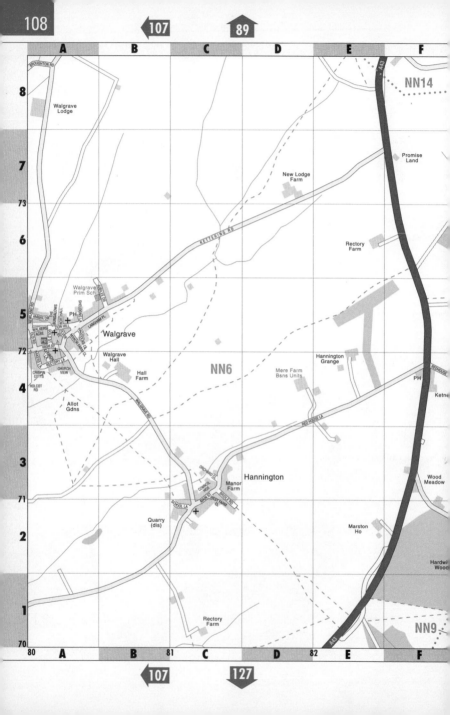

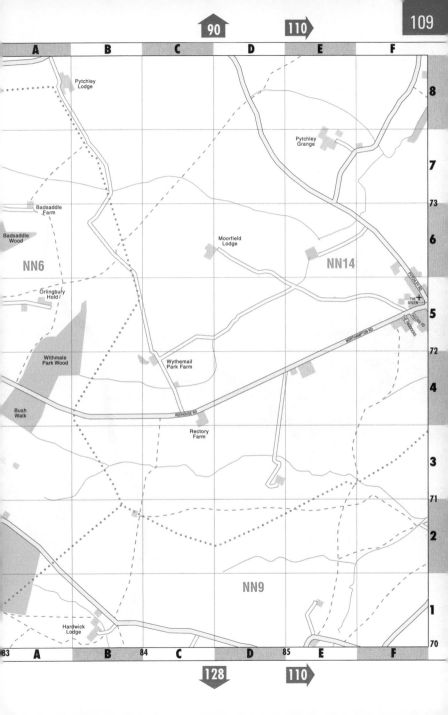

A B C D E F

8

7

73

6

NN6

NN14

Pytchley
Lodge

Badsaddle
Farm

Badsaddle
Wood

Moorfield
Lodge

Pytchley
Grange

PYTCHLEY RD

THE
GREEN

Orlingbury
Hold

Withmale
Park Wood

Wythemail
Park Farm

NORTHAMPTON RD

THE PADDOCKS

IGHTON RD

5

72

Bush
Walk

REDHOUSE RD

Rectory
Farm

4

3

71

NN9

2

Hardwick
Lodge

1

70

83 A B 84 C D 85 E F

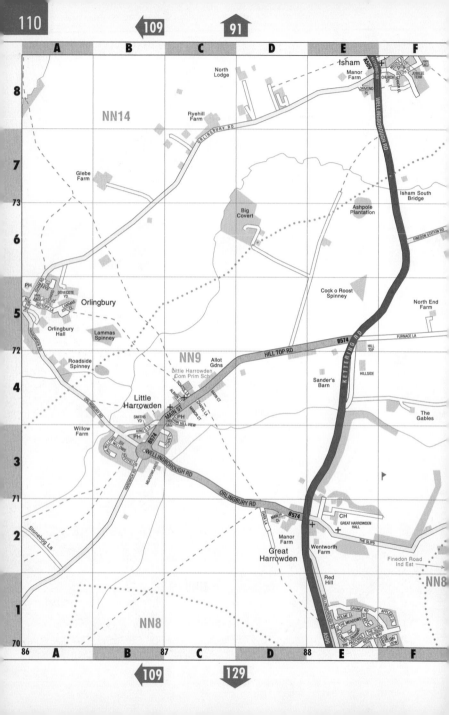

109
91

Isham

NN14

North Lodge

Manor Farm

Ryehill Farm

ORLINGBURY RD

Glebe Farm

Big Covert

Ashpole Plantation

Isham South Bridge

FINEDON STATION RD

WELLINGBOROUGH RD

A5095

Cock o Roost Spinney

North End Farm

PH

DOVECOTE YD
LAMMAS
RECTORY LA

Orlingbury

FURNACE LA

Orlingbury Hall

Lammas Spinney

HILL TOP RD

B574

HILL TOP

HILLSIDE

KETTERING RD

Roadside Spinney

NN9

Allot Gdns

Sander's Barn

Little Harrowden Com Prim Sch

SCHOOL LA

BARN CT

The Gables

Little Harrowden

MAIN ST

PH

CHAPEL LA

MANOR CT

ORCHARD RD

SMITHS YD

PH

KINGS

PH

OAK HILL VIEW

Willow Farm

SIX BELLOWS

DOVEHOUSE

WELLINGBOROUGH RD

B574

ORLINGBURY RD

BRIDLE RD

MEADOW

B574

MANOR CL

CH

GREAT HARROWDEN HALL

THE SLIPS

Finedon Road Ind Est

NN8

Stonebrig La

CORK LA

Manor Farm

Wentworth Farm

Great Harrowden

WELLINGBOROUGH RD

Red Hill

GRANGE RD

APPLEBY CL

HOLME CL

THE MEADOWS

THE BLACK

PASTURES

KENTWELL WAY

OAK

A5095

NN8

109
129

A B C D E F

8

New Barn
Farm

BRICK KILN RD

Northdale
Farm

7

Scalley
Farm

Kepwick

Cemy

YORK WAY

FAIROAKS DR

1 PENNY LA
2 BRIDGE ST
3 TITHE BARN CL
4 DOVECOTE CL

Brooks
Farm

MIDLAND RD

73

Scalley
Farm

MEADOW LA

Windmill
Prim
Sch

Libv

RAUNDS

Mast

LONDON RD

MARSHALL ST

WINDMILL AVE

ST PETERS WAY

WESLEY

B663

6

BELMONT GDNS

OLD AVE

DRYDEN ST

RED ROW

SMITHFIELD

SPINNEY ST
EVALYN WLK
CHRISTINE CT
SHELMERDINE
RISE

CLARE ST

HARCOURT ST

Schs

Manor
Farm

Sewage
Works

Hog Dyke

MACKENZIE RD

FIELD CT

TITTY RD

GROVE ST

WELLINGTON RD

SMITH
CT

FORESTERS

Thorpe House
Farm

5

CHERRY WLK

CHAMBERLAIN

MAPLETOFT
ST

NN9

72

FRANCIS
TERR

LAWRENCE
CL

P

Darsdale
Farm

4

Potter

CUMBERLAND

RAUNDS RD

WESTFIELD AVE

ANTONA
GDNS

CHELVESTON RD

SHELTON RD

Stanwick

Stanwick
Prim Sch

3

CHAPEL LA

BROOKSIDE

THE AVENUE

EAST ST

MARKS CL

CHELVESTON RD

Cemy

71

2

Pastures Lodge
Farm

Pastures
Cottage

New Covert

1

Pasture
Barn

B663

Stanwick
Pastures

70

98 A B 99 C D 00 E F

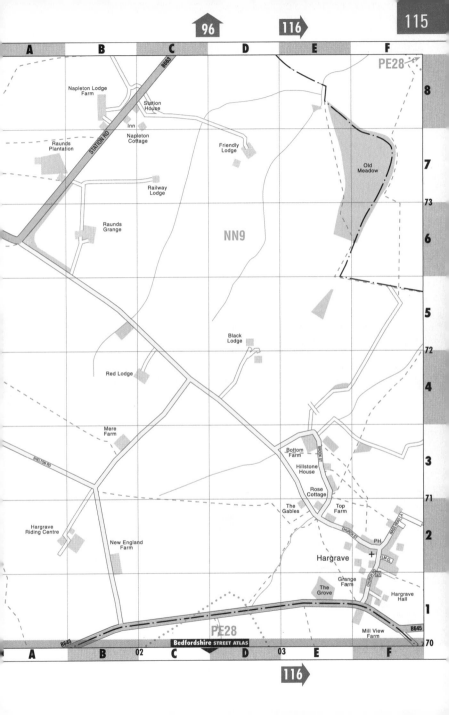

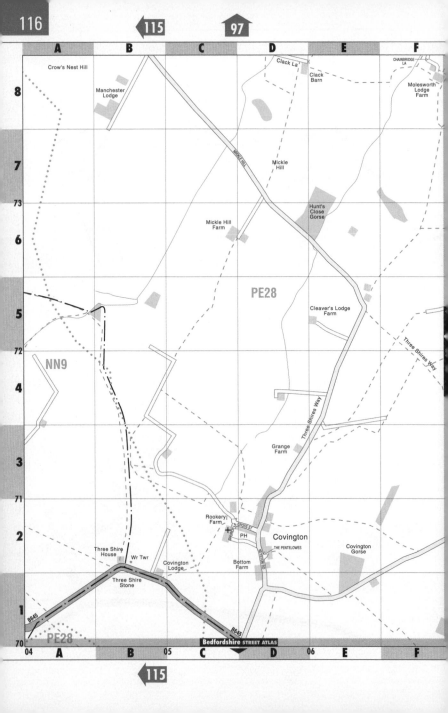

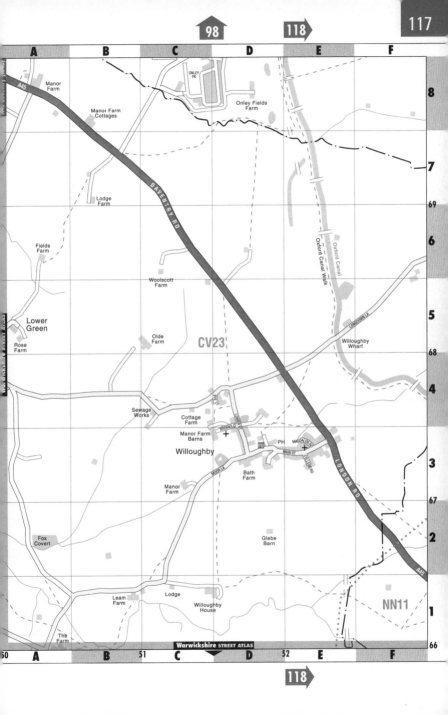

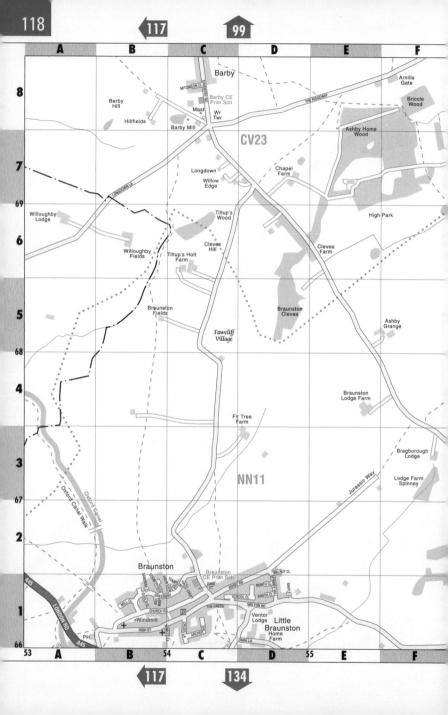

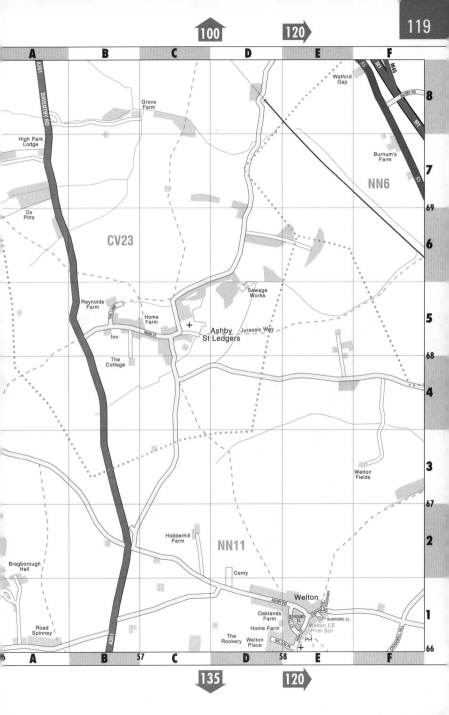

119
101

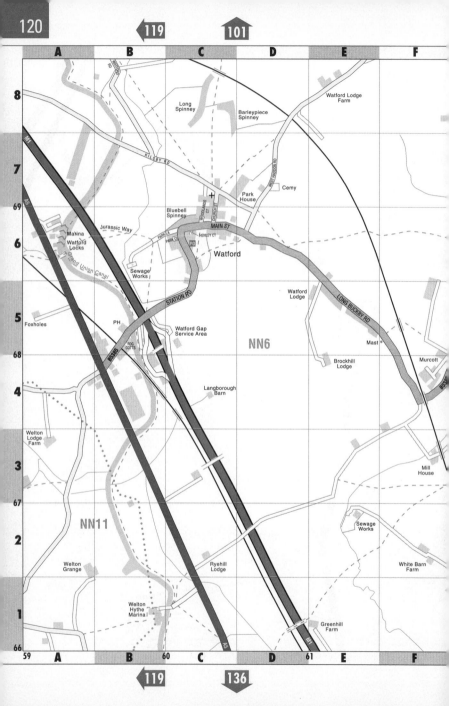

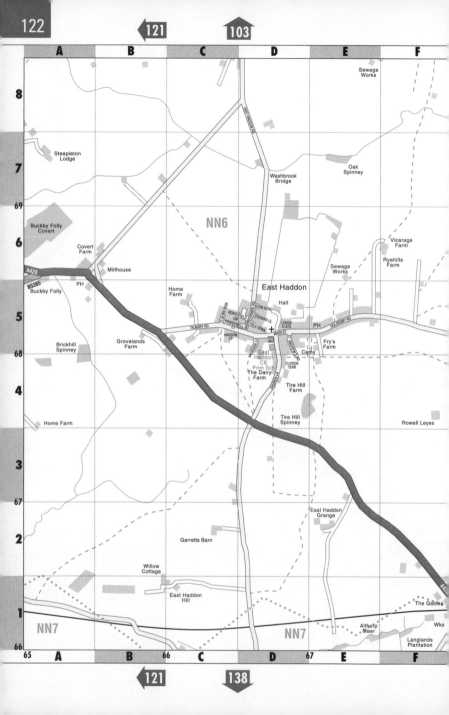

121
103

A B C D E F

8

7

69

NN6

6

Steepleton
Lodge

Sewage
Works

Oak
Spinney

Washbrook
Bridge

Buckby Folly
Covert

Covert
Farm

Millhouse

Vicarage
Farm

Ryehills
Farm

A428

B5385

PH

Buckby Folly

Home
Farm

East Haddon

Hall

Sewage
Works

5

Brickhill
Spinney

Grovelands
Farm

BACH ACRE

NORTHFIELD

ORCHARD CL

PRIESTWELL ST

TILBURY ROAD

HALL CLOSE

TILBURY RISE

HADDON
CT

MOORLEY LA

CRESTON LA

ST ANDREWS RD

MAIN ST

PO

LODGE
FLATS

PH

HOLDENBY RD

Fry's
Farm

68

East
Haddon
CE
Prim Sch

CLIFDEN
TERR

Cemy

The Dairy
Farm

Tire Hill
Farm

4

Tire Hill
Spinney

Rowell Leyes

Home Farm

3

67

East Haddon
Grange

2

Garretts Barn

Willow
Cottage

East Haddon
Hill

The Gables

Wks

1

NN7

NN7

Althorp
Meer

Langlands
Plantation

66

65 **A** 66 **B** **C** 66 **D** 67 **E** **F**

121
138

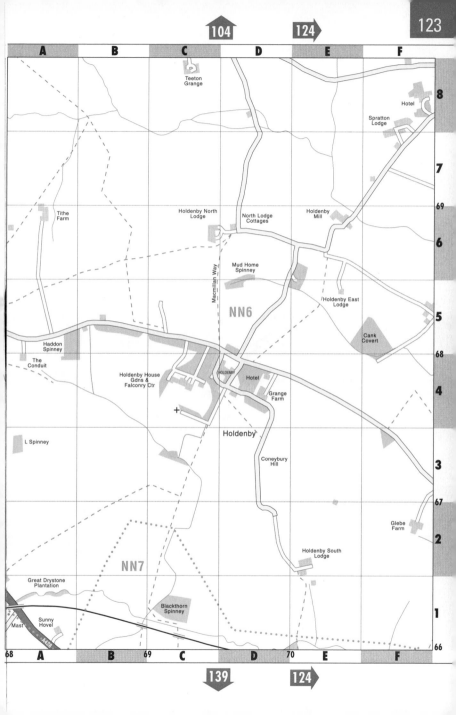

104
124
139
124

Teeton Grange

Hotel

Spratton Lodge

Tithe Farm

Holdenby North Lodge

North Lodge Cottages

Holdenby Mill

Mud Home Spinney

Macmillan Way

NN6

Holdenby East Lodge

Cank Covert

Haddon Spinney

The Conduit

Holdenby House Gdns & Falconry Ctr

HOLDENBY

Hotel

Grange Farm

L Spinney

Holdenby

Coneybury Hill

Glebe Farm

NN7

Holdenby South Lodge

Great Drystone Plantation

Blackthorn Spinney

Mast

Sunny Hovel

A428

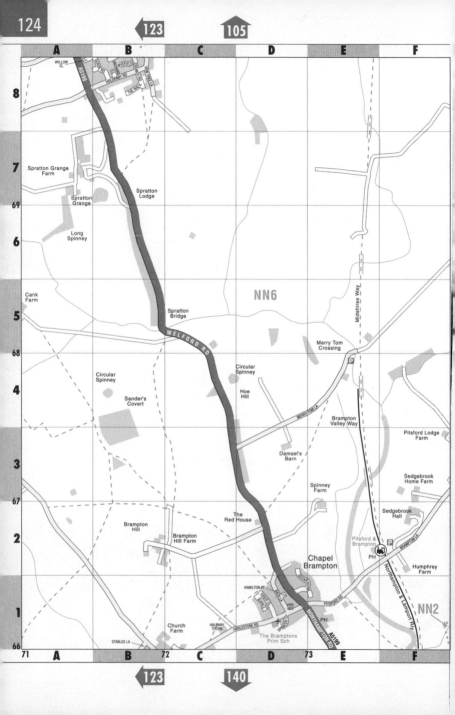

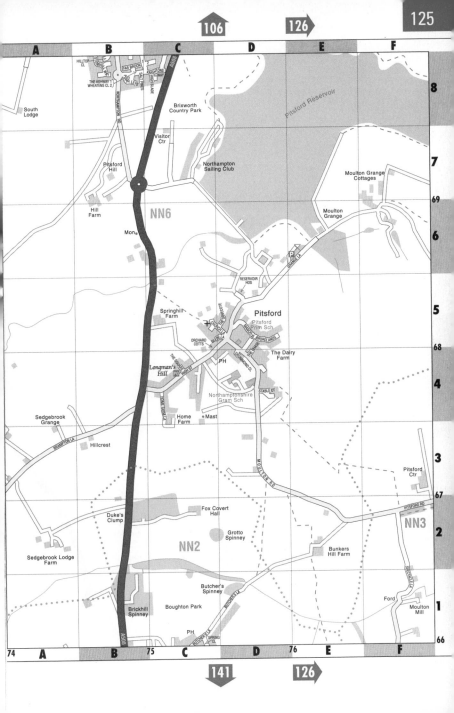

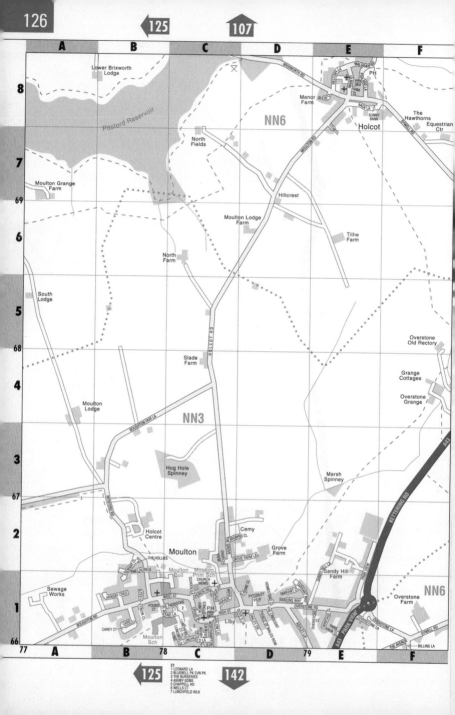

A **B** **C** **D** **E** **F**

8

Lower Brixworth Lodge

Pitsford Reservoir

Manor Farm

NN6

WALGRAVE
PH

Holcot

The Hawthorns
Equestrian Ctr

SUNNY BANK

SYBELL RD

North Fields

7

Moulton Grange Farm

69

Hillcrest

Moulton Lodge Farm

Tithe Farm

6

North Farm

MOULTON RD

South Lodge

5

Overstone Old Rectory

68

Slade Farm

Grange Cottages

Overstone Grange

HOLCOT RD

4

Moulton Lodge

NN3

BOUGHTON FAIR LA

Hog Hole Spinney

Marsh Spinney

A43

KETTERING RD

3

67

Holcot Centre

Cemy

PECTOR RD

Moulton

Grove Farm

THE HOLLIES

Sandy Hill Farm

NN6

2

Sewage Works

Moulton Coll

Moulton Prim Sch

Grove Farm

Overstone Farm

ARNSBY CRES

THE LAURELS

CHURCH MEWS

Overstone Rd

PARK VIEW

A43

NN6

1

WEST ST

POUND CT

PH

Liby

Moulton Sch

CAREY CT CAREY

BROUGHTON RD

HIGH ST

PYTCHLEY VIEW

OVERSTONE LA

BILLING LA

THE AVENUE

SYBELL RD

66

77 **A** **B** **78** **C** **D** **79** **E** **F**

C1
1 LEONARD LA
2 BLUEBELL PK CVN PK
3 THE NURSERIES
4 ASHBY GDNS
5 CHAPPELL HO
6 WELLS CT
7 LUNCHFIELD WLK

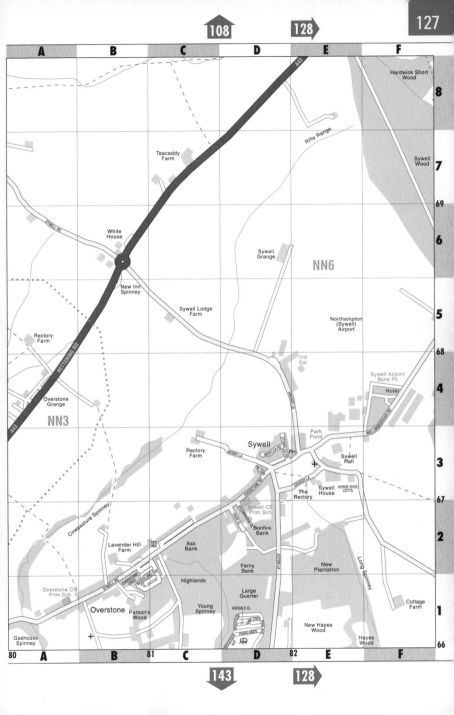

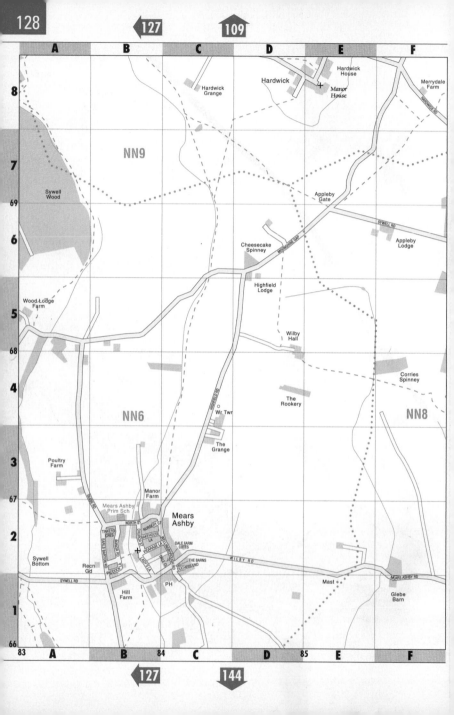

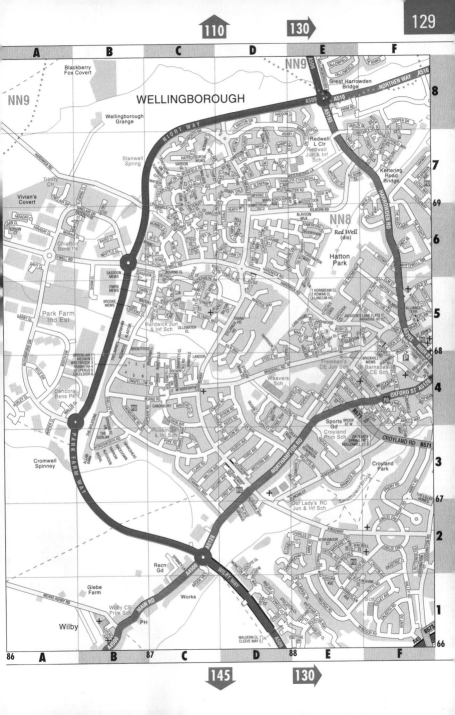

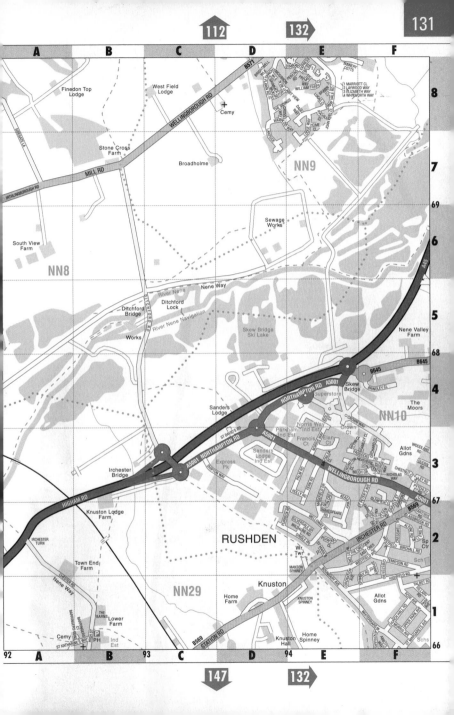

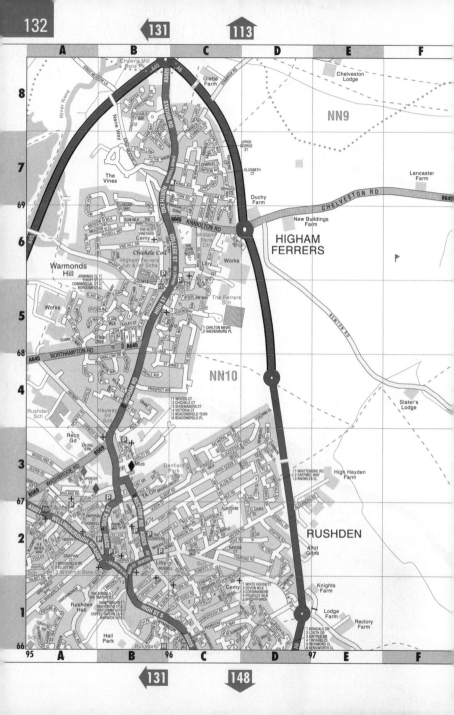

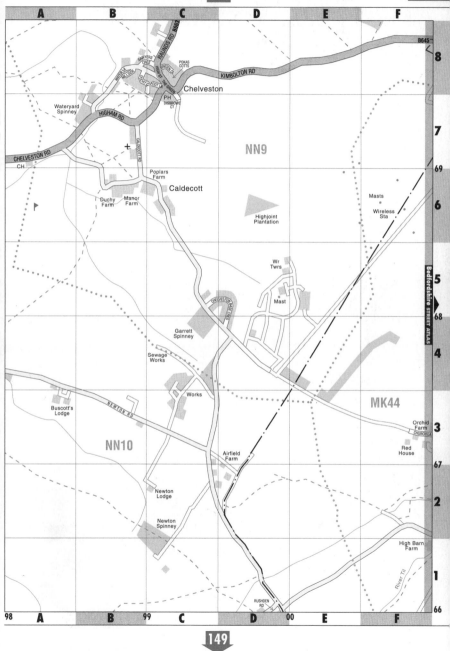

B645

8

Chelveston

KIMBOLTON RD

POKAS COTTS

ROUNDS RD B663

SMITHFIELD CRES
WINDSETT
FOOT LN

WEDDELL

IRETONS

HIGHAM RD

Wateryard
Spinney

PH
DISBROWE
CT

7

69

CHELVESTON RD

CH

NN9

CALDECOTT RD

Poplars
Farm

Caldecott

6

Duchy
Farm

Manor
Farm

Masts

Wireless
Sta

Highjoint
Plantation

Wr
Twrs

5

68

CHELVESTON PK CRES

Mast

Garrett
Spinney

4

Sewage
Works

Works

Buscott's
Lodge

NEWTON RD

MK44

Orchid
Farm

3

CHURCH LA

Red
House

NN10

Newton
Lodge

Airfield
Farm

67

2

Newton
Spinney

High Barn
Farm

1

River Till

66

RUSHDEN
RD

118

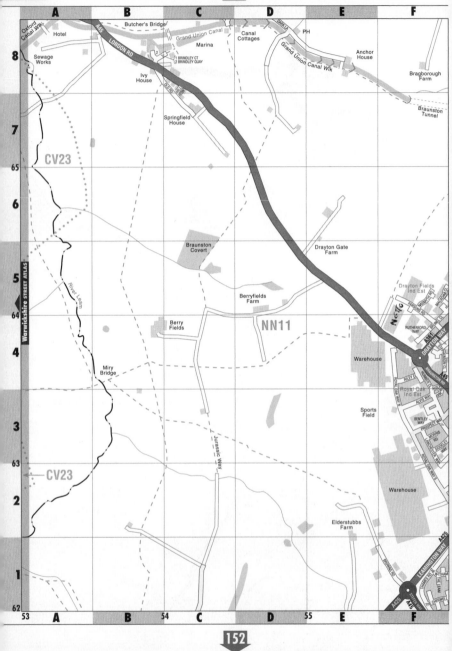

152

B3
1 CHANTELLE CT
2 HENRY SMITH HO
3 EDINBURGH SQ

B4
1 ROCKINGHAM CL
2 SALCEY CL
3 ARDEN CL
4 EPPING WLK
5 CHARNWOOD CL
6 DEAN WLK
7 RODERICK WAY
8 BROWNING SQ

C1
1 TAVERN LA
2 ST JAMES CL
3 NEWLANDS
4 FOUNDRY WLK
5 FOUNDRY CT
6 JOSEPH PRIESTLEY CT
7 BOWEN SQ
8 CHARLES TERR
9 THE LIMES

C2
1 RIDLEY CT
2 WARDENS LODGE
3 MARKET SQ
4 BISHOPS CT
5 REGENCY CT
6 THE ALBANY
7 BRAMLEY HO
8 CRABTREE HO
9 BROOK ST

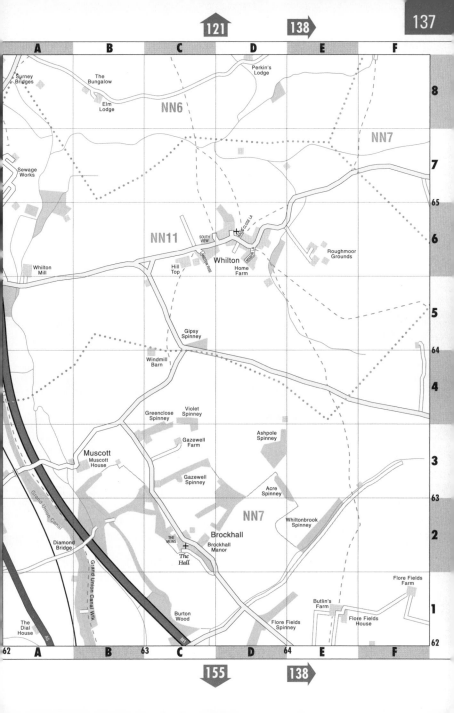

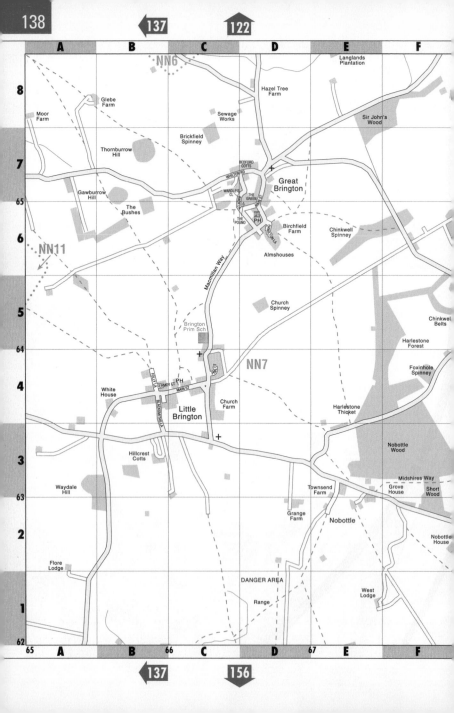

139
124

	A	B	C	D	E	F

8

Church Brampton

Manor Farm House

Brampton Brook Plantation

Brampton Grange

Boughton Mill

NORTHAMPTON RD

Cold Store

7

CH

CH

NN6

RAILWAY COTTS

BRAMPTON LA.

P

Sewage Works

65

Meadow View

Fox Covert

6

NN7

WELFORD RD

THE AVENUE

HARROW WAY

NN2

MEADHILLS WAY

5

Saw Mill

HARVEST WAY 1
MARTINDALE 2
ARNDALE 3
WESTERDALE 4
GLAISDALE CL 5
CROXDALE CL 6

64

A428

Harlestone Heath

Dallington Heath

Grange Farm

CATTON CRES

4

Round Oak Plantation

3

DALLINGTON BROOK

NN5

Heath Spinney

63

King's Heath

WHARFE GN

E M Regis

Lodge Farm Ind Est

HARLESTONE RD

2

DORCHESTER CT

New Duston

Britannia Trad Ctr

LENNOX WLK

PARK SQ

DERWENT CL

1

VELOCETTE WAY

Sch

ASHCROFT CL

Hopping Hill

TRESHAM GN

1 ROKEBY WLK
2 STONELEIGH CHASE
3 WENLOCK WAY

Allot Gdns

WOODSIDE WLK

WOODSIDE GN

HEATH CL

ST MARY'S RC LOWER SCH

62

Cemy

A428

71	A	B	72	C	D	73	E	F

139
158

F1
1 THE CROFT
2 THE BARTONS CL
3 ST MARGARET'S GDNS
4 KG House Bsns Ctr

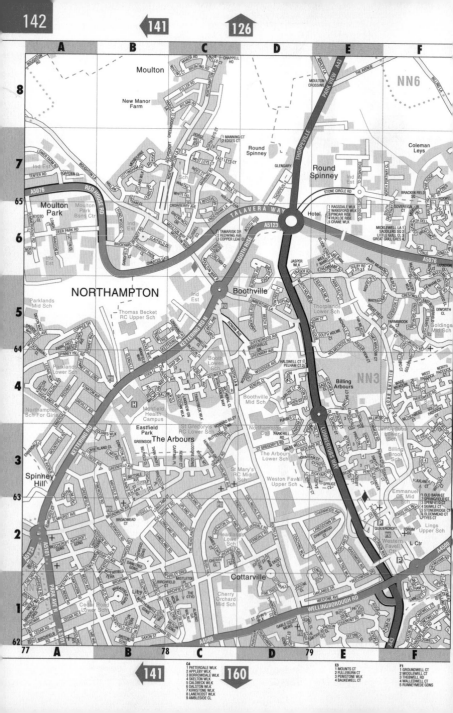

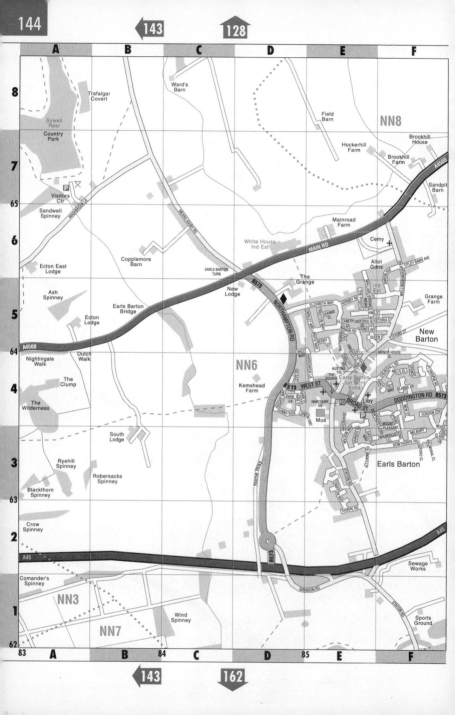

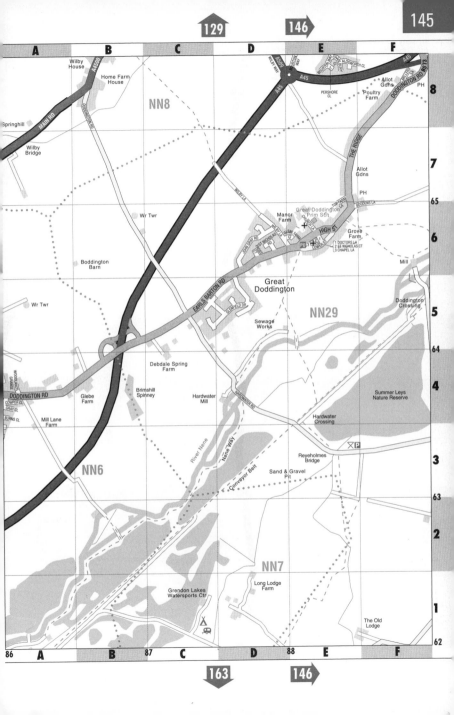

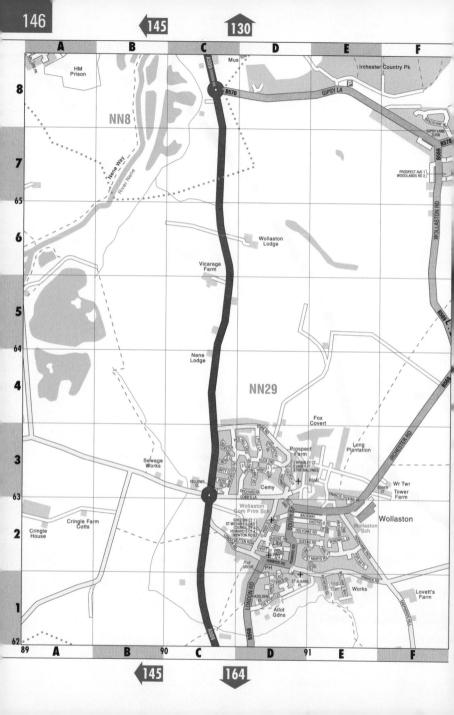

147
132

	A	B	C	D	E	F

8

Rushden
BLUEBELL CL
Schs

1 OAKHAM CL
2 HADDON CL

MANOR CT

DAISY CROFT

Jubilee
Park

1 ASCOT RD
2 GOODWOOD RD
3 SUNNINGDALE DR
4 TEWKESBURY DR

1 BARLEY CT
2 RYE CL
3 BELVOIR CL
4 OAKLETS WAY
5 CHELTENHAM CL

Eastfields
Farm

Allot
Gdns

CELANDINE CL

Allot Gdns

7

65

Little
Wymington

RUSHDEN

6

NN10

St Lawrence
Lower Sch

MANOR LA

Sports
Gd

5

CHURCH

1 BROOK FARM CL
2 ST LAWRENCE WLK
3 THE BRAMBLES

Poplar
Farm

Wr
Twr

HIGH ST

3 CHESTNUT CL

Wymington

New
Buildings

BEDFORD RD

64

4

Works

Goosey's
Lodge

River Til

Ravensden
Farm

North
Lodge

Bencroft
Grange

3

63

Darnell's
Dene

Whitland's
Barn

Sharnbrook Tunnel

MK44

Blackmere
Farm

2

Three Shires Way

1

NN29

Sharnbrook
Summit

62

95	A	B	96	C	D	97	E	F

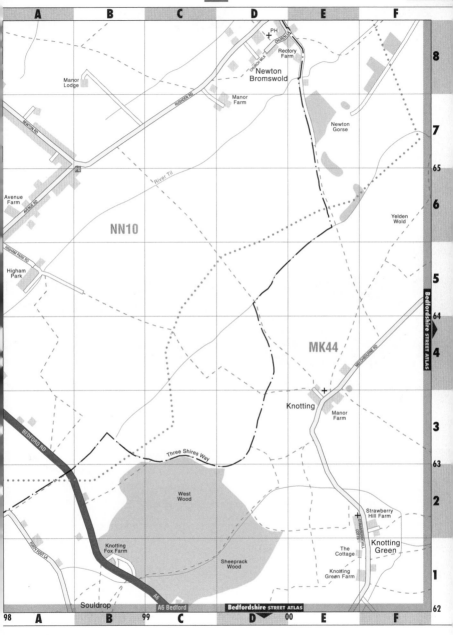

Manor Lodge

Newton Bromswold

PH

Rectory Farm

CHURCH WLK

SUSPEN RD

NEWTON RD

PO

Manor Farm

Newton Gorse

River Til

Avenue Farm

AVENUE RD

NN10

Yelden Wold

HIGHAM PARK RD

Higham Park

MK44

MELCHBOURNE RD

Knotting

Manor Farm

BEDFORD RD

Three Shires Way

West Wood

63

FORTY FOOT LA

Knotting Fox Farm

STRAWBERRY HILL

Strawberry Hill Farm

Knotting Green

The Cottage

Sheeprack Wood

Knotting Green Farm

A6

Souldrop

A6 Bedford

98

99

00

62

8

7

65

6

5

64

4

3

2

1

A B C D E F

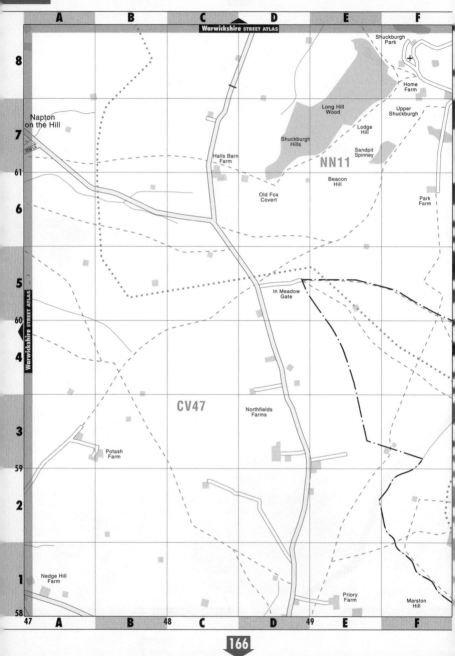

Warwickshire STREET ATLAS

Napton
on the Hill

Shuckburgh
Park

Home
Farm

Long Hill
Wood

Upper
Shuckburgh

Lodge
Hill

Shuckburgh
Hills

Sandpit
Spinney

NN11

Halls Barn
Farm

Beacon
Hill

Park
Farm

Old Fox
Covert

In Meadow
Gate

CV47

Northfields
Farms

Potash
Farm

Nedge Hill
Farm

Priory
Farm

Marston
Hill

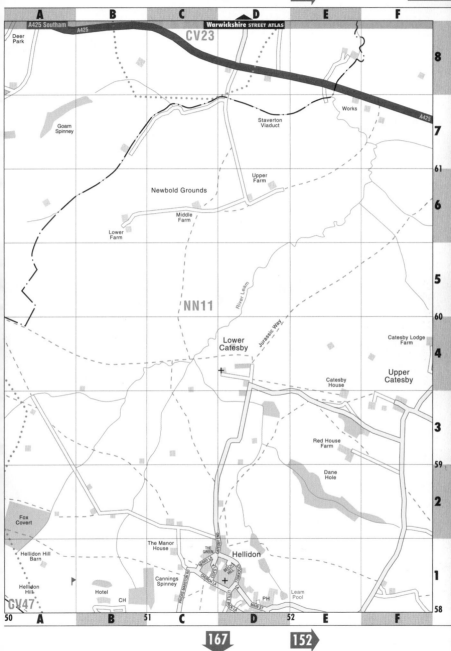

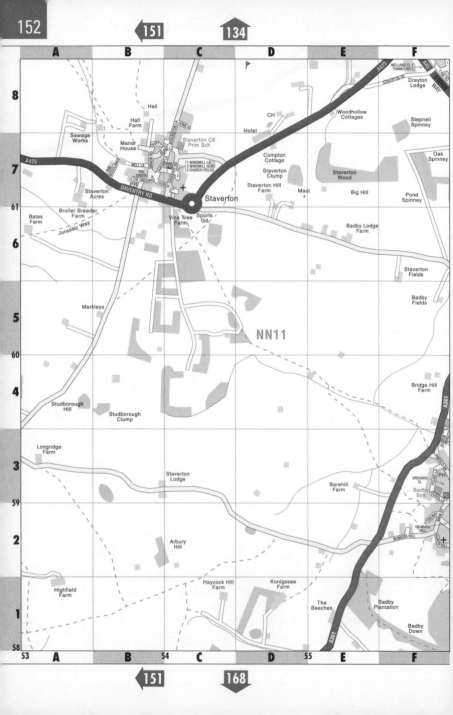

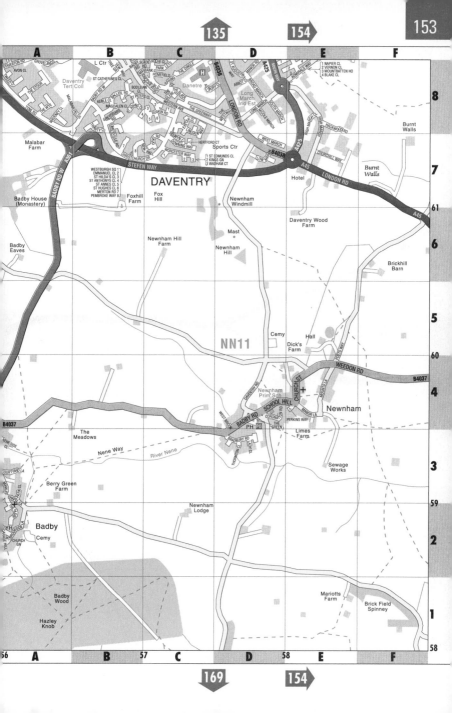

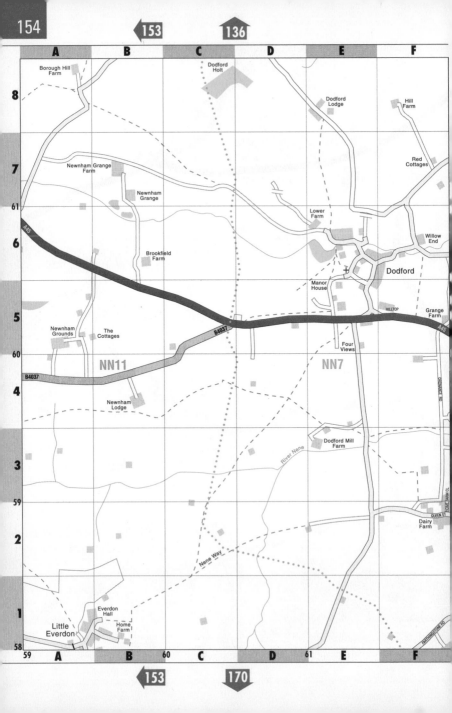

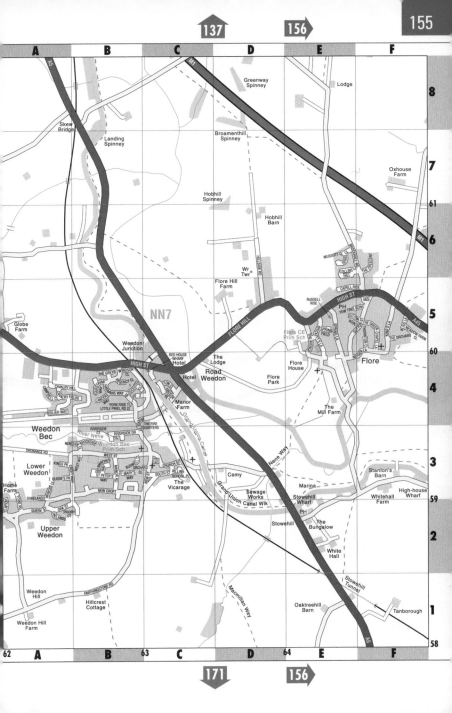

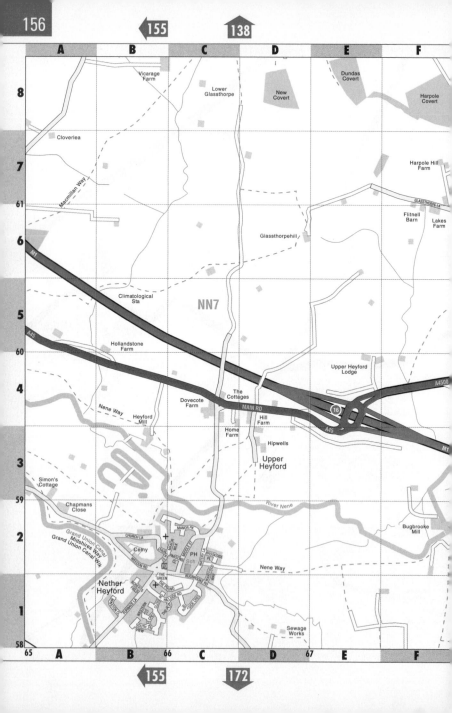

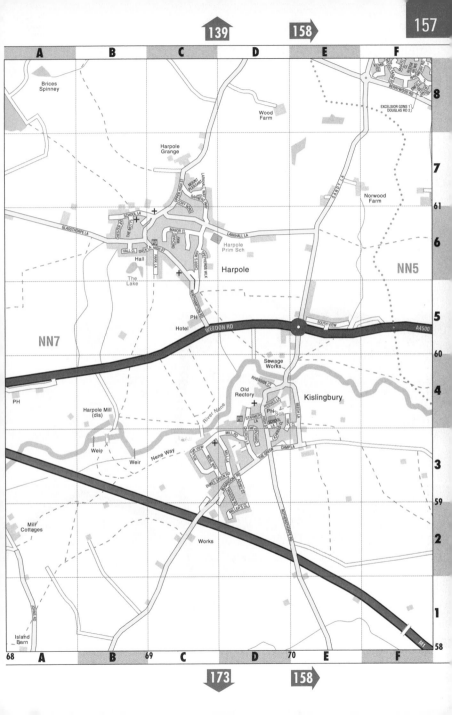

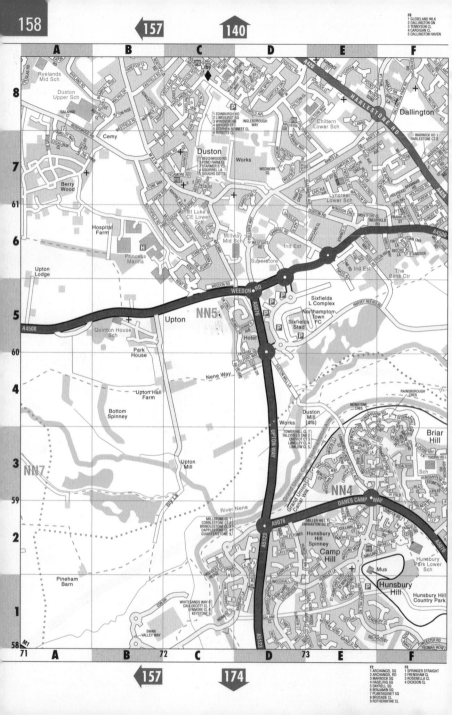

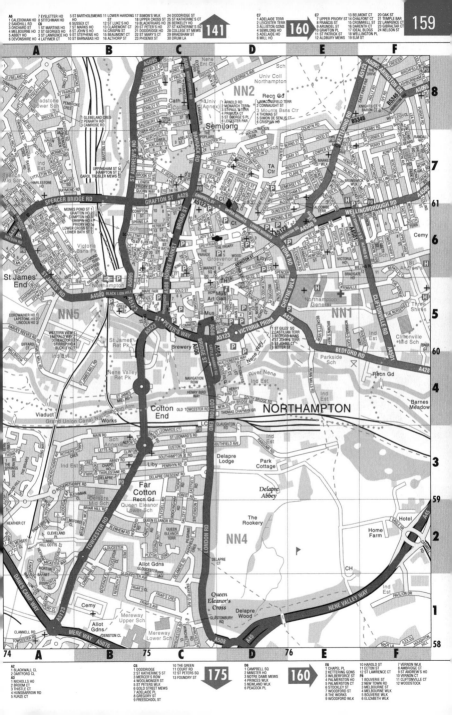

A6
1 CALEDONIAN RD
2 SANDHILL RD
3 ORCHARD ST
4 MELBOURNE HO
5 ABBEY HO
6 DEVONSHIRE HO
7 EYELETTER HO
8 STITCHMAN HO

C6
1 ST MARTINS HO
2 ST GEORGES HO
3 ST LAWRENCE HO
4 LATYMER CT
5 ST BARTHOLEMEWS HO
6 SUSSEX CT
7 ST MARKS HO
8 ST JOHN'S HO
9 ST STEPHENS HO
10 ST BARNABAS HO
11 LOWER HARDING ST
12 ST LUKE'S HO
13 CLAREMONT CT
14 CRISPIN ST
15 BEAUMONT CT
16 ALTHORP ST
17 SIMON'S WLK
18 UPPER CROSS ST
19 BLACKFRIARS HO
20 ST PETER'S HO
21 DODDRIDGE ST
22 ST MARY'S CT
23 PHOENIX ST
24 DODDRIDGE ST
25 ST KATHERINE'S SQ
26 BERKELEY HO
27 ST KATHERINE'S SQ
28 COLLEGE ST MEWS
29 BRADSHAW ST
30 DRUM LA

141

C7
1 ADELAIDE TERR
2 LEICESTER TERR
3 ALLISTON GDNS
4 SEMILONG HO
5 ADELAIDE HO
6 MILL HO

160

C7
7 UPPER PRIORY ST
8 FRANCIS ST
9 ARUNDEL ST
10 GRAFTON ST
11 ST PATRICK ST
12 ALDBURY MEWS
13 BELMONT CT
14 CHALFONT CT
15 CROMWELL ST
16 DARENTH CT
17 IDEAL BLDGS
18 WELLINGTON PL
19 ELM ST
20 OAK ST
21 TEMPLE BAR
22 LAWRENCE CT
23 GIBRALTAR CT
24 NELSON ST

159

A2
1 BLACKWALL CL
2 DARTFORD CL
A3
1 NICHOLLS HO
2 BROOM CT
3 THISTLE CT
4 HUNSBARROW RD
5 FURZE CT

C6
1 DODDRIDGE
2 ST KATHERINE'S SQ
3 MERCER'S ROW
4 WOOLMERGER ST
5 ST PETERS WLK
6 GOLD STREET MEWS
7 ADELAIDE PL
8 GREGORY ST
9 FREESCHOOL ST
10 THE GREEN
11 COURT RD
12 ST PETERS SQ
13 FOUNDRY ST

175

D6
1 CAMPBELL SQ
2 MINSTER HO
3 NOTRE DAME MEWS
4 PRINCES WLK
5 NEWLAND WLK
6 PEACOCK PL

160

E6
1 CHAPEL PL
2 KETTERING GDNS
3 WILBERFORCE ST
4 PALMERSTON HO
5 PALMERSTON CT
6 STOCKLEY ST
7 WOODFORD ST
8 THE WORKS
9 WOODFORD WLK
10 HAROLD ST
11 ECTON ST
12 ST LAWRENCE CT
F6
1 BOUVERIE ST
2 NEW TOWN RD
3 MELBOURNE ST
4 MELBOURNE WLK
5 BOUVERIE WLK
6 ELIZABETH WLK
7 VERNON WLK
8 AMBRIDGE CT
9 ST ANDREW'S HO
10 VERNON CT
11 CLIFTONVILLE CT
12 WOODSTOCK

159

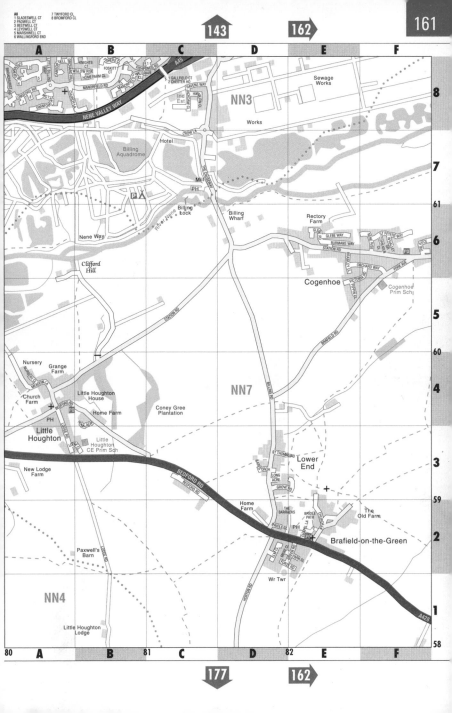

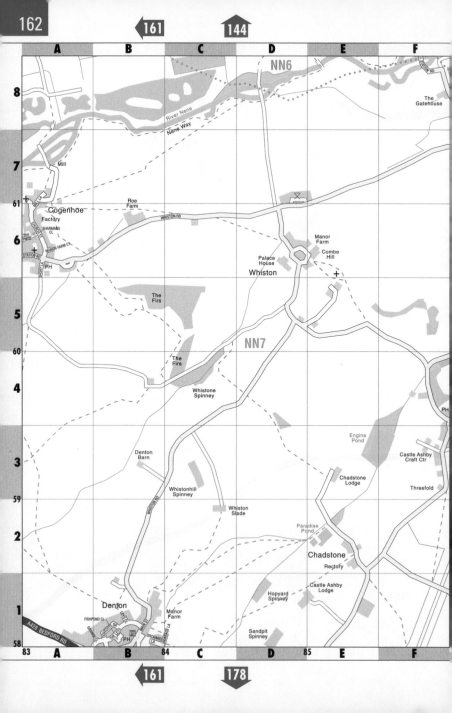

A   B   C   D   E   F

NN6

The
Gatehouse

8

River Nene

Nene Way

Mill

7

61

Cogenhoe

Roe
Farm

Factory

SHARMANS
CL.

WHISTON RD

Manor
Farm

THE PIECE

MANOR FARM CT.

STATION RD

PH

Palace
House

Combe
Hill

Whiston

6

The
Firs

5

60

The
Firs

NN7

Whistone
Spinney

4

Engine
Pond

Castle Ashby
Craft Ctr

PH

Denton
Barn

3

Chadstone
Lodge

Threefold

Whistonhill
Spinney

WHISTON RD

Whiston
Slade

59

Paradise
Pond

Chadstone

2

Rectory

Denton

Manor
Farm

Hopyard
Spinney

Castle Ashby
Lodge

A428 BEDFORD RD

FISHPOND CL.

LITTLE END

MILL LA

ORCHARD

DENTON LA

PH

1

Sandpit
Spinney

58

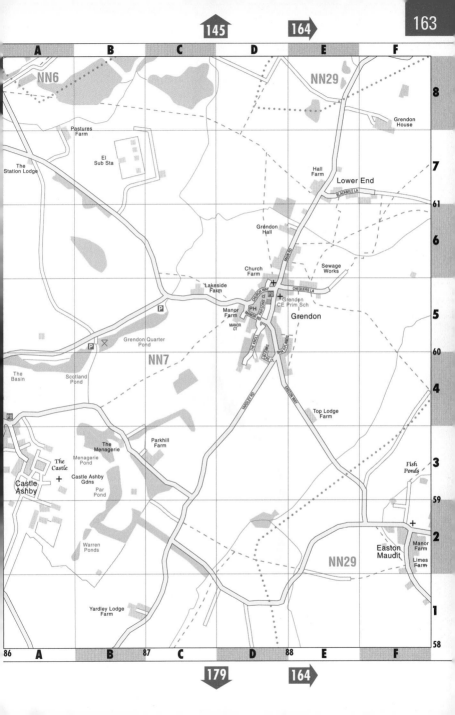

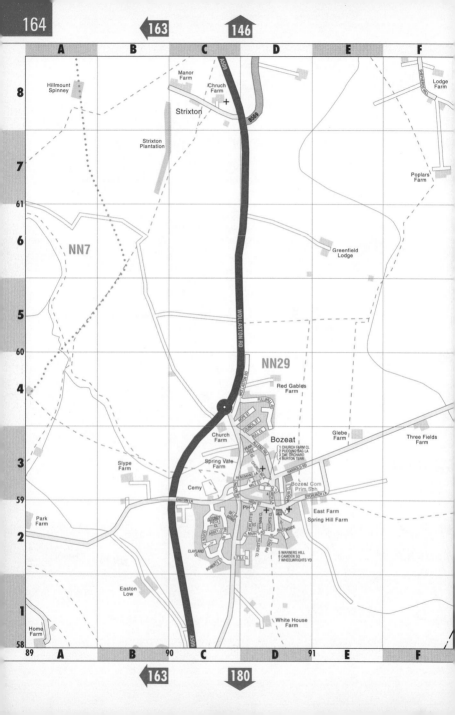

Hillmount
Spinney

Manor
Farm

Chruch
Farm

Strixton

Strixton
Plantation

NN7

Lodge
Farm

Poplars
Farm

Greenfield
Lodge

NN29

Red Gables
Farm

FULLMEAD RD

HOPE ST

COUNCIL ST

HILL CR

Church
Farm

Bozeat

1 CHURCH FARM CL
2 PUDDING BAG LA
3 THE ORCHARD
4 BURTON TERR

Glebe
Farm

Three Fields
Farm

Slype
Farm

Spring Vale
Farm

Cemy

EASTON LA

HARROLD RD

Bozeat Com
Prim Sch

CHURCH LA

Park
Farm

PH

HIGH ST

East Farm
Spring Hill Farm

CLAYLAND
CL

LITTLE CL

ROBERTS

5 WARNERS HILL
6 CAMDEN SQ
7 WHEELWRIGHTS YD

Easton
Low

Home
Farm

White House
Farm

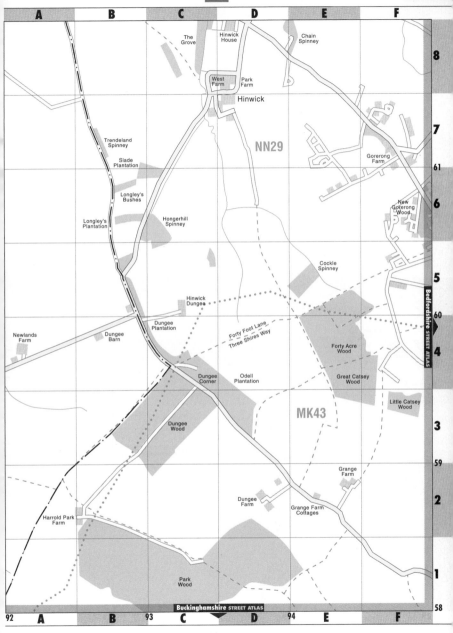

Bedfordshire STREET ATLAS

The Grove
Hinwick House
Chain Spinney

West Farm
Park Farm

Hinwick

NN29

Trendeland Spinney

Slade Plantation

Gorerong Farm

Longley's Bushes

New Gorerong Wood

Longley's Plantation

Hongerhill Spinney

Cockle Spinney

Hinwick Dungee

Dungee Plantation

Forty Foot Lane
Three Shires Way

Forty Acre Wood

Newlands Farm

Dungee Barn

Dungee Corner

Odell Plantation

Great Catsey Wood

Little Catsey Wood

MK43

Dungee Wood

Grange Farm

Dungee Farm

Grange Farm Cottages

Harrold Park Farm

Park Wood

150

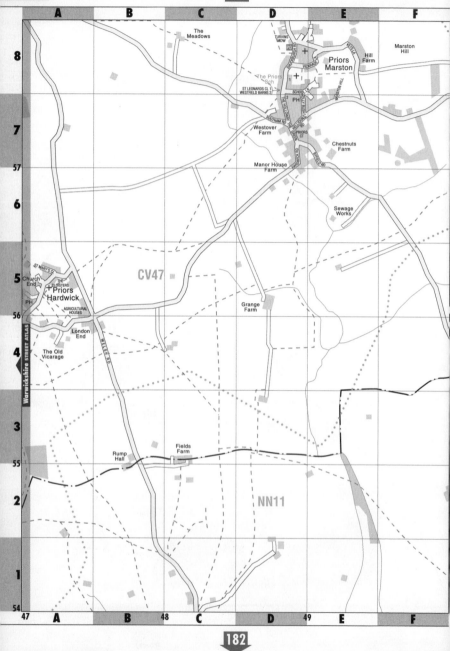

182

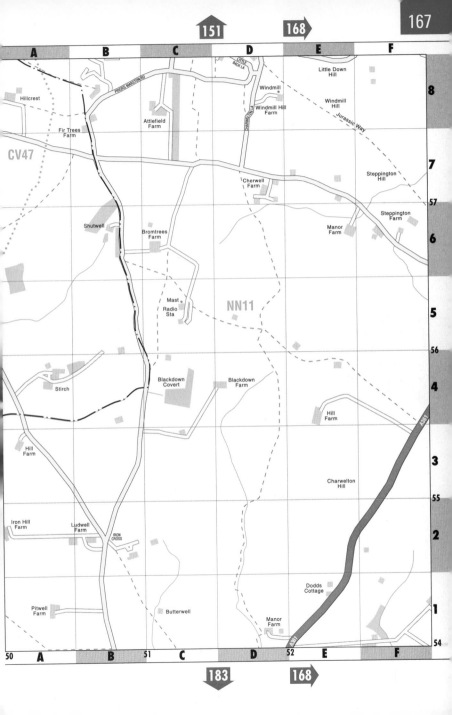

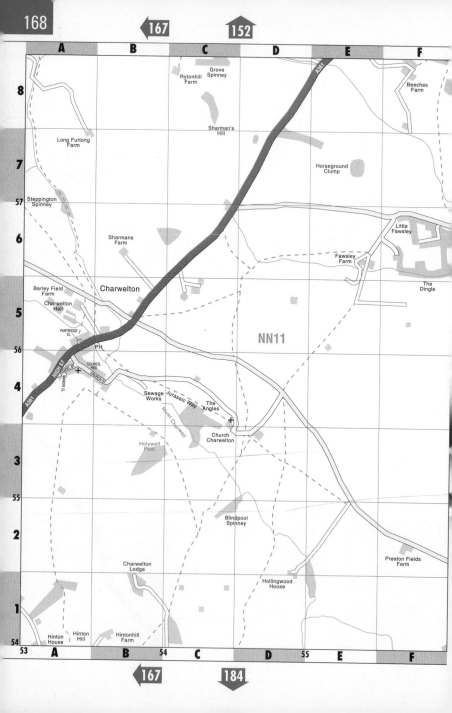

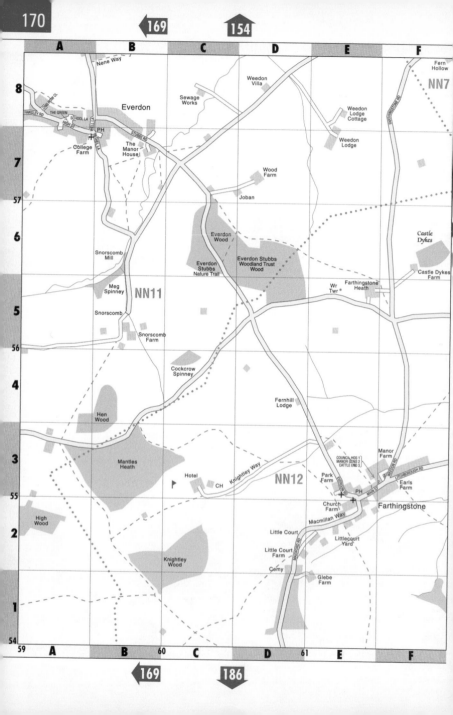

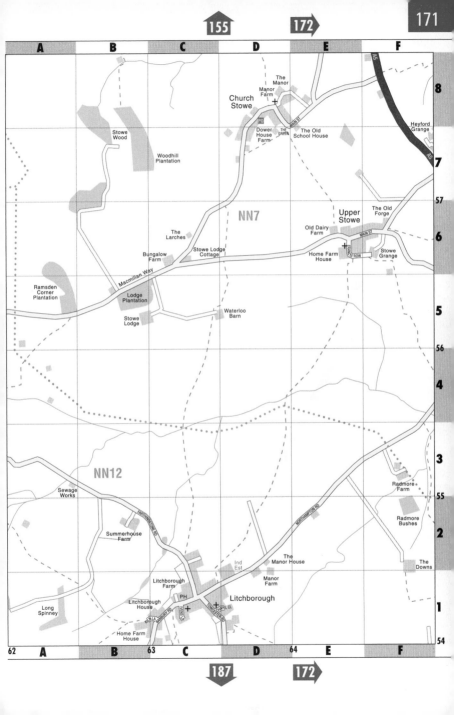

A **B** **C** **D** **E** **F**

8

The Manor
Manor Farm
Church Stowe
Heyford Grange

Stowe Wood
Dower House Farm
The Old School House
7

Woodhill Plantation
THE GREEN
57

NN7
Upper Stowe
The Old Forge
6
The Larches
Old Dairy Farm
MAIN ST
Bungalow Farm
Stowe Lodge Cottage
Home Farm House
Stowe Grange

Macmillan Way
Ramsden Corner Plantation
Lodge Plantation
5
Stowe Lodge
Waterloo Barn
56

4

NN12
3
Radmore Farm
55
Sewage Works
Radmore Bushes
Summerhouse Farm
2
The Manor House
The Downs
Litchborough Farm
Ind Est
Manor Farm
Litchborough House
PH
Litchborough
1
Long Spinney
Home Farm House
54

62 **A** **B** 63 **C** **D** 64 **E** **F**

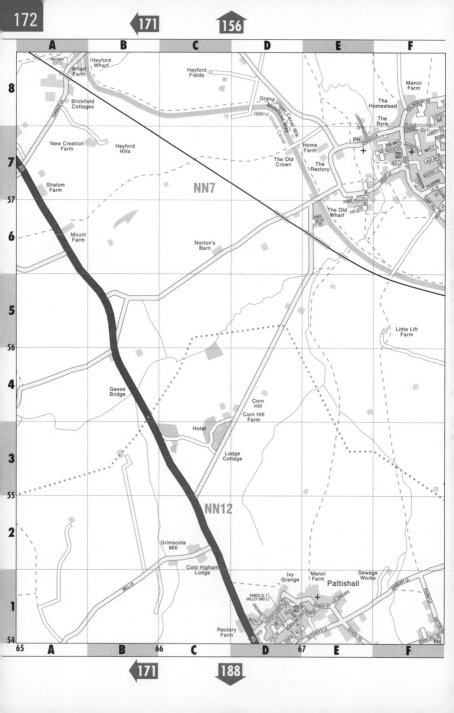

171
156

A B C D E F

8

RAILWAY
COTTS
Wharf
Farm
Heyford
Wharf
Heyford
Fields

The
Homestead
Manor
Farm

The Byre
Bugbrooke
Prim Sch

Brickfield
Cottages

New Creation
Farm

Heyford
Hills

7

57

Shalom
Farm

NN7

Home
Farm

The Old
Crown

The
Rectory

PH

The Old
Wharf

6

Mount
Farm

Norton's
Barn

HALL
MEAD
CL

Grand Union Canal Wlk
Midshires Way
Grand Union Canal

5

56

Little Lift
Farm

4

Geese
Bridge

Corn
Hill

Corn Hill
Farm

Hotel

3

Lodge
Cottage

55

NN12

2

Grimscote
Mill

Cold Higham
Lodge

Ivy
Grange

Manor
Farm

Pattishall

Sewage
Works

MILL LA

SANDS CL 1
VALLEY END 2

CROUCH ST

1

Rectory
Farm

PH

54

65 A B 66 C D 67 E F

171
188

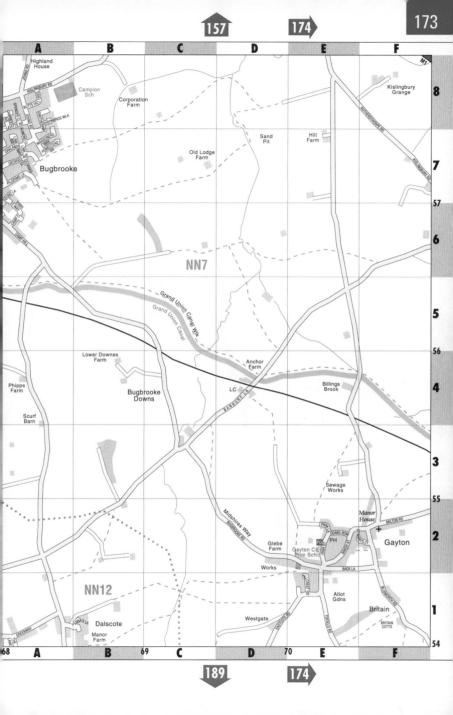

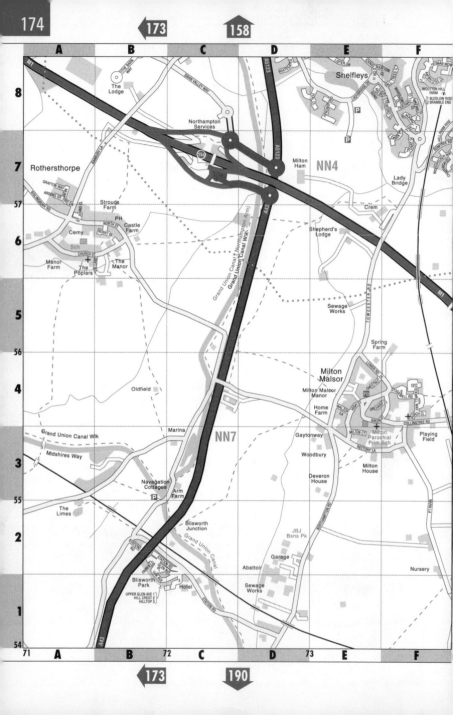

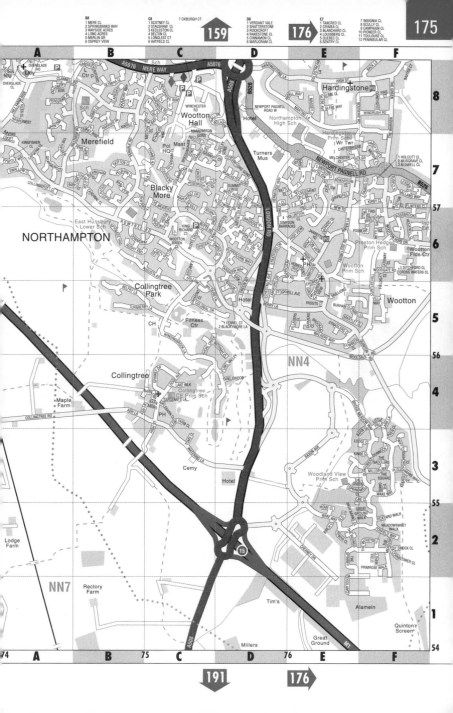

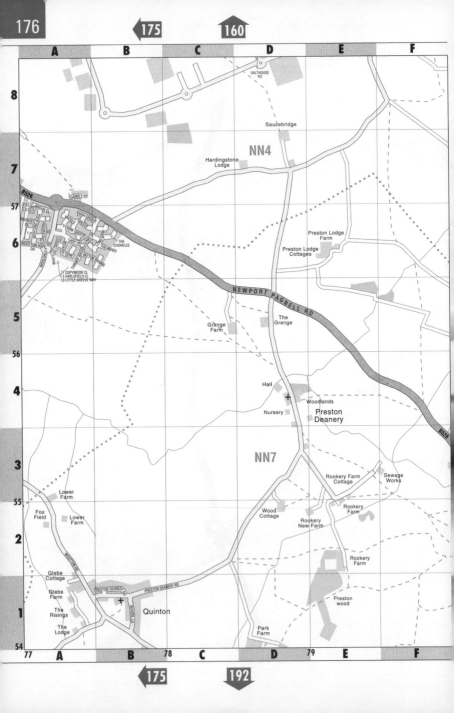

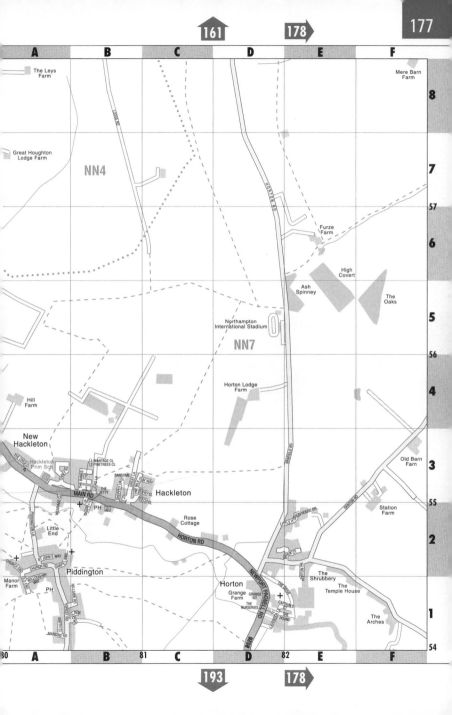

Map Grid

	A	B	C	D	E	F

A428

THE LEYS
Denton
Nursery
SOUTHAMPTON LANE
RING'S LANE
CHURCH WAY
OXFORD RD
MARGET LA
Vicarage Farm
Denton Prim Sch

Grange Farm

WARBING LA 1
WINDMILL LA 2
BY PASS WAY 3

Stonepit House

The Elms

Denton Lodge

Avenue Lodges

Forest Lodge

Avenue Villa

A428

Whiston Pike Copse

Old Ausway

Chestnut Star

Young Ausway

Freewood Copse

Dentonwood Lodge

Chase View Farm

Shortgrove Copse

Little Hay Copse

NN7

Ninneway-ats

Allot Gdns

Blenley Lodge

CHASE PARK RD

Buntingsea Copse

Hops Copse

New Hay Farm

Chase Park

Northampton Copse

Yardley Chase

Newhay Copse

House Wood

Chase Park Farm

The Park Sawmills

HIGHDAI LA

Victoria Star

Park Pond

Arniss Copse

Collier's Hern

The Wold

Sane Copse

DENTON RD

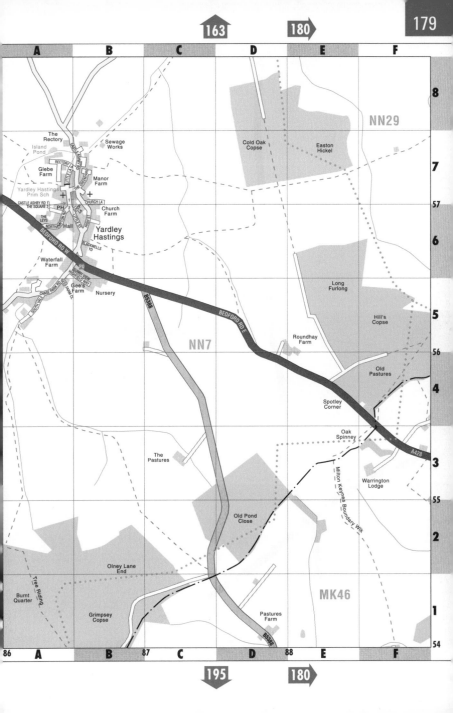

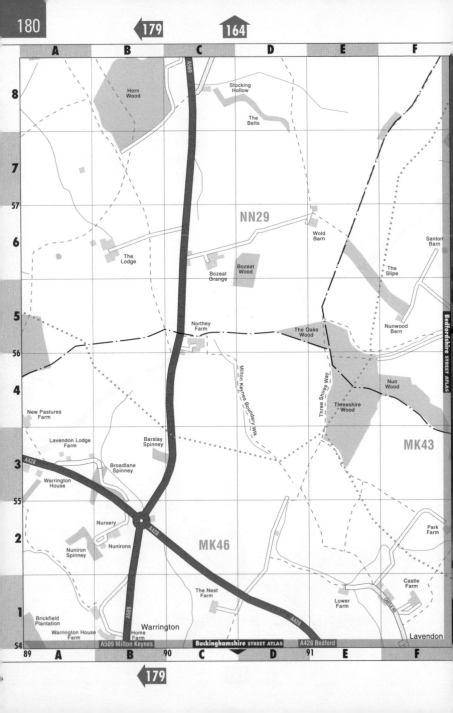

8

7

57

6

56

5

4

55

3

2

1

54

A   B   C   D   E   F

Horn
Wood

Stocking
Hollow

The Belts

NN29

Wold
Barn

Santon
Barn

The Lodge

Bozeat
Grange

Bozeat
Wood

The
Slipe

Nunwood
Barn

Northey
Farm

The Oaks
Wood

Nun
Wood

New Pastures
Farm

Milton Keynes Boundary Wk

Three Shires Way

Threeshire
Wood

MK43

Lavendon Lodge
Farm

Barslay
Spinney

A428

Broadlane
Spinney

Warrington
House

Nursery

MK46

Park
Farm

A428

Nuniron
Spinney

Nunirons

Castle
Farm

The Nest
Farm

CASTLE RD

Brickfield
Plantation

Home
Farm

Warrington

Lower
Farm

A428

Lavendon

Warrington House
Farm

A509

A509 Milton Keynes

Buckinghamshire STREET ATLAS

A428 Bedford

Bedfordshire STREET ATLAS

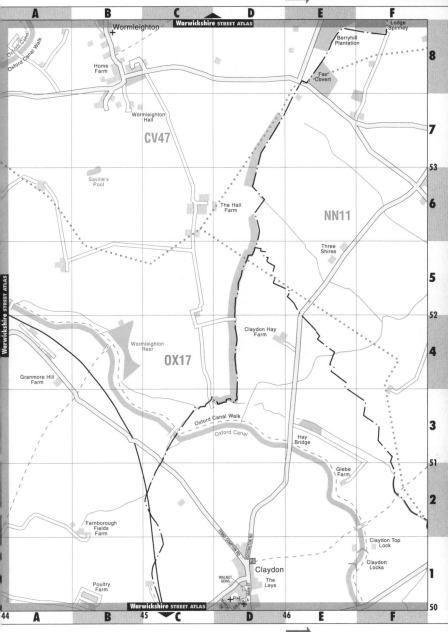

Wormleighton

Home Farm

Oxford Canal
Oxford Canal Walk

Wormleighton Hall

CV47

Berryhill Plantation

Lodge Spinney

Fox Covert

Saville's Pool

The Hall Farm

NN11

Three Shires

Claydon Hay Farm

Wormleighton Resr

OX17

Granmore Hill Farm

Oxford Canal Walk

Oxford Canal

Hay Bridge

Glebe Farm

Farnborough Fields Farm

Claydon Top Lock

Claydon Locks

Poultry Farm

WALNUT GDNS

Claydon

The Leys

PH

Warwickshire STREET ATLAS

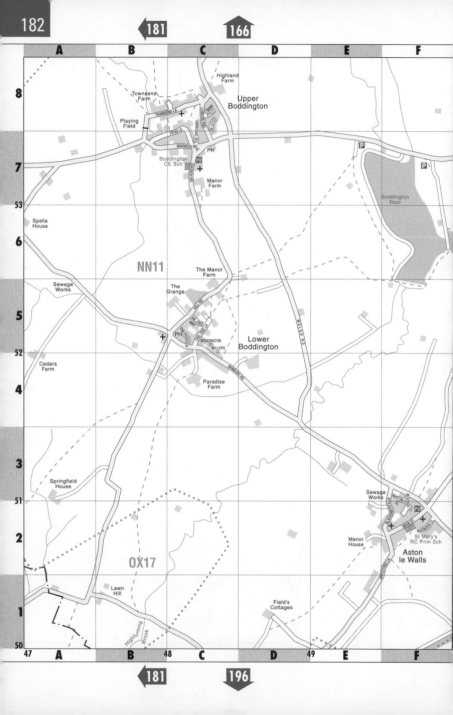

181
166

A   B   C   D   E   F

8

Highland Farm

Townsend Farm

Upper Boddington

Playing Field

TOWNSEND LA

PRIOR LA

THE GREEN

LONDON RD

WARWICK RD

PH

7

Boddington CE Sch

PO

Manor Farm

53

Spella House

6

NN11

The Manor Farm

The Grange

Sewage Works

5

MILL RD

HILL RD

PH

THE GROVE

LANE END

LANE END LA

BODDINGTON MILLERS CL

Lower Boddington

WELSH RD

52

Cedars Farm

4

Paradise Farm

BANBURY RD

3

Springfield House

51

Sewage Works

Aston le Walls

MAIN ST

PO

St Mary's RC Prim Sch

2

OX17

Manor House

1

Lawn Hill

Field's Cottages

50

Highfurlong Brook

47   A   B   48   C   D   49   E   F

181
196

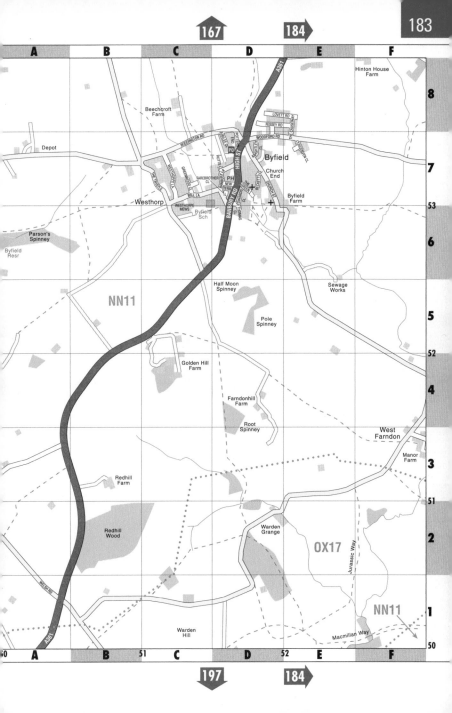

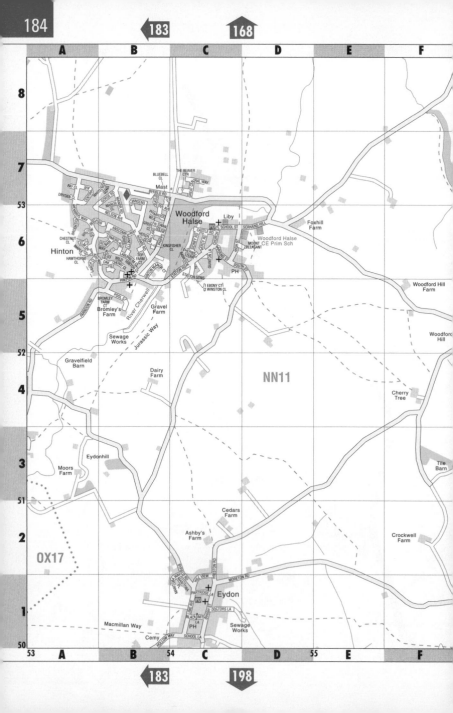

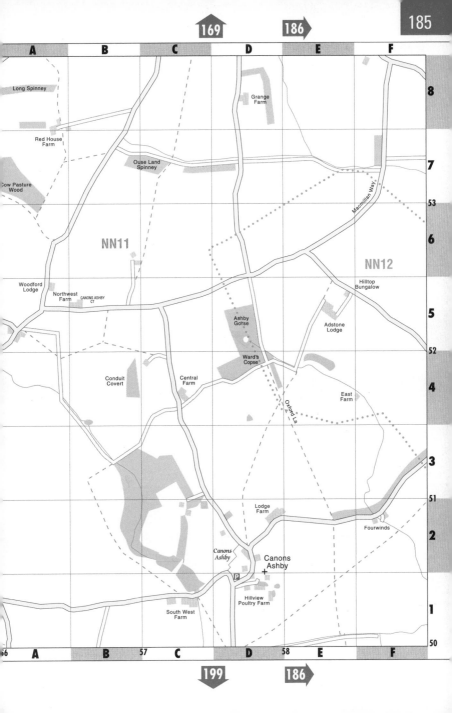

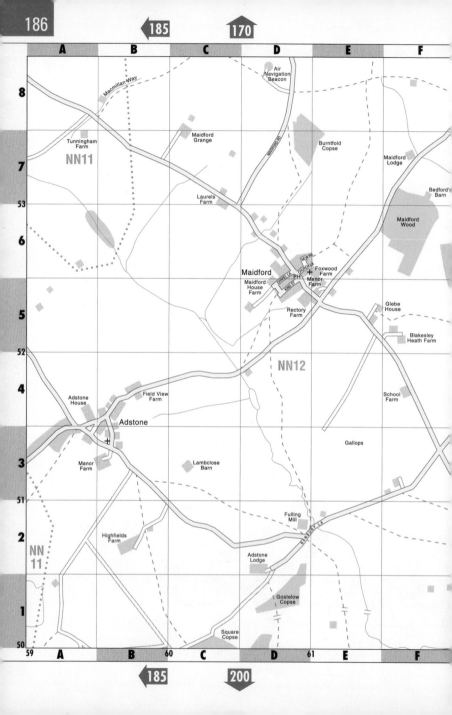

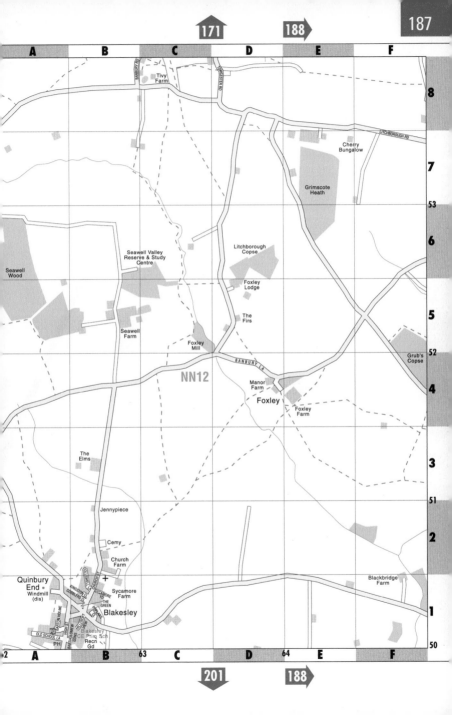

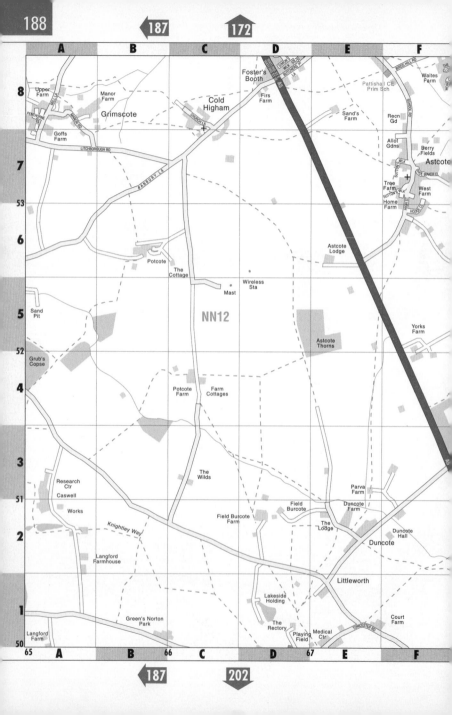

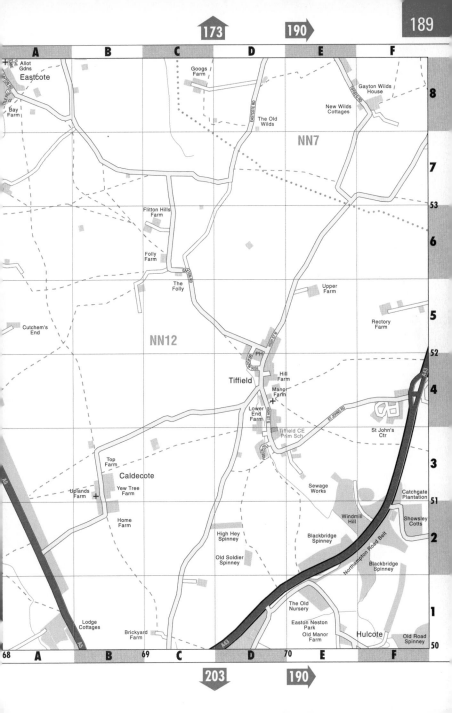

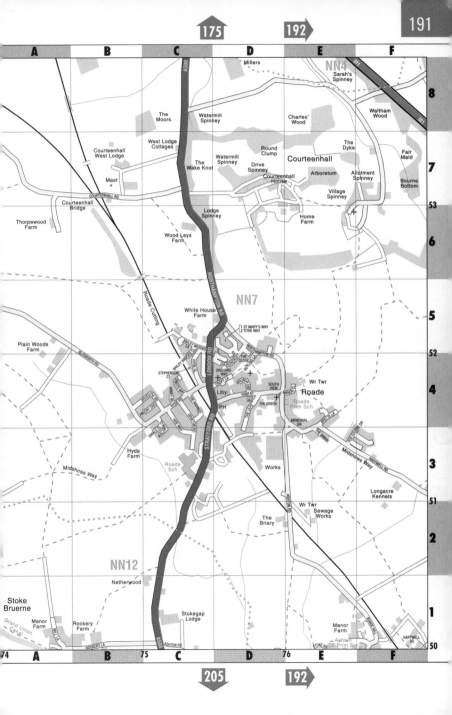

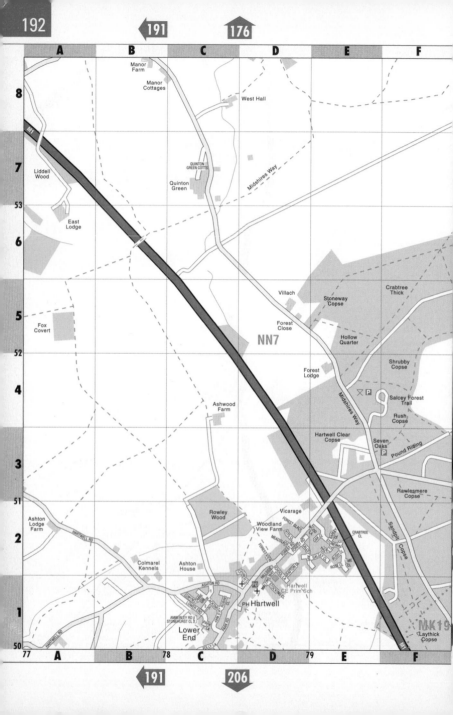

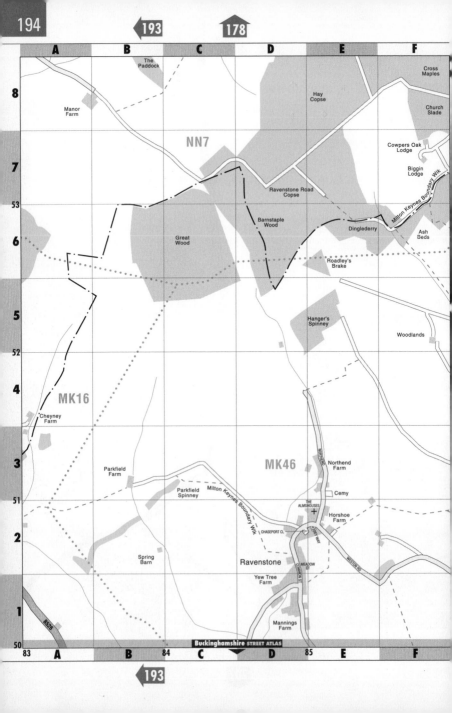

A   B   C   D   E   F

8

The Paddock

Cross Maples

Manor Farm

Hay Copse

Church Slade

7

NN7

Cowpers Oak Lodge

Biggin Lodge

53

Ravenstone Road Copse

Milton Keynes Boundary Wlk

Barnstaple Wood

6

Great Wood

Dinglederry

Ash Beds

Roadley's Brake

5

Hanger's Spinney

Woodlands

52

4

MK16

Cheyney Farm

3

Parkfield Farm

MK46

Northend Farm

Parkfield Spinney

Milton Keynes Boundary Wlk

Cemy

51

THE ALMSHOUSES

Horshoe Farm

2

CHASEPORT CL

Spring Barn

Ravenstone

MEADOW CT

Yew Tree Farm

1

B526

Mannings Farm

50

8

7

53

6

5

52

4

Liby

51

3

2

1

50

NN7

Howbrook
Copse

Kilwick
Wood

Olney Park
Farm

Milton Keynes Boundary Wlk

Olney
Hyde

Smith's
Farm

Court
Farm

B5388

Buckinghamshire STREET ATLAS

A509 Wellingborough

Allot
Gdns

Sewage
Works

Warrington
Road
Farm

Ind
Est

Hungary
Hall

Dickens
Spinney

MK46

Olney

Olney
Mid Sch

LONG MASSEY 1
SHORT MASSEY 2
CRAB TREE CL 3
HAWKSWOOD 4
MAYBUSH WLK 5
FISHERMANS CL 6

KENSINGTON

MIDLAND RD

NEWTON

B5388

DARTMOUTH RD

HIGH ST

Milton Keynes Boundary Wlk

Pheasants
Nest

FLAGGS MDW 1
STOCKEN CL 2
OVERHILLS 3
CHERRY ORCH 4
WHITMEES CL 5
DICKENS SPINNEY 6
ANDING CL 7
COURT CNR 8
BACON HILL 9

Long La

Long La

SPRINGFIELD

JOHNSONS
FIELD

COBBS
GDN

Olney
Fst Sch

ORCHARD
RISE

SPRING LA

The
Alcove

Overbrook
Spinney

Weston
Park

Flamingo Gardens
& Zoo Park

Weston Rd

STONE PIT
CL

BEECH AVE

OAKDOWN
CL

Recn
Gd

Mus

P

P

HIGH ST

The
Wilderness

Goosey
Bridge

MARKET PL 1
OSBORNE'S CT 2
PEMBROKE'RD 3
CHURCH ST 4

Works

Weston
Underwood

PH

Laundry
Cottage

Church
Farm

COWPERS ORCH

THE CLOSE

River Great Ouse

Grebe
Lake

Otter
Pool

Heron
Water

Emberton
Country Park
& Visitor Centre

The
Willows

Snipe
Pool

CH

Emberton

A509 Milton Keynes

HARVEY DR

BRIDGE ST

A

B

C

D

E

F

6

87

88

50

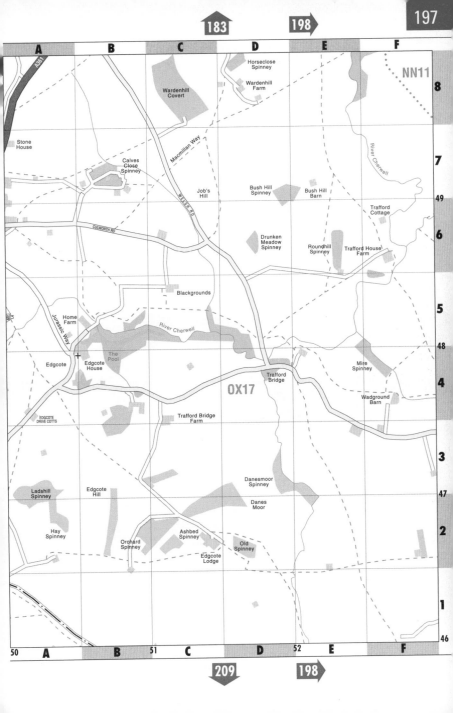

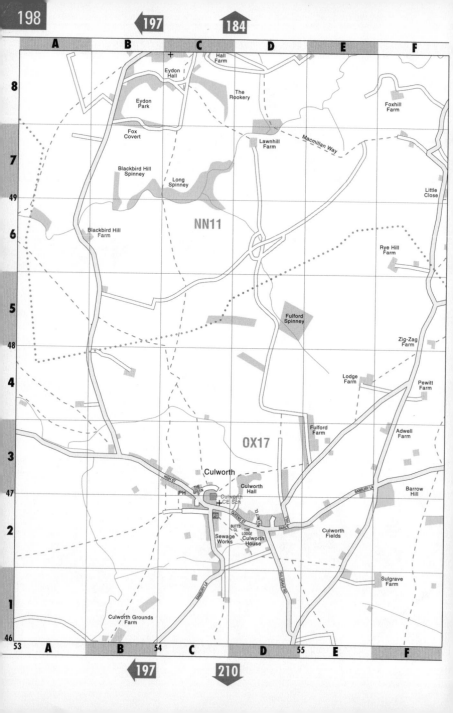

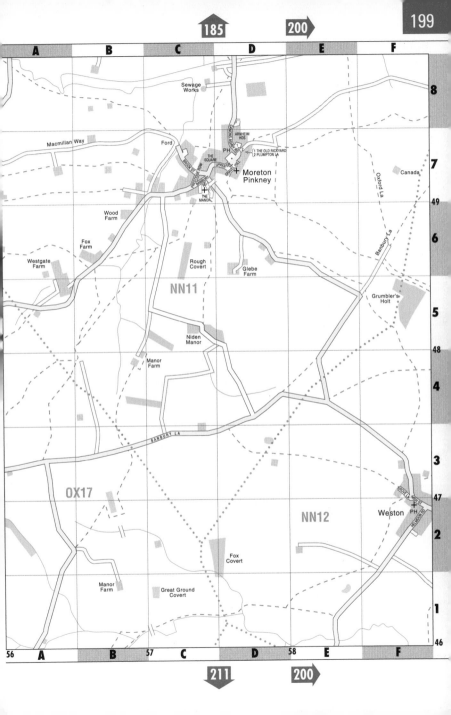

A   B   C   D   E   F

8

Sewage Works

Macmillan Way

Ford

ARNHEIM HOS

PH

1 THE OLD RICKYARD
2 PLUMPTON LA

7

Oxford La

Canada

THE SQUARE

UPPER

Moreton
Pinkney

49

THE MANOR

Wood Farm

Fox Farm

6

Westgate Farm

Rough Covert

Glebe Farm

Banbury La

NN11

Grumbler's Holt

5

48

Niden Manor

4

Manor Farm

BANBURY LA

3

OX17

47

NN12

Weston   PH

2

Fox Covert

Manor Farm

Great Ground Covert

1

46

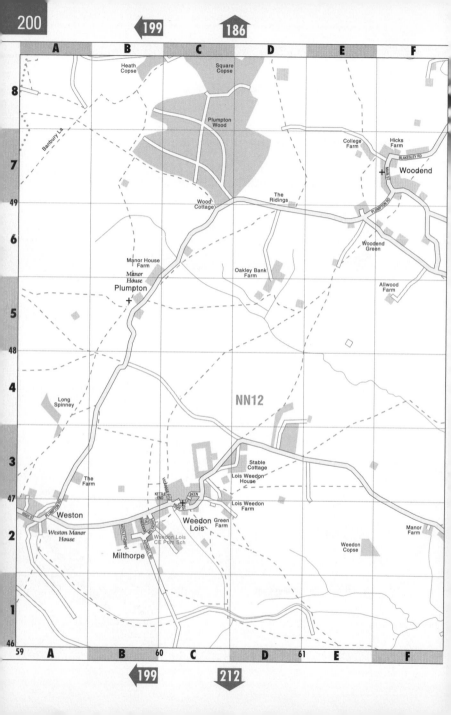

A B C D E F

8
7
49
6
5
48
4
3
47
2
1
46

Heath Copse
Square Copse
Plumpton Wood

Banbury La

College Farm
Hicks Farm
Woodend

BLAKESLEY RD

MAIN ST

Wood Cottage
The Ridings

PLUMPTON RD

Woodend Green

Manor House Farm
Manor House
Plumpton

Oakley Bank Farm

Allwood Farm

Long Spinney

NN12

Stable Cottage
Lois Weedon House

The Farm

VICARAGE RISE

KETTLE END

HIGH ST

GREEN

Lois Weedon Farm

Lois Weedon Farm

PLUMPTON RD

HIGH ST

Weston

MIDDLE THORPE

Weedon Lois

Green Farm

Manor Farm

Weston Manor House

DOCKELL RD

DOCKELL RD

Weedon Lois CE Prim Sch

Milthorpe

Weedon Copse

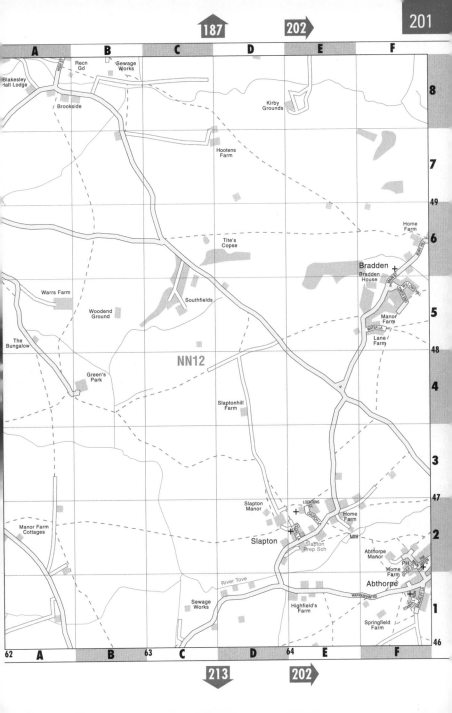

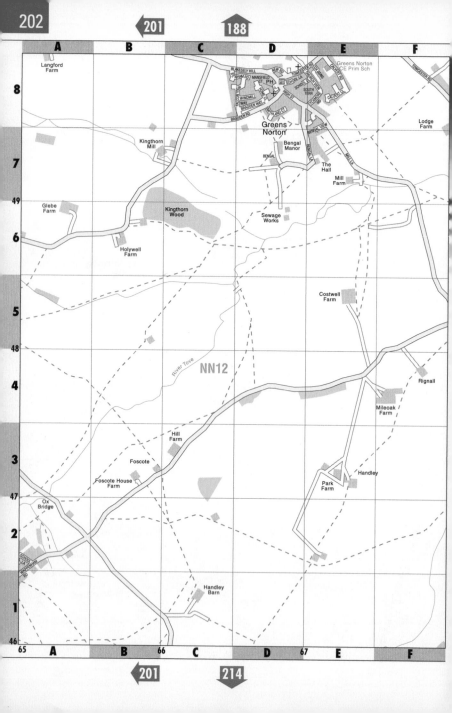

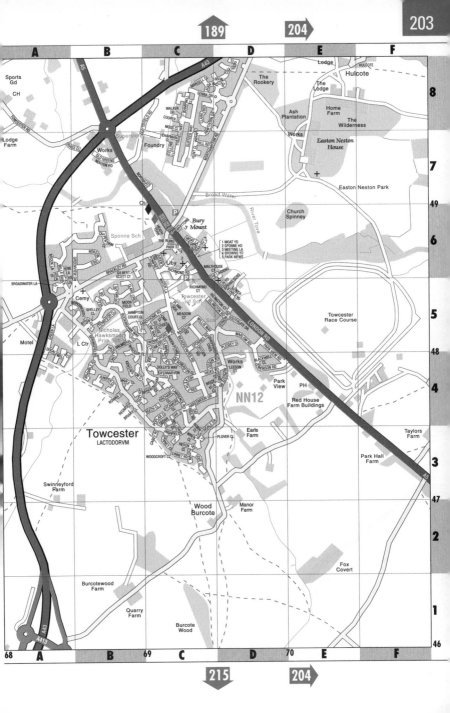

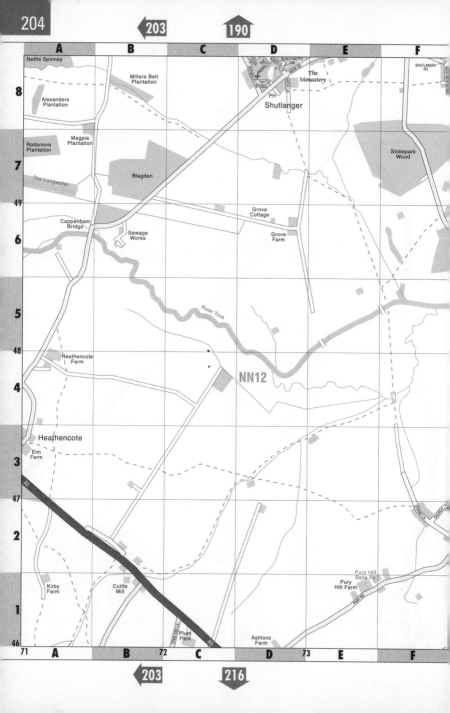

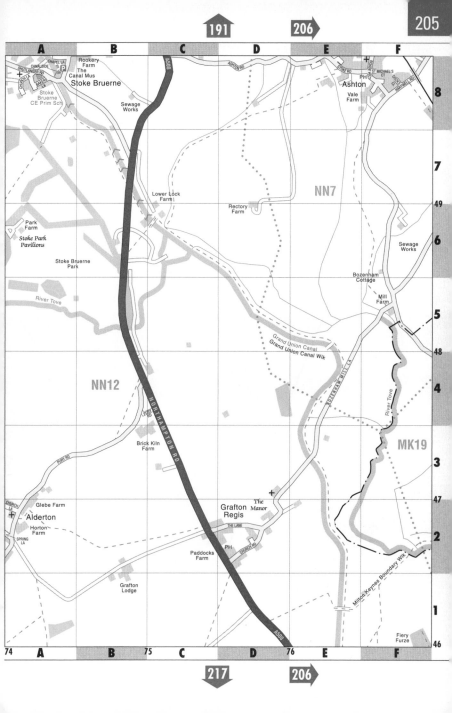

191
206

A   **B**   **C**   **D**   **E**   **F**

CHAPEL LA
CANALSIDE
RUTLANGER LA
BAKERS LA
Rookery Farm
The Canal Mus
Stoke Bruerne
Stoke Bruerne CE Prim Sch
ASHTON RD
STORE RD
PH
ST MICHAEL'S CT
HARTWELL RD
Ashton
Vale Farm
Sewage Works

8

7

NN7

Lower Lock Farm
Rectory Farm
49

Park Farm
Stoke Park Pavilions
Stoke Bruerne Park
Sewage Works
6

Bozenham Cottage
Mill Farm

River Tove
Grand Union Canal
Grand Union Canal Wlk
5

48

NN12
FERRY RD
4

PURT RD
Brick Kiln Farm
NORTHAMPTON RD
River Tove
MK19
3

CHURCH LA
Glebe Farm
The Manor
47

Alderton
Horton Farm
SPRING LA
Grafton Regis
THE LANE
CHURCH RD
2

PH
Paddocks Farm
Milton Keynes Boundary Wlk

Grafton Lodge
1

A508
Fiery Furze
46

74   **A**   **B**   75   **C**   **D**   76   **E**   **F**

217
206

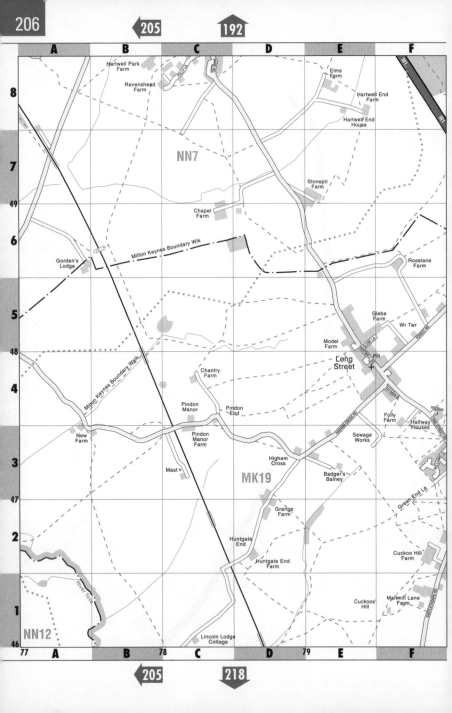

A B C D E F

8

NN7

7

49

6

5

48

4

3

47

2

1

46

77 A B 78 C D 79 E F

Hartwell Park Farm
Ravenshead Farm
Elms Farm
Hartwell End Farm
Hartwell End House
Stonepit Farm
Chapel Farm
Milton Keynes Boundary Wlk
Gorden's Lodge
Roselane Farm
Glebe Farm
Wr Twr
Model Farm
Long Street
PH
Chantry Farm
Milton Keynes Boundary Walk
Pindon Manor
Pindon End
Folly Farm
Halfway Houses
New Farm
Pindon Manor Farm
Sewage Works
Higham Cross
Mast
MK19
Badger's Balney
Green End La
Grange Farm
Cuckoo Hill Farm
Huntgate End
Huntgate End Farm
Cuckoos' Hill
Malmill Lane Farm
River Tove
NN12
Lincoln Lodge Cottage

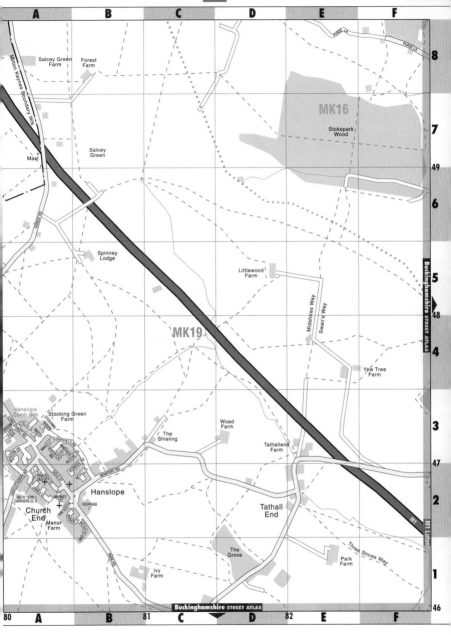

A **B** **C** **D** **E** **F**

8

Salcey Green Farm | Forest Farm

MK16

7

Stokepark Wood

Salcey Green

49

Mast

Milton Keynes Boundary Wlk

6

Spinney Lodge

Littlewood Farm

5

Midshires Way | Swan's Way

48

MK19

4

Yew Tree Farm

Hanslope Comb Sch | Stocking Green Farm

Woad Farm

3

The Shieling

Tathallend Farm

47

Newport Rd

Hanslope

Church End

Manor Farm

Tathall End

M1 Luton

2

Vicarage Ct

The Grove

Ivy Farm

Park Farm

Three Shires Way

1

46

80 **A** 81 **B** **C** 82 **D** **E** **F**

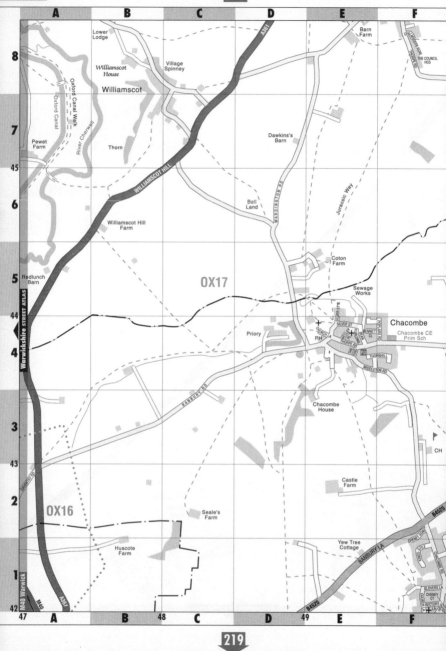

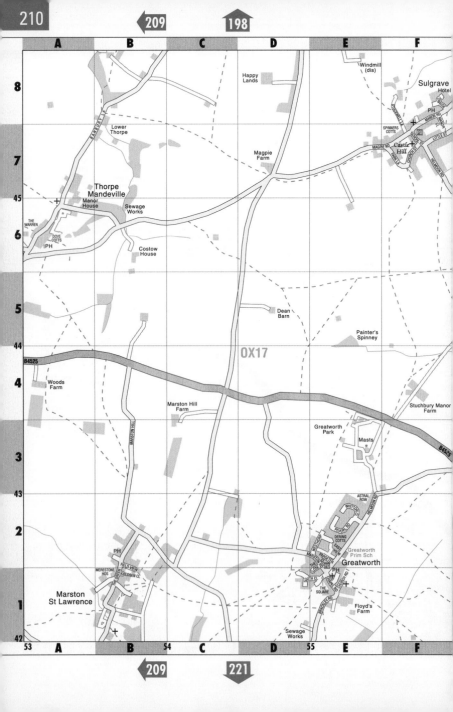

209
198

A **B** **C** **D** **E** **F**

8

Windmill (dis)

Sulgrave
Hotel

Happy
Lands

PH

7

Lower
Thorpe

SPINNERS
COTTS

Magpie
Farm

Castle
Hill

MAGPIE RD

45

Thorpe
Mandeville

Manor
House

Sewage
Works

THE
WARREN

6

DOVE
COTTS

PH

Costow
House

OX17

5

Dean
Barn

Painter's
Spinney

44

B4525

4

Woods
Farm

Marston Hill
Farm

Stuchbury Manor
Farm

MARSTON HILL

Greatworth
Park

Masts

B4525

3

43

ASTRAL
ROW

2

DERING
COTTS

Greatworth
Prim Sch

Greatworth

PH

Marston
St Lawrence

MERESTONE
HOS

FIELD VIEW

Floyd's
Farm

1

THE
SQUARE

Sewage
Works

42

53 **A** **B** 54 **C** **D** 55 **E** **F**

209
221

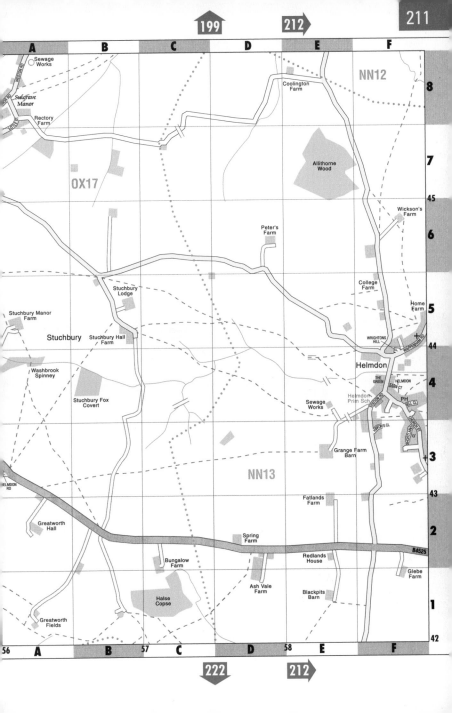

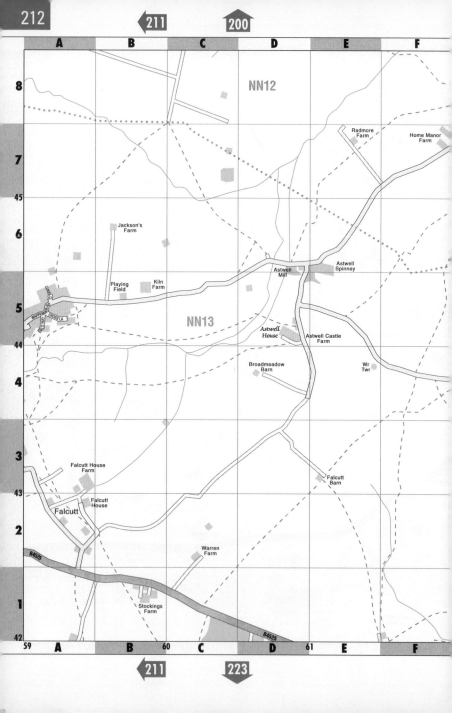

NN12

Radmore
Farm

Home Manor
Farm

Jackson's
Farm

Astwell
Spinney

Astwell
Mill

Playing
Field

Kiln
Farm

NN13

Astwell
House

Astwell Castle
Farm

Broadmeadow
Barn

Wr
Twr

Falcutt House
Farm

Falcutt
Barn

Falcutt
House

Falcutt

Warren
Farm

B4525

Stockings
Farm

B4525

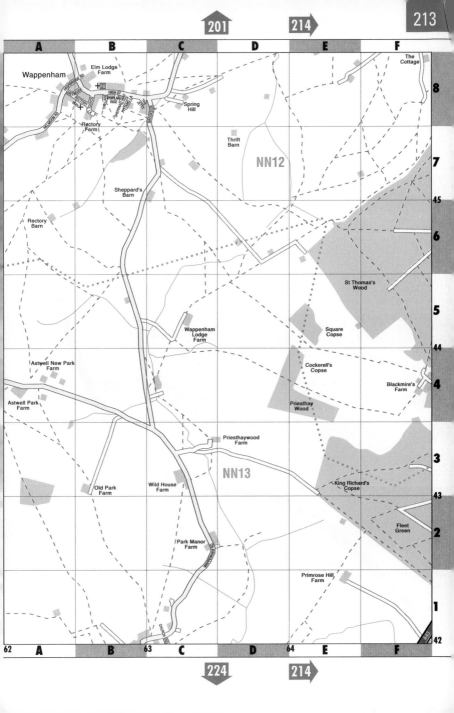

Wappenham

Elm Lodge Farm

The Cottage

Spring Hill

Rectory Farm

Thrift Barn

NN12

Sheppard's Barn

Rectory Barn

St Thomas's Wood

Wappenham Lodge Farm

Square Copse

Astwell New Park Farm

Cockerell's Copse

Blackmire's Farm

Astwell Park Farm

Priesthay Wood

Priesthaywood Farm

Old Park Farm

Wild House Farm

NN13

King Richard's Copse

Fleet Green

Park Manor Farm

Primrose Hill Farm

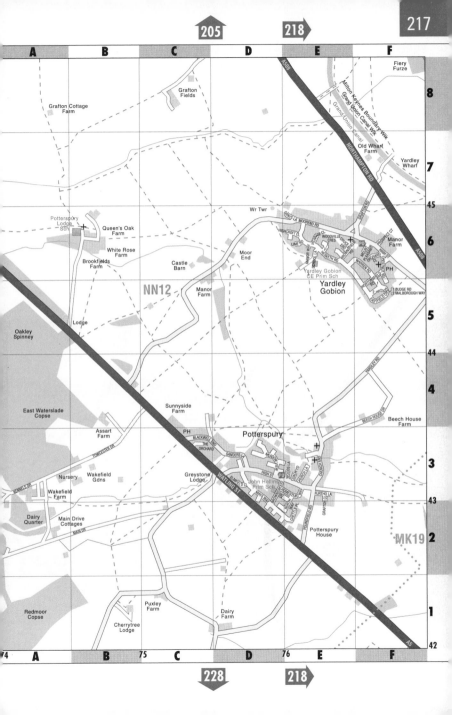

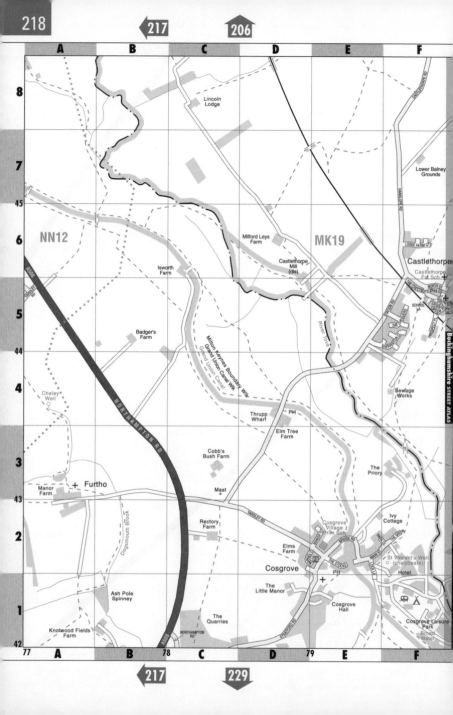

217
206

A B C D E F

8

Lincoln
Lodge

Lower Balney
Grounds

7

45

NN12

Milford Leys
Farm

MK19

Isworth
Farm

Castlethorpe
Mill
(dis)

Castlethorpe

LODGE FARM CT

Castlethorpe
Fst Sch

NORTH ST
THE CHESTNUTS
PH

SCHOOL LA

6

5

Badger's
Farm

Milton Keynes Boundary Wlk
Grand Union Canal Wlk
Grand Union Canal

River Tove

STATION RD
THE HEDGES

THE ELMS
SHEPPERTON

44

4

Cheley
Well

NORTHAMPTON RD

Thrupp
Wharf

PH

Sewage
Works

Buckinghamshire STREET ATLAS

Elm Tree
Farm

3

Cobb's
Bush Farm

The
Priory

Manor
Farm

Furtho

Mast

43

Dogsmouth Brook

TARDLEY RD

Ivy
Cottage

2

Rectory
Farm

Cosgrove
Village
Prim Sch

BRIDGE RD

St Vincent's Well
(chalybeate)

Hotel

Elms
Farm

THE STOCKS

MAIN ST
THE GREEN

LOCK LA

Cosgrove

PH

1

Ash Pole
Spinney

The
Little Manor

Cosgrove
Hall

Cosgrove
Leisure
Park
Broad
Water

Knotwood Fields
Farm

The
Quarries

NORTHAMPTON RD

A508

42

77 A B 78 C D 79 E F

217
229

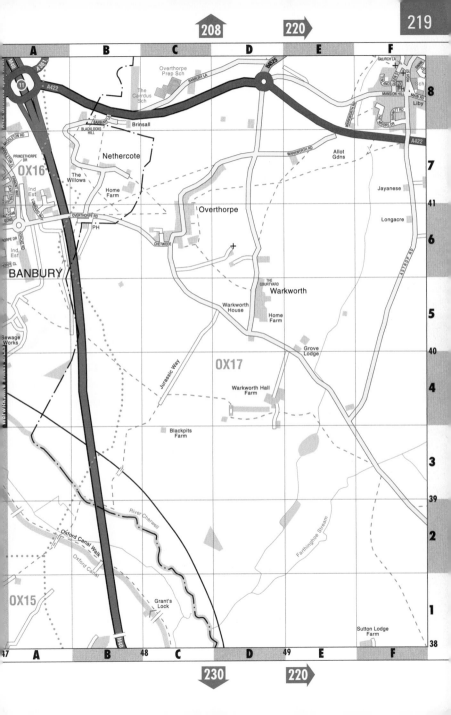

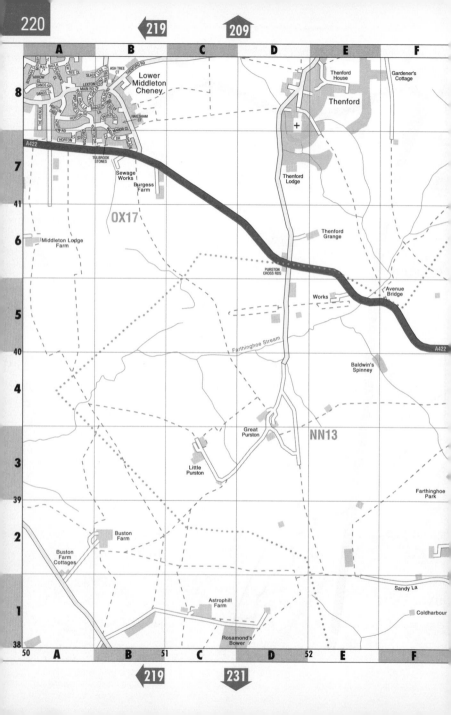

219
209

A   B   C   D   E   F

8

Bull Balk
Arrow Cl
Dands Cl
Tree Cl
Slade Cl
Ash Tree Ct
Thenford Rd
Lexton
Main Rd
Poplars
Horton Cl
Nailsham Ct
Manor Cl
The Avenue
Main Rd
Horton Rd
Horton
The Dr

Lower
Middleton
Cheney

Thenford House

Thenford

Gardener's
Cottage

7

A422

Tolbrook
Stones

Sewage
Works

Burgess
Farm

Thenford
Lodge

41

OX17

6

Middleton Lodge
Farm

Thenford
Grange

PURSTON
CROSS RDS

Works

Avenue
Bridge

5

Farthinghoe Stream

Baldwin's
Spinney

A422

40

4

Great
Purston

NN13

3

Little
Purston

Farthinghoe
Park

39

2

Buston
Farm

Buston
Farm
Cottages

Sandy La

1

Astrophill
Farm

Coldharbour

38

Rosamond's
Bower

50   A   B   51   C   D   52   E   F

219
231

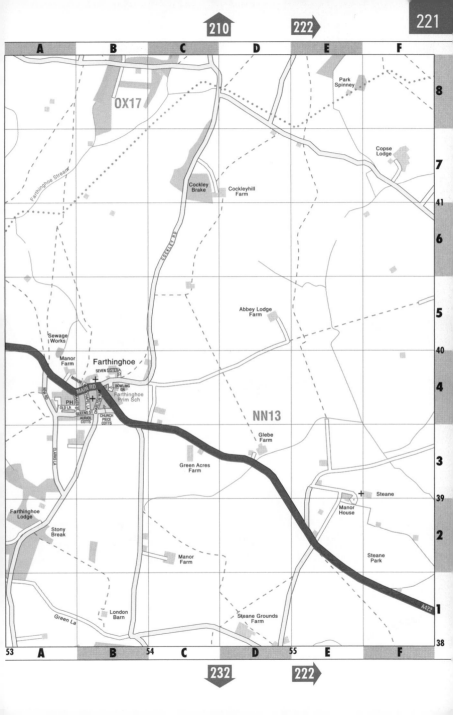

A B C D E F

8
7
41
6
5
40
4
3
39
2
1
38

OX17

Park
Spinney

Copse
Lodge

Farthinghoe Stream

Cockley
Brake

Cockleyhill
Farm

COCKLEY RD

Abbey Lodge
Farm

Sewage
Works

Manor
Farm

Farthinghoe

SEVEN SISTERS

BOWLING
GN
Farthinghoe
Prim Sch

MAIN RD

KINGS RD

PH

OLD LA

QUEENS ST

AURIOL
COTTS

CHURCH
PIECE
COTTS

CLARKS LA

NN13

Glebe
Farm

Green Acres
Farm

Steane

Manor
House

Farthinghoe
Lodge

Stony
Break

Manor
Farm

Steane
Park

Green La

London
Barn

Steane Grounds
Farm

A422

53 A B 54 C D 55 E F 38

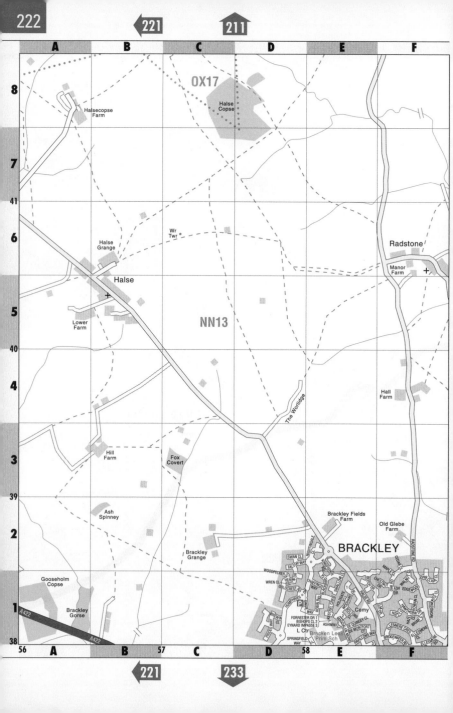

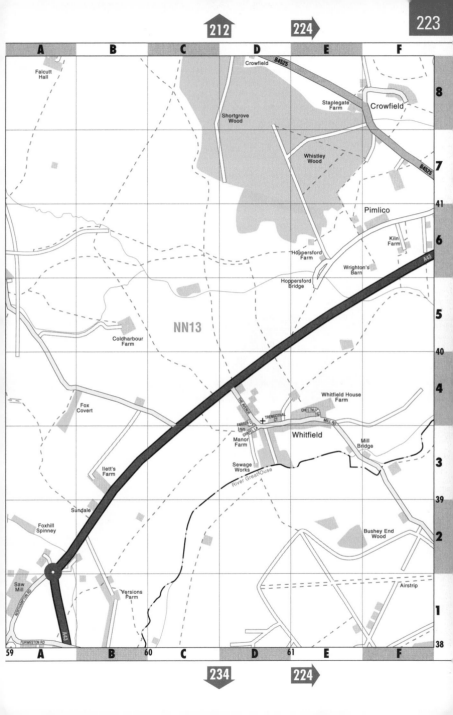

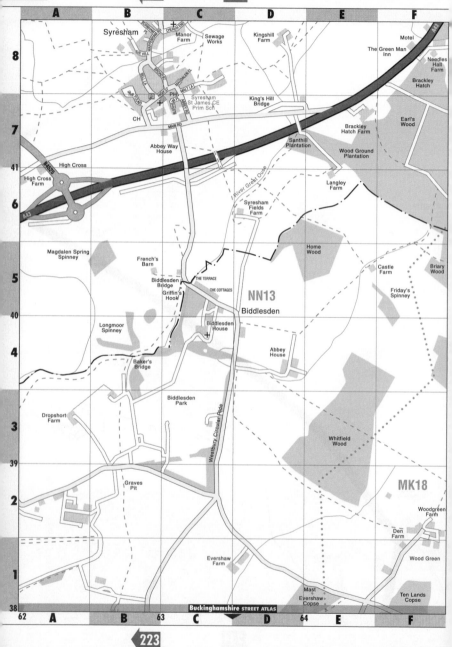

Syresham

Manor Farm

Sewage Works

Kingshill Farm

Motel

The Green Man Inn

Needles Hall Farm

Brackley Hatch

8

PH

Syresham St James CE Prim Sch

King's Hill Bridge

Earl's Wood

7

CH

MAIN RD

Brackley Hatch Farm

Abbey Way House

Santhill Plantation

Wood Ground Plantation

41

High Cross

High Cross Farm

Langley Farm

A43

6

Syresham Fields Farm

Magdalen Spring Spinney

French's Barn

Home Wood

Castle Farm

Briary Wood

5

Biddlesden Bridge

THE TERRACE

Friday's Spinney

Griffin's Hook

THE COTTAGES

NN13

40

Biddlesden

Longmoor Spinney

Biddlesden House

4

Baker's Bridge

Abbey House

Biddlesden Park

Westbury Circular Ride

3

Dropshort Farm

Whitfield Wood

39

MK18

2

Graves Pit

Woodgreen Farm

Den Farm

Wood Green

1

Evershaw Farm

Mast

Ten Lands Copse

Evershaw Copse

38

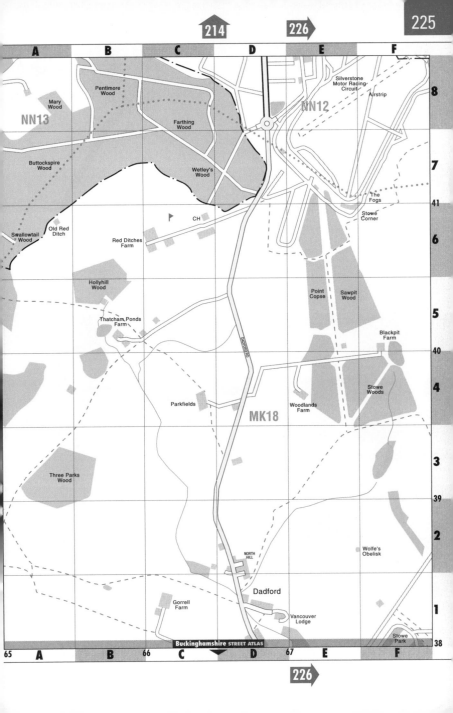

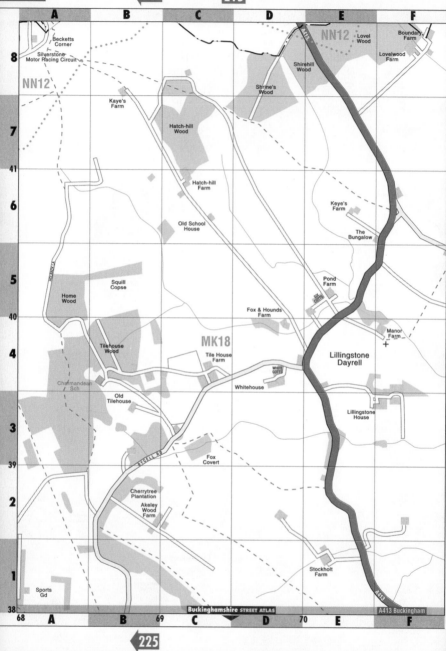

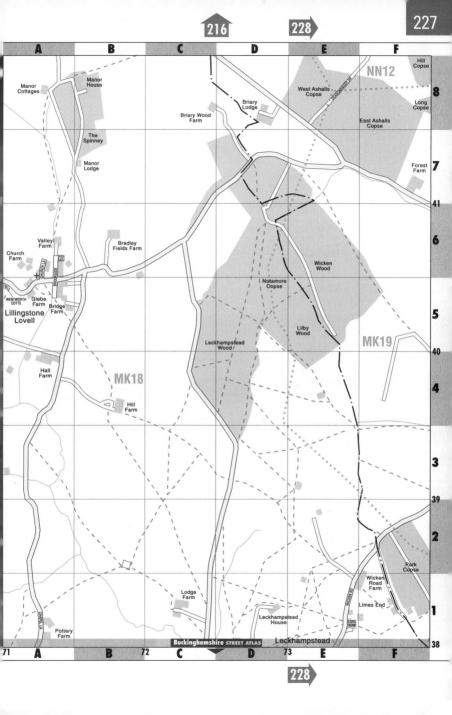

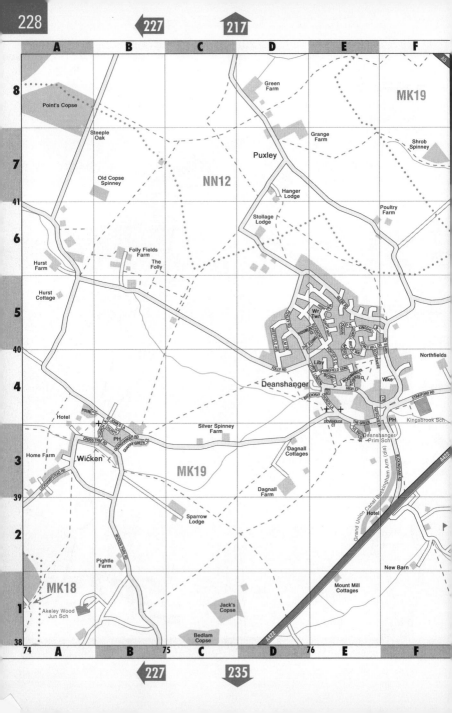

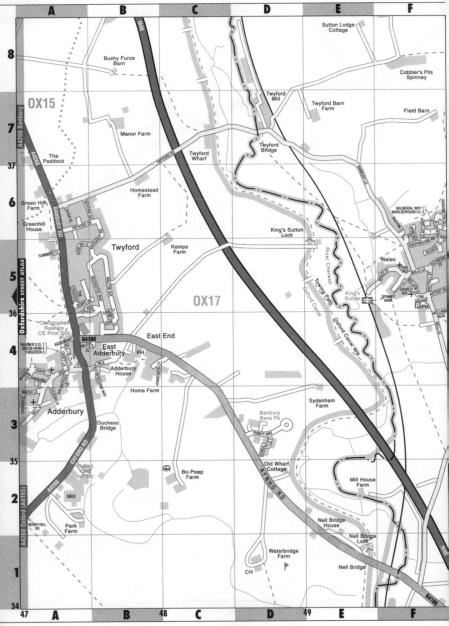

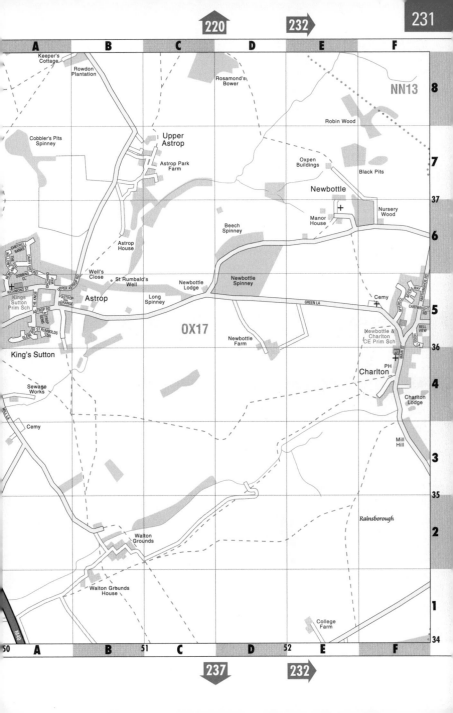

NN13

8

Keeper's Cottage

Rowdon Plantation

Rosamond's Bower

Robin Wood

7

Cobbler's Pits Spinney

Upper Astrop

Astrop Park Farm

Oxpen Buildings

Black Pits

Newbottle

37

Nursery Wood

Manor House

6

Beech Spinney

Astrop House

Well's Close

St Rumbald's Well

Newbottle Lodge

Newbottle Spinney

Cemy

Astrop

Long Spinney

GREEN LA

5

Kings Sutton Prim Sch

OX17

Newbottle & Charlton CE Prim Sch

BELL VIEW

King's Sutton

Newbottle Farm

36

PH

Charlton

Sewage Works

4

Charlton Lodge

Cemy

Mill Hill

3

35

Rainsborough

2

Walton Grounds

Walton Grounds House

1

College Farm

34

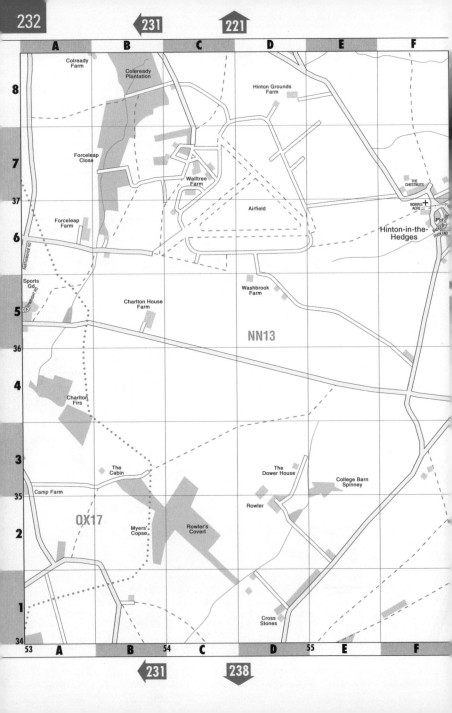

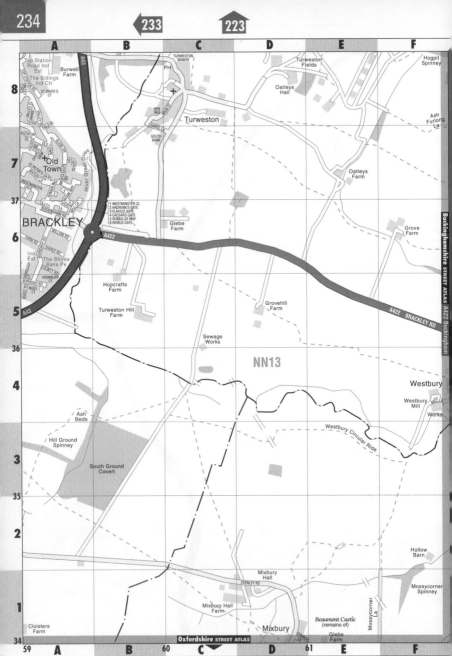

8

7

37

6

5

36

4

3

35

2

1

34

A   B   C   D   E   F

Top Station
Road Ind
Est

Burwell
Farm

The Sidings
Ind Ctr

St David's
Ct

TURWESTON
MANOR

PH

PO

CHAPEL LA

SOUTH
BANK

Turweston

Turweston
Fields

Oatleys
Hall

Hogpit
Spinney

Ash
Furlong
La

Old
Town

St Peter's La

BRACKLEY

WILLOW RD

SHIRES RD

Ind
Est

The Shires
Bsns Pk

COUNTY RD

AVONBURY
CT

BOROUGH RD

NIGEL
CT

River Great Ouse

A43

A422

1 WESTMINSTER CL
2 HADRIAN'S GATE
3 FLAVIUS GATE
4 CAESARS GATE
5 ROMULUS WAY
6 REMUS GATE

Glebe
Farm

Oatleys
Farm

Grove
Farm

Hopcrafts
Farm

Turweston Hill
Farm

A43

Grovehill
Farm

A422   BRACKLEY RD

Sewage
Works

NN13

Westbury

Westbury
Mill

Works

Ash
Beds

Hill Ground
Spinney

South Ground
Covert

Westbury Circular Ride

Hollow
Barn

Mixbury
Hall

EVENLEY RD

Mixbury Hall
Farm

Beaumont Castle
(remains of)

Mossycorner
Spinney

Mossycorner La

Cloisters
Farm

Mixbury

Glebe
Farm

Buckinghamshire STREET ATLAS A422 Buckingham

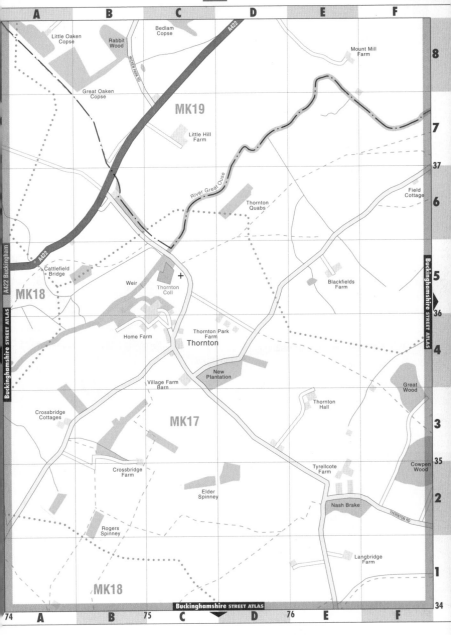

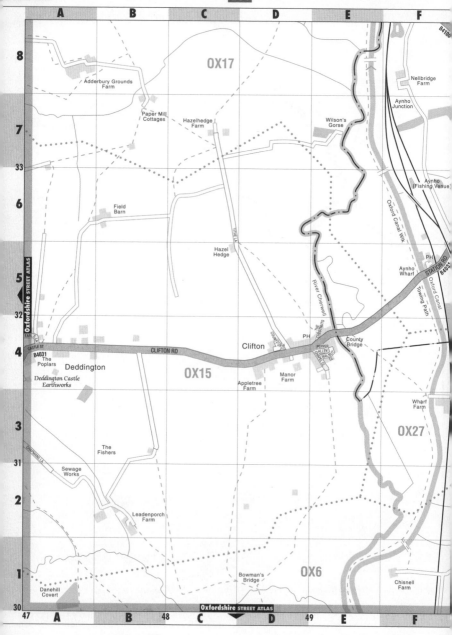

OX17

Adderbury Grounds Farm

Paper Mill Cottages

Hazelhedge Farm

Wilson's Gorse

Nellbridge Farm

Aynho Junction

Field Barn

Aynho (Fishing Venue)

Hazel Hedge

Oxford Canal Wlk

Aynho Wharf

PH

STATION RD

B4031

Oxfordshire STREET ATLAS

River Cherwell

Towing Path

Oxford Canal

Clifton

PH

County Bridge

Wharf Farm

CASTLE ST

Deddington

The Poplars

B4031

CLIFTON RD

OX15

Deddington Castle Earthworks

Appletree Farm

Manor Farm

PEPPER ALLEY

OX27

CHAPMAN LA

The Fishers

OX15

Sewage Works

Leadenporch Farm

Bowman's Bridge

OX6

Danehill Covert

Chisnell Farm

8
7
33
6
5
32
4
3
31
2
1
30

A   B   C   D   E   F

47   48   49

NN13

8

Pesthouse Wood

Ox House

Allot Gdns

Bricklands Farm

Recn Gd

BLACKSMITHS HILL 1
SKITTLE ALLEY 2
THE HILL 3
THE SQUARE 4

BANBURY RD

B4100   B4031   B4031   7

COLLEGE FIELDS

College Farm

B4031

STATION RD

Friar's Well

AYNHOE PK

OX17

Aynho

Aynho Fields   33

CROUGHTON RD

THE BOTHY

AYNHO CT

Ryeland Hill

Northcotehill Covert   6

Ash Grove

Puckwell

Aynho Park

Lower Aynho Grounds

The Firs

The Mill House

Keeper's Hill

Park Flat

Holloway's Flat   5

The Oaks

Ockley Brook   32

Sewage Works

Risley's Corner

Upper Aynho Grounds

Souldern Mill

Old Shaws

4

WHARF LA

OX27

PO

Souldern Manor

PH

1 THE PADDOCKS
2 COTSWOLD CT

Souldern   3

PH

Mast   31

Ploughley Hill

B4100

Foxhill La

2

Souldern Grounds

Holtage La

Fox Hill

Foxhill Barn

Inkerman Farm

OX25

Upper Souldern Grounds Farm

1

M40

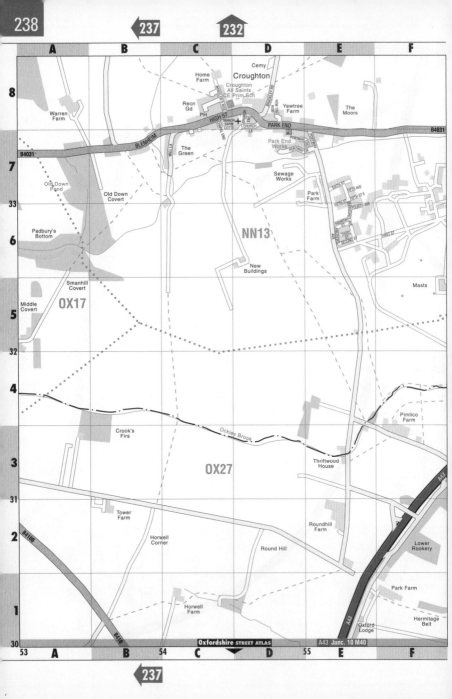

Croughton

Home Farm

Cemy

Croughton All Saints CE Prim Sch

Recn Gd

PH

Warren Farm

HIGH ST

BLENHEIM

MANOR FARM COTTS

CHURCH

PARK END

Yewtree Farm

The Moors

B4031

B4031

The Green

Park End Works

PORTWAY

PORTWAY

Old Down Pond

Old Down Covert

Sewage Works

SIXTH AVE

FIFTH AVE

FIFTH ST E

FIFTH ST

Park Farm

FOURTH AVE

FOURTH ST

FOURTH ST E

NN13

Padbury's Bottom

THIRD AVE

SECOND ST

THIRD ST

FIRST ST

Smanhill Covert

New Buildings

Masts

Middle Covert

OX17

OX27

Ockley Brook

Pimlico Farm

Crook's Firs

Thriftwood House

Tower Farm

Round Hill

Roundhill Farm

Lower Rookery

Horwell Corner

Horwell Farm

Park Farm

B4100

A43

Oxford Lodge

Hermitage Belt

B4100

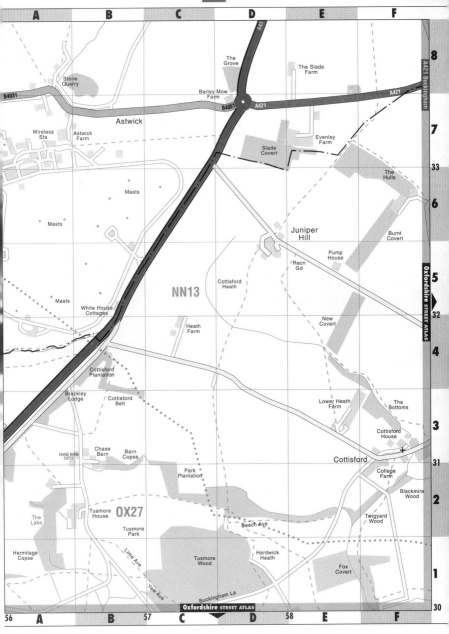

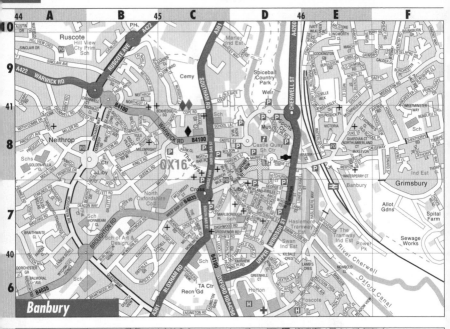

Banbury

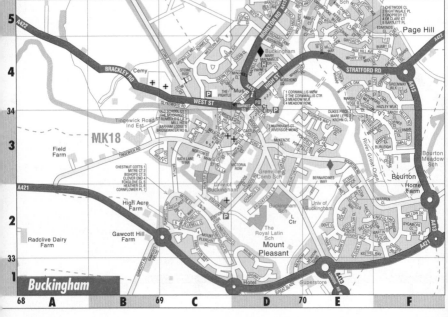

Buckingham

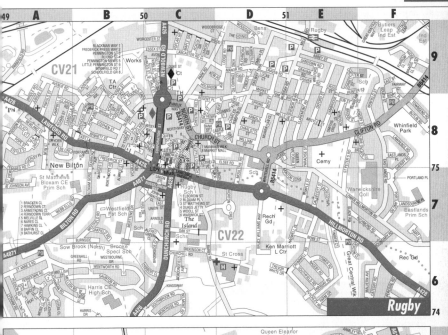

Rugby

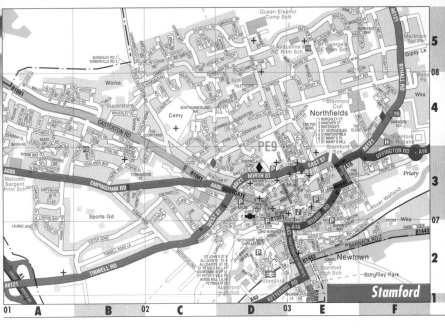

Stamford

Index

Church Rd **6** Beckenham BR2..........**53** C6

Place name
May be abbreviated
on the map

Location number
Present when a number
indicates the place's
position in a crowded
area of mapping

Locality, town or village
Shown when more than
one place has the same
name

Postcode district
District for the indexed
place

Page and grid square
Page number and grid
reference for the standard
mapping

Public and commercial buildings are highlighted in magenta. Places of interest are highlighted in blue with a star★

Abbreviations used in the index

Acad	**Academy**	Comm	**Common**	Gd	**Ground**	L	**Leisure**	Prom	**Promenade**
App	**Approach**	Cott	**Cottage**	Gdn	**Garden**	La	**Lane**	Rd	**Road**
Arc	**Arcade**	Cres	**Crescent**	Gn	**Green**	Liby	**Library**	Recn	**Recreation**
Ave	**Avenue**	Cswy	**Causeway**	Gr	**Grove**	Mdw	**Meadow**	Ret	**Retail**
Bglw	**Bungalow**	Ct	**Court**	H	**Hall**	Meml	**Memorial**	Sh	**Shopping**
Bldg	**Building**	Ctr	**Centre**	Ho	**House**	Mkt	**Market**	Sq	**Square**
Bsns, Bus	**Business**	Ctry	**Country**	Hospl	**Hospital**	Mus	**Museum**	St	**Street**
Bvd	**Boulevard**	Cty	**County**	HQ	**Headquarters**	Orch	**Orchard**	Sta	**Station**
Cath	**Cathedral**	Dr	**Drive**	Hts	**Heights**	Pal	**Palace**	Terr	**Terrace**
Cir	**Circus**	Dro	**Drove**	Ind	**Industrial**	Par	**Parade**	TH	**Town Hall**
Cl	**Close**	Ed	**Education**	Inst	**Institute**	Pas	**Passage**	Univ	**University**
Cnr	**Corner**	Emb	**Embankment**	Int	**International**	Pk	**Park**	Wk, Wlk	**Walk**
Coll	**College**	Est	**Estate**	Intc	**Interchange**	Pl	**Place**	Wr	**Water**
Com	**Community**	Ex	**Exhibition**	Junc	**Junction**	Prec	**Precinct**	Yd	**Yard**

Index of localities, towns and villages

Abthorpe 201 F1
Adderbury 230 A3
Alderton 205 A2
Aldwincle 76 F8
Apethorpe 14 C3
Arthingworth 68 C8
Ashby St Ledgers 119 D5
Ashley 18 E2
Ashton 205 E8
Astcote 188 F7
Aston le Walls 182 F2
Aynho 237 D7
Badby 153 A2
Banbury 219 A6
Barby 99 D1
Barnwell 59 B6
Barrowden 3 F5
Biddlesham 224 D5
Blakesley 187 B1
Blisworth 190 E7
Boughton 141 D8
Bozeat 164 D3
Brackley 233 E7
Bradden 201 F6
Brafield-on-the-Green .161 E2
Brampton Ash 33 E3
Braunston 118 B2
Braybrooke 49 F5
Brigstock 55 E7
Bringhurst 20 C5
Brixworth 106 A2
Brockhall 137 D2
Broughton 90 B4
Bugbrooke 173 A7
Bulwick 12 C1
Burton Latimer 92 A1
Byfield 183 D7
Bythorn 97 D4
Caldecott 21 C8
Canons Ashby 185 D2
Castlethorpe 218 F6
Chacombe 208 F4
Chapel Brampton 124 E2
Charlton 231 F4
Charwelton 168 B5
Chelveston 133 C8
Chipping Warden 196 F6
Church Brampton 140 C8
Church Stowe 171 D8
Claydon 181 D1
Clifton 236 D4
Clifton upon Dunsmore .80 A6
Clipston 66 F8
Clopton 79 B5
Cogenhoe 162 A6
Cold Ashby 84 B5
Cold Higham 188 C8
Collyweston 1 D2
Corby 36 E4
Cosgrove 218 D2
Cottesbrooke 104 F8
Cottingham 20 D1
Cottisford 239 E3
Covington 116 D2

Cranford 93 A7
Creaton 104 E4
Crick 101 A5
Cropredy 196 A2
Croughton 238 D8
Culworth 198 C3
Dadford 225 D1
Daventry 135 D3
Deanshanger 228 D4
Deddington 236 A4
Deene 23 F6
Deenethorpe 24 B4
Denford 95 C5
Denton 178 A8
Desborough 51 C2
Dingley 33 A4
Dodford 154 F6
Draughton 87 E6
Drayton 20 A5
Duddington 5 B6
Earls Barton 144 F3
East Carlton 35 A7
Eastcote 189 A8
East Farndon 48 B7
East Haddon 122 D5
Easton on the Hill 2 A4
Ecton 143 F4
Elton 28 E8
Emberton 195 F1
Evenley 233 E2
Everdon 170 B8
Eydon 184 C1
Farthinghoe 221 B4
Farthingstone 170 F2
Finedon 111 E4
Flore 155 F4
Fotheringhay 27 D7
Foxton 30 E8
Gayton 173 F2
Geddington 54 B3
Glapthorn 26 C2
Grafton Regis 205 D2
Great Addington 94 B2
Great Bowden 32 A6
Great Brington 138 D7
Great Doddington 145 D5
Great Easton 20 E7
Great Gidding 61 E3
Great Harrowden 110 D2
Great Houghton 160 F2
Great Oxendon 48 E3
Greatworth 210 E2
Greens Norton 202 D8
Grendon 163 E5
Gretton 10 C1
Grimscote 188 B8
Guilsborough 103 E6
Gumley 30 A8
Hackleton 177 C3
Hanging Houghton 106 C8
Hannington 108 D3
Hanslope 207 B2
Hargrave 115 E2
Harpole 157 D6

Harrington 69 B4
Harringworth 10 F7
Hartwell 192 D1
Hellidon 151 D1
Helmdon 211 F4
Higham Ferrers 132 D6
Hinton 184 A6
Hinton-in-the-Hedges .232 F6
Holcot 126 E8
Holdenby 123 D3
Hollowell 104 B5
Horton 177 D1
Husbands Bosworth 45 D5
Irchester 147 B7
Irthlingborough 112 D2
Isham 110 E8
Islip 96 B3
Kelmarsh 67 F3
Kettering 72 E3
Ketton 1 A6
Keyston 97 A4
Kilsby 100 A3
King's Cliffe 13 E8
King's Sutton 231 A4
Kislingbury 157 E4
Knotting Green 149 F1
Lamport 87 D2
Lavendon 180 F1
Leckhampstead 227 E1
Lilbourne 81 A6
Lillingstone Dayrell . . .226 E4
Lillingstone Lovell 227 A5
Litchborough 171 D1
Little Addington 113 B7
Little Brington 138 C4
Little Harrowden 110 B4
Little Houghton 161 A3
Little Irchester 130 C1
Loddington 70 C2
Long Buckby 121 B4
Long Buckby Wharf . . .136 E7
Lower Benefield 40 C6
Lower Boddington 182 D5
Lower Harlestone 139 F5
Lowick 75 F6
Lubenham 30 E3
Lutton 44 C4
Lyddington 9 C7
Maidford 186 D6
Maidwell 87 B7
Market Harborough 31 C2
Marston St Lawrence . .210 A1
Marston Trussell 47 C8
Mawsley Village 89 B4
Mears Ashby 128 C2
Medbourne 18 F6
Middleton 35 B8
Middleton Cheney 209 A1
Milton Malsor 158 E4
Mixbury 234 D1
Morcott 3 A5
Moreton Pinkney 199 D7
Moulton 126 C2
Napton on the Hill 150 A7

Naseby 66 B1
Nassington 15 E5
Nether Heyford 156 B1
New Hackleton 177 A3
Newnham 153 E4
Newton Bromswold . . .149 D8
Northampton 159 D4
North Kilworth 45 A3
Norton 136 C4
Old 107 D7
Old Stratford 229 B7
Olney 195 E4
Orlingbury 110 A5
Orton 70 A3
Oundle 42 A6
Overstone 127 B1
Pattishall 172 E1
Paulerspury 216 C8
Piddington 177 B2
Pitsford 125 D5
Podington 147 E2
Polebrook 43 A3
Potterspury 217 D3
Preston Capes 169 D2
Priors Hardwick 166 A5
Priors Marston 166 E8
Pury End 215 F8
Pytchley 90 F2
Quinton 176 B1
Raunds 114 C6
Ravensthorpe 103 E1
Ravenstone 194 D2
Ringstead 95 B3
Roade 191 E4
Rockingham 21 B4
Rothersthorpe 174 A7
Rothwell 70 D8
Rugby 99 A7
Rushden 132 E2
Rushton 52 C2
Scaldwell 106 F6
Shutlanger 204 D8
Sibbertoft 46 F2
Silverstone 214 D4
Slapton 201 D2
Slipton 75 A3
Souldern 237 E3
Souldrop 149 B1
South Kilworth 63 D8
South Luffenham 3 D8
Southwick 26 B5
Spratton 105 C1
Stanion 37 F2
Stanwick 113 E4
Staverton 152 C7
Stibbington 8 D2
Stoke Albany 34 A4
Stoke Bruerne 205 B8
Stoke Doyle 41 C1
Stony Stratford 229 E5
Sulgrave 210 F8
Sutton 8 F2
Sutton Bassett 18 A1
Swinford 62 C3

Syresham 224 B8
Sywell 127 D3
Tansor 27 D2
Theddingworth 46 C8
Thornby 84 E4
Thornhaugh 7 F5
Thornton 235 C9
Thorpe by Water 10 A6
Thorpe Langton 17 A5
Thorpe Malsor 71 B3
Thorpe Mandeville . . .210 B7
Thorpe Waterville 77 C8
Thrapston 76 E1
Thurning 60 D2
Tiffield 189 D4
Titchmarsh 77 D4
Towcester 203 B3
Turweston 234 C8
Twyford 230 B5
Twywell 75 A1
Upper Benefield 39 F7
Upper Boddington 182 C8
Upper Harlestone 139 D4
Upper Heyford 156 D3
Upper Stowe 171 E6
Wadenhoe 58 A4
Wakerley 4 A3
Walgrave 108 B5
Wansford 8 B4
Wappenham 213 A8
Wardington 196 D2
Warmington 28 C3
Watford 120 C6
Weedon 155 A3
Weedon Lois 200 C2
Weldon 38 C8
Welford 64 E5
Welham 17 E5
Wellingborough 130 D6
Welton 119 E1
Westbury 234 F4
West Haddon 102 C4
Weston 200 A2
Weston by Welland 18 A3
Weston Underwood . . .195 A2
Whilton 137 D6
Whitfield 223 D3
Whittlebury 215 C4
Wicken 228 B3
Wilbarston 34 C5
Wilby 129 A1
Willoughby 117 C3
Wittering 7 D8
Wollaston 146 F2
Woodend 200 F7
Woodford 94 D6
Woodford Halse 184 C6
Woodnewton 14 F2
Wothorpe 2 C8
Wymington 148 B5
Yardley Gobion 217 E5
Yardley Hastings 179 B6
Yarwell 16 A8
Yelvertoft 82 C4

Badby Leys CV22 ....98 A2
Badby Pk NN11 ....135 A5
Badby Rd Daventry NN11 .135 C1
Newnham NN11 ....153 D4
Badby Rd W
Daventry NN11 ....153 A2
Daventry NN11 ....153 B8
Badby Sch NN11 ....152 F3
Baden Powell Cres
NN12 ....203 C4
Badgers Cl NN17 ....172 F7
Badgers Hyde NN13 ..232 F6
Badgers Way MK18 ....240 E2
Badgers Wlk NN2 ....141 B5
Baffin Cl Rothwell NN14 ...70 E7
Rugby CV22 ....241 A6
Bailey Brooks Cl NN7 ..191 C5
Bailey Brooks La NN7 ..191 C5
Bailey Ct NN10 ....132 B5
Bailiff St NN1 ....159 D7
Bain Cl PE9 ....241 E5
Baird Ave NN5 ....158 D4
Baird Cl NN13 ....159 B8
Baird Ct NN8 ....135 B5
Baird Rd NN17 ....22 D1
Bairstow Rd NN12 ....203 C5
Bakehouse Hill
Geddington NN14 ....54 A3
Little Addington NN14 ..113 B8
Bakehouse La
Burton Latimer NN15 ....92 C3
Mears Ashby NN6 ....128 B2
Rugby CV21 ....241 B8
Bakehouse Rise NN6 .....85 B8
Baker Ave NN14 ....90 A3
Baker Ct NN14 ....76 D1
Baker St
Farthinghoe NN13 ....221 B4
Gayton NN7 ....173 E2
Irthlingborough NN9 ..112 E1
Northampton NN2 ....159 C8
3 Wellingborough NN8 ..130 A5
Baker's La NN11 ....204 D8
Bakers Cres NN29 ....147 A8
Bakers La Norton NN11 ..136 C4
Spratton NN6 ....105 B1
Stoke Bruerne NN12 ..205 A8
Walgrave NN6 ....108 A4
Woodford NN14 ....94 D6
Bakewell Cl NN14 ....174 F8
Balcombe Cl CV22 ....98 E8
Balcombe Pl NN18 ....36 A5
Balcombe Rd CV22 ....98 D8
Balding Cl CV23 ....99 C1
Baldwin Cl NN3 ....142 B4
Baler Cl NN11 ....135 C6
Balfour Dr NN14 ....70 E7
Balfour Gdns LE16 ....31 D1
Balfour Rd NN2 ....141 D1
Balfour St NN16 ....72 C4
Balham Cl NN10 ....147 F8
Balland Way NN4 ....175 F7
Ballantyne Rd NN12 ..132 A1
Balliol Rd Brackley NN13 ..233 D8
Daventry NN11 ....153 B8
Balmoral Cl NN8 ....36 C3
Balmoral Ave
Earls Barton NN6 ....144 F3
Market Harborough LE16 ..32 B2
Towcester NN12 ....203 B5
Wellingborough NN8 ..129 E1
Balmoral Ct NN15 ....91 C5
Balmoral Dr NN13 ....233 E7
Balmoral Ho NN11 ....141 C1
Balmoral Rd NN2 ....141 C1
Balmoral Way OX17 ..230 F6
Baltic Cl NN18 ....36 A2
Bamburgh Cl LE16 ....32 B3
Bampton Ct NN18 ....36 A4
Banbury Bsns Pk OX17 .230 D3
Banbury Cl
Northampton NN8 ....158 D2
Wellingborough NN8 ..129 E1
Banbury La
Banbury OX17 ....219 B8
Banbury OX17 ....219 C8
Blakesley NN12 ....186 D2
Byfield NN11 ....183 D7
Cold Higham NN12 ....188 B7
Culworth OX17 ....198 E3
Gayton NN7 ....173 D4
Great Easton LE16 ....20 D6
Kings Sutton OX17 ..230 B6
Middleton Cheney OX17 .209 C4
Northampton NN4 ....173 F1
Rothersthorpe NN7 ....174 B7
Thorpe Mandeville OX17 .210 B8
Weston NN12 ....199 C2
Banbury Mus* OX17 ..240 D8
Banbury Rd Aynho OX17 .237 C7
Brackley NN13 ....233 E6
Byfield NN11 ....183 D7
Chacombe OX17 ....208 C3
Chipping Warden OX17 ..196 F6
Litchborough NN12 ....171 C1
Lower Boddington NN11 ..182 C4
Moreton Pinkney NN11 ..199 C7
Twyford OX17 ....230 A6
Banbury Sta OX16 ....240 A6
Banbury Sta OX16 ....240 E7
Bancroft Rd LE16 ....20 D1

Bangrave Rd NN17 ....37 F8
Bank Hill View NN9 ....110 C4
Bank St CV21 ....241 C8
Bank View NN4 ....175 B7
Bankfield Dr LE16 ....32 A5
Banks The
Broughton NN14 ....90 B5
Hackleton NN7 ....177 B3
Kilsby CV23 ....100 A2
Long Buckby NN6 ....121 B4
Wellingborough NN9 ..129 F8
Bankside Banbury OX16 ..240 E6
Corby NN18 ....36 D3
Northampton NN1 ....141 F3
Woodford Halse NN11 ..184 C6
Banner Cl NN10 ....132 A1
Bannerman Dr NN13 ..233 E7
Bantock La NN5 ....158 E7
Barby CE Prim Sch
CV23 ....118 C8
Barby La CV23 ....99 B5
Barby Rd Kilsby CV23 ......99 F3
Rugby CV22 ....241 C6
Bardsley Rd NN17 ....21 E1
Barford MK11 ....229 F4
Barley Ct NN10 ....148 C8
Barley Hill OX17 ....198 D2
Barley Hill Rd NN3 ..142 F6
Barley La NN7 ....141 B5
Barlow Cl NN14 ....15 C5
Barlow Ct NN15 ....92 B1
Barlow La NN3 ....126 C1
Barlows La LE16 ....32 B1
Barn Acre NN6 ....122 D5
Barn Cl Corby NN18 ....36 A1
Barn Cnr NN4 ....175 C4
Barn Cl Helmdon NN13 ..211 F4
Little Harrowden NN9 ..110 C4
Barn Hill PE9 ....241 D3
Barn La NN7 ....174 F2
Barn Mews NN4 ....175 C4
Barn Owl Cl NN4 ....175 A8
Barn Way NN5 ....140 C2
Barnack Rd PE9 ....241 E2
Barnard NN18 ....36 C3
Barnard Cl NN5 ....158 A8
Barnard Gdns LE16 ....48 D8
Barnard's Way NN14 ....56 A4
Barnes Dr Daventry NN11 .135 B3
Kettering NN15 ....91 B7
Old NN6 ....107 D7
Barnes Mdw* NN4 ....159 A1
Barnes Meadow Intc
NN4 ....160 A4
Barneswell Ct NN4 ....106 B2
Barnet Cl NN4 ....159 A2
Barnet Cres NN13 ..184 B6
Barnett Rd OX17 ....219 F8
Barnfield Cl NN12 ....141 B4
Barnhill Sq NN3 ....143 A6
Barns The
Irchester NN29 ....131 B1
Mears Ashby NN6 ....128 C2
Barnsdale LE16 ....20 D6
Barnsdale Cl LE16 ....20 D6
Barnsley Sq NN18 ....36 C4
Barnstaple Ct NN13 ..233 D7
Barnwell CE Prim Sch
PE8 ....59 B6
Barnwell Ctry Pk* PE8 ..41 E3
Barnwell Ctry Pk Visitor Ctr*
PE8 ....41 E3
Barnwell Dr NN10 ....148 A8
Barnwell Gdns NN8 ....122 C8
Barnwell Rd
Northampton NN2 ....141 D4
Oundle PE8 ....41 F3
Stamford PE9 ....241 A4
Barnwell St NN16 ....72 D2
Baron Ave
Earls Barton NN6 ....144 F6
Kettering NN16 ....71 E3
Baron Ct Corby NN17 ......59 F7
Northampton NN5 ....159 F8
Barons Way NN7 ....141 A4
Baronson Gdns NN1 ..159 F8
Barrack Rd NN1,NN2 ..159 C7
Barracks The NN7 ....161 D7
Barratt Cl NN13 ....132 B5
Barrett Cl NN8 ....124 C7
Barringers Ct NN29 ..131 B1
Barringers Gdns NN29 .131 B1
Barrington Ct NN11 ..233 E6
Barrington Rd NN10 ..148 C8
Barron Cl NN15 ....91 C6
Barrowden La LE15 ....43 B6
Barrowden Rd
Barrowden PE9 ....4 C8
Ketton PE9 ....1 A4
South Luffenham LE15 ....3 F7
Barry Green Ct NN11 ......84 F7
Barry Lower Sch NN11 ..160 A7
Barry Rd NN1 ....160 A6
Barth Cl NN18 ....36 B2

Bartholomew Gdns
NN12 ....187 A1
Bartlett Cl NN13 ....152 B4
Bartlett Cl NN13 ....233 D7
Bartlett Pl MK18 ....240 E4
Bartley Dr NN16 ....71 F4
Barton Cl OX17 ....230 F6
Barton Fields NN6 ....143 F3
Barton Holme NN12 ..187 A1
Barton Rd NN9 ....91 E7
Barton Seagrave Prim Sch
NN15 ....92 A6
Bartons Cl The 2 NN5 ..140 F1
Barwick Ho NN10 ....132 B2
Barwick Rd NN10 ....132 B2
Bassett Ford Rd PE8 ......42 A4
Bassett Pl PE8 ....42 A4
Bassett Way LE16 ....67 A8
Bates Ave NN16 ....71 D3
Bates Cl
Higham Ferrers NN10 ..132 B5
Market Harborough LE16 ..31 E5
Bates La OX27 ....237 D3
Bath La
Buckingham MK18 ....240 C3
Kettering NN16 ....72 C3
Bath Lane Terr MK18 ..240 C3
Bath Rd Banbury OX16 ..240 C7
Northampton NN5 ....72 C4
Bath Row NN7 ....241 D2
Bath St
Market Harborough LE16 ...31 E1
Northampton NN5 ....158 E2
Bathurst Cl CV22 ....241 A6
Battalion Dr NN4 ....175 E7
Battle Cl Cranford NN14 ....93 A6
Northampton NN5 ....175 D7
Bauknewit Ct 3 NN3 ..142 E3
Baunhill Cl NN3 ....160 D7
Baxter Cl NN14 ....175 F8
Bayard Brow NN3 ....233 E8
Bayes St NN16 ....72 A3
Baysdale Ave NN17 ....36 E6
Beacon Cl NN4 ....158 E3
Beaconsfield Ave CV22 .241 C6
Beaconsfield Pl NN10 ..132 B3
Beaconsfield Terr
Rushden NN10 ....159 D7
Rushden NN10 ....132 B3
Bean Furlong OX17 ..208 E4
Beanfield Ave NN18 ....36 B5
Beanfield Jun & Inf Sch
NN18 ....36 A5
Beardsley Cl NN14 ....36 D5
Beardsley Gdns NN14 ...36 D5
Beargarden Rd OX16 ..240 C7
Beatrice Dr OX16 ....240 B7
Beatrice Rd NN16 ....72 B5
Beatty Cl NN11 ....135 E1
Beatty Gdns NN17 ....36 B7
Beaufort Dr
Kettering NN15 ....92 A6
Northampton NN5 ....140 C1
Beaulieu Cl OX16 ....240 F8
Beauly Ct NN15 ....91 E8
Beaumaris Cl NN10 ..132 C1
Beaumont Cl NN13 ....233 E7
Beaumont Ct 1 NN11 ..159 C6
Beaumont Dr NN13 ..143 C3
Beaune Ct NN5 ....139 F1
Beausais Ct NN5 ....139 F1
Beaver Cl MK18 ....240 E2
Beaver Cse The NN11 ..184 C7
Beck Ct NN8 ....129 D6
Becket Way NN3 ....142 B4
Beckett's View NN1 ..159 F5
Becketts Cl NN11 ....183 D7
Bective Rd NN2 ....141 C4
Bective Way NN2 ....141 C4
Bedale Rd NN8 ....130 A6
Beddoes Cl NN4 ....176 A6
Bede Cl Corby NN18 ....36 A1
Bedford Cl NN15 ....91 F5
Bedford Cotts NN7 ....138 D7
Bedford Mans NN1 ..159 D5
Bedford Pl NN1 ....159 D6
Bedford Rd Denton NN7 ..178 B8
Little Houghton NN7 ..160 F3
Northampton NN1 ....159 D5
Rushden NN10 ....148 D5
Bedford Rd E NN7 ....179 C6
Bedford Rd W NN7 ....179 A6
Beech Ave
Northampton NN3 ....142 A1
Olney MK46 ....195 E3
Beech Cl
Buckingham MK18 ....240 D3
Bugbrooke NN7 ....172 F7
Corby NN17 ....21 E1
Desborough NN14 ....51 A3
Hackleton NN7 ....155 A3
Towcester NN12 ....203 C4
Beech Cres
Irchester NN29 ....147 A7
Kettering NN16 ....72 D1
Beech Cl Rugby CV22 ......98 F8
Thrapston NN14 ....76 D2
Beech Dr Brackley NN13 ..222 E1
Rushden NN10 ....184 B6
Wellingborough NN9 ..129 E5
Beech Gr
Northampton NN3 ....160 F1
Rushden NN10 ....131 F3
Beech Hill NN11 ....151 D1
Beech House Dr NN12 ..217 F4

Beech La NN7 ....157 E4
Beech St NN5 ....132 B4
Beechcroft Gdns NN3 ..142 A2
Beeches Cl LE16 ....46 F2
Beechwood Cl
Deanshanger MK19 ..228 E3
Pattishall NN12 ....172 E1
Beechwood Dr NN3 ..142 E1
Beechwood Rd NN5 ....158 C7
Beesley Rd OX16 ....240 A8
Beeston Ave NN3 ....160 F8
Beeston Pl NN18 ....36 C5
Belfield Cl NN3 ....142 B3
Belfry La NN4 ....175 B5
Belgrave Cl NN15 ....92 A5
Bell Cl NN13 ....211 F4
Bell Ct Corby NN18 ....36 A4
5 Wellingborough NN8 ..130 A4
Bell End NN29 ....146 D2
Bell Hill Finedon NN9 ..111 E4
Rothwell NN14 ....70 D7
Bell La Byfield NN11 ..183 C7
Husbands Bosworth LE17 ..45 E5
Syresham NN13 ....224 B8
Bell St NN8 ....130 A5
Bell View OX17 ....231 F5
Bell Wlk CV21 ....99 A8
Bellamy Rd PE8 ....41 F7
Belle Baulk NN12 ....203 A6
Bellfields La LE16 ....32 A2
Bellfields St LE16 ....32 A2
Bellfoundry La 4 NN10 ..158 C7
Bellinge Lower Sch
NN3 ....143 B1
Bellropes Sq 5 NN3 ..143 D2
Bells Cl NN14 ....55 E8
Belmont Cl NN8 ....130 A5
Belmont Dr NN11 ..114 C6
Belmont Rd CV22 ....241 C6
Belstead Rd NN3 ....160 D6
Belton Cl 4 NN4 ....175 C8
Belton St PE9 ....241 E3
Belvedere Cl NN5 ....158 F7
Belvedere Rd NN15 ....92 D1
Belvoir Cl
Northampton NN5 ....140 B1
Rushden NN10 ....148 C8
Stamford PE9 ....241 A4
Belvoir Dr NN15 ....92 A6
Bembridge Dr NN12 ..141 B1
Benbow Cl NN11 ....135 E2
Benedict Cl NN10 ....147 F8
Benefield Rd
Brigstock NN14 ....39 B2
Deenethorpe NN17 ....24 C4
Oundle PE8 ....41 C5
Bengal Cl NN12 ....202 D7
Bengal La NN12 ....202 E7
Benham Cl NN12 ....202 D8
Benham Rd NN12 ..202 D8
Benjamin Sq 6 NN4 ..158 F2
Benn St CV22 ....241 E7
Bennet Cl MK11 ....229 D4
Bennett St CV21 ....241 B8
Bennfield Rd CV21 ....241 C8
Bentley Cl NN13 ....218 F5
Bentley Cl NN3 ....143 C3
Bentley Cres NN13 ....139 F1
Bentley Ct NN10 ....111 B1
Bentley St PE9 ....241 E4
Bentley Way NN11 ....134 F3
Bergen Wlk NN18 ....36 C5
Bergerac Cl NN5 ....139 F2
Berkeley Cl NN11 ....159 F6
Berkeley Pl PE9 ....241 F4
Berkeley Ho NN10 ....159 C6
Berkeley St LE16 ....46 F2
Bern Links NN5 ....159 A3
Bern Side NN4 ....159 A3
Bernardines Way MK18 ..240 E2
Berneshaw Cl NN18 ....36 A4
Berridges La LE17 ....45 E5
Berrill St NN29 ....147 A7
Berrister Pl NN10 ....148 A8
Berry Cl Earls Barton NN6 .144 E5
Great Bowden LE16 ....32 A5
Hackleton NN7 ....154 F1
Rotherthorpe NN7 ....174 B6
Berry Field Rd OX16 ..240 A7
Berry Green Rd NN14 ......78 E6
Berry Green Rd NN9 ..111 E5
Berry Hill Rd OX17 ....230 A2
Berry La Hellidon NN11 ..151 C1
Northampton NN5 ....175 D5
Berry Rd NN5 ....20 C1
Berrybut Way PE9 ....241 D8
Berrydale NN3 ....143 D4
Berrymoor Ct NN10 ....148 A8
Berrymoor Rd NN10 ..129 C2
Berrymoor Rd
Banbury OX16 ....240 A7
Wellingborough NN9 ..129 C2
Berrywood Rd NN5 ..158 A3
Bertha Way NN10 ....132 B5
Berwick Ho NN7 ....141 D5
Berwick Rd NN5 ....141 D5
Berwick Way NN15 ....92 A8
Bestwell Cl 3 NN3 ..161 A8
Bestwood Gn NN18 ....36 C5
Bethany Homestead 1
NN2 ....141 A1
Bethel La NN11 ....155 A3
Betjeman Cl
Daventry NN11 ....135 A3

Betjeman Cl continued
Higham Ferrers NN10 ..132 A5
Betony Wlk NN10 ....148 B8
Bettycroft Ct NN6 ....103 E1
Bevan Cl Warmington PE8 ..28 B3
Wellingborough NN8 ....130 C7
Beverley Cl NN14 ....142 C1
Beverley Cres NN11 ..142 C1
Beverley Gdns PE9 ....241 B4
Beverley Rd NN15 ....91 D8
Beverley Wlk NN14 ....36 C5
Bewick Cl NN18 ....36 E4
Bewick Rd NN3 ....160 E8
Bexhill Wlk NN18 ....36 B4
Biart Pl CV21 ....241 F8
Bibury Cl NN8 ....129 D1
Bibury Cres NN3 ....142 D6
Bicester Hill NN13 ....233 F2
Bickerstaffes Rd NN12 .203 C5
Bidders Cl NN1 ....159 D4
Bideford Cl NN3 ....160 D7
Bideford Sq NN18 ....36 E5
Bies Cl NN18 ....36 C2
Big Gn PE8 ....28 C3
Bignal Ct NN15 ....90 E8
Billing Aquadrome NN7 .161 B7
Billing Brook Rd NN3 ..142 F3
Billing Brook Sch NN3 .142 F3
Billing La Moulton NN6 ..126 F1
Northampton NN3 ....143 A7
Billing Rd
Brafield-on-t-G NN7 ..161 D4
Northampton NN1 ....159 F6
Billing Rd E NN3 ....160 D7
Billing School Pl NN7 ..155 C3
Billing Way NN3 ....143 C5
Bilsdon Cl NN10 ....129 D5
Bilton Cl NN8 ....129 D5
Bilton Rd CV22 ....241 A7
Binbrook Wlk NN14 ....36 C4
Binders Cl NN14 ....37 F8
Bingham Wlk NN14 ....36 C5
Birch Ave NN18 ....36 A5
Birch Barn Way NN11 ..141 B6
Birch Cl Hinton NN11 ..184 B6
Northampton NN5 ....175 E2
Birch Dr Kettering NN16 ...72 D3
Northampton NN3 ....132 C2
Birch Tree Gdns LE16 ....36 A1
Birchall Rd NN10 ....131 F2
Birchfield Cres NN13 ..142 C2
Birchfield Ct 142 B1
Birchfield Rd
Northampton NN1,NN3 ..142 C2
Wellingborough NN8 ..129 E4
Birchfield Rd E NN1 ....142 C2
Birchington Rd NN17 ......22 C1
Birchlea Cl NN14 ....50 E4
Bird Cl OX16 ....240 B8
Bird St NN15 ....92 D3
Birds End Cl
Eastcote NN12 ....188 F8
Northampton NN5 ....142 F3
Birds Hill Wlk NN12 ..142 F2
Birkdale Cl
Daventry NN11 ....135 C2
Northampton NN2 ....141 F3
Birkdale Dr NN10 ....132 D1
Birling Pl MK18 ....36 B5
Birtley Coppice LE16 ......36 E8
Bishop Cl LE16 ....48 E8
Bishop Stopford CE Sch
NN15 ....91 B7
Bishop Wulstan RC Sch
CV22 ....241 C7
Bishop's Dr NN15 ....91 B6
Bishops Ct NN13 ....222 E1
Bishops Cl
Buckingham MK18 ....240 C3
4 Daventry NN11 ....135 C2
Higham Ferrers NN10 ..132 C7
Bishops Dr NN2 ....141 B3
Bishops Rd NN14 ....36 A4
Bitten Ct NN3 ....142 C2
Black Lion Hill NN1 ..159 B5
Black Swan Spinney PE8 ...8 A4
Blackberry Cl NN16 ....72 B6
Blackberry La NN4 ....158 F3
Blackbird Ct NN13 ....222 E1
Blackdown MK11 ....229 F4
Blackfriars NN10 ....147 F8
Blackfriars 10 NN1 ..159 C6
Blacklocks Hill OX17 ..219 B8
Blackmile La NN7 ....163 E7
Blackmires La NN12 ..214 B5
Blackmoor Ave NN18 ....36 A4
Blackpool La PE8 ....42 A5
Blacksmith's La
Aston le W NN11 ....182 F2
Pytchley NN14 ....90 F2
Blacksmith's Way NN7 ..192 C1
Blacksmiths End NN8 ..240 D8
Blacksmiths Hill OX17 .237 C7
Blacksmiths La
Eydon NN11 ....184 C1
Little Brington NN7 ..138 B4
Blackthorn Bridge Ct 4
NN3 ....143 B4
Blackthorn Cl
Kettering NN16 ....72 C6
Spratton NN6 ....105 A1
Blackthorn Mid Sch
NN3 ....143 C5
Blackthorn Rd NN3 ..143 B4

Blackthorne Lower Sch
NN3 . . . . .143 B4
Blackwall CI **1** NN4 . . . . .159 A2
Blackwell CI NN12 . . . . . . .203 D4
Blackwell End NN12 . . . . . .217 C3
Blackwells NN7 . . . . .179 B6
Blackymore La NN4 . . . . . .175 D5
Bladon CI NN3 . . . . .142 C4
Blake CI NN11 . . . . .153 E8
Blake CI NN15 . . . . .92 A8
Blake Rd NN18 . . . . .36 D4
Blake Wlk NN10 . . . . .132 A5
Blakesely Hill NN12 . . . . . .202 D8
Blakesley CE Prim Sch
NN12 . . . . .187 B1
Blakesley Rd NN12 . . . . . . .141 C5
Blakesley Rd NN12 . . . . . . .200 F7
Blanchard CI **3** NN4 . . . . .175 F7
Blandford Ave NN3 . . . . .72 B5
Blandford CI NN18 . . . . .36 A6
Blashfield CI PE9 . . . . .241 C4
Blatherwycke Rd PE8 . . . . . .13 E7
Blaydon Wlk NN8 . . . . .129 E6
Bleaklow CI NN14 . . . . .50 E3
Bledlow Rise NN14 . . . . . . .174 F8
Blencowe Dr NN13 . . . . . . .233 D7
Blenheim CI NN3 . . . . .238 B7
Blenheim Ave NN11 . . . . . . .229 E4
Blenheim CI NN10 . . . . .148 A8
Blenheim Croft NN13 . . . . . .233 F6
Blenheim PI NN13 . . . . .224 C7
Blenheim Rd
Northampton NN4 . . . . . . .159 B2
Wellingborough NN8 . . . . . .129 D7
Blenheim Rise OX17 . . . . . .236 B4
Blenheim Way
Kettering NN15 . . . . .91 C5
Market Harborough LE16 . . . .31 E1
Blenheim Wlk NN18 . . . . . . .36 C3
Blinco Rd NN10 . . . . .132 C3
Blind La LE16 . . . . .20 D1
Bliss Charity Sch The
NN7 . . . . .156 C2
Bliss La NN7 . . . . .155 F5
Blisworth CI NN4 . . . . .159 A2
Blisworth Mill NN7 . . . . . . .190 C7
Blisworth Prim Sch
NN7 . . . . .190 D8
Blisworth Rd Gayton NN7 . .173 F1
Roade NN7 . . . . .191 B4
Bloomfield CI NN10 . . . . . . .132 A2
Blossac Ct NN5 . . . . .139 F1
Blossom Way NN3 . . . . .143 A1
Bloxam Gdns CV22 . . . . . . .241 B7
Bloxam PI CV21 . . . . .241 C8
Bloxham Rd OX16 . . . . .240 C6
Bluebell CI
Buckingham MK18 . . . . .240 C2
Corby NN18 . . . . .36 D2
Hinton NN11 . . . . .184 B7
Kettering NN16 . . . . .72 E4
Rushden NN10 . . . . .200 D8
Bluebell CI NN3 . . . . .160 C6
Bluebell Pk Cvn Pk **2**
NN3 . . . . .126 C1
Bluebell Rise NN10 . . . . . . .148 B8
Blueberry CI NN6 . . . . .87 B6
Blueberry Rise **3** NN3 . . .143 C2
Bluecoat La LE15 . . . . .9 D7
Bluecoat Sch The PE9 . . . . .241 C6
Blythe CI NN14 . . . . .70 E6
Blyton CI NN18 . . . . .36 C4
Board St NN9 . . . . .112 F2
Boarden Ct NN3 . . . . .142 A7
Boardman Rd NN15 . . . . .90 F8
Boat Horse La NN6 . . . . . . .101 A5
Boathouse The LE16 . . . . . . .31 F4
Bobtail Ct NN15 . . . . .140 C1
Boddington CE Sch
NN11 . . . . .182 C2
Boddington Ct NN11 . . . . . .182 C5
Boddington Mews NN15 . . . .91 C8
Boddington Rd
Byfield NN11 . . . . .183 C2
Claydon OX17 . . . . .181 D1
Kettering NN15 . . . . .91 C8
Boddington Way NN13 . . . . .233 A8
Boden CI NN18 . . . . .33 A2
Bodenham CI MK18 . . . . . . .240 F3
Bodiam CI, NN14 . . . . .76 E2
Bodiam PI NN18 . . . . .36 A5
Bodleian CI NN11 . . . . .153 B8
Bognor Rd NN18 . . . . .36 B4
Bollinger CI NN5 . . . . .139 F1
Bolton Rd OX16 . . . . .240 C8
Boltons CI NN13 . . . . .222 E1
Bond St CV21 . . . . .241 B8
Bondfield Ave NN4 . . . . . . .141 D3
Bonham Rd NN18 . . . . .72 C3
Bonington Wlk NN18 . . . . . . .36 D5
Bonnington Ct CV21 . . . . . . .80 B1
Bonsor Gdns NN14 . . . . .95 A3
Boon Wlk NN17 . . . . .37 B7
Booth CI NN12 . . . . .172 D1
Booth Dr NN8 . . . . .129 A4
Booth La N NN3 . . . . .142 C4
Booth La S NN3 . . . . .142 D2
Booth Lower Sch NN3 . . . . .142 C4
Booth Meadow Ct NN3 . . . .142 E5
Booth Rise NN3 . . . . .142 D6
Boothville Gn NN3 . . . . . . .142 D5
Boothville Mid Sch
NN3 . . . . .142 D4
Bordeaux Ct NN15 . . . . . . .139 F1
Borough Ct
Brackley NN13 . . . . .234 A5

Borough Ct *continued*
Higham Ferrers NN10 . . . . . .132 B5
Borough Rd NN11 . . . . .234 A5
Borrowdale Rd 36 D8
Borrowdale Wlk **3** NN3 . .142 C4
Bostock Ave NN1 . . . . .159 F7
Boston CI NN18 . . . . .91 D4
Boswell CI MK18 . . . . .240 E5
Boswell La NN15 . . . . .228 E4
Bosworth CI
Northampton NN4 . . . . .159 A1
Warmington PE8 . . . . .28 B3
Bosworth Independent Coll
NN2 . . . . .159 C8
Bosworth Rd
Husbands Bosworth LE17 . . .45 A8
Theddingworth LE17 . . . . . . .46 C7
Bothy The OX17 . . . . .237 D7
Botmead Rd NN3 . . . . .143 D4
Bottom La LE16 . . . . .19 E1
Bougainvillea Dr NN3 . . . . .160 C6
Boughton NN15 . . . . .91 D4
Boughton Dr NN10 . . . . . . .148 A8
Boughton Fair La NN11 . . . . .56 C6
Boughton Green Rd
NN2,NN3 . . . . .141 D5
Boughton Ho* NN14 . . . . . . .73 A8
Boughton La NN3 . . . . .141 F7
Boughton Prim Sch
NN2 . . . . .141 D8
Boughton Rd
Boughton NN2,NN3 . . . . . . .141 F8
Moulton NN3 . . . . .126 A1
Boundary Ave NN10 . . . . . . .131 E1
Boundary Cres MK11 . . . . . .229 E6
Boundary Rd
Brackley NN13 . . . . .234 A6
Rugby CV21,CV22 . . . . .241 F7
Bourne CI Corby NN18 . . . . .36 D2
Wellingborough NN8 . . . . . . .129 C6
Bourne Cres NN5 . . . . .140 C1
Bourton CI NN4 . . . . .174 E8
Bourton Meadow Sch
MK18 . . . . .240 F3
Bourton Rd NN18 . . . . .240 E3
Bourton Way NN8 . . . . .129 E1
Bourtonville MK18 . . . . .240 F3
Bouverie Rd NN4 . . . . .175 E8
Bouverie St NN1 . . . . .159 F6
Bouverie Wlk **5** NN1 . . . .159 F6
Bowell CI OX27 . . . . .237 E3
Bow Ct NN4 . . . . .158 E3
Bowden La
Market Harborough LE16 . . . .31 E4
Welham LE16 . . . . .17 E5
Bowden Rd
Northampton NN5 . . . . .159 A6
Bowden Ridge LE16 . . . . . . .31 E4
Bowen CI CV22 . . . . .98 D8
Bowen Sq **7** NN11 . . . . . .135 C1
Bowhill NN5 . . . . .72 A1
Bowland Dr NN15 . . . . .92 A5
Bowling Gn NN13 . . . . .221 B4
Bowling Green Ave NN15 . . .72 B1
Bowling Green Rd NN15 . . . .72 B1
Bowman CI OX17 . . . . .220 A8
Bowmans St NN4 . . . . .158 D1
Bowmens Lea OX17 . . . . . . .237 C7
Bowness NN8 . . . . .129 D5
Bowthorpe CI NN3 . . . . .160 D6
Boxhedge Rd OX16 . . . . . . .240 B8
Boxhedge Rd W OX16 . . . . .240 B8
Boxhedge Sq OX16 . . . . . . .240 B8
Boxwood Dr CV23 . . . . .100 A3
Boyle Rd NN17 . . . . .22 C1
Bozeat Com Prim Sch
NN29 . . . . .164 D3
Bozenham Mill La NN7 . . . .205 E4
Brabham CI NN12 . . . . .214 D4
Bracadale Wlk NN17 . . . . . . .21 C1
Bracken Borough Rd NN6 . .106 C2
Bracken CI Kettering NN16 . .72 B5
Rugby CV22 . . . . .241 A6
Bracken Dr CV23 . . . . .99 C1
Brackendale Dr CV23 . . . . . .99 C1
Brackenhill CI NN2 . . . . .141 E3
Brackley CE Jun Sch
NN13 . . . . .233 F8
Brackley CI NN4 . . . . .141 C3
Brackley Cottage Hospl
NN13 . . . . .233 F7
Brackley La NN12 . . . . .201 F1
Brackley Lodge Mews
NN13 . . . . .233 E6
Brackley Magdalen College
Sch (St John's) NN13 . . . . .233 F2
Brackley Magdalen College
Sch (Waynflete) NN13 . . . . .233 E7
Brackley Rd
Buckingham MK18 . . . . .240 B4
Croughton NN13 . . . . .238 D8
Greatworth OX17 . . . . .210 E1
Silverstone NN12 . . . . .214 D3
Towcester NN12 . . . . .203 B6
Westbury NN13 . . . . .234 F5
Brackley Wayneflete Inf Sch
NN13 . . . . .233 E6
Brackmills Ind Est NN4 . . . .160 A2
Bracknell CI NN3 . . . . .129 C4
Bradbury Rd NN11 . . . . .153 D3
Bradden CI NN2 . . . . .141 D5

Bradden Rd NN12 . . . . .202 D8
Bradden Way NN12 . . . . . . .202 D8
Bradden Wlk MK18 . . . . . . .240 D5
Bradfield CI
Rushden NN10 . . . . .132 D3
Wellingborough NN8 . . . . . . .111 A1
Bradfield Rd NN6 . . . . .121 E1
Bradford Wlk NN18 . . . . .36 C5
Bradgate Ho NN1 . . . . .159 E6
Bradmoore Ct NN3 . . . . . . .143 B5
Bradmore Gdns NN18 . . . . . .36 C6
Bradshaw St **20** NN1 . . . .159 C6
Bradshaw Way NN9 . . . . . . .146 F8
Braemar CI
Kettering NN15 . . . . .91 E8
Stamford PE9 . . . . .241 A4
Braemar Cres NN4 . . . . .175 C8
Brafield Leys CV22 . . . . .98 A6
Brafield CI
Cogenhoe NN7 . . . . .161 E5
Horton NN7 . . . . .177 E3
Braggintons La OX17 . . . . . .220 B8
Braid Ct NN8 . . . . .129 F7
Braids CI CV21 . . . . .241 F9
Braithwaite CI
Banbury OX16 . . . . .240 A7
Kettering NN15 . . . . .90 F8
Brakey Rd NN17 . . . . .37 F8
Bramber CI NN18 . . . . .36 A5
Bramble CI Kettering NN16 . .72 D4
Ringstead NN14 . . . . .95 A3
Bramble End NN4 . . . . .174 F8
Bramble Rd NN12 . . . . .203 B4
Brambleside
Kettering NN16 . . . . .72 C6
Thrapston NN14 . . . . .76 D1
Brambleside Com Prim Sch
NN16 . . . . .72 B6
Bramblewood CI NN11 . . . . .184 B5
Bramcote CI NN3 . . . . .160 F8
Bramhall Rise NN5 . . . . . . .158 B8
Bramley CI
Cogenhoe NN7 . . . . .161 E6
Market Harborough LE16 . . . .31 F5
Rushden NN10 . . . . .131 F3
Bramley CI NN4 . . . . .159 A2
Bramley Dr NN3 . . . . .146 D3
Bramley Gr NN3 . . . . .143 B2
Bramley Ho **7** NN1 . . . . .135 C2
Brammar Ho NN5 . . . . .158 A6
Brampton CI
Kettering NN15 . . . . .92 A5
Wellingborough NN8 . . . . . . .129 D7
Brampton Hill LE16 . . . . . . .32 A4
Brampton La
Boughton NN2,NN6 . . . . . . .141 A7
Chapel Brampton NN6 . . . . .125 A7
Brampton Valley Way* . . . .
NN6 . . . . .124 E4
Brampton Way NN6 . . . . . . .106 B1
Brampton Wlk NN3 . . . . . . .141 F5
Brampton Wood La NN7 . . . .124 B6
Bramptons Prim Sch The
NN6 . . . . .124 D1
Bramshill Ave NN16 . . . . .72 A6
Bramston CI PE8 . . . . .42 A4
Brandenburg Rd NN18 . . . . . .35 F2
Brangwyn Wlk NN18 . . . . . . .36 A3
Branksome Ave NN2 . . . . . .141 B1
Branksome Ct NN18 . . . . . . .36 A6
Branson CI NN3 . . . . .72 A3
Brantwood Rise OX16 . . . . .240 B6
Brasenose Dr NN3 . . . . .233 D8
Brasiland Dr NN4 . . . . .175 C8
Braunston CE Prim Sch
NN11 . . . . .118 C1
Braunston La NN11 . . . . . . .152 C8
Braunston PI CV22 . . . . .98 D8
Braunston Rd NN11 . . . . . . .135 B2
Braunston PI NN18 . . . . .36 C4
Brawn CI NN9 . . . . .131 E8
Brawn Way PE8 . . . . .16 D1
Braybrooke CI NN14 . . . . . . .95 C3
Braybrooke Prim Sch
LE16 . . . . .49 E6
Braybrooke Rd
Arthingworth LE16 . . . . .68 D8
Desborough LE16 . . . . .50 F4
Dingley LE16 . . . . .33 A3
Great Oxendon LE16 . . . . . .49 A3
Market Harborough LE16 . . . .32 B1
Brayford Ave NN18 . . . . .36 F5
Brayford CI NN3 . . . . .160 C7
Brazenose La PE9 . . . . .241 E3
Breach CI NN6 . . . . .106 C2
Breakleys Rd NN14 . . . . .51 B2
Breck CI NN17 . . . . .53 B8
Brecon CI NN15 . . . . .159 A8
Breedon CI NN18 . . . . .36 A1
Breezehill NN14 . . . . .175 F6
Brembridge CI NN6 . . . . . . .127 D2
Brendon CI NN17 . . . . .160 D7
Brent CI NN15 . . . . .92 A2
Brentford Wlk NN18 . . . . .36 A3
Brer Ct NN4 . . . . .159 F5
Bressingham Gdns NN4 . . . .175 C7
Bretch CI NN16 . . . . .240 A6
Breton MK11 . . . . .229 E6
Bretton CI NN5 . . . . .140 A1
Bretts La NN7 . . . . .191 E4
Brewery Ct PE8 . . . . .41 F4
Brewin CI NN13 . . . . .222 D1
Briar Ct NN13 . . . . .222 F1

Briar Rd NN18 . . . . .72 E5
Briars The NN4 . . . . .159 A3
Briary CI NN12 . . . . .203 B4
Brick Kiln CI NN12 . . . . .203 D4
Brick Kiln La NN12 . . . . .159 D8
Brick Kiln Rd NN9 . . . . .114 D8
Brickett's La NN7 . . . . .155 E5
Brickhill Mews NN8 . . . . . . .129 E4
Brickhill Rd NN8 . . . . .129 D4
Brickwell CI NN3 . . . . .143 A1
Brickyard Spinney Rd
NN3 . . . . .142 B6
Bridewell La **1** NN10 . . . . .72 B2
Bridge Ct Corby NN17 . . . . . .37 A7
Thrapston NN14 . . . . .76 C2
Bridge End PE8 . . . . .8 A3
Bridge Ho NN10 . . . . .70 D7
Bridge Mdw NN7 . . . . .178 B8
Bridge Meadow Way
NN4 . . . . .175 F4
Bridge Rd
Cosgrove NN12 . . . . .218 E2
Desborough NN14 . . . . .50 F5
Bridge St Apethorpe PE8 . . .14 D4
Banbury OX16 . . . . .240 D8
Brackley NN13 . . . . .233 E6
Brigstock NN14 . . . . .57 E7
Buckingham MK18 . . . . .240 D3
Geddington NN14 . . . . .54 A2
Kettering NN16 . . . . .72 C3
King's Cliffe PE8 . . . . .14 F7
Northampton NN1 . . . . .159 C5
Olney MK46 . . . . .195 F2
Raunds NN9 . . . . .114 D7
Rothwell NN14 . . . . .70 D7
Rugby CV21 . . . . .241 E8
Weedon NN7 . . . . .155 B4
Weldon NN17 . . . . .38 B8
Bridgend NN6 . . . . .82 B4
Bridget St CV22 . . . . .241 B8
Bridgewater CI NN13 . . . . . .233 F8
Bridgewater Cres NN13 . . . .233 F8
Bridgewater Ct NN13 . . . . . .233 F8
Bridgewater Dr NN3 . . . . . . .160 D7
Bridgewater Ho
Brackley NN13 . . . . .233 F8
Buckingham MK18 . . . . .240 D3
Bridgewater Rd NN13 . . . . . .233 F8
Bridgewater Rise NN13 . . . .233 F8
Bridgford PI NN13 . . . . .36 C5
Bridgwater Ct NN18 . . . . . . .36 A6
Bridle CI
Brafield-on-t-G NN7 . . . . . . .161 D2
Wellingborough NN8 . . . . . . .111 A1
Bridle La NN6 . . . . .84 B6
Bridle Path NN7 . . . . .161 E2
Bridle Rd
Burton Latimer NN15 . . . . . .92 A2
Hannington NN6 . . . . .108 C3
Old NN6 . . . . .107 D7
Rugby CV23 . . . . .241 A9
Bridle Way NN14 . . . . .90 A6
Briery CI NN18 . . . . .36 B1
Brigg Ct NN18 . . . . .36 C4
Brighouse CI NN18 . . . . .36 C4
Bright Trees Rd NN14 . . . . . .54 B3
Brighton Rd NN18 . . . . .36 B4
Brightwell Wlk NN9 . . . . . . .131 D8
Brigstock Ctry Pk*
NN14 . . . . .56 A7
Brigstock Latham's CE Prim
Sch NN14 . . . . .57 E6
Brigstock Rd NN14 . . . . .38 A2
Brindlestone CI NN4 . . . . . .158 D2
Brindley CI
Daventry NN11 . . . . .135 A5
Rushden NN10 . . . . .134 B8
Brindley Quay NN11 . . . . . . .134 B8
Brindley Rd CV21 . . . . .80 B1
Bringhurst Prim Sch
LE16 . . . . .91 F5
Brington Dr NN3 . . . . .160 D7
Brington Prim Sch NN7 . . . .138 C5
Brington Rd NN6 . . . . .121 C3
Brinkburn Gr OX16 . . . . . . .240 F10
Brinkhill Wlk NN18 . . . . .36 C4
Brinklow Rd NN11 . . . . .134 B8
Brisbane Gdns NN18 . . . . . . .36 B2
Briscoe CI NN2 . . . . .141 E6
Bristol Hill NN18 . . . . .240 C3
Britannia Gdns NN8 . . . . . . .130 C4
Britannia Rd
Kettering NN16 . . . . .72 B5
Britannia Trad Ctr NN5 . . . .140 D2
Britannia Wlk LE16 . . . . .31 F2
British La **1** NN10 . . . . . .131 C3
Briton Gdns NN3 . . . . .142 B1
Briton Rd NN3 . . . . .142 B1
Briton Terr NN3 . . . . .142 B1
Britten CI NN9 . . . . .133 A7
Brittens Dr NN3 . . . . .143 A7
Brixham Wlk NN18 . . . . .36 B2
Brixworth CE Prim Sch
NN6 . . . . .106 B1
Brixworth Ctry Pk*
NN6 . . . . .125 C3
Brixworth Ctry Pk Visitor
Ctr* NN6 . . . . .125 C7
Brixworth Hall Pk NN6 . . . . .106 B2
Brixworth Rd
Creaton NN6 . . . . .104 F4
Holcot NN6 . . . . .126 D8
Spratton NN6 . . . . .105 E3
Broad La NN13 . . . . .233 E3

Broad March NN11 . . . . . . .153 D8
Broad St Banbury OX16 . . . .240 D7
Brixworth NN6 . . . . .106 B1
Earls Barton NN6 . . . . .144 E4
Northampton NN1 . . . . .159 C6
Stamford PE9 . . . . .241 D3
Syresham NN13 . . . . .224 B8
Broadgate LE10 . . . . .20 D7
Broadgate Way PE8 . . . . . . .28 C2
Broadhurst Dr NN3 . . . . . . .161 A8
Broadlands
Desborough NN14 . . . . .106 A1
Pitsford NN6 . . . . .125 C5
Rounds NN9 . . . . .114 E6
Rushden NN10 . . . . .132 B3
Broadmead Ave NN3 . . . . . .142 B2
Broadmead CI NN3 . . . . . . .142 B2
Broadstone CI NN18 . . . . . . .36 A6
Broadwater La NN12 . . . . . .203 A5
Broadway Kettering NN15 . . .91 B8
Northampton NN1,NN3 . . . . .142 A1
Wellingborough NN8 . . . . . . .130 A3
Broadway E NN3 . . . . .142 B1
Broadway Ter LE16 . . . . .31 F4
Broadway The
Market Harborough LE16 . . . .31 F4
Northampton NN1 . . . . .136 C4
Brocade CI **3** NN4 . . . . . .158 F2
Brockhall CI NN2 . . . . .141 E6
Brockhall Rd Flore NN7 . . . .155 E6
Northampton NN2 . . . . .141 E4
Brockhill CI NN15 . . . . .72 E1
Brockton St NN2 . . . . .141 D1
Brockwood CI NN5 . . . . .140 A1
Bromford CI **8** NN3 . . . . .161 A8
Bromley Farm Ct NN11 . . . .184 B5
Bromley CI Kettering NN16 . .72 C6
Bronte CI Kettering NN16 . . .72 C6
Rugby CV21 . . . . .241 F8
Brontes The NN7 . . . . .36 D8
Brook CI Horton NN7 . . . . . .177 E2
Silverstone NN12 . . . . .214 D5
Brook Farm CI NN10 . . . . . .148 B5
Brook La
Great Easton LE16 . . . . .20 D6
Northampton NN5 . . . . .158 F8
Towcester NN12 . . . . .203 A6
Brook St
9 Daventry NN11 . . . . . . .135 C2
Hargrave NN9 . . . . .115 E3
Moreton Pinkney NN11 . . . . .199 C7
Northampton NN1 . . . . .159 B7
Raunds NN9 . . . . .114 D6
Brook St E NN8 . . . . .130 B4
Brook St W NN8 . . . . .129 F4
Brook Terr
1 Irthlingborough NN9 . . .112 F2
Medbourne LE16 . . . . .18 F6
Brook Vale NN8 . . . . .129 C2
Brook Wlk NN14 . . . . .95 A3
Brooke Ave PE9 . . . . .241 A2
Brooke CI Rushden NN10 . . .132 B1
Wellingborough NN8 . . . . . . .129 B5
Brooke Gn NN8 . . . . .129 B5
Brooke Ho NN17 . . . . .29 B6
Brooke House Sixth Form
Coll LE16 . . . . .31 E4
Brooke Mews NN8 . . . . .129 B5
Brooke Rd NN18 . . . . .53 B8
Brooke Speci Sch CV22 . . . .241 B6
Brooke Weston City Tech
Coll NN18 . . . . .36 B3
Brookend NN4 . . . . .175 E5
Brookes Gr NN17 . . . . .21 E1
Brookes Mews NN14 . . . . . .144 E5
Brookfield La MK18 . . . . . . .240 D2
Brookfield Rd
Market Harborough LE16 . . . .31 C2
Northampton NN2 . . . . .141 E2
Rushden NN10 . . . . .132 B2
Brookhaven NN14 . . . . .90 A4
Brookland Cres NN3 . . . . . .142 A1
Brookland Rd NN1,NN3 . . . .142 A1
Brooklands CI NN11 . . . . . . .135 C1
Brooklands Gdns LE16 . . . . .31 D5
Brooks CI
Burton Latimer NN15 . . . . . .92 C1
Willoughby CV23 . . . . .117 D4
Brooks Rd MK18 . . . . .240 D3
Brookside Bozeat NN29 . . . .164 D2
Desborough NN14 . . . . .51 B2
Glapthorn PE8 . . . . .26 C1
Hinton NN11 . . . . .184 A6
Lillingstone Lovell MK18 . . . .227 A6
Southwick PE8 . . . . .25 F4
Stanwick NN9 . . . . .114 D6
Wappenham NN12 . . . . .213 C8
Brookside Cl
Old Stratford MK19 . . . . . . .229 B6
Rugby CV22 . . . . .241 C6
Yelvertoft NN6 . . . . .82 B4
Brookside La NN11 . . . . . . .153 A2
Brookside Mews NN15 . . . . .140 E1
Brookside Mews NN6 . . . . . . .72 B6
Brookside PI NN7 . . . . .126 C2
Brookway MK19 . . . . .228 C4
Broom CI CV22 . . . . .241 A6
Broom CI **7** NN9 . . . . .159 A3
Broom Way NN15 . . . . .90 F8
Broome Way OX16 . . . . .240 E9
Broomhill Cres NN3 . . . . . . .143 A6

Brough Cl NN5 ....**139** F1
Broughton Hill NN14 ....90 A6
Broughton Pl NN3 ....**142** B3
Broughton Prim Sch
NN14 ....90 A4
Broughton Rd
Banbury OX16 ....**240** B7
Mawsley Village NN14 ....89 B3
Old NN6 ....107 E8
Pytchley NN14 ....90 E2
Brown's La NN14 ....95 C6
Brown's Way NN1 ....**159** E5
Browne's Hospl PE9 ......**241** D3
Browning Ave NN16 ....72 C5
Browning Cl ⬛ NN11 .....**135** B4
Browning Rd Rugby CV21 ..99 B8
Wellingborough NN8 ....**129** C4
Browning Wlk NN17 ....36 D8
Brownlow Ct NN3 ....**142** E4
Brownlow Quay PE9 ......**241** E3
Brownlow Pl PE9 ....**241** E3
Browns Cl NN3 ....**126** D2
Browns Rd NN12 ....**134** F1
Brownsfield Rd NN12 .....**203** C6
Brownswood Dr NN12 ....**217** D3
Bruce St NN5 ....**158** F6
Bruce Williams Way
CV23 ....**241** D7
Brundall Cl NN3 ....**160** D7
Brunel Cl Daventry NN11 ..**134** F4
Kettering NN16 ....72 A1
Wellingborough NN8 ....**129** B6
Brunel Ct NN17 ....22 A2
Brunel Dr NN5 ....**158** D5
Brunel Rd NN17 ....22 A2
Brunswick Gdns NN18 ....35 F2
Brunswick Pl
Banbury OX16 ....**240** E8
Northampton NN1 ....**159** E7
Brunswick Wlk NN11 .....**159** E7
Brunting Rd NN3 ....**142** C8
Bryant Av NN15 ....91 C7
Bryant Way NN10 ....**132** B6
Bsns Ctr The NN5 ....**158** F5
Buccleuch St NN16 ....72 B3
Buchanan Cl NN4 ....**159** A3
Buchanan Rd CV22 ....**241** A6
Buckfast Sq NN18 ....36 F4
Buckingham Ct
Northampton NN4 ....**175** B7
Wellingborough NN8 ....**129** E1
Buckingham Ct NN15 ......91 F7
Buckingham Hospl
MK18 ....**240** D4
Buckingham Prim Sch
MK18 ....**240** D4
Buckingham Rd
Brackley NN13 ....**234** A6
Deanshanger MK19 ....**228** F3
Buckingham Sch MK18 ...**240** D2
Buckingham Way NN12 ..**203** B5
Buckle Ho NN1 ....**159** B5
Buckley Ct MK11 ....**229** F4
Bucknell Wood Forest Wlk*
NN12 ....**214** B6
Bucknill Cres CV21 ....99 B7
Bucknills La NN6 ....**100** F5
Buckwell Cl
Desborough NN14 ....51 A3
Wellingborough NN8 ....**129** E5
Buckwell End NN8 ....**129** E4
Buckwell La CV23 ....80 B6
Buckwell Pl NN8 ....**129** F4
Budge Rd NN12 ....**217** F5
Bugbrooke Com Prim Sch
NN12 ....**172** F7
Bugbrooke Rd
Gayton NN7 ....**173** D2
Kislingbury NN7 ....**157** D3
Nether Heyford NN7 ....**156** C1
Bugby Dr NN9 ....**113** B5
Bugby Way NN9 ....**114** D7
Bull Baulk OX17 ....**220** A8
Bull Cl NN3 ....**164** D3
Bull La PE9 ....1 A6
Bullock Rd PE7 ....29 D5
Bulls La OX17 ....**230** F5
Bulwell Gn NN18 ....36 C4
Bungalows The
Theddingworth LE17 ....46 D8
Walgrave NN6 ....**108** A5
Bunkers Hill Badby NN11 .**152** F2
Gumley LE17 ....30 A5
Bunsty Ct MK11 ....**229** F5
Bunting Cl NN15 ....92 A2
Bunting Rd NN2 ....**141** D1
Bunting's La PE8 ....**228** E3
Burchester Pl OX16 ....**240** F9
Burcote Rd NN12 ....**203** D4
Burditt Cl NN14 ....70 F6
Burford Ave NN3 ....**142** D5
Burford Cl LE16 ....31 D1
Burford Way NN8 ....**129** D1
Burgess Ct NN18 ....36 A4
Burgess Row LE16 ....36 F4
Burghley Cl Corby NN18 ...36 F4
Desborough NN14 ....51 A4
Market Harborough LE16 ...32 A3
Burghley Ct PE9 ....**241** E3
Burghley Dr NN18 ....36 F5
Burghley La PE9 ....**241** E2
Burghley Rd PE9 ....**241** B5
Burghley St NN16 ....72 C4
Burham Cl NN4 ....**175** E5

Burkitt Rd NN17 ....21 F3
Burleigh Ct MK18 ....**240** F3
Burleigh Piece MK18 .....**240** E4
Burleigh Rd NN2 ....**141** C1
Burlington Gdns OX16 ...**240** B6
Burmans Way NN7 ....**161** E6
Burnell Cl NN14 ....95 B3
Burnham Pl NN13 ....**224** B8
Burnmill Rd LE16 ....31 E5
Burns Cl NN6 ....**145** A4
Burns Dr NN17 ....36 D8
Burns Rd Daventry NN11 .**135** B4
Kettering NN16 ....72 C5
Burns St NN1 ....**159** E7
Burnside CV22 ....**241** B7
Burrows Ct NN11 ....**119** E1
Burrows Ct NN3 ....**142** E4
Burrows Farm La NN14 ..**113** B8
Burrows Vale NN6 ....**106** C2
Burryport Rd NN4 ....**160** B2
Burton Cl NN11 ....**135** C5
Burton Ho NN15 ....92 C2
Burton Rd NN9 ....**111** F6
Burton Terr NN29 ....**164** D3
Burwell Ct NN4 ....90 A4
Burtram Cl NN3 ....**142** E1
Burwell Hill NN13 ....**233** F8
Burwell Hill Cl NN13 .....**233** F8
Burwell Wlk NN18 ....36 C4
Burwood Rd NN12 ....**218** A4
Bury Cl Cottingham LE16 ..20 C1
Higham Ferrers NN10 ......**132** C6
Bury Dyke NN5 ....**101** A6
Bury Hill NN12 ....**201** F6
Burystead Pl NN8 ....**129** C4
Burystead Rise NN9 ......**114** E7
Busby Cl MK18 ....**240** F4
Bush Cl NN8 ....**129** E5
Bush Hill NN3 ....**142** C2
Bushacre Ct NN16 ....71 F3
Bushey Baik Cl NN18 ....36 B1
Bushey Cl MK18 ....**240** F4
Bushland Rd NN2 ....**141** C2
Buswell Cl NN7 ....**155** B3
Buswell Rise NN14 ....70 E7
Butcher's La
Boughton NN2 ....**125** C1
Pattishall NN12 ....**172** E1
Pytchley NN14 ....90 F2
Butcher's Row OX16 .....**240** D8
Butchers Paddock NN14 ..93 A7
Bute Cl NN17 ....36 B8
Butland Cl NN10 ....**36** D2
Canada Sq NN18 ....36 C4
Butler Gdns LE16 ....31 C1
Butlers Cl NN7 ....**141** C4
Butlers Leap Ind Est
CV21 ....**241** F9
Butlin Cl Daventry NN11 .**135** B3
Rothwell NN14 ....70 E6
Butlin Cl NN11 ....**130** C1
Butlin Rd CV21 ....**241** F8
Butlins La NN7 ....**191** D4
Butt La LE17 ....45 E5
Butterfields NN8 ....**129** F2
Buttermere NN8 ....**129** C5
Buttermere Cl
Kettering NN16 ....71 E3
Northampton NN3 ....**142** C3
Butterwick Wlk NN18 ....36 C4
Buttmead NN7 ....**190** D7
Butts Cl Aynho OX17 .....**237** C7
Culworth OX17 ....**198** D2
Butts Croft Cl NN4 ....**175** C6
Butts Hill Cres NN13 ......**173** A8
Butts Rd
Northampton NN4 ....**175** C6
Raunds NN9 ....**114** E6
Wellingborough NN8 ....**129** F1
Butts The OX17 ....**237** D8
Buxton Dr NN14 ....50 E4
By Pass Way NN7 ....**178** B8
Bycell Rd MK18 ....**226** B3
Byfield By Pass OX16 ....**240** F9
Byfield Rd
Chipping Warden OX17 ....**196** F7
Eydon NN11 ....**184** C2
Hinton NN11 ....**184** B7
Northampton NN5 ....**159** A5
Priors Marston CV47 ....**166** E7
Byfield Sch NN11 ....**183** C7
Byron Cl NN11 ....**203** B5
Byron Cres
Higham Ferrers NN10 .....**132** A8
Rushden NN10 ....**131** E2
Byron Rd Corby NN17 ......36 B8
Kettering NN16 ....72 C5
Wellingborough NN8 ....**129** D4
Byron St NN2 ....**141** C1
Byron Way PE9 ....**241** A3
Byron Wlk NN13 ....**135** B3

C

Cabot Cl Daventry NN11 .**135** C5
Rothwell NN14 ....70 E6
Caernarvon Cl NN14 ....70 F6
Caesars Gate NN13 ....**234** A6
Caistor Rd NN17 ....10 C1
Caithness Rd PE9 ....**241** A4
Caldbeck Wlk ⬛ NN3 ....**142** C4
Caldecott Pl CV21 ....**241** E7
Caldecott Rd
Chelveston NN9 ....**133** B7
Rockingham LE16 ....21 B5
Caldecott St CV21,CV22 .**241** E7

Calder Cl Banbury OX16 .**240** F9
Corby NN17 ....21 D1
Calder Gn NN5 ....**140** E1
Caledonian Ho ⬛ NN5 ..**159** A6
Callcott Dr NN15 ....92 A8
Calstock Cl NN3 ....**160** D7
Calthorpe Rd OX16 ....**240** F7
Calthorpe St OX16 ....**240** C7
Calvert Cl NN12 ....**202** E8
Calvert Rd NN12 ....**202** E8
Calverton Rd MK11 ....**229** D4
Cam Cl NN17 ....21 C1
Camberley Cl NN14 ....**143** B2
Cambium Cl NN16 ....72 C6
Camborne Cl NN4 ....**159** B2
Cambria Cres NN3 ....**142** C1
Cambridge Rd NN7 ....36 B6
Cambridge Rd PE9 ....**241** C5
Cambridge St
Kettering NN16 ....72 C3
Northampton NN2 ....**159** C8
Rothwell NN14 ....70 D8
Rushden NN10 ....**131** C5
Wellingborough NN8 ....**130** A5
Camden Sq NN29 ....**164** D2
Camelot Way NN5 ....**158** A7
Cameron Cl
Daventry NN11 ....**135** B1
Northampton NN5 ....**158** E7
Cameron Cres NN5 ....**158** E7
Cameron Ct NN17 ....36 F5
Camp Cl NN7 ....**173** A6
Camp Dr NN7 ....**173** A6
Camp La NN7 ....**157** D3
Campaign Cl ⬛ NN4 ....**175** E7
Campana Cl ⬛ NN11 ...**160** C6
Campbell Cl
Buckingham MK18 ....**240** F3
Weedon NN7 ....**155** A4
Campbell Rd Corby NN17 ..36 F5
Wellingborough NN8 ....**130** A4
Campbell Sq ⬛ NN1 ....**159** D6
Campbell St
Northampton NN1 ....**159** C7
Rugby CV21 ....**241** A8
Campion Cl NN10 ....**148** B8
Campion Dr NN3 ....**143** B1
Campion Sch NN12 ....**173** A8
Camrose Rd NN5 ....**159** A6
Camsdale Wlk LE16 ....35 C8
Canada Cl OX16 ....**240** D9
Canada Sq NN18 ....36 C4
Canal Mus The* NN12 ...**205** A8
Canal St OX16 ....**240** D7
Canalside
Old Stratford MK19 ....**229** C7
Stoke Bruerne NN12 ....**205** A8
Canberra Ho NN17 ....22 F1
Candace Cl NN5 ....**158** E8
Candleford NN3 ....**143** B4
Canham Cl LE16 ....36 A6
Cannam Cl LE16 ....20 B1
Cannock Rd NN12 ....**36** F8
Cannon St NN8 ....**130** A5
Canon Harnett Ct MK12 .**229** F6
Canons Ashby NN6 ....72 B3
Canonbury NN8 ....**129** C4
Canons Ashby* NN11 ....**185** D9
Canons Ashby Rd NN11 .**199** D7
Canons Ashby Rd NN11 .**185** D6
Cansfield Ho NN6 ....**141** B4
Cantell Cl NN18 ....**240** D4
Canterbury Ct OX16 ......**219** A7
Cantle Cl NN18 ....36 D3
Capell Gdns NN18 ....36 C4
Capell Rise NN7 ....**155** E5
Cappenham Cl NN12 .....**203** B6
Captain's Ct NN7 ....**177** E1
Cardigan Cl ⬛ NN5 ......**158** F8
Cardigan Ho NN17 ....36 C5
Cardigan Pl Corby NN17 ..36 E5
Kettering NN16 ....72 C2
Cardigan Rd NN14 ....37 E2
Cardinal Cl NN4 ....**175** B7
Cares Orch NN7 ....**161** D3
Carey Cl NN3 ....**126** B1
Carey Ct NN3 ....**126** B1
Carey Dr NN12 ....36 C6
Carey Ho ⬛ NN16 ....70 B2
Carey Rd Hackleton NN7 .**177** A3
Towcester NN12 ....**203** C3
Carey St Kettering NN16 ..72 C2
Northampton NN1 ....**159** E7
Carey Way NN10 ....**132** D3
Careys Rd NN12 ....**215** F7
Carina Rd NN15 ....91 C5
Carisbrooke Cl NN5 ....91 F8
Carisbrooke Ct NN18 ....**240** A8
Carisbrooke Dr PE9 ......**241** A3
Carline Ct NN3 ....**142** D4
Carlow Rd NN14 ....95 A3
Carlow St NN14 ....95 A3
Carlton Cl NN10 ....**148** A7
Carlton Gdns NN7 ....**141** E2
Carlton Mews NN10 ......**132** C5
Carlton Rd NN18 ....36 B6
Carlton Rd
Northampton NN2 ....**141** E2
Wibarston LE16 ....34 D5
Carlton St NN16 ....72 A3
Carlyle Ave NN5 ....**158** E7
Carmarthen Way NN14 ..**148** C8
Carne The MK11 ....**229** E5
Carnegie St NN10 ....**132** A2

Carol Trusler Mews
NN2 ....**159** B7
Carousel Way NN3 ....**160** F7
Carpetbegar+Northants
Aviation Mus* NN6 ....68 F3
Carr's Way NN7 ....**157** C6
Carradale Cl NN16 ....72 A6
Carrdus Sch The OX17 ...**219** C8
Carriage Dr NN16 ....72 C6
Carriers Cl MK19 ....**207** A2
Carrington Gdns ⬛
NN3 ....**160** F8
Carrington St NN16 ....72 B2
Carron Cl NN17 ....21 C1
Carsington Cl NN16 ....71 E3
Carter Ave NN14 ....90 A3
Carter Cl NN8 ....**130** B4
Cartmel Pl NN3 ....**142** C3
Cartwell Way NN10 ....**132** D3
Cartrill St NN9 ....**114** C6
Cartwright Cres NN13 ...**233** D7
Cartwright Gdns OX17 ..**237** D7
Cartwright Rd
Charlton OX17 ....**231** F5
Northampton NN2 ....**141** C1
Casterbridge Ct NN4 ....**175** E7
Casterton Cl NN4 ....**175** B7
Casterton Rd PE9 ....**241** B4
Castilian St NN1 ....**159** D5
Castilian Terr NN1 ....**159** D5
Castle Ashby Craft Ctr*
NN7 ....**163** B3
Castle Ashby Gdns*
NN7 ....**163** B3
Castle Ashby Rd NN7 ....**179** B7
Castle Ave NN5 ....**158** C8
Castle Bush NN5 ....**158** C8
Castle Dyke NN7 ....**173** A6
Castle Mews NN8 ....**130** B4
Castle Mound CV23 ....99 C2
Castle Mount NN13 ....**233** E8
Castle
Buckingham MK18 ....**240** D3
Rushden NN10 ....**148** A8
Wellingborough NN8 ....**130** B4
Castle Hill
Daventry NN11 ....**135** B1
Rothwell NN14 ....70 D7
Castle La NN10 ....**148** A8
Castle Mews NN8 ....**130** B4
Castle Mount NN13 ....**233** E8
Castle Quay Sh Ctr
OX16 ....**240** D8
Castle Rd Lavendon MK46 .**180** F1
Wellingborough NN8 ....**130** B4
Woodford Halse NN11 ...**164** D8
Castle St
Buckingham MK18 ....**240** D3
Deddington OX15 ....**236** A4
Northampton NN1 ....**159** C6
Rugby CV21 ....**241** D3
Stamford PE9 ....**241** D3
Wellingborough NN8 ....**130** B4
Castle Way Kettering NN15 .91 C4
Wellingborough NN8 ....**130** A4
Castlethorpe Fst Sch
MK19 ....**206** F1
Castlethorpe Rd MK19 ..**206** F1
Castleton Rd NN14 ....50 E4
Caswell Rd NN4 ....**160** B1
Catchland Cl NN18 ....36 C2
Catchpole Cl NN18 ....36 D3
Catesby Cl NN2 ....**141** E4
Catesby End NN11 ....**151** D1
Catesby Rd Rothwell NN14 .70 E7
Rugby CV22 ....**241** F6
Catesby St NN16 ....72 C3
Catherine Cl NN18 ....**240** E5
Catlow Cl NN9 ....**114** C8
Cattle End
Farthingstone NN12 ....**170** F3
Silverstone NN12 ....**214** C4
Cattle Market Rd NN1 ...**159** C4
Catton Cl NN6 ....85 B8
Catton Cres NN12 ....**140** F5
Cauldecott Cl NN4 ....**158** D1
Causeway NN10 ....**240** F8
Causeway Rd NN17 ....21 E2
Causeway The
Brigstock NN14 ....**183** E8
Northampton NN1 ....**161** C7
Causin Cl NN14 ....55 F8
Causin Way NN8 ....40 C6
Cavalry Dr NN11 ....**135** B1
Cavalry Fields NN7 ....**155** A4
Cavalry Hill NN7 ....**155** A4
Cavendish Cl NN15 ....91 F5
Cavendish Ctyd NN7 ......22 E1
Cavendish Dr NN3 ....**160** D6
Cawley Rd NN7 ....**230** B5
Caxton Cl NN11 ....**135** A4
Caxton St LE16 ....31 F1
Caythorpe Sq NN18 ....36 B6
Cecil Cl NN18 ....36 E4
Cecil Dr PE9 ....**241** E3
Cecil Rd NN2 ....**141** C2
Cecil St Kettering NN16 ...72 C4
Rothwell NN14 ....70 D7
Cedar Cl Brackley NN13 ..**222** F2
Daventry NN11 ....**135** C5
Desborough NN14 ....51 C2
Irchester NN29 ....**147** A7
Rushden NN10 ....**148** A8

Cedar Cl continued
Sywell NN6 ....**143** D8
Towcester NN12 ....**203** C4
Cedar Ct NN12 ....21 E1
Cedar Dr NN14 ....76 D1
Cedar Hythe NN6 ....**124** D1
Cedar Rd Kettering NN16 ..72 C4
Northampton NN1,NN3 ..**142** A1
Cedar Rd NN3 ....**142** A1
Cedar Road Lower Sch
NN3 ....**142** A1
Cedar Villa OX16 ....**240** F9
Cedar Way
Higham Ferrers NN10 .....**132** B6
Wellingborough NN8 ....**130** A7
Cedrus Ct NN2 ....**140** F6
Celandine Cl NN10 ....**148** C7
Celeborn Pl NN3 ....**143** B5
Celtic Way NN6 ....**100** C6
Cemetery La NN10 ....**132** B6
Centaine Rd NN10 ....**132** A1
Centec Ct MK19 ....**229** B7
Central Ave Hinton NN4 .**184** A7
Kettering NN16 ....72 D2
Northampton NN2 ....**141** B6
Wellingborough NN8 ....**129** E2
Central Mus & Art Gall*
NN1 ....**159** D5
Centre 2000 NN16 ....71 F4
Centre Par NN16 ....72 D4
Centre St NN3 ....**240** E9
Chace Rd NN8 ....**130** C4
Chacombe CE Prim Sch
OX17 ....**208** F4
Chacombe Rd OX17 ......**208** F1
Chadleigh Cl NN13 ....**233** E6
Chadstone Ave NN2 ......**141** D6
Chadwick Gdns NN5 .....**140** D1
Chaffinch Cl NN4 ....**174** F7
Chaffinch Way NN13 .....**222** E1
Chainbridge La PE28 ......97 F1
Chalcombe Ave NN2 .....**141** C5
Chalcombe Rd NN2 ......**141** C4
Chalfont Cl ⬛ NN1 ....**159** C7
Chalk La NN1 ....**159** B6
Chamberlain Ave NN8 ...**129** E1
Chamberlain Rd CV21 ....99 B8
Chamberlain Way
Higham Ferrers NN10 .....**132** C5
Raunds NN9 ....**114** C5
Chambers Hill NN14 ....89 B4
Champion Ct NN13 ....**233** E8
Chancel Terr PE8 ....59 B5
Chancery La NN14 ....76 D2
Chandler Gdns NN14 ......76 E1
Chandlers Way NN4 ....36 E5
Chandos Cl MK18 ....**240** D2
Chandos Ct NN18 ....**240** D2
Chandos St MK18 ....**240** D2
Channing St ⬛ NN11 ....72 C2
Chantelle Ct ⬛ NN11 ..**135** B3
Chantry Cl NN3 ....**143** B3
Chantry La NN12 ....**203** C6
Chapel Cl Clifton OX15 ..**236** E4
Great Addington NN14 .....94 B2
Litchborough NN12 ....**171** C1
Silverstone NN12 ....**214** D4
Chapel Ct PE8 ....8 B2
Chapel End
Croughton NN13 ....**238** C8
Great Gidding PE27 ....61 D2
Piddington NN7 ....**177** A2
Chapel Fields LE17 ....62 B3
Chapel Gn NN5 ....**141** A2
Chapel Hill
Higham Ferrers NN10 ....**132** B7
Irchester NN29 ....**147** B8
Islip NN14 ....76 B2
Little Addington NN14 ....**113** B7
Silverstone NN12 ....**214** D4
Chapel Ho NN4 ....**159** B3
Chapel La
Adderbury OX17 ....**230** A4
Badby NN11 ....**153** A3
Barrowden LE15 ....3 F5
Blisworth NN7 ....**190** D8
Brafield-on-t-G NN7 ......**161** E2
Clipston LE16 ....66 F8
Corby NN17 ....37 B6
Crick NN6 ....**101** A5
Daventry NN11 ....**135** C2
Denford NN14 ....**113** E5
Elton PE8 ....28 C8
Farthingstone NN13 ......**221** B4
Flore NN7 ....**155** F5
Geddington NN14 ....54 A2
Great Doddington NN29 .**145** E6
Hackleton NN7 ....**177** B2
Ketton PE9 ....1 A5
Lilbourne CV23 ....81 A6
Lillingstone Lovell MK18 .**227** A1
Little Harrowden NN9 ....**110** C4
Maidford NN12 ....**186** D6
Old NN6 ....**107** C7
Rushton NN14 ....52 C2
Slapton NN12 ....**201** E2
Stanion NN14 ....37 E2
Stanwick NN9 ....**114** A3
Stoke Albany LE16 ....34 B4
Stoke Bruerne NN12 .....**205** A8
Turweston NN13 ....**234** B7
Whitfield NN13 ....**223** D3
Wilbarston LE16 ....34 C5
Chapel Pl ⬛ NN1 ....**159** E6
Chapel Rd
Greatworth OX17 ....**210** E1
Weldon NN17 ....38 A8
Chapel Row NN3 ....**143** C2

Chapel St
Charwelton NN11 ...168 A4
Kisby CV23 ...100 A2
Ringstead NN14 ...95 A3
Rugby CV21 ...241 C8
Swinford LE17 ...62 B3
Titchmarsh NN14 ...77 C4
Warmington PE8 ...28 B3
Chapel View NN14 ...90 B5
Chapel Yd PE9 ...241 D3
Chaplins La NN14 ...51 A3
Chapman CI NN12 ...203 C7
Chapman Gr NN17 ...36 E8
Chapmans CI
Irchester NN27 ...147 B8
Stoke Albany LE16 ...34 B4
Chapmans Dr MK19 ...229 B7
Chapmans La OX15 ...236 A3
Chappell Ho **8** NN3 ...126 C1
Chardonnay CI NN5 ...140 A2
Charlbury CI NN8 ...145 C8
Charles CI
Higham Ferrers NN10 ...132 C7
Long Buckby NN6 ...121 B3
Old NN6 ...107 D7
Charles Ct OX16 ...240 C7
Charles Rd PE9 ...241 C5
Charles Robinson Ct
NN6 ...129 C3
Charles St Corby NN17 ...36 F1
Kettering NN16 ...72 B4
Market Harborough LE16 ...31 D3
Northampton NN1 ...70 C6
Rothwell NN14 ...241 B8
Rugby CV21 ...241 B8
Thrapston NN14 ...76 E2
Wellingborough NN8 ...129 E2
Charles Terr **8** NN1 ...135 C1
Charles Warren CI
CV21 ...
Charlesfield Rd CV22 ...98 A8
Charlotte PI NN11 ...72 E4
Charlotte St CV21 ...241 D2
Charlton CI NN2 ...141 C5
Charlton Rd OX17 ...237 C7
Charlton Way NN13 ...221 B4
Charmandean Sch
MK18 ...226 B4
Charnwood **8** NN6 ...130 A5
Charnwood Ave NN3 ...142 C2
Charnwood CI **8** NN11 ...135 B4
Charnwood Ct NN12 ...142 C2
Charnwood Dr NN3 ...142 E2
Charnwood Rd NN7 ...92 A5
Charnwood Rd NN17 ...36 F7
Charter Gate NN1 ...142 B6
Charter Rd CV22 ...98 E8
Charterhouse CI NN3 ...233 E7
Chartwell Ave NN3 ...142 C5
Charwelton La NN11 ...167 D8
Charwelton Rd NN12 ...169 C2
Chase Barn Cotts OX27 ...239 B3
Chase CI NN14 ...37 E3
Chase Farm NN14 ...54 B2
Chase Hill NN14 ...54 A3
Chase Park Rd NN7 ...179 A5
The Chase
Long Buckby NN6 ...121 B4
Pitsford NN6 ...125 C4
Chase View Rd NN14 ...54 B3
Chassport CI MK46 ...194 D2
Chaston PI NN16 ...72 E5
Chatellerault Ct NN17 ...36 E8
Chater CI LE16 ...32 A6
Chatsworth Ave
Kettering NN15 ...91 C5
Northampton NN3 ...142 F5
Chatsworth Dr
Market Harborough LE16 ...32 B3
Wellingborough NN8 ...129 C7
Chatsworth Rd PE9 ...241 B4
Chaucer CI NN2 ...141 F1
Chaucer Ho NN12 ...141 F1
Chaucer Rd Rugby CV22 ...98 A7
Wellingborough NN8 ...129 D4
Chaucer St NN2 ...141 F1
Chaucer Way NN11 ...135 B2
Cheaney Dr NN14 ...175 E2
Cheddar CI NN5 ...158 D7
Cheddar Wlk NN16 ...36 A6
Chedworth Ct NN3 ...130 A4
Cheese La **8** NN6 ...125 B4
Chelfham CI NN3 ...160 D7
Chelmorton Vale NN14 ...50 E4
Chelmscote Row OX17 ...208 F8
Chelmsford CI NN14 ...159 A2
Cheltenham CI NN10 ...148 C8
Chelveston Base Cres
NN9 ...133 D5
Chelveston Dr NN1 ...132 E7
Chelveston Rd
Higham Ferrers NN10 ...132 E7
Raunds NN9 ...114 C4
Stanwick NN9 ...114 B3
Chenderit Sch OX17 ...208 F1
Cheney CI NN11 ...208 F1
Cheney Gdns OX17 ...208 F7
Cheney Rd OX16 ...240 F10
Chepstow CI
Kettering NN15 ...91 F8
Northampton NN5 ...159 A7
Chepstow Dr NN16 ...129 C7
Chequers La
Grendon NN7 ...163 E5
Ravensthorpe NN6 ...103 E1
Wellingborough NN8 ...130 A5
Chequers The MK19 ...218 F5
Cheriton CI NN11 ...135 C6
Cheriton Rd NN18 ...36 F4

Cheriton Way NN1 ...160 C6
Cherry Ave NN8 ...130 A7
Cherry Blossom CI NN3 ...143 B2
Cherry CI NN1 ...142 C2
Cherry Ct NN9 ...112 E1
Cherry Hill NN6 ...107 E6
Cherry Lodge Rd NN3 ...143 B3
Cherry Orch Olney MK46 ...159 F4
Rushden NN10 ...132 C1
Cherry Orchard Mid Sch
NN3 ...142 C1
Cherry Rd Banbury OX16 ...240 A9
Kettering NN16 ...72 D4
Cherry St
Irthlingborough NN9 ...112 E1
Ringstead NN14 ...95 B3
Cherry Tree CI
Desborough NN14 ...51 B2
Husbands Bosworth LE17 ...45 E5
Cherry Tree La NN4 ...160 E3
Cherry Wlk NN9 ...114 B5
Cherryholt La PE9 ...241 E3
Cherryholt Rd PE9 ...241 F3
Cherrytree Wlk NN6 ...143 D8
Cherwell Banks OX17 ...231 A6
Cherwell Gn NN5 ...140 F1
Cherwell St OX16 ...240 D9
Cherwell Terr NN11 ...184 C6
Cherwell The NN11 ...134 F1
Cherwell Wlk NN17 ...21 C1
Chesham Rise NN3 ...143 B4
Chesil Wlk NN18 ...36 A6
Chester Ave NN7 ...157 B6
Chester Ct NN15 ...91 B6
Chester Ho NN1 ...161 B8
Chester Rd
Irchester NN29 ...131 A1
Rushden NN10 ...130 C4
Chester St CV21 ...241 E9
Chestnut Ave Corby NN17 ...21 D1
Kettering NN15 ...72 B1
Northampton NN4 ...175 D5
Chestnut CI Hinton NN11 ...184 A6
Long Buckby NN6 ...121 B3
Milton Malsor NN7 ...174 E4
Rushden NN10 ...131 F3
Stony Stratford MK11 ...229 D5
Wymington NN10 ...148 B5
Chestnut Cotts MK18 ...240 C2
Chestnut Dr
Brackley NN13 ...222 F1
Desborough NN14 ...51 B2
Chestnut Field CV21 ...241 C8
Chestnut Gn NN13 ...223 E4
Chestnut Gr NN8 ...67 A8
Chestnut Rd
Northampton NN3 ...142 A1
Yardley Gobion NN12 ...217 F6
Chestnut Terr NN3 ...142 A2
Chestnuts The
Castlethorpe MK19 ...218 F5
Clifton OX15 ...236 D8
Chettle PI NN12 ...217 E2
Chetwode OX17 ...219 C6
Chetwode CI MK18 ...240 E5
Cheviot CI NN14 ...72 B7
Cheviot CI NN4 ...158 E3
Cheviot Ho NN2 ...141 F1
Chewton CI NN5 ...158 D7
Cheyne CI NN18 ...240 F4
Cheyne Wlk
Kettering NN15 ...91 E8
Chichele CI NN10 ...132 B5
Chichele Coll **8** NN9 ...132 B6
Chichele St NN10 ...132 B5
Chichele St NN10 ...132 C6
Chicherley Cotts NN14 ...76 D2
Chichester CI
Daventry NN11 ...135 D1
Rothwell NN14 ...70 C6
Chieftan Bsns Pk NN6 ...129 A6
Child's St NN14 ...95 C6
Chiltern Ave NN15 ...158 B8
Chiltern CI
Market Harborough LE16 ...31 F5
Northampton NN5 ...158 C8
Chiltern Lower Sch
NN5 ...158 A8
Chiltern Rd
Daventry NN11 ...135 B5
Kettering NN16 ...72 B6
Chiltern Way NN5 ...158 B8
Chilwell CI **8** NN3 ...160 F8
Chipping Warden Sch
OX17 ...196 F7
Chipsey Ave
Brigstock NN7 ...172 F8
Northampton NN5 ...160 B6
Choakles The NN14 ...176 B6
Chowns Mill Bsns Pk
NN9 ...113 B1
Christchurch Ct OX16 ...240 D8
Christchurch Dr NN11 ...135 C2
Christchurch Rd NN1 ...160 A7
Christie Way NN15 ...158 B8
Christine CI NN9 ...114 D6
Christopher Rawlins CE Prim
Sch OX17 ...230 A4
Christopher Reeves Lower
Sch NN29 ...148 A5
Chulmleigh Wlk NN13 ...160 C7
Church Ave OX17 ...230 F5
Church Bank NN16 ...20 D7
Church CI
Adderbury OX17 ...230 A3
Braybrooke LE16 ...49 E6

Church CI continued
Caldecott LE16 ...21 B8
Clipston LE16 ...67 A8
Hartwell NN7 ...192 D2
Milton Malsor NN7 ...174 F4
Wardington OX17 ...196 E1
West Haddon NN6 ...102 C5
Wicken MK19 ...228 B3
Wymington NN10 ...148 B5
Church Ct PE9 ...241 D2
Church Dr NN18 ...53 C8
Church End
Croughton NN13 ...238 D8
Piddington NN7 ...177 A2
Roade NN7 ...191 D4
Syresham NN13 ...264 D3
Church Farm CI NN29 ...164 D3
Church Farm Way LE16 ...68 C7
Church Fields NN11 ...152 C7
Church Gdns NN6 ...103 E1
Church Gn Badby NN11 ...153 A2
Barnwell PE8 ...59 B6
Northampton NN5 ...140 F2
Woodford NN14 ...94 D6
Church Hall Rd NN10 ...131 F1
Church Hill Badby NN11 ...152 F2
Barnwell PE8 ...59 B6
Finedon NN9 ...111 E4
Geddington NN14 ...54 A3
Hollowell NN6 ...104 B4
Moulton NN3 ...126 C1
Northampton NN4 ...175 E6
Ravensthorpe NN6 ...103 D1
Church La
Adderbury OX17 ...230 A3
Alderton NN7 ...204 F2
Banbury OX16 ...240 D8
Barnwell PE8 ...59 B6
Barrowden LE15 ...3 F4
Blisworth NN7 ...190 D7
Bozeat NN29 ...164 D3
Brafield-on-t-G NN7 ...161 E2
Broughton NN14 ...89 F6
Bugbrooke NN7 ...172 E7
Burton Latimer NN15 ...92 C2
Bythorn PE28 ...97 D4
Caldecott LE16 ...21 B8
Cold Ashby NN6 ...133 F3
Chacombe OX17 ...208 E4
Church Brampton NN6 ...140 B8
Claydon OX17 ...181 D1
Clipston LE16 ...67 A8
Cold Ashby NN6 ...84 A5
Cold Higham NN12 ...188 C8
Covington PE18 ...116 C2
Cranford NN7 ...93 B7
Croughton NN13 ...238 D8
Deanshanger MK19 ...208 E4
Denford NN14 ...95 C6
Dingley LE16 ...33 A4
Duddington PE9 ...5 B6
East Carlton NN17 ...35 A7
East Haddon NN6 ...122 D4
Evenley NN13 ...233 F3
Great Doddington NN29 ...145 E6
Harrington NN6 ...69 B6
Helidon NN11 ...151 C1
Husbands Bosworth LE17 ...45 E5
Kislingbury NN7 ...174 D7
Lillingstone Lovell MK18 ...227 A6
Lower Harlestone NN7 ...139 D4
Lyddington LE15 ...
Maidford NN12 ...186 D6
Middleton Cheney OX17 ...208 F1
Morcott LE15 ...
Nether Heyford NN7 ...156 B2
Newton Bromswold NN10 ...149 D8
Northampton NN1 ...159 C6
Northampton,Billing NN3 ...161 A4
Pitsford NN6 ...125 D5
Pottersbury NN12 ...217 E3
Slapton NN12 ...201 E2
Slipton NN14 ...76 C4
South Kilworth LE17 ...63 C8
South Luffenham LE15 ...3 A8
Spratton NN6 ...105 B1
Stamford PE9 ...241 E2
Stibbington PE8 ...
Stoke Bruerne NN12 ...205 A8
Stoke Doyle PE8 ...41 D1
Swinford NN6 ...62 F2
Sywell NN6 ...127 E3
Thornby NN6 ...84 D4
Walgrave NN6 ...160 E8
Warmington PE8 ...28 B3
Welford NN6 ...64 C5
Wicken MK19 ...228 B3
Wilby NN8 ...129 B1
Wollaston NN29 ...146 D3
Wymington NN10 ...148 B5
Yardley Hastings NN7 ...179 B2
Church Leys NN3 ...233 E3
Church Mount NN6 ...103 F6
Piece Piece Cotts
NN13 ...221 B4
Church Pk PE8 ...42 F3
Church Rd Brackley NN13 ...233 F7
Braunston NN11 ...118 B1
Grafton Regis NN12 ...205 D2
Greatworth OX17 ...210 C1
Hargrave NN9 ...115 F1
Ketton PE9 ...1 A5
Piddington NN7 ...177 A2
Pytchley NN14 ...91 A8
Spratton NN6 ...124 B8
Upper Boddington NN11 ...182 C7
Church Sq **8** LE16 ...31 E3

Church St continued
Blakesley NN12 ...187 B1
Boughton NN2 ...141 C8
Brigstock NN14 ...55 F7
Brixworth NN6 ...106 B3
Broughton NN14 ...90 B4
Buckingham MK18 ...240 C3
Burton Latimer NN15 ...92 C3
Byfield NN11 ...183 D7
Charwelton NN11 ...168 B4
Clifton u D CV23 ...80 A1
Cogenhoe NN7 ...162 A6
Cottingham LE16 ...20 D1
Crick NN6 ...100 F6
Easton o t H PE9 ...2 A6
Finedon NN9 ...111 E2
Hargrave NN9 ...115 F2
Helmdon NN13 ...211 D1
Husbands Bosworth LE17 ...45 E5
Isham NN14 ...91 F1
Long Buckby NN6 ...121 B4
Market Harborough LE16 ...31 E3
Mears Ashby NN6 ...128 B2
Moulton NN3 ...126 C1
Naseby NN6 ...66 C3
Nassington PE8 ...15 F5
Nether Heyford NN7 ...156 B2
Newnham NN11 ...153 C4
Olney NN6 ...195 F3
Oundle PE8 ...42 F3
Pattishall NN12 ...172 C1
Polebrook PE8 ...42 F3
Raunds NN9 ...114 E7
Ringstead NN14 ...95 B3
Rothersthorpe NN7 ...174 A6
Rugby CV21 ...241 C8
Rushden NN10 ...132 B2
Sibbertoft LE16 ...47 A2
Silverstone NN12 ...214 D5
Stamford PE9 ...241 E2
Stanwick NN9 ...114 A3
Staverton NN11 ...152 C7
Stony Stratford MK11 ...229 D5
Sulgrave OX17 ...210 F7
Titchmarsh NN14 ...77 C4
Wadenhoe PE8 ...58 A3
Warmington PE8 ...28 B2
Watford NN6 ...120 C6
Weedon NN7 ...155 C3
Weldon NN17 ...38 B7
Wellingborough NN8 ...130 A4
Wilbarston LE16 ...34 C1
Woodford NN14 ...94 D6
Woodford Halse NN11 ...184 C6
Church View
Banbury OX16 ...240 B6
Brackley NN13 ...90 A4
Broughton NN14 ...90 A4
Burton Latimer NN15 ...92 C3
Ecton NN6 ...143 F4
Greens Norton NN12 ...202 E8
Keyston PE28 ...97 A3
Moulton NN3 ...126 C2
Northampton NN4 ...175 D4
Raunds NN9 ...114 D7
Walgrave NN6 ...105 B6
Weldon NN17 ...38 B7
Church View Rd NN14 ...51 B2
Church Way Denton NN7 ...161 E5
Ecton NN6 ...143 F4
Grendon NN7 ...163 D5
Northampton NN3 ...160 F8
Preston Capes NN11 ...169 D2
Thorpe Malsor NN14 ...71 A3
Whittlebury NN12 ...215 C5
Church Way Ct NN13 ...160 D8
Church Wlk
Banbury OX16 ...240 C7
Barby CV23 ...99 C1
Bozeat NN29 ...164 D3
Corby NN17 ...135 C2
Denford NN14 ...95 C6
8 Irthlingborough NN9 ...112 F2
8 Kettering NN16 ...72 B2
Kilsby CV23 ...100 A2
Little Addington NN14 ...113 B8
Lubenham LE16 ...30 E3
Market Harborough LE16 ...32 A2
Newton Bromswold NN10 ...149 D8
Northampton NN3 ...143 B2
Rugby CV21,CV22 ...241 C7
Weldon NN17 ...38 B7
Churchcroft NN3 ...191 D4
Churchfield CI NN2 ...141 E4
Churchill Ave
Irthlingborough NN9 ...113 B5
Northampton NN3 ...142 B4
Wellingborough NN8 ...129 C7
Churchill CI NN14 ...70 C7
Churchill Rd
Earls Barton NN6 ...144 F4
Rugby CV22 ...241 D5
Stamford PE9 ...241 C5
Welton NN11 ...135 E8
Churchill Way
Brackley NN13 ...233 F6
Burton Latimer NN15 ...92 B2
Daventry NN11 ...153 E7
Kettering NN15 ...72 F1
Churchway NN11 ...169 D2
Cider CI LE11 ...3 C5
Cinnamon CI **8** NN4 ...175 D6
Circus End NN11 ...140 C1
Circus Gr PE8 ...42 F2

Cissbury Rd NN4 ...158 F4
Clailey Ct NN11 ...229 F5
Clannell Rd NN4 ...175 A8
Clare Ave NN11 ...229 F5
Clare CI Earls Barton NN6 ...144 F3
Stamford PE9 ...241 C3
Clare Cres NN12 ...203 B5
Clare Ct CV21 ...241 B8
Clare Dr NN14 ...76 E3
Clare Rd NN8 ...129 C3
Clare St
Northampton NN1 ...159 E7
Raunds NN9 ...114 D6
Clare Wlk NN10 ...132 B5
Claregate NN4 ...175 B8
Claremont Ave MK11 ...229 E4
Claremont Ct **13** NN1 ...159 C6
Claremont Ct NN16 ...32 A3
Claremont Rd PE9 ...241 E8
Clarence Ave NN12 ...141 C2
Clarence Ct NN10 ...148 A8
Clarence Rd
Kettering NN16 ...72 C3
Rugby CV21 ...241 A8
Stony Stratford MK11 ...229 E5
Clarence St LE16 ...31 F3
Clark CI NN9 ...113 B4
Clark Cres NN12 ...203 C8
Clarke CI NN6 ...72 A4
Clarke CI NN6 ...144 F4
Clarke Ho NN1 ...160 A8
Clarke Rd Corby NN17 ...36 D8
Northampton NN1 ...160 A8
Clarke St LE16 ...31 D3
Clarkes Dale LE16 ...20 D1
Clarkes Way
Brackley NN13 ...233 D7
Welton NN11 ...135 D8
Clarks La NN13 ...233 D7
Claughton Rd NN4 ...159 D3
Clay La NN17 ...10 B1
Claydon CI NN8 ...129 E5
Clayfield CI NN13 ...142 B6
Clayland CI NN29 ...164 C2
Claystones NN6 ...158 D2
Cleaver St NN15 ...72 A1
Cleavers La NN6 ...107 D7
Cleburne St NN9 ...114 A4
Clee Rise NN5 ...158 D8
Cleeve Way NN8 ...129 D1
Clement Bois NN13 ...233 E8
Cleveland Ave NN16 ...72 C6
Cleveland PI NN4 ...159 A2
Clickers Yd NN4 ...195 F4
Cliften Terr NN6 ...122 D4
Cliff Cres PE9 ...241 D3
Cliff Rd PE9 ...241 D3
Cliffe Rd **8** NN4 ...2 A3
Clifton CI Kettering NN15 ...72 C1
Long Buckby NN6 ...121 C4
Clifton Dr PE9 ...41 E5
Clifton Gr NN15 ...72 C1
Clifton Rd
Deddington OX15 ...236 B4
Rugby CV21 ...241 F8
Clifton Sq NN17 ...36 E8
Cliftonville NN1 ...159 E6
Cliftonville Mid Sch
NN1 ...159 F5
Cliftonville Rd NN1 ...159 F5
Clinton Rd NN14 ...51 B2
Clipston Endowed Prim Sch
NN16 ...67 A8
Clipston Field PI **7**
NN13 ...143 C2
Clipston La LE16 ...48 E3
Clipston Rd
East Farndon LE16 ...48 B4
Great Oxendon LE16 ...48 D2
Clipston St LE16 ...31 C2
Clipston Way NN6 ...140 D1
Clipstone CI NN14 ...70 C6
Clive CI NN15 ...72 A1
Clock Tower Ct NN3 ...142 E6
Cloisters The
Irthlingborough NN9 ...113 D2
Priors Hardwick CV47 ...166 A5
Rushden NN10 ...132 B2
Wellingborough NN8 ...130 B4
Close NN7 ...192 C6
Close Rd NN7 ...156 B1
Close The
Chipping Warden OX17 ...196 F6
Eastcote NN12 ...188 F8
Easton o t H PE9 ...
Greatworth OX17 ...210 D1
Hargrave NN9 ...115 F2
Irthlingborough NN9 ...112 F1
Kettering NN16 ...91 B8
Northampton NN2 ...141 C4
Roade NN7 ...191 D4
Swinford LE17 ...62 A8
Weston Underwood MK46 ...195 A1
Cloutsham St NN1 ...159 C7
Clovelly Ct NN14 ...36 F4
Clover Dr Rushden NN10 ...148 C8
Thrapston NN14 ...76 D2
Clover End NN8 ...240 C2
Clover Field NN4 ...175 F2
Clover Gdns NN16 ...72 B4
Clover La NN2 ...141 E4
Club La NN14 ...94 C6
Club St NN15 ...72 A1
Clumber Ct NN18 ...36 F6
Clumber Dr NN11 ...160 E7

Clun Wlk NN17 .... 21 C1
Clwyd Wlk NN17 .... 21 C1
Clydesdale Rd NN17 .... 36 D7
Co-operative Row
NN10 .... 132 B1
Coach Ho The NN3 ..... 160 B7
Coach Yd NN12 .... 217 E3
Coaching Wlk NN3 ...... 142 D2
Coales Gdns LE16 .... 31 D5
Coalport Cl NN14 .... 50 F3
Cob Dr NN4 .... 158 B1
Cobb's La NN29 .... 146 D3
Cobblers Ct NN12 .... 187 B1
Cobblestone Ct NN4 .... 158 D2
Cobbs Gdn NN16 .... 195 F4
Cobden St NN16 .... 72 A3
Cobham Cl MK18 .... 240 C4
Cockbrook La PE17 ...... 79 C2
Cockerell Rd NN17 ...... 37 B8
Cockerill's Mdw CV21 .. 99 A8
Cockington Cl OX16 .... 240 E9
Cockley Rd NN13 .... 221 C6
Codlin Cl NN3 .... 143 B1
Coffee Tavern La NN10 132 B2
Cofferidge Cl MK11 ..... 229 D5
Cogan Cres NN14 .... 70 B6
Cogenhoe Prim Sch
NN7 .... 161 F5
Coggins Cl NN9 .... 114 C6
Cold Ashby Rd
Guilsborough NN6 ...... 103 E7
Thornby NN6 .... 64 A5
Coldermeadow Ave
NN18 .... 36 A3
Coldstream Cl NN11 .... 135 B1
Coldstream La NN4 ..... 175 E8
Cole Ct NN9 .... 114 C5
Cole St NN10 .... 131 E4
Coleman Cl NN6 .... 101 A6
Coleman St NN9 .... 114 D6
Coleraine Cl NN2 .... 141 A5
Coleridge Way NN17 .... 36 C3
Coleridge Wlk NN11 .... 135 B4
Coles Rise NN13 .... 233 D7
College Field Cl NN3 ... 143 C3
College Fields NN4 ...... 237 C7
College Rd CV23 .... 117 E3
College St
Higham Ferrers NN10 .. 132 C6
Irthlingborough NN9 ... 112 F2
Northampton NN1 .... 159 C6
Rushden NN10 .... 132 B2
Wellingborough NN8 ... 129 E4
Wollaston NN29 .... 164 C7
College St Mews 28
NN1 .... 159 C6
Colley Rise LE15 .... 9 C7
Collingcroft Cl NN4 ..... 175 A7
Collingdale Rd NN3 ..... 142 D2
Collingham Cl NN9 ...... 114 A5
Collingtree CE Prim Sch
NN4 .... 175 C4
Collingtree Rd NN4,NN7 175 A4
Collingwood Ave NN17 36 A7
Collingwood Rd NN1 ... 141 F1
Collingwood Way NN11 135 E3
Collins Cl NN12 .... 203 C7
Collins Hill NN7 .... 155 E6
Collins St NN1 .... 159 F7
Collmead Ct NN3 .... 143 B4
Collswell La NN12 .... 187 B1
Collyweston Cross Roads
PE8 .... 6 A6
Collyweston Rd NN3 ... 143 C5
Colmar Cl NN11 .... 135 A4
Colne Cl NN17 .... 21 C1
Colne Way NN5 .... 140 E1
Colonial Dr NN4 .... 175 C5
Colsons Way NN4 .... 195 F5
Coltsfoot Rd NN10 ...... 148 C7
Columbia Cres NN14 ... 70 E6
Columbus Ct NN11 ..... 135 B5
Colville Wlk OX16 .... 240 E9
Colwell Rd NN8 .... 130 C4
Colwyn Rd NN1 .... 159 E8
Colyers Ave NN18 .... 36 B3
Comfrey Cl NN10 .... 148 B7
Commercial Rd
Corby NN17 .... 37 B6
Kettering NN16 .... 72 B2
Commercial St
Higham Ferrers NN10 .. 132 B5
Northampton NN1 .... 159 C5
Commercial Way NN16 72 A3
Common St MK46 ...... 194 D1
Compton Gn NN18 ...... 36 A6
Compton Ho NN1 .... 159 B6
Compton Pl NN16 .... 72 C2
Compton St NN10 ...... 130 C5
Compton St
Desborough NN14 ...... 51 A3
Northampton NN1 .... 159 B6
Compton Way NN6 ..... 144 E3
Conduit Rd PE9 .... 241 E4
Coneygree Ave NN4 .... 175 F8
Coneygree Ct NN4 ...... 143 B1
Conifer Rise NN11 ...... 142 C1
Coniston Ave NN3 ...... 142 D3
Coniston Cl
Daventry NN11 .... 135 B2
Higham Ferrers NN10 .. 132 B8
Wellingborough NN8 ... 129 C5
Coniston Rd NN16 ...... 71 F2
Connaught Rd LE16 .... 31 F4

Connaught St
Kettering NN16 .... 72 D3
Northampton NN1 .... 159 A5
Connegar Leys NN7 .... 190 E7
Connell Cl LE16 .... 30 F3
Connell Ct NN17 .... 36 F5
Connolly Cl NN4 .... 70 F7
Connolly Dr NN14 ...... 70 F7
Constable Dr
Kettering NN15 .... 92 A7
Wellingborough NN8 ... 129 F7
Constable Rd Corby NN18 36 E5
Rugby CV21 .... 80 B1
Constable Wlk NN4 .... 94 D7
Conway Cl
Northampton NN5 ...... 140 E2
Rushden NN10 .... 148 A8
Wellingborough NN8 ... 129 C6
Conway Dr
Burton Latimer NN15 .. 92 B2
Thrapston NN14 .... 76 F2
Conway Wlk NN17 ...... 21 D1
Conyngham Rd NN3 ... 142 F2
Cook Cl Daventry NN11 135 C5
Rothwell NN14 .... 70 E6
Cook's Terr NN6 .... 121 A3
Cook's Way NN6 .... 121 A3
Cooks Cl NN7 .... 205 F8
Cooks Rd NN17 .... 37 F8
Coomb Rd NN18 .... 36 D1
Cooper Cl NN12 .... 203 C8
Cooper Ct NN14 .... 76 D1
Cooper Dr NN8 .... 129 F8
Coopers Gate OX16 .... 240 C9
Coots Cl MK18 .... 240 E2
Cope Rd OX16 .... 240 C8
Copelands Rd NN14 .... 51 C3
Copenhagen Rd NN18 .. 36 A1
Copper Leaf Cl NN1 .... 142 C6
Copperfield Cl NN16 ... 72 D3
Coppice Cl Banbury OX16 240 E6
Wellingborough NN8 ... 129 C8
Coppice Dr NN3 .... 142 A5
Copse Cl
Burton Latimer NN15 .. 92 C3
Northampton NN2 ...... 140 F5
Copymoor Cl NN4 ...... 176 A6
Cora Rd NN16 .... 72 E4
Corbett St CV21 .... 241 E9
Corbieres Ct NN5 .... 140 A2
Corby Com Coll NN17 .. 22 E5
Corby Cstm Hospl NN17 36 D6
Corby Gate NN17 .... 22 D1
Corby Gate Bsns Pk
NN17 .... 22 F1
Corby Rd Cottingham LE16 36 F8
Gretton NN17 .... 22 B6
Stanion NN14 .... 37 E3
Weldon NN17 .... 38 A7
Cordon Cl NN3 .... 143 B3
Cordon Cres NN6 .... 144 F4
Cordwainer Gr NN14 ... 76 D1
Cordwainer Ho NN5 .... 159 A5
Cordwainers NN10 ...... 132 C1
Corn Kiln Cl NN7 .... 161 F6
Corn La 7 NN8 .... 130 A4
Corner Cl NN29 .... 77 E7
Cornfield Cl NN12 ...... 241 B5
Cornfield Way NN15 .... 92 C1
Cornflower Cl NN4 ...... 175 F7
Cornflower Pl MK18 .... 240 E2
Cornhill Cl NN5 .... 140 C3
Cornstalk Bldgs PE9 ... 241 E3
Cornwall Cl NN17 .... 36 C6
Cornwall Rd
Kettering NN16 .... 72 D3
Stamford PE9 .... 241 D4
Cornwalls Ctr The
MK18 .... 240 D4
Cornwalls Mdw MK18 .. 240 D4
Cornwell Bsns Pk NN4 .. 168 D2
Coronation Ave
Rothwell NN14 .... 70 D7
Rushden NN10 .... 131 E1
Coronation Cres PE8 ... 39 E7
Coronation Rd
Newnham NN11 .... 153 D4
Stony Stratford MK11 .. 229 E5
Corporation St
Corby NN17 .... 36 E6
Rugby CV21 .... 241 C8
Corran Cl NN5 .... 158 E8
Cory Gdns NN7 .... 157 C7
Cosgrove L Pk* MK19 .. 218 F1
Cosgrove Rd
Northampton NN2 ...... 141 C5
Old Stratford MK19 .... 229 C7
Cosgrove Village Prim Sch
MK19 .... 218 D2
Cosgrove Way NN2 ..... 141 C5
Cosy Nook NN14 .... 76 C2
Coton Cl NN6 .... 103 E1
Coton Manor Gdns*
NN6 .... 103 A4
Coton Rd
Guilsborough NN6 ...... 103 F5
Rugby CV21 .... 80 A1
Cotswold Ave
Kettering NN16 .... 72 B1
Northampton NN5 ...... 158 D8
Cotswold Cl NN11 ...... 135 B5
Cotswold Ct OX27 ...... 237 E3
Cotswold Dr NN10 ..... 129 D1
Cottage Cl NN12 .... 141 A4
Cottage Gdns NN3 ..... 143 B3
Cottage Leap CV21 .... 241 F9
Cottages The NN13 .... 224 C5

Cottagewell Ct NN3 .... 142 F1
Cottarville NN3 .... 142 D1
Cotterstock Rd PE8 .... 41 F7
Cottesbrooke Gdns
NN4 .... 175 D7
Cottesbrooke Grange
NN6 .... 105 A8
Cottesbrooke Hall*
NN6 .... 105 A8
Cottesbrooke Pk NN11 135 A5
Cottesbrooke Rd NN17 36 E5
Cottesloe Ct MK11 ..... 229 F5
Cottesmore Ave NN15 92 A6
Cottesmore Cl NN5 .... 140 B1
Cottesmore Rd PE9 .... 241 A3
Cottesmore Way NN8 .. 129 D4
Cottingham CE Prim Sch
LE16 .... 20 C1
Cottingham Dr NN3 .... 142 B7
Cottingham Rd
Corby NN17 .... 36 E6
Corby NN18 .... 36 B7
Rockingham LE16 ...... 21 A4
Cottingham Way NN4 .. 76 C2
Cotton End
Long Buckby NN6 .... 121 D4
Northampton NN4 ...... 159 C4
Cottons The
Rockingham LE16 ...... 21 A4
Wellingborough NN8 ... 129 D7
Coulon Cl NN29 .... 147 A7
Coulthard Cl NN12 ..... 203 D8
Council Ho's LE16 ...... 48 B8
Council Hos
Farthingstone NN12 .... 170 E3
Guilsborough NN6 ...... 103 F7
Hannington NN6 .... 108 C3
Podington NN29 .... 147 E1
Council Hos The
Long Buckby Wharf NN6 136 E7
Wardington OX17 .... 208 F8
Council Houses NN6 .. 106 F6
Council St Bozeat NN29 164 C4
Wollaston NN29 .... 146 D2
Countess Cres NN5 .... 159 A7
Countess Rd NN5 ...... 159 A7
Countryside NN11 ...... 118 B1
Counts Farm Rd NN18 36 D4
County Rd NN13 .... 234 A6
County View NN15 ..... 236 D4
Courier Rd NN17 .... 37 B8
Court Ave NN4 .... 195 E4
Court Dr NN16 .... 72 B6
Court House Cl NN6 ... 104 F4
Court La NN6 .... 64 D3
Court Mews NN8 .... 130 B4
Courtenhall Cl NN7 .... 159 C5
Courtenhall Rd NN7 ... 191 A7
Courtman Rd NN9 ..... 114 A4
Courtney Rd NN10 ..... 132 A1
Courtyard La NN11 ..... 153 A3
Courtyard The Islip NN14 76 B3
Middleton Cheney OX17 219 D5
Stamford PE9 .... 241 C3
Courtyard Workshops
LE16 .... 31 D3
Coventry Rd NN11 ..... 135 B3
Coverack Cl NN4 .... 159 B1
Coverdale NN2 .... 140 F5
Coverley Pl CV22 .... 241 A8
Covert Cl NN2 .... 141 A6
Covington Gr NN8 ...... 130 A6
Covington St NN1 ...... 160 A7
Cow Yd NN2 .... 141 B3
Cowbeck Cl NN4 .... 175 E5
Cowgill Cl NN3 .... 143 B3
Cowley Cl NN16 .... 72 D6
Cowley Rd NN11 .... 135 B3
Cowley Way CV23 ...... 99 F2
Cowper & Newton Mus The*
MK46 .... 195 F3
Cowper Cl
Earls Barton NN6 ...... 145 A4
Irthlingborough NN9 ... 112 D1
Cowper Rd
Daventry NN11 .... 135 B2
Wellingborough NN8 ... 130 C3
Cowper St Kettering NN16 72 B4
Northampton NN1 .... 159 F7
Cowper Terr NN1 .... 121 A3
Cowpers Orch NN4 .... 195 A1
Cowslip Cl NN10 .... 148 C8
Cowslip Hill NN14 ...... 89 B5
Cox Gdns NN12 .... 202 E8
Cox's Cl NN6 .... 121 B3
Cox's La NN14 .... 90 A5
Cox's La NN11 .... 135 C1
Coxwell Cl MK18 .... 240 F4
Crab Apple Way NN14 76 E1
Crab Tree Cl NN6 ...... 145 B5
Crabb St NN10 .... 132 B1
Crabb Tree Dr NN3 .... 143 A2
Crabtree CI Hartwell NN7 197 E2
Wellingborough NN8 ... 129 F2
Crabtree Ho NN11 ..... 135 C4
Crabtree La NN6 .... 84 B5
Cracknuts La NN14 .... 160 E2
Craddock Cl NN29 ..... 147 B8
Cragside NN8 .... 129 C6
Craigie NN6 .... 121 C3
Cranbrooke Rd NN2 ... 141 C1
Crane Cl Broughton NN14 92 E8
Rushden NN10 .... 132 B4
Crane Wlk NN3 .... 142 E6

Cranford CE Prim Sch
NN14 .... 93 B7
Cranford Ho 1 NN2 .... 141 C3
Cranford Rd
Burton Latimer NN15 .. 92 D4
Great Addington NN14 . 92 C6
Kettering NN16 .... 72 A2
Northampton NN2 ...... 141 C3
Cranleigh Rd NN15 .... 91 B7
Cranmere Ave NN1 .... 160 B6
Cransley Gdns NN17 .. 36 B7
Cransley Hill NN14 ..... 90 A4
Cransley Rd NN14 ..... 70 C1
Cranstoun St NN1 ..... 159 D7
Craven Rd CV21 .... 241 E9
Craven St NN1 .... 159 D7
Cravford Ave NN5 ...... 158 C7
Crawford Gr NN17 ..... 36 E8
Crawley Ave NN8 ...... 129 D7
Crawley Rd NN17 ...... 10 B1
Creampot Cl OX17 ..... 196 A2
Creampot La OX17 .... 196 A2
Creaton Rd NN6 .... 104 D5
Crediton Cl NN3 .... 160 D7
Creed Rd PE8 .... 41 F7
Creighton Cres NN15 . 91 F6
Crescent Cl LE16 ...... 31 F4
Crescent The
Burton Latimer NN15 .. 92 C4
Easton o t H PE9 ...... 1 F5
Flore NN7 .... 155 F6
Hackleton NN7 .... 177 A3
Kettering NN15 .... 91 B8
Ketton PE9 .... 1 A7
Market Harborough LE16 31 F4
Moulton NN3 .... 126 D1
Northampton NN1 ...... 159 F8
Pattishall NN12 .... 172 E1
Rothwell NN14 .... 70 C6
Rushden NN10 .... 131 E2
Twyford OX17 .... 230 A5
Whittlebury NN12 ...... 215 C5
Cresswell Rd NN10 ... 131 F2
Cresswell Wlk NN11 ... 135 E3
Crestline Ct NN14 ..... 143 A5
Crestwood Gdns NN3 142 F5
Crestwood Rd NN3 ... 142 F5
Creswell Wlk NN17 .... 21 C1
Crick Cl NN17 .... 22 A1
Crick Prim Sch NN6 .. 100 C6
Crick Rd Rugby CV21,CV23 99 D7
West Haddon NN6 ..... 102 A5
Yelvertoft NN6 .... 82 A2
Cricketers Gn NN17 ... 38 C8
Cricklade Cl NN3 ...... 160 D6
Crickley Cres NN4 ..... 158 E3
Crimea Cl 2 NN4 ..... 175 E7
Crispian Cl NN10 ...... 159 D7
Crispian Ho NN1 ...... 159 D7
Crispin Cotts NN6 .... 108 A4
Crispin Ho NN1 .... 159 B6
Crispin Pl 14 NN16 ... 72 A7
Crispin St
14 Northampton NN1 . 140 F1
Rugby CV21 .... 99 A8
Stamford PE9 .... 241 E3
Croft Way Rushden NN10 132 D3
Weedon NN7 .... 155 A3
Crofters Cl NN4 .... 175 B7
Croftmeadow Ct NN3 143 B4
Cromarty Cl NN7 ...... 36 F5
Cromarty Rd NN17 .... 36 F5
Cromarty Rd PE9 ...... 241 A4
Cromer Rd NN0 .... 111 F4
Cromwell Cl NN14 .... 91 C8
Cromwell Cres LE16 .. 31 D1
Cromwell Ct
Banbury OX16 .... 240 B9
Buckingham MK18 .... 240 E5
Cromwell Ho NN8 ..... 130 B4
Cromwell Rd
Banbury OX16 .... 240 A8
Kettering NN16 .... 72 A2
Rugby CV22 .... 241 E6
Rushden NN10 .... 132 C2
Cromwell St 16 NN1 . 141 C4
Cronin Cpt NN13 ...... 37 E7
Cropredy Ct MK18 .... 240 E5
Cronin Rd NN3 .... 37 E7
Crosby Rd LE16 .... 31 F1
Cross Bank LE16 ...... 20 D6
Cross Ct NN16 .... 72 A3
Cross Hill NN6 .... 106 B3
Cross Keys Ct NN13 .. 233 F7
Cross La Aldwincle NN14 74 F5
Braunston NN11 ...... 118 C5
Helmdon NN13 .... 212 A5
Weston Underwood MK46 195 B2
Cross Rd NN4 .... 160 B6
Cross St Covington PE18 116 D2
Daventry NN11 .... 135 B3
Kettering NN16 .... 72 A3
Market Harborough LE16 31 F2
Moulton NN3 .... 126 C1
Rothwell NN14 .... 70 D7

Cross St continued
Rugby CV21 .... 241 E9
Cross The NN4 .... 160 E2
Cross Tree Rd MK19 .. 228 B3
Cross Waters Cl NN4 . 175 F6
Cross Way NN9 .... 131 D8
Crossbrooks NN4 ..... 175 F6
Crosse Cl NN7 .... 155 C4
Crosshills MK11 .... 229 D4
Crouch Rd NN9 .... 112 F1
Crouch St OX16 .... 240 C7
Croughton All Saints CE Prim
Sch NN13 .... 228 D7
Croughton Cl NN2 .... 141 C5
Croughton Rd OX17 .. 237 D7
Crow La NN3 .... 161 C7
Crowberry Ave NN3 ... 142 C6
Crown Ct Corby NN18 36 E5
Rushden NN10 .... 131 E3
Crown La Barrowden LE15 3 F5
Rothwell NN14 .... 70 C7
West Haddon NN6 .... 102 C4
Crown St Kettering NN16 72 B3
Stamford PE9 .... 241 D3
Crown Way NN10 ..... 131 E4
Crownsmead NN4 .... 158 D1
Crowthorp Rd NN3 ... 143 C5
Croxdale Cl NN2 ...... 140 F5
Croxen Cl NN15 .... 92 C2
Croyde Ave NN18 ..... 36 A1
Croyland Hall Her Ctr Mus*
NN8 .... 130 A4
Croyland Prim Sch NN8 129 E3
Croyland Rd NN8 ..... 129 F3
Crucible Rd NN17 .... 37 B7
Ctyd The NN3 .... 142 C1
Cubleigh Cl NN3 ...... 142 C6
Cuckoo Cl LE15 .... 3 E5
Cullahill Cl NN4 .... 158 E2
Culloden Ct NN17 .... 36 F5
Culloden Dr NN15 .... 91 F8
Culme Cl PE8 .... 41 C7
Culross Wlk NN18 .... 36 A3
Culworth CE Sch OX17 198 C2
Culworth Cres NN2 ... 141 D5
Culworth Rd OX17 .... 197 B6
Cumberland Ave NN9 114 A4
Cumberland Cl NN13 142 A3
Cumbrae Dr NN3 ...... 142 B5
Cunliffe Dr NN16 ..... 72 A4
Cunningham
Daventry NN11 .... 135 E2
Higham Ferrers NN10 . 132 C8
Cupar Cres NN17 ...... 36 F5
Curgenven Ct NN11 .. 183 E7
Curie Cl CV21 .... 241 F8
Curlbrook Cl NN4 ..... 176 A6
Curlew Way NN11 .... 183 E7
Curie Rd NN2 .... 141 C1
Curtis Mews NN8 ..... 129 C7
Curtlee Hill NN4 ...... 175 F5
Curver Way NN17 .... 22 D1
Cyclamen Cl NN14 ... 91 E6
Cypress Cl NN14 ..... 50 F3
Cypress Ct NN3 .... 142 E3
Cyril St NN1 .... 159 E6
Cytringen Cl NN15 ... 91 A7

D

D'albini Cl LE16 .... 34 B4
Da Vinci Cl NN5 .... 158 C5
Dadford Rd NN12,MK18 225 D5
Daffodil Dr NN10 ..... 148 B7
Dagnall Rd NN4 ...... 195 E3
Dahlia Rd NN16 ...... 72 D4
Daimler Cl
Daventry NN11 .... 135 A3
Northampton NN3 ..... 142 E7
Dairy Cl Brixworth NN6 106 A1
West Haddon NN6 .... 102 D4
Dairy Cotts LE17 ..... 45 A4
Dairy Farm Cl NN6 .. 121 B3
Dairy Ground OX17 .. 231 A6
Dairy Meadow Ct NN3 142 F6
Dairy Way NN9 .... 131 E8
Daisy Bank Ave NN4 70 C7
Daisy Croft NN10 .... 148 C8
Dakin Cl PE8 .... 13 F8
Dalby Cl NN16 .... 72 A6
Dale Ave NN8 .... 129 C5
Dale Cl Brackley NN13 234 A7
Daventry NN11 .... 135 B5
Mears Ashby NN6 .... 128 C5
Wellingborough NN8 . 129 C5
Dale Farm Cotts NN6 128 C2
Dale Ho NN8 .... 129 F4
Dale St Corby NN17 . 36 D7
Rugby CV21 .... 241 C9
Wellingborough NN8 . 129 F4
Dale The NN6 .... 121 C3
Dalestones NN4 ..... 158 D2
Daleswood Rise PE8 13 E7
Dalkeith Ave 20 NN11 72 B2
Dalkeith Pl NN16 .... 72 B2
Dalkeith Rd NN8 .... 129 C6
Dallacre Dr LE16 .... 34 C4
Dallington Cl NN14 . 54 A2
Dallington Gn 2 NN5 158 F8
Dallington Haven 8
NN5 .... 158 F8
Dallington Park Rd NN5 158 F8
Dallington Rd NN5 .. 159 A7
Dallison Ct LE16 ..... 48 E8
Dalmeny Rd NN14 .. 91 C8
Dalston Wlk 6 NN3 . 142 C4
Dalton Rd NN17 ..... 21 E2
Damherst Piece NN6 106 C2

Damson Cl NN14 .....76 E1
Damson Dell NN3 ....161 A8
Dando Cl NN29 ....146 D1
Dands Cl OX17 ....220 A8
Dands Dr OX17 ....220 A8
Dane Ct NN11 ....118 C1
Dane Ridge NN5 .....158 C6
Danefield Rd NN3 ...142 B2
Daneholme Ave NN11 .135 C4
Danes Backside NN12 .141 B3
Danes Camp Way NN4 .158 E3
Danes Way NN6 ......100 C7
Daneholme Jun & Inf Sch
  NN18 ....36 A2
Daneholme Rd NN18 ..36 A2
Danetre Comp Sch
  NN11 ....135 E1
Danetre Dr NN11 .....135 D1
Danetre Hospl NN11 ..153 C8
Danetree Gdns NN12 .142 B2
Danewood Rd NN3 ....142 B2
Danford Cl PE8 ......41 F4
Danfords PE8 ....41 F5
Daniaud Ct NN13 ....233 E8
Daniel Ct PE9 ....241 E2
Daniell Wlk NN18 ....36 D5
Daniels Rd NN8 ......130 C1
Dapplestone Cl NN4 .158 D2
Darby Cl NN5 ....129 A5
Dardis Cl 2 NN12 ...141 E1
Darenth Ct 12 NN11 .159 C7
Darescroft LE16 ....20 B1
Dark La Braunston NN11 .118 D1
  Great Harrowden NN9 .110 D2
Darley Cl NN16 ......74 C4
Darley Dale Rd NN17 .36 C8
Dart Cl NN17 ....72 C2
Dartford Cl 2 NN4 ..159 A2
Dartmouth Rd NN46 ..195 F4
Dartmouth Row NN11 .135 C1
Darwin Cl PE9 ....241 C5
Darwin Cl 1 NN17 ...37 C8
Darwin Ho NN17 .....22 F1
Darwin Rd NN17 .....37 C8
Darwin Wlk NN5 .....140 C1
Dash Farm Cl NN17 ..38 A8
Dashwood Rd OX16 ...240 C7
Daventry Country Pk*
  NN11 ....135 D5
Daventry Rd
  Banbury OX16 ....208 A2
  Banbury OX16 ....240 F9
  Barby CV23 ....118 C8
  Kilsby CV23 ....100 A1
  Newnham NN11 ....153 D4
  Norton NN11 ....136 C5
  Staverton NN11 .....152 B7
  Staverton NN11 .....152 C7
  Willoughby CV23 ....117 C7
Daventry Tert Coll
  NN11 ....153 B8
Daventry William Parker Sch
  NN11 ....135 C3
Davey Rd NN17 ......37 C8
Davies Cl NN15 .....90 F8
Davis Cl NN14 ......70 E6
Davis Ct NN17 ......37 A6
Davy Cl NN8 ....129 A6
Dawkins Ct NN14 ....90 A4
Dayrell Rd NN4 .....158 F2
Dayrell Sq 5 NN4 ..158 F2
Dayton St NN10 .....132 A2
De Capel Ct NN14 ...94 D6
De Clare Ct MK18 ...240 D6
De Ferneus Dr NN9 ..114 D7
De Lisle Cl LE16 ...31 D2
De Montfort Ct NN13 .222 E1
De Quincey Cl NN14 .222 E1
De Roos Way LE16 ...34 B4
De Vere Rd NN14 ....76 D2
Deacon Cl
  Market Harborough LE16 .31 D5
  Rugby CV22 ....241 E6
  Rushden NN10 ....132 D3
Deacon Way OX16 ....240 A7
Deacons Ct NN3 .....143 C4
Deal Ct NN1 ....159 D7
Deal St NN1 ....159 C7
Dean Cl NN10 ....148 A8
Dean Wlk 8 LE16 ...167 A8
Deancourt Dr NN5 ..140 A1
Deane Par CV21 ....99 A8
Deane Rd CV21 .....99 B8
Deans Row NN7 .....139 A6
Deanshanger Dr NN12 .216 F1
Deanshanger Prim Sch
  MK19 ....228 E2
Deanshanger Rd
  Old Stratford MK19 .229 B6
  Wicken MK19 ....228 B3
Deansway NN3 ......143 C4
Debbs Cl MK11 ......229 E5
Debdale Rd
  Northampton NN3 ...142 D2
  Wellingborough NN8 .129 F5
Deben Rd NN17 .....72 C2
Deddington Castle
  Earthworks* OX15 ..236 A4
Dee Wlk NN11 ......135 A1
Deeble Rd NN15 ....72 F1
Deene Cl Adderbury OX17 .230 B4
  Corby NN17 ....56 D6
  Market Harborough LE16 .32 A3
Deene End NN17 ....38 C8
Deene Hall* NN17 ..223 F6
Deene Rd NN17 .....10 F7
Deeneside NN17 ....38 B8
Deepdale LE16 .....20 D7

Deer Park Rd NN3 ...142 A6
Deerfield Cl MK18 ..240 E2
Deerings Rd NN17 ..99 A8
Delamere Dr NN15 ..92 A5
Delamere Rd NN14 ..159 D3
Delapre Abbey* NN4 .159 D3
Delapre Cres NN4 ..159 D3
Delapre Crescent Rd
  NN4 ....159 C3
Delapre Ct NN4 ....159 C2
Delapre Dr OX16 ...240 F9
Delapre Mid Sch Annexe
  NN4 ....159 B3
Delapre Pl NN18 ...36 A3
Delapre St NN18 ...159 B3
Dell Cres NN3 ......143 B5
Dell Pl NN10 ....132 C2
Dells MK46 ....195 F4
Dells Cl PE17 ......61 D2
Delta Way NN3 .....141 A5
Delves The NN9 ....114 C6
Dempsey Dr NN10 ..70 F6
Demswell NN6 ......106 C2
Denbigh Rd NN3 ....160 D6
Denby Dale NN8 ....129 D7
Dencora Bsns Pk NN10 .107 A2
Dene Cl Kettering NN16 .72 A1
  Wellingborough NN8 .129 C6
Denethorpe La NN17 .24 B5
Denfield Park Jun Sch
  NN10 ....132 C3
Denford Dr NN15 ...72 F1
Denford Rd Corby NN17 .36 B8
  Ringstead NN14 ....95 C4
  Thrapston NN14 ....95 D8
Denford Way NN8 ..129 D7
Denington Cl NN8 ..130 B3
Denington Ind Est NN8 .130 B2
Denington Rd NN8 ..130 A2
Denman Cl LE16 ....34 A4
Denmark Ct NN18 ..36 C5
Denmark St NN10 ..132 C1
Denmark Rd
  Northampton NN1 ..159 E6
  Rushden NN10 .....132 C1
Denne Cl NN18 .....36 C1
Denney Cres NN11 .135 B2
Denston Cl NN4 ....159 B1
Denton Cl
  Irchester NN29 ....147 B8
  Rushden NN10 .....132 C3
Denton Ct NN15 ...92 B2
Denton Prim Sch NN7 .178 C8
Denton Rd NN7 ....178 B6
Derby Rd NN1 .....159 F8
Dering Cotts OX17 .210 E2
Derngate NN1 .....159 D5
Derry The NN6 .....100 F5
Derwent Cl
  Daventry NN11 ....135 A1
  Northampton NN8 .129 C6
Derwent Cres NN16 .71 F2
Derwent Dr NN5 ....140 F2
Derwent Ho PE8 ...42 A6
Derwent Wlk NN17 .21 D2
Desborough Rd
  Arthingworth LE16 .49 F1
  Braybrooke LE16 ..49 F5
  Rothwell NN14 ....70 C7
  Rushton NN14 .....52 B2
  Stoke Albany LE16 .343 B3
Deveron Wlk NN7 ..21 D1
Devon Cl NN15 .....91 C6
Devon Ox Rd CV23 .99 F2
Devon Way NN3 ....142 A5
Devon Wlk NN10 ...132 C1
Devonshire Cl
  Boughton NN2 .....141 C8
  Wellingborough NN8 .129 C6
Devonshire Ho 6 NN5 .159 A6
Dewar Dr NN11 ....233 C6
Dexter Cl OX16 ....240 D6
Dexter Way PE8 ...28 B3
Diamond Dr NN13 ..131 E8
Diamond Way NN9 .113 A2
Diana Ho NN8 .....129 D5
Diana Way NN15 ..92 B1
Dibbin Cl NN17 ...37 B8
Dick's Hill LE16 ...34 A3
Dickens Dr Kettering NN16 .72 B6
  Old Stratford MK19 .229 B6
  Stamford PE9 ....241 E2
Dickens Spinney MK46 .195 E4
Dickinson Ct CV22 .241 C6
Dickson Cl 4 NN14 .158 F3
Digby St NN16 ....72 C3
Dimock Sq NN4 ....158 F2
Dingle Rd NN10 ...131 E2
Dingle The NN11 ..153 C8
Dinglederry MK46 ..195 F4
Dingley La LE16 ...32 F6
Dingley Rd LE16 ...32 B6
Dingley Terr LE16 ..31 F3
Disbrowe Ct NN9 ..133 C7
Diswell Brook Way
  MK19 ....228 E5
Ditchford Cl NN14 ..158 F4
Ditchford Rd NN13 .131 C5
Dixon Rd NN12 ....141 E6
Dixon Wlk NN17 ..37 A6
Dobbins Cl OX17 ..231 A6
Dobson Cl NN18 ..36 D5
Dobson Wlk NN18 ..36 D5
Dockhouse The LE16 ..31 D4
Docklewell Cl NN12 .203 A4

Doctors La Eydon NN11 .184 C1
  Great Doddington NN29 .145 E6
Doddington Cl NN8 .129 F2
Doddington Rd
  Earls Barton NN6 .145 A4
  Wellingborough NN8 .145 F8
  Wellingborough NN8 .145 F8
  Wilby NN8 ....145 B8
Doddridge 1 NN1 ..159 C5
Doddridge Ho 2 NN1 .159 C5
Doddridge Rd LE16 .31 E4
Doddridge St 24 NN1 .159 C5
Dog La
  Napton on t H CV47 .150 A7
  South Kilworth LE17 .63 C8
Dolben Ave NN4 ...113 F4
Dolben Cl NN4 .....111 E4
Dolben Sq NN9 ....111 F4
Dolver Ct NN18 ...36 C2
Don Cl NN17 ......21 D1
Donald Greaves Ho
  NN17 ....21 D1
Donaldson Ave NN14 .90 A3
Donellan Gn NN3 ..142 A6
Donne Cl
  Higham Ferrers NN10 .132 A5
  Kettering NN16 ...72 A6
Donovan Ct NN3 ...160 E8
Dorcas Rd OX16 ...219 A6
Dorchester Cl NN5 .140 B2
Dorchester Gr OX16 .240 A6
Dore Cl NN6 ......143 A5
Doris Rd NN16 ....72 C4
Dorking Wlk NN18 ..36 C3
Dorothy Rd NN16 ..72 E3
Dorset Gdns NN2 ..141 D3
Dorset Rd Corby NN17 .36 C6
  Oundle PE8 ......42 A5
Doubles The NN11 ..135 B1
Doughty St PE9 ...241 F5
Douglas Ct NN16 ..91 E8
Douglas Rd NN5 ...157 F8
Douglas Dr LE16 ..31 F4
Doulton Cl NN14 ..50 F3
Dove Cl
  Buckingham MK18 .240 E2
  Northampton NN7 .125 D4
Dove Cotts OX17 ..203 C3
Dove Cotts OX17 ..210 A6
Dove's La NN3 ....126 D1
Dovecote Cl
  Barrowden LE15 ...3 F5
  Nassington NN15 ..91 F7
  Raunds NN9 ......117 A6
  Yarwell PE8 ......16 A8
Dovecote Dr Denton NN7 .162 B1
  Little Addington NN14 .113 B7
Dovecote Rd NN7 ..191 C4
Dovecote The NN6 .125 D5
Dovecote Yd NN10 .110 A5
Dovedale Gr NN14 .50 E4
Dovedale Rd NN17 .36 F7
Dovehouse Cl
  Brackley NN13 .....113 F3
  Stanwick NN9 .....113 F3
Dovehouse Ct MK19 .228 E4
Dover Cl NN10 ....132 D1
Dovercourt NN5 ...159 B5
Downer Cl MK18 ..240 E6
Downing Cres NN6 .241 D5
Downing Way NN11 .153 C7
Downs The NN9 ....110 E1
Downsway NN4 ....175 B6
Downwood Cl NN3 .143 C3
Dowthorpe End NN6 .144 F3
Dowthorpe Hill NN6 .144 F3
Drake Cl Corby NN17 .36 B8
  Daventry NN11 ....135 E1
  Rothwell NN14 ...70 E7
Drake Lee Mews NN16 .72 B1
Draper's Ct PE8 ...28 C3
Drapery NN1 ......159 C6
Draughton Rd NN6 .87 B7
Draycott Cl NN3 ..160 D7
Draymans Wlk NN13 .233 E6
Drayton Cl Corby NN17 .36 B4
  Islip NN14 ....76 B3
Drayton Fields Ind Est
  NN11 ....148 A8
Drayton Leys CV22 .98 A7
Drayton Pk NN11 ..135 B5
Drayton Pl NN9 ...112 F3
Drayton Rd
  Bringhurst LE16 ..20 B5
  Drayton LE16 .....19 D7
  Irthlingborough NN9 .112 F3
  Lowick NN14 .....75 E6
  Medbourne LE16 ..19 A5
  Wigston Wlk NN11 .135 A8
Dresden Cl NN10 ..35 F2
Driffield Gr NN17 ..36 F7
Drift Ave PE9 .....241 F4
Drift Gdns PE9 ...241 E4
Drift Rd PE9 ......241 E4
Drift The Collyweston PE9 .1 D2
  Sutton PE5 ....20 B5
Drift Way NN14 ...195 F5
Drill Hall Ct NN15 .72 A1
Drive The Horton NN7 .177 E1
  Kettering NN15 ...72 B1
  Northampton, Duston NN5 .158 A7
  Northampton, Phippsville
  NN1 ....159 E6
  Rushden NN10 ....132 C1
Wellingborough NN8 .130 A3
Droue Ct NN14 ....70 C7

Drove The Collyweston PE9 .1 D1
  Nassington PE8 ...15 E5
Drovers Wlk NN2 ..141 A5
Druce Rd NN12 ....217 E6
Druids Way NN3 ...141 F5
Drum La 23 NN1 ...159 C6
Drumming Well La PE8 .42 A5
Drummond Ct NN6 .125 D4
Drury La CV21 ....241 E8
Drydale Ave NN3 ..142 B3
Dryden Ave NN11 ..135 B2
Dryden Cl NN11 ...184 A7
Dryden Pl CV22 ...241 A8
Dryden Rd
  Northampton NN5 .158 F7
  Towcester NN12 ..203 C5
  Wellingborough NN8 .129 C5
Dryden St Kettering NN16 .72 B3
  Raunds NN9 ......114 C6
Dryden Way Corby NN17 .36 B8
  Higham Ferrers NN10 .132 B5
Dryden Wlk CV22 ..241 A8
Dryden's Cl NN14 ..77 C4
Dryden's Cl NN14 ..77 C4
Dryland Rd NN3 ...142 C2
Dryland St NN16 ..72 B2
Drylees Ct NN14 ..143 B5
Drywell Ct NN3 ...143 B5
Duchess Cl NN16 ..72 B4
Duchess End NN6 ..128 C2
Duchy Cl Chelveston NN9 .133 B8
  Higham Ferrers NN10 .132 C5
Duck End Cranford NN14 .93 B7
  Denford NN14 ....95 D6
  Hinton-in-t-H NN14 .232 F6
  Wollaston NN29 ..146 D3
Duck La Harpole NN7 .157 C6
  Oundle PE8 ......42 A5
Duck St Elton PE8 .16 F8
  Kislingbury NN7 ..107 C2
Duckworth Dell NN3 .142 F6
Duckworth Rd NN17 .36 B7
Duffy Pl CV21 ....99 A8
Duke St Banbury OX16 .240 E8
  Burton Latimer NN15 .92 B2
  Kettering NN16 ..72 B3
  Northampton NN1 .159 D7
Dukelands NN3 ...143 B5
Dukes Green Rd NN7 .157 D3
Dukes Jetty CV21 .241 C8
Dukes Piece MK18 .240 F3
Duke Rd NN5 .....158 C8
Dulley Ave NN8 ...129 F1
Dulverton Dr NN3 .160 D7
Dumas Cul-De-Sac
  NN13 ....222 E1
Dumble Cl NN18 ..36 D2
Dunbar Cl NN15 ...91 F8
Duncan Cl NN3 ....141 F7
Duncan Ct NN8 ...129 D3
Duncan Rd NN17 ..36 B7
Dunchurch Rd CV22 .241 C6
Dundee Dr PE9 ...241 A4
Dundee St NN5 ...158 F6
Dunedin Rd NN16 ..36 C2
Dunkirk Ave NN14 ..51 B3
Dunn Cl NN6 ......101 A6
Dunnock La NN4 ..175 F3
Dunslade Cl LE16 .32 B2
Dunslade Gr LE16 .32 B2
Dunslade Rd LE16 .32 A2
Dunsmore Ave CV22 .241 B5
Dunster St NN1 ...159 D6
Durban Rd NN16 ..72 D2
Durham Rd NN16 ..72 D2
Durness Cl NN15 ..91 E8
Duston Cl NN11 ...135 A8
Duston Eldean Lower Sch
  NN5 ....140 B1
Duston Mill La NN5 .158 D4
Duston Rd NN5 ...158 D6
Duston Upper Sch NN5 .158 A8
Duston Wildes NN5 .140 A2
Dychurch La
  Bozeat NN29 ......164 E3
  Northampton NN1 .159 D6
Dyson Cl CV21 ....80 A1
Dyson Dr NN16 ...72 A4

E

Eady Rd NN15 ....92 B1
Eady's Row NN4 ..94 D7
Eagle Dr NN4 .....159 F2
Eagle La NN14 ....71 B1
Eaglehurst NN6 ...106 C2
Eaglesfield NN11 ..136 C4
Ealing Terr NN11 ..132 A3
Earl St Northampton NN1 .159 D7
Earl's La CV22 ....236 A4
Rugby CV21 ......236 A4
Earls Barton Inf Sch
  NN6 ....144 E4
Earls Barton Jun Sch
  NN6 ....144 E4
Earls Barton Mus*
  NN6 ....144 E4
Earls Barton Rd
  Great Addington NN29 .145 C5
  Mears Ashby NN6 .128 E8
Earlsfield Cl NN4 ..176 A6
Earlstoke Cl OX16 .240 E10
Earlstrees Ct NN17 .21 F2

Earlstrees Ind Est NN17 .21 E2
Earlstrees Rd NN17 .21 E2
Easington Gdns OX16 .240 C6
Easington Rd OX16 .240 C6
East Ave
  Burton Latimer NN15 .92 B3
  Corby NN17 ....36 F5
  Kettering NN15 ...72 D2
East Bank NN3 ....143 A6
East Butterfield Ct NN3 .142 F5
East Carlton Countryside
  Pk* LE16 ....35 B8
East Carlton Pk LE16 .35 B8
East Cl Banbury OX16 .240 F9
  Kettering NN15 ...72 D2
East Cres Rushden NN10 .131 F2
  Weldon NN17 .....38 C8
East Dr NN15 ......72 E2
East End NN6 .....106 F5
East Gr NN11 .....132 B3
East Haddon CE Prim Sch
  NN6 ....122 D5
East Haddon Rd NN6 .122 D8
East Hunsbury Lower Sch
  NN4 ....175 D7
East Langham Rd NN9 .114 D7
East Leys Cl NN3 ..142 C7
East Oval NN5 ....140 F2
East Paddock Ct NN3 .143 A4
East Park Par NN1 .159 F8
East Priors Ct NN3 .143 A4
East Rd NN5 ......42 A5
East Rising NN4 ...175 D7
East St Banbury OX16 .240 F8
  Irchester NN29 ...147 B8
  Long Buckby NN6 .121 D4
  Market Harborough LE16 .31 D3
  Northampton NN1 .159 F6
  Olney MK46 ......195 F4
  Rugby CV21 ......241 E3
  Stamford PE9 ....241 E3
  Stanwick NN9 ....114 A3
East Union St CV22 .241 C7
East View OX17 ...210 E2
East Wlk NN15 ....72 E2
Eastbourne Ave NN18 .36 B5
Eastbrook NN18 ...36 B4
Eastbrook Hill NN5 .51 C3
Eastcote Rd NN7 ..189 D8
Eastern Ave N NN2 .141 D3
Eastern Ave S NN2 .141 D3
Eastern Way NN11 .135 C2
Eastfield NN7 .....190 D7
Eastfield Cl NN5 ..140 C1
Eastfield Cres
  Finedon NN9 .....112 A5
  Yardley Gobion NN12 .217 F5
Eastfield Lower Sch
  NN3 ....142 B3
Eastfield Pl CV21 ..241 C8
Eastfield Rd
  Brixworth NN6 ....106 B1
  8 Irthlingborough NN9 .112 F2
  Northampton, Duston NN5 .158 A8
  Northampton,Far Cotton
  NN4 ....159 C3
  Wellingborough NN8 .130 C6
  Wollaston NN29 ..146 E2
Eastfields Cres PE8 .15 E6
Easthill Cl NN13 ...233 F7
Eastlands Pl CV21 .241 F8
Eastlands Prim Sch
  CV21 ....241 F7
Eastlands Rd
  Finedon NN9 .....112 A5
  Rugby CV21 ......241 F8
Eastleigh Rd NN15 .91 D7
Eastman Ct NN3 ..143 A1
Eastmead St NN14 ..70 E7
Eaton Garfords Charity Sch
  PE9 ....2 A4
Easton La NN29 ...164 C3
Easton Way NN7 ..163 E4
Easton Wlk NN17 ..37 B6
Eastwood Gr CV21 .99 C8
Eastwood Rd PE8 ..42 A5
Easy La CV21 .....241 B8
Eaton Rd NN5 .....158 A8
Eaton Wlk NN10 ...132 B2
Ebbw Vale Rd NN17 .131 E8
Ebenezer Pl 8 NN10 .131 E2
Ebony Ct NN11 ...184 D5
Eccles Rd NN8 ....7 D8
Ecton Brook Lower Sch
  NN3 ....143 D1
Ecton Brook Mid Sch
  NN3 ....143 D1
Ecton Brook Rd NN3 .143 D2
Ecton Hall NN6 ...143 F4
Ecton La NN6 .....127 D2
Ecton Leys CV22 ..98 A7
Ecton Pk Rd NN3 ..143 C3
Ecton Prim Sch NN6 .143 F4
Ecton St 11 NN1 ..159 E6
Edale Gn NN14 ...50 E4
Eden Cl Daventry NN11 .135 A1
  Northampton NN3 .142 B4
Eden St NN16 ....72 B2
Edgar Rd NN16 ...72 D3
Edgcote Drive Cotts
  OX17 ....197 A4
Edge Hill Ct MK18 .240 E5
Edgehill Dr NN5 ..135 D6
Edgehill Rd NN5 ..140 D1

Edgell St NN16 ....72 C2
Edgemead Cl NN3 ....142 E7
Edgemont Rd NN3 ....142 E1
Edges Ct NN3 ....142 C7
Edgewood NN13 ....222 F1
Edinburgh Cl
  Market Harborough LE16 ......31 F4
  Rothwell NN14 ....70 C6
Edinburgh Ho NN5 ....158 C8
Edinburgh Mews NN2 ....141 C2
Edinburgh Rd
  Kettering NN16 ....72 D3
  Northampton NN2 ....141 C2
  Stamford PE9 ....241 D5
  Wellingborough NN8 ....129 E1
Edinburgh Sq 3 NN11 ....135 B3
Edison Cl NN8 ....129 A6
Edison Ct NN8 ....129 A6
Edison Ctyd NN17 ....21 F3
Edison Dr NN5 ....158 D4
Edith Ave NN16 ....72 E4
Edith St NN1 ....159 E6
Edmonds Cl
  Buckingham MK18 ....240 F4
  Burton Latimer NN15 ....241 F4
  Wellingborough NN8 ....130 A2
Edmonds Dr PE9 ....1 A5
Edmund St NN16 ....72 D2
Edmunds Rd OX16 ....240 A7
Edward Cl
  Higham Ferrers NN10 ....132 C7
  Kettering NN15 ....91 C7
Edward Rd
  Irchester NN29 ....147 B7
  Kettering NN15 ....91 C7
  Market Harborough LE16 ....31 D5
  Stamford PE9 ....241 D5
Edward St Banbury OX16 ....240 F8
  Rugby CV21 ....241 B9
Edward Watson Cl NN2 ....141 B5
Edwardian Cl NN4 ....175 E7
Edwards Cl NN11 ....183 D7
Edwards Dr NN8 ....129 D5
Edwinstowe Cl NN4 ....160 E7
Egerton Cl NN13 ....234 A7
Egmont Ave MK11 ....229 E4
Eider Cl
  Buckingham MK18 ....240 E3
  Burton Latimer NN15 ....92 A2
  Daventry NN11 ....135 C3
Eismann Way NN17 ....37 C7
Ekins Cl NN3 ....142 D2
Elan Ct NN10 ....131 E3
Elborow St CV21 ....241 C8
Eldean Rd NN5 ....140 B1
Elder Cl NN11 ....135 C4
Elderberry Ct NN3 ....143 C3
Eldon Cl NN6 ....100 E6
Eldon Way NN6 ....100 E6
Eleanor Cl PE9 ....241 C4
Eleanor Ct NN6 ....102 C4
Elgin St NN5 ....158 F6
Eliot Cl NN16 ....72 C6
Eliot Ct CV22 ....241 A8
Eliot Way NN10 ....132 A5
Elizabeth Cl
  Earls Barton NN6 ....144 E5
  Wellingborough NN8 ....129 D2
Elizabeth Ct NN10 ....132 C7
Elizabeth Rd
  Daventry NN11 ....135 B3
  Kettering NN16 ....72 D3
  Rothwell NN14 ....70 C6
  Stamford PE9 ....241 C4
  West Haddon NN6 ....102 C5
Elizabeth St Corby NN17 ....36 E6
  Northampton NN1 ....159 F6
Elizabeth Way
  Earls Barton NN6 ....144 E5
  Higham Ferrers NN10 ....132 C7
  Irthlingborough NN9 ....131 E8
Elizabeth Wlk 6 NN1 ....159 F6
Elkington Cl CV23 ....99 B1
Elkington Rd NN6 ....82 B4
Elkins Cl NN6 ....82 B4
Ellen Cl NN6 ....100 F6
Ellesmere Ave
  Brackley NN13 ....233 F8
  Northampton NN5 ....158 E7
Ellesmere Cl NN13 ....222 F1
Ellesmere Cres NN13 ....222 F1
Ellesmere Rd NN13 ....222 F1
Ellfield Ct NN3 ....142 F3
Elliot Ho NN10 ....132 A4
Ellis La NN14 ....89 B4
Ellison Cl NN9 ....114 C7
Elm Cl
  Brafield-on-t-G NN7 ....161 D2
  Hargrave NN9 ....115 F2
Elm Ct NN14 ....76 D1
Elm Dr Brackley NN13 ....233 D5
  Deanshanger MK19 ....228 D5
  Hinton NN11 ....184 A6
  Market Harborough LE16 ....31 C2
Elm Rd
  Burton Latimer NN15 ....92 C4
  Kettering NN15 ....72 D1
Elm St Buckingham MK18 ......240 D3
  18 Northampton NN1 ....159 C7
  Stamford PE9 ....241 D5
  Wellingborough NN8 ....129 F5
Elm Way NN7 ....177 C3
Elm Wlk Corby NN17 ....21 D1
  Higham Ferrers NN10 ....132 B6

Elmfield Cl NN12 ....217 D3
Elmhurst Ave NN3 ....142 A7
Elmhurst Ct NN3 ....142 A2
Elmington Cotts PE8 ....42 C8
Elmington Rd NN3 ....143 C5
Elmlea Dr MK46 ....195 F4
Elmore Rd CV22 ....241 B6
Elms Dr CV22 ....98 F8
Elms Dyke NN11 ....135 E8
Elmwood Wlk NN5 ....140 A1
Elsden Rd NN8 ....130 C5
Elsee Rd CV21 ....241 D8
Elton CE Prim Sch PE8 ....28 D8
Elton Cl
  Northampton NN3 ....143 B5
  Stamford PE9 ....241 B4
Elton Hall* PE8 ....28 D6
Elton Rd PE8 ....16 C7
Elwes Way NN3 ....143 B2
Elysium Terr NN2 ....159 C8
Embankment NN8 ....130 C2
Emberton Ctry Pk & Visitor
  Ctr* MK46 ....195 E1
Embleton Way MK18 ....240 C2
Emerald Way NN11 ....159 B5
Emerton Gdns MK11 ....229 D5
Emery Cl NN11 ....135 E8
Emley Cl NN3 ....142 F1
Emlyns Gdns PE9 ....241 E4
Emlyns St 7 PE9 ....241 D4
Emmanuel CE Mid Sch
  NN3 ....142 F2
Emmanuel Cl NN11 ....153 C8
Emmanuel Rd PE9 ....241 D5
Empingham Rd PE9 ....241 B3
Encon Ct NN3 ....141 F7
Enfield Cl NN5 ....157 F8
English Martyrs RC Prim Sch
  NN1 ....99 A7
Ennerdale Cl
  Daventry NN11 ....135 A2
  Kettering NN16 ....72 A2
  Northampton NN3 ....142 A3
  Rushden NN10 ....132 D3
Ensleigh Cl NN15 ....91 C7
Enstone Ct NN8 ....129 C1
Enterprise Cl NN16 ....71 F4
Enterprise Ct NN8 ....129 B6
Enterprise Ind Pk NN17 ....22 F1
Enterprise Rd NN9 ....114 E7
Entwood Dr NN3 ....143 B5
Epping Cl NN15 ....92 A5
Epping Wlk 4 NN11 ....135 B4
Epsom Cl NN10 ....148 D8
Epsom Wlk NN18 ....36 C1
Equestrian Way NN7 ....155 B4
Ericsson Cl NN11 ....135 C5
Ermine Cl NN8 ....241 B3
Ermine Rd NN3 ....143 C5
Ermine Way PE9 ....241 B3
Ermont Way
  Banbury OX16 ....219 A7
  Banbury OX16 ....240 F9
Erskin Wood NN6 ....105 B1
Esher Ct NN3 ....142 D4
Eskdaill Pl NN16 ....72 B3
Eskdaill St NN16 ....72 B3
Eskdale Cl Corby NN17 ....36 E7
  Northampton NN3 ....142 B3
Eskdale Cl NN8 ....129 C6
Essen La CV23 ....100 A6
Essenden Ct MK11 ....229 F5
Essex Cl NN17 ....36 B6
Essex Gdns LE16 ....31 D1
Essex Pl NN15 ....91 D6
Essex Rd Rushden NN10 ....132 C1
  Stamford PE9 ....241 B4
Essex St
  Northampton NN2 ....159 C8
  Rugby CV21 ....241 C9
Estel St NN1 ....159 E6
Eton Cl NN3 ....155 C4
Eton Ct 3 NN2 ....141 C3
Ettrick Cl NN16 ....72 A6
Euro Bsns Pk LE16 ....32 B2
Euro Hub NN18 ....37 A4
Euston Rd NN4 ....159 C3
Eva Rd NN16 ....72 E3
Evanwil Wlk NN9 ....114 D6
Evans Cl NN11 ....135 C1
Evelyn Way NN29 ....147 C7
Evenley Rd
  Mixbury NN13 ....234 D1
  Northampton NN1 ....141 C5
Evenlode Cl NN10 ....240 B9
Evensford Wlk NN9 ....131 D8
Everard Cl CV23 ....80 A5
Everdon Cl
  Northampton NN1 ....141 E4
  Rugby CV22 ....98 E8
Everdon Pk NN11 ....135 A6
Everdon Rd NN2 ....170 E3
Everdon Stubbs Nature
  Trail* NN11 ....170 C2
Everest Ho NN17 ....36 B6
Everest La NN17 ....36 E6
Evergreen Dr NN14 ....113 B7
Everitt Cl NN8 ....130 B2
Evesham Cl NN16 ....129 C1
Evesham Ct NN11 ....143 A7
Evison Rd NN14 ....70 C6
Evreux Way CV21 ....241 C8
Ewenfield Rd NN9 ....111 F4
Excalibur Cl NN3 ....158 A7

Excelsior NN8 ....129 B4
Excelsior Ct NN9 ....112 E2
Excelsior Gdns NN5 ....157 F8
Exeter Cl NN11 ....153 C8
Exeter Gdns PE9 ....241 B2
Exeter Jun & Inf Sch
  NN18 ....36 F5
Exeter Pl NN1 ....159 E7
Exeter St NN16 ....72 C5
Exmoor Cl NN3 ....160 D7
Exmouth Ave NN18 ....36 F4
Express Cl NN9 ....131 E8
Express Pk Kettering NN16 ....71 F3
  Rushden NN10 ....131 D3
Exton Cl PE9 ....241 A3
Eyam Cl NN14 ....50 E3
Eyelletter Ho 7 NN5 ....159 A6
Eynard Impasse NN13 ....222 E1
Eynon Cl NN3 ....126 B1

F

Factory La 9 LE16 ....31 E3
Fair La NN14 ....76 E3
Fair Mile NN7 ....141 A6
Fairfax Cl OX16 ....240 A6
Fairfax Rd LE16 ....31 E1
Fairfax Rise NN4 ....85 B8
Fairfield NN7 ....174 B2
Fairfield Rd Isham NN14 ....91 E1
  Market Harborough LE16 ....31 D4
  Northampton NN2 ....141 F2
  Paulerspury NN12 ....216 B7
Fairfields Sch NN2 ....141 E1
Fairground Way NN3 ....160 E7
Fairhurst Way NN6 ....144 F4
Fairlight Ct 8 NN18 ....36 B5
Fairmead Cres NN10 ....147 F8
Fairmead Rise NN2 ....140 F6
Fairoaks Dr NN6 ....114 C7
Fairoaks The NN3 ....160 F8
Fairview Rd OX16 ....240 D6
Fairway
  Market Harborough LE16 ....31 D4
  Northampton NN1 ....141 E2
  Rugby CV21 ....241 F9
Fairway The
  Banbury OX16 ....240 A8
  Daventry NN11 ....135 F2
Fernie Cl NN15 ....92 A5
Faith Terr MK19 ....207 A2
Falcon View NN12 ....202 D8
Falcon Way NN11 ....222 D2
Falconer's Hill Jun & Inf Schs
  NN11 ....135 C3
Falconers Cl NN11 ....135 C3
Falconers Rise NN4 ....175 A8
Falcutt Way NN7 ....141 D5
Falkirk Cl PE9 ....241 A4
Falkner's Cl OX17 ....230 A4
Fallow Wlk NN2 ....141 A6
Fallowfield NN9 ....129 E8
Fallowfield Rd NN9 ....129 E8
Fallowfields NN16 ....101 A6
Falmer Wlk NN18 ....36 B4
Falsgrave Cl NN18 ....36 B4
Fane Cl PE9 ....241 D5
Far Brook NN6 ....125 B8
Far Meadow Cl NN3 ....142 E5
Faracre Ct NN3 ....143 B1
Faraday Cl
  Daventry NN11 ....135 A4
  Northampton NN5 ....158 D5
  Wellingborough NN8 ....129 A6
Faraday Ct
  Thrapston NN14 ....76 E2
  Wellingborough NN8 ....129 A6
Faraday Gr NN17 ....37 A8
Faraday Rd CV22 ....241 E6
Faramir Pl NN3 ....143 B6
Farebrother Cl NN11 ....183 D7
Fareham Ave CV22 ....98 E8
Faringdon Ct NN3 ....143 A7
Farm Cl Brigstock NN14 ....55 F7
  Holcot NN6 ....126 E8
  Northampton NN1 ....141 B4
Farm Close Rd NN4 ....175 C6
Farm Field Ct NN11 ....142 E5
Farm Gr CV22 ....241 E6
Farm Rd Brackley NN13 ....234 A6
  Wellingborough NN8 ....129 E8
Farm Stile NN11 ....182 C8
Farmbrook Ct NN8 ....142 F5
Farmers Cl NN4 ....175 C5
Farmers Dr NN13 ....233 D8
Farmfield Cl NN3 ....191 F4
Farmhill Rd NN10 ....143 A6
Farmstead Rd NN18 ....36 A6
Farnborough Cl NN15 ....91 D5
Farndale Ave NN17 ....36 E7
Farndale View LE16 ....31 C2
Farndish Rd NN10 ....147 B7
Farndish Rd NN9 ....147 B7
Farndon Cl NN13 ....142 F6
Farndon Ct NN11 ....153 C8

Farrer Cl NN13 ....223 D4
Farthing Cl NN13 ....233 D7
Farthinghoe Prim Sch
  NN13 ....221 B4
Farthinghoe Rd OX17 ....231 F5
Farthingstone Rd
  Litchborough NN12 ....171 B2
  Weedon NN7 ....155 A1
Faugere Cl NN14 ....233 F8
Favell Way NN4 ....160 D8
Fawsley Leys CV22 ....98 A7
Fawsley Rd
  Everdon NN11 ....170 A8
  Northampton NN4 ....159 C2
Faxton Cl NN4 ....141 D4
Faxton End NN6 ....107 D7
Fay Cl NN11 ....184 A7
Feast Field CE NN29 ....146 D1
Featherbed La
  Geddington NN18 ....37 B1
  Rugby CV21 ....80 A1
Federation Ave NN14 ....50 F2
Fegans Ct NN11 ....229 D6
Fell Wlk NN8 ....129 D6
Fellmead Rd NN3 ....143 C5
Fellows Cl NN29 ....146 C3
Fellows Way CV21 ....98 F8
Fengate Cl NN3 ....143 C5
Fenn Ct PE8 ....15 E5
Fennel Ct NN4 ....175 D5
Fenners Ct NN10 ....132 D2
Fenny Compton Rd
  OX17 ....181 D1
Fenton Rise NN13 ....233 D7
Fenwick Dr CV21 ....99 A8
Ferdown Cl CV22 ....241 A6
Ferndown Ct CV22 ....241 A6
Ferndown Rd CV22 ....241 A6
Ferndown Terr CV22 ....241 A6
Ferne Furlong MK46 ....195 F5
Fernfield Cl LE16 ....32 B4
Fernie Chase LE16 ....17 A6
Fernie Cl NN15 ....92 A5
Fernie Field NN3 ....142 C6
Fernie Rd LE16 ....31 F3
Fernie Way NN8 ....129 D4
Ferrers Ct NN10 ....132 C7
Ferrers Sch The NN10 ....132 C5
Ferrestone Rd NN8 ....130 A6
Ferris Row NN3 ....160 F7
Fern Fields NN6 ....106 C3
Fessey Rd NN11 ....183 D8
Festival Cl NN9 ....113 B5
Festival Rd NN12 ....172 D1
Fetter St NN1 ....113 B5
Fettledine Rd NN9 ....116 C6
Field Cl NN6 ....102 C4
Field Cotts NN18 ....53 B8
Field Rose Sq 4 NN3 ....143 C2
Field St NN16 ....72 B3
Field Street Ave NN16 ....72 B3
Field View
  Brackley NN13 ....233 D7
  Braunston NN11 ....118 C1
  Marston St Lawrence
    OX17 ....210 B2
Field Way NN13 ....212 A5
Fieldgate Cl NN4 ....175 F6
Fieldhead Cl LE16 ....31 C3
Fieldmill Rd NN3 ....143 B1
Fields View NN6 ....130 B4
Fieldway NN3 ....142 B1
Fiennes Ct NN11 ....135 B6
Fiennes Rd OX16 ....240 D6
Fiensgate NN4 ....158 D1
Fife St NN5 ....158 F7
First Ave Kilby NN13 ....238 E7
Fifth Cl NN11 ....238 E7
Fifth St E NN13 ....238 E7
Filleigh Way NN10 ....160 C7
Finch Dr NN15 ....92 A6
Finch-Hatton Dr NN7 ....10 C1
Finedon Hall NN9 ....111 F5
Finedon Inf Sch NN9 ....111 F5
Finedon Mulso CE Jun Sch
  NN9 ....112 A5
Finedon Rd
  Burton Latimer NN15 ....92 C3
  Irthlingborough NN9 ....112 C3
  Wellingborough NN8 ....130 B6
Finedon Road Ind Est
  NN8 ....130 B8
Finedon St NN15 ....92 B1
Finedon Station Rd NN9 ....111 A6
Fineshade Cl
  Kettering NN15 ....92 A5
  King's Cliffe PE8 ....13 E7
Fineshade Gr NN17 ....36 A2
Finland Way NN13 ....36 A2
Fir Rd NN16 ....72 D2
Fir Tree Gr NN29 ....164 D2
Fir Tree La LE17 ....47 C4
Fir Tree Wlk
  Market Harborough LE16 ....31 E4
  Northampton NN3 ....142 E2
Firbank Ct NN6 ....160 F8
Firbank Gr Ave NN10 ....132 B4
Fire Quarters The NN7 ....155 C4
Firs Ct NN4 ....175 F8

Firs Dr CV22 ....241 B7
Firs The Daventry NN11 ....135 C3
  Market Harborough LE16 ....31 C3
First Ave NN13 ....129 D3
First La NN15 ....158 F6
First St NN13 ....238 F6
Firsview Dr NN5 ....140 C1
Fish St NN1 ....159 D6
Fisher Ave CV22 ....98 E8
Fisher Cl NN14 ....76 E1
Fishermans Cl MK46 ....195 E4
Fishers Cl Kilsby CV23 ....99 F2
  Northampton NN3 ....143 B1
Fishers Field MK18 ....240 C3
Fishpond Cl NN7 ....162 B1
Fishponds Rd NN3 ....143 B1
Fishton Cl NN15 ....91 D5
Fitzroy Pl NN1 ....159 B6
Fitzwilliam Dr NN15 ....92 A5
Fitzwilliam Leys NN10 ....132 B7
Fitzwilliam Rd
  Irthlingborough NN9 ....112 F3
  Stamford PE9 ....241 C5
Fitzwilliam St NN10 ....132 A2
Five Acres Fold NN4 ....158 F3
Fjord Wlk NN18 ....36 A2
Flaggs Mdw NN4 ....195 E4
Flamingo Gardens & Zoo
  Pk* MK46 ....195 B3
Flatlets The NN9 ....112 F2
Flavius Gate NN13 ....234 A7
Flaxland Cl LE16 ....32 B3
Flaxlands Ct NN3 ....142 E3
Flaxwell Ct NN3 ....160 F8
Fleet Cl MK18 ....240 F5
Fleet St NN16 ....72 A2
Fleetwind Dr NN4 ....175 D7
Fleetwood Cl LE16 ....31 D1
Fleetwood Gdns LE16 ....31 D1
Fleming Cl NN8 ....129 B7
Fleming Rd NN12 ....22 A2
Flensburg Cl NN18 ....36 B2
Fletcher Gdns NN14 ....76 D1
Fletcher Rd NN10 ....132 A3
Fletton Way PE8 ....41 F6
Flintcomb Rise NN3 ....143 B3
Flinters Cl NN4 ....175 F7
Flitton Ct MK11 ....229 F5
Flora Thompson Dr
  NN13 ....233 D8
Flore CE Prim Sch NN7 ....155 C5
Flore Hill NN7 ....155 D5
Florence Rd NN1 ....159 F7
Floribunda Dr NN4 ....158 F2
Fog Cotts NN6 ....120 B5
Folly La Hartwell NN7 ....206 C8
  Little Brington NN7 ....138 B4
Folly Rd MK19 ....228 D4
Fontwell Gdns PE9 ....241 C5
Foot La NN9 ....133 C8
Ford Bank LE16 ....20 D6
Ford Dr NN3 ....233 D8
Ford St
  Buckingham MK18 ....240 D3
  Northampton NN16 ....72 C2
Forest App PE8 ....13 F7
Forest Cl NN15 ....92 D3
Forest Ct NN10 ....132 D3
Forest Dr NN7 ....36 E7
Forest Glade
  Hartwell NN7 ....192 D2
  Kettering NN16 ....72 D3
Forest Rd
  Hanslope MK19 ....207 A6
  Hartwell NN7 ....192 D2
  Northampton NN4 ....159 C3
  Piddington NN7 ....177 A1
Forest View NN7 ....192 D2
Foresters Pl CV21 ....99 B7
Foresters The NN9 ....114 E5
Forfar St NN5 ....158 F7
Forge Ho NN14 ....70 D7
Forge The NN10 ....132 B1
Forrester Dr NN13 ....222 E1
Forrester Gr NN14 ....76 E1
Forstall Cl NN18 ....36 D3
Fort Pl NN1 ....159 B6
Forty Foot La MK44 ....149 A1
Fosberry Cl NN4 ....175 F6
Foscote Hospl OX16 ....240 D6
Foscote Rise OX16 ....240 D6
Foskett Cl NN10 ....132 A3
Foskitt Ct NN6 ....143 B1
Fosse Cl NN8 ....129 D1
Fosse Gn NN10 ....132 C3
Foster Ct NN18 ....36 E5
Foster's Booth Rd NN12 ....172 D1
Fothergill Cl LE16 ....32 B3
Fothergill Rd NN7 ....27 D7
Fotheringay Castle*
  PE8 ....27 E6
Fotheringhay Rd
  Corby NN17 ....36 B8
  Nassington PE8 ....13 E7
Foundry Pl 8 NN11 ....135 C1
Foundry PI NN11 ....135 C1
Foundry Rd PE9 ....241 C3
Foundry St
  Banbury OX16 ....240 C8
  18 Northampton NN1 ....159 C5
Foundry Wlk
  4 Daventry NN11 ....135 C1
  Thrapston NN14 ....76 C1
Fourth Ave
  Croughton NN13 ....238 E6
  Wellingborough NN8 ....129 D3
Fourth St NN13 ....238 E6

Fowey Cl NN8 ....129 C6
Fowler Rd OX16 ....240 E9
Fox Cl CV21 ....80 B1
Fox Covert Dr NN7 ....191 E3
Fox Coverts NN14 ....89 A4
Fox Dale PE9 ....241 B4
Fox Hill Rd NN13 ......143 D2
Fox La Brackley NN13 ..233 E7
  Souldern OX27 ....237 E3
Fox St NN11 ....70 C7
Fox Way MK18 ....240 E2
Fox Yd **7** LE16 ....31 E3
Foxcovert Rd NN3 .....143 B6
Foxendale Sq NN4 .....143 D2
Foxfield Way NN7 ......175 F2
Foxford Cl NN11 ....174 F8
Foxglove Ave NN11 ....184 B6
Foxglove Cl

  Buckingham MK18 ....240 C2
  Rushden NN10 ....148 C8
Foxglove Ave NN2 ......141 B4
Foxhill NN46 ....195 E5
Foxhill Cl OX27 ....237 E3
Foxhill Rd NN6 ....102 B3
Foxlands NN11 ....51 B2
Foxton Canal Mus*
  LE16 ....30 C7
Foxton Ct NN15 ....72 A1
Foxton Locks Ctry Pk*
  LE16 ....30 B7
Foxton Prim Sch LE16 ..30 D8
Foxton Rd Gumley LE16 ..30 B7
  Lubenham LE16 ....30 D5
Foxwell Sq NN3 ....142 F7
Foxwood Cl NN10 ......131 E2
Francis Cl NN11 ....131 E3
Francis Dickins Cl

  NN29 ....146 E3
Francis St

  8 Northampton NN1 ..159 C7
  Raunds NN9 ....114 B4
Francis Terr NN9 ....114 B4
Franciscan Cl NN10 ...147 F8
Frank Wise Sch OX16 ..222 E7
Franklin Cres NN5 .....158 D7
Franklin Fields NN7 ....37 A8
Franklin Way NN11 ....135 B5
Franklin's Cl NN6 ......143 F4
Frankston Ave MK11 ..229 E5
Fraser Cl Banbury OX16 ..240 F9
  Daventry NN11 ....135 D2
Fraser Rd NN3 ....142 D6
Frederick Press Way

  CV21 ....241 B8
Frederick St CV21 ......241 B8
Freehold St NN3 ....159 C8
Freeman Way NN9 .....112 B5
Freeman's Endowed CE Jun
  Sch NN8 ....129 C6
Freeman's La NN14 .....59 E6
Freeschool St **9** NN1 ..159 C5
Fremeaux Terr NN2 ....141 B2
French Dr NN1 ....72 F1
Frensham Ct **4** NN4 ..158 F3
Friar's Ave NN11 ....159 C1
Friar's Cl NN8 ....159 B1
Friar's Cres NN11 .....159 C1
Friars Cl NN5 ....130 A3
Friars St NN8 ....159 B1
Friary Cl NN11 ....135 D2
Friary The NN1 ....159 D6
Frinton Cl NN10 ....147 F8
Frisby La LE15 ....3 D8
Frobisher Cl NN11 ....135 E2
Frog Hall Brixworth NN6 ..106 A2
  Silverstone NN12 .....214 C5
Frog La NN11 ....182 C7
Front St NN11 ....95 C6
Frost Cl NN29 ....145 D6
Frosts Ct NN4 ....175 E5
Frosty Hollow NN4 ....175 C6
Froxhill Cres NN6 .....106 A1
Froxhill Wlk NN6 ......106 A1
Fuchsd Dr VN11 ....160 C6
Fulford Cl NN14 ....161 E3
Fulleburn Ct **2** NN1 ..142 E3
Fullen La NN17 ....22 D8
Fuller Rd NN3 ....142 C8
Fuller St NN16 ....72 C2
Fullers Cl NN14 ....76 F8
Fullingdale Rd NN3 ...142 B2
Fullwell Rd NN7 ....164 D4
Fulmar La NN8 ....130 A8
Fulwell Ave NN11 ....10 C1
Furber Ct NN3 ....142 D4
Furlong Rd NN4 ....51 C3
Furlongs The LE16 .....32 B3
Furnace Cotts NN9 ....111 A5
Furnace Dr NN11 ......135 A4
Furnace La Finedon NN9 ..72 A5
  Kettering NN16 ....72 E1
  Nether Heyford NN7 ..172 A8
Furnace Lane Ind Est

  NN16 ....72 A5
Furnells Cl NN9 ....114 D7
Furrow Cl CV21 ....241 F9
Furtho Ct MK19 ....229 B7
Furtho La NN12 ....217 E3
Furze Ct **3** NN4 ....159 A3
Furze Rd NN7 ....161 D2
Furze Wlk NN2 ....141 E2
Fushia Way NN10 .....148 B7
Fusilier Rd NN11 ......135 B1
Fusilier Way NN7 ......155 A4
Fyfe Rd NN7 ....36 B8
Fylingdale NN2 ....140 F5

G

Gable Cl NN11 ....135 B1
Gable Court Mews NN3 ..142 C1
Gables The NN15 ....72 B1
Gadesby Ct NN3 ....142 E3
Gainage Cl NN18 ....36 C1
Gains La PE17 ....61 D2
Gainsborough Ave NN15 ..92 A7
Gainsborough Cres CV21 ..80 B1
Gainsborough Dr NN8 ..36 D5
Gainsborough Dr NN9 ..129 F7
Gainsborough Rd

  Corby NN18 ....36 C4
  Stamford PE9 ....241 B5
Gainsborough Way

  NN1 ....135 C6
Galahad Ct NN5 ....158 A8
Galance Cl NN4 ....158 D1
Gallery Cl NN3 ....143 A6
Galley Hill MK11 ......229 F5
Gallfield Ct NN14 ......143 A6
Galliard Ct NN1 ....159 F7
Gallow Field Rd LE16 ..30 E7
Gallowhill Rd NN4 .....160 B1
Gambrel Rd NN5 ....158 D6
Gamston Wlk NN14 ....51 A4
Gander Cl NN17 ....38 A7
Gannet La NN8 ....130 A8
Ganton Cl NN11 ......135 F3
Gap The NN29 ....146 E2
Gapstile Cl NN14 ......51 A4
Garden Cl OX16 ....240 F9
Garden Fields Cl NN29 ..147 C8
Gardenfield NN10 .....132 B5
Gardenfields CE **1** NN3 ..113 B5
Gardens The

  East Carlton LE16 ......35 A7
  Kettering NN16 ....72 A4
Gardiner St LE16 ....31 C3
Gardner Cl NN14 ......114 C7
Gardner Rise NN13 ...233 D7
Garfield Cl NN7 ....2 A5
Garfield St Kettering NN15 ..91 B8
  Northampton NN2 .....141 B3
Garford La PE9 ....2 A5
Garners Way NN7 .....157 C2
Garrard Way NN16 .....71 F3
Garratt Rd PE9 ....241 D2
Garrick Rd NN1 ....160 B7
Garrow Cl NN3 ....112 E3
Garsdale NN2 ....140 F5
Garston Rd NN18 ....36 C1
Gas La PE9 ....241 E3
Gas St Rugby CV21 ...241 D8
  Stamford PE9 ....241 E3
Gatcombe Ho NN10 ...132 B2
Gate La NN14 ....90 B5
Gatehouse Cl CV21 ...99 A8
Gatehouse La LE16 ....20 F6
Gatelodge Cl NN3 .....142 E6
Gates Cl NN9 ....112 E3
Gateway Cl NN4 ....240 D7
Gatteridge St OX16 ...240 D7
Gaultney The NN14 ....51 A3
Gawcott Fields MK18 ..240 B2
Gawcott Rd MK18 .....240 B1
Gaydon Ho NN17 ......22 C1
Gayhurst Cl NN13 .....142 B7
Gayton CE Prim Sch

  NN7 ....173 E2
Gayton Rd Blisworth NN7 ..190 C8
  Eastcote NN12 ....172 F1
  Tiffield NN12 ....172 C6
Geddington CE Prim Sch

  NN14 ....54 B2
Geddington Rd NN18 ..37 D5
Gedling Cl NN3 ....160 F8
Gees Farm Cl NN7 ...179 A5
Geeston Rd PE9 ....1 B5
Geldock Rd NN3 ......143 A1
Genner Rd NN17 ....72 B1
Gentian Cl NN11 ......135 B4
George Blackall Ct NN17 ..36 C8
George Nutt La NN4 ..159 C2
George Row NN1 .....159 C5
George St Banbury OX16 ..240 F9
  Burton Latimer NN15 ..92 D3
  Corby NN17 ....36 C4
  Higham Ferrers NN10 ..132 C7
  Irthlingborough NN9 ..112 D1
  Kettering NN16 ....72 B1
  Rugby CV21 ....241 B8
  Rushden NN10 ....132 C7
  Wellingborough NN8 ..130 A5
George Yd MK11 ....229 D5
Georges Ave NN7 .....173 A7
Georges Cl NN7 ....173 A7
Gerandria Ct CV22 ....98 E2
Gerrard Gdns LE16 ....48 D8
Gervase Sq NN4 ......143 C1
Gharana Nivas NN8 ..130 B5
Gibbons Dr NN14 ....70 E7
Gibbs Rd OX16 ....240 E9
Gibbsacre Ct NN3 ....143 C1
Gibraltar St **28** NN11 ..159 C7
Gibson Dr Rugby CV21 ..80 A1
  Upper Benefield PE8 ..39 F7
Gifford Ct

  Market Harborough LE16 ..31 D3
  Northampton NN5 .....159 A5
Gifford Pl MK18 ....240 E4
Gifford Rd NN18 ....32 B2
Gilbert La NN5 ....158 C8
Gilbert Pl NN11 ....159 A5
Gilbert Scott Ct NN12 ..203 B6

Gilberts Rugby Football
  Mus* CV21 ....241 C8
Gilbey Cl NN11 ....110 E1
Gilchrist Ave NN17 ....37 A8
Gilkes Yd OX16 ....240 B7
Gillett Cl OX16 ....240 B7
Gillett Rd OX16 ....240 B7
Gillingham Rd NN15 ...90 F8
Gillitts Rd NN16 ......129 E3
Gillsway NN11 ....141 A4
Gilson's Cl LE15 ....3 A6
Gingles Ct CV21 ....99 A8
Gipsy La Irchester NN29 ..148 C6
  Kettering NN16 ....71 E2
Gipsy Lane Turn NN29 ..146 F7
Girton Way PE9 ....241 C5
Gisburne Rd NN18 ....130 A6
Glade Cl

  Burton Latimer NN15 ..92 C3
  Northampton NN3 .....143 B1
Glade The NN9 ....110 E1
Gladstone Cl NN15 ...141 A1
Gladstone Ct **7** NN12 ..72 C2
Gladstone Lower Sch

  NN5 ....159 A8
Gladstone Rd NN10 ..159 A8
Gladstone St

  Desborough NN14 ......51 A4
  Kettering NN16 ....72 C2
  Market Harborough LE16 ..31 F2
  Raunds NN9 ....114 D6
  Ringstead NN14 ....95 C3
  Rothwell NN14 ....73 C4
Glaisdale Ct NN4 .....140 F5
Glaister Pl NN16 ....72 D2
Glamis Cl NN10 ....132 D1
Glan y Mor Terr NN2 ..141 C5
Glanville Gdns NN2 ..140 C6
Glapthorn CE Lower Sch

  PE8 ....26 B2
Glapthorn Rd PE8 .....41 F6
Glasgow St NN5 ......158 F6
Glassbrook Rd NN10 ..131 C1
Glasshorpe La NN7 ..157 A6
Glaston Rd LE15 ....3 A5
Glastonbury Cl NN15 ..91 F8
Glastonbury Rd

  Kettering NN16 ....36 A6
  Northampton NN4 .....159 C1
Glebe Ave Broughton NN14 ..90 B4
  Kettering NN15 ....91 B8
  Northampton NN5 .....175 E8
Glebe Cl Holcot NN6 ..106 C8
  Northampton NN5 .....175 E8
Glebe Farm Cl NN14 ..241 A8
Glebe Farm Dr NN29 ..145 E6
Glebe La

  Great Houghton NN4 ..160 E2
  Hanslope NN4 ....206 E5
  Lower Harlestone NN7 ..139 E7
  Pitsford NN6 ....125 D5
  Staverton NN11 ....152 C7
Glebe Rd

  Burton Latimer NN15 ..92 A2
  Cogenhoe NN7 ....211 E6
  Deanshanger MK19 ..229 D7
  Market Harborough LE16 ..32 A2
  Mears Ashby NN6 .....128 B2
Glebe Rise OX17 .....231 A5
Glebe The Aynho OX17 ..237 D7
  Badby NN11 ....153 A2
  Daventry NN11 ....153 C8
Glebe Way

  Cogenhoe NN7 ....161 E6
  Northampton NN5 .....175 E8
Glebeland Cres NN5 ..140 F1
Glebeland Gdns NN5 ..158 F1
Glebeland Wlk **1** NN5 ..158 F1
Glebelands NN6 ....105 B1
Glen Ave NN7 ....174 B2
Glen Bank NN8 ....130 A4
Glen Baulk Rd NN14,

  NN16 ....71 C4
Glen Cres PE9 ....241 E5
Glencoe Dr NN5 ......140 C3
Glendon Rd NN14 .....70 E7
Glendower Cl NN11 ..135 A4
Gleneagles Cl

  Daventry NN11 ....135 E3
  Kettering NN15 ....91 F8
Gleneagles Dr NN8 ..129 D7
Glenfield Cl NN10 ....131 F2
Glenfield Dr NN29 ...145 D5
Glengarry NN7 ....142 D7
Glenhills Ct NN15 .....91 F8
Glenville Cl NN8 ......142 B4
Gloucester Ave NN14 ..159 B1
Gloucester Cl

  2 Kettering NN16 ..72 C2
  Northampton NN5 .....159 B2
  Weedon NN7 ....155 B4
Gloucester Cres

  Northampton NN5 .....159 B2
  Rushden NN10 ....132 C3
Gloucester Ct NN14 ...70 D6
Gloucester La NN6 ...159 C2
Gloucester Pl NN8 ...130 A4
Gloucester Rd PE9 ...241 D4
Glover Cl LE15 ....20 C1
Glovers La OX17 .....208 F1
Glyndebourne Gdns

  NN18 ....36 A4

Glynswood Rd MK18 ..240 C4
Goadby's Yd **6** NN16 ..72 B2
Gocker Wood Cl NN18 ..36 B1
Godwin Rd NN2 ....21 F3
Godwin Wlk NN5 ......140 D2
Gold St Clipston LE16 ..66 F8
  Desborough NN14 ....151 A3
  Hanslope MK19 ....207 A2
  Kettering NN16 ....72 B2
  Northampton NN1 .....159 C5
  Podington NN29 ....147 E2
  Walgrave NN6 ....108 A5
  Wellingborough NN8 ..130 A6
Gold Street Mews **6**

  NN1 ....159 C5
Goldcrest Cl NN3 .....143 A5
Goldcrest Rd NN11 ...222 D1
Golden Villa Cl OX16 ..240 A7
Goldenash Ct NN3 ...142 F5
Golding Cl NN11 .....135 C2
Goldings Mid Sch NN3 ..142 F5
Goldings Rd NN3 .....143 A5
Goldsmith Dr NN17 ...36 D8
Goldsmith Rd NN4 ...129 C4
Golf La NN6 ....140 C8
Good Shepherd RC Lower

  Sch The NN2 ....141 C3
Goodacre Cl CV23 .....80 A5
Goodens La NN10 ....145 F6
Goodhew Cl NN15 ......90 F8
Goodrington Cl OX16 ..240 B8
Goodwood Ave NN11 ..141 F5
Goodwood Cl LE16 ...32 B3
Goodwood Rd NN10 ..148 D8
Goose Gn NN13 ....233 E6
Goosemere MK19 ....228 E4
Goran Ave NN11 .....229 E4
Gordon Dr Oundle PE8 ..42 A6
  Wellingborough NN8 ..130 B5
Gordon St Kettering NN16 ..72 C2
  Northampton NN5 .....159 C8
  Rothwell NN14 ....70 D6
  Rushden NN10 ....131 F2
Gordon Way NN13 ....233 D6
Gosforth NN6 ....129 E3
Gosler The NN8 ....129 B3
Gotch Cl NN15 ....91 F4
Gotch Rd NN15 ....91 F5
Gough Cl NN15 ....72 E1
Goughs Cotts NN15 ..128 C2
Gould Cl NN11 ....118 B1
Goulds Villas OX16 ..240 A7
Goward St LE16 ....31 E3
Gower Cl NN11 ....91 C6
Gowers Yd WN19 ....229 B7
Grace Ct NN15 ....31 C2
Gracelands LE16 ......31 C2
Graeme Rd PE5 ....8 A8
Grafton Cl Hartwell NN7 ..192 D2
  Pottersbury NN12 .....217 E3
Grafton Cl NN7 ....36 B8
Grafton Dr NN7 ....36 B8
Grafton Pl NN1 ....159 C7
Grafton Rd Brigstock NN14 ..56 E8
  Cranford NN14 ....93 A7
Grafton St Kettering NN16 ..72 B4
  Northampton NN1 .....159 C7
Grafton View NN4 ....175 B6
Grafton Way

  Northampton NN4 .....140 B2
  Rothersthorpe NN7 ..174 A7
Graham Hill NN12 ....214 D4
Graham Hill NN12 ....203 C3
Graham Rd CV21 .....241 E9
Granary Cl LE16 ....31 F6
Granary Ct NN4 ....175 C7
Granary Rd NN4 ......175 C7
Granby Cl NN18 ....36 B6
Grandborough Cl NN6 ..106 C1
Grange Ave NN5 .....162 B1
Grange Cl **2** Denton NN7 ..190 F8
  Earls Barton NN6 .....144 E5
  Irchester NN29 ....147 B7
Grange Com Sch NN3 ..129 F7
Grange Ct Brixworth NN6 ..106 B2
Grange Dr NN7 ....177 D1
Grange Jun & Inf Schs The

  NN11 ....135 A1
Grange La Pitsford NN6 ..125 C6
  Thorpe Langton LE16 ..17 A5
Grange Pk NN16 ......72 E4
Grange Rd

  Broughton NN14 ....90 B5
  Geddington NN14 ....54 B3
  Islip NN14 ....76 B1
  Kettering NN16 ....72 A3
  Northampton NN3 .....142 C3
  Stanion NN14 ....37 C4
  Wollaston NN9 ....114 A3
  Wellingborough NN9 ..110 E1
Grange Road Workshops

  NN14 ....53 F2

Grange Way NN29 ....147 B3
Grangeway NN10 ....148 A8
Grangewood NN4 ....175 A7
Grant Cl NN15 ....90 F7
Grant Rd NN8 ....130 B5
Grantham Wlk NN18 ..36 B4
Grantown Cl NN15 ....91 E8
Granville St

  Kettering NN16 ....72 C2
  Market Harborough LE16 ..31 F2
Grasmere Gn NN8 ...129 B4
Grasmere Rd NN16 ...71 F2
Grasmere Way NN10 ..132 B8
Graspin La NN3 ....160 D8
Grass Cl NN12 ....203 B7
Grass Croft NN6 ......121 A3
Grass Slade NN6 .....106 C2
Grasscroft NN11 ......141 A4
Grasmere Ave NN18 ..142 E2
Gravel Hill NN11 .....199 D7
Gravely St NN10 ......131 F2
Gray La NN6 ....145 A4
Gray St Irchester NN29 ..147 A2
  Northampton NN1 .....159 E7
Gray's Cl NN1 ....31 D5
Grays Cl NN12 ....216 D8
Grays Dr NN14 ....37 E3
Grays La

  Paulerspury NN12 ....216 D8
  Yardley Gobion OX17 ..217 E6
Greasley Wlk NN18 ...36 B6
Great Addington CE Prim Sch

  NN14 ....94 B3
Great Billing CE Lower Sch

  NN3 ....143 C2
Great Billing Way NN3 ..143 C4
Great Bowden CE Sch

  LE16 ....32 A5
Great Bowden Hall LE16 ..31 E7
Great Bowden Rd LE16 ..32 A4
Great Central Walk Nature
  Trail* CV21 ....98 D6
Great Central Way

  Rugby CV21 ....241 F9
  Woodford Halse NN11 ..184 C7
Great Creaton Prim Sch

  NN6 ....104 F4
Great Doddington Prim Sch

  NN29 ....145 E6
Great Easton CE Prim Sch
  Bringhurst LE16 ....20 C6
  Caldecott LE16 ....21 A7
  Drayton LE16 ....20 A5
  Great Easton LE16 ....20 F6
Great Field Ct NN12 ..90 E3
Great Folds Rd NN18 ..35 F1
Great Gidding CE Prim Sch

  PE17 ....61 D3
Great Ground Wlk NN5 ..175 F2
Great Gull Cres NN3 ..143 C6
Great Holme Ct NN14 ..142 E5
Great La Bugbrooke NN7 ..172 F7
  Hackleton NN7 ....177 B3
Great North Rd

  Stamford PE9 ....241 A2
  Stibbington PE8 ....8 C2
  Wothorpe PE9 ....2 B8
Great Park St NN8 ...130 A5
Great Russell St NN1 ..159 D7
Great Slade MK18 ...240 D1
Greatmeadow NN3 ..143 C4
Greatmeadow Rd NN3 ..143 B4
Greatworth Prim Sch

  OX17 ....210 A2
Greaves Cl NN5 ....139 F1
Grebe Cl Hinton NN11 ..84 B6
  Thrapston NN14 ....76 E3
Green Cl NN6 ....129 C7
Green End La NN11 ..207 A3
Green Farm CE Lower Sch
  NN7 ....230 A4
Green Farm Ct CV23 ..230 A4
Green La Ashley LE16 ..18 F2
  Banbury OX16 ....240 D6
  Braybrooke LE16 ....49 F5
  Charlton OX17 ....231 E5
  Desborough NN14 ....150 E3
  Duddington PE9 ....1 F5
  Husbands Bosworth LE17 ..45 E5
  Kettering NN16 ....72 B2
  Market Harborough LE16 ..31 E1
  Northampton NN5 .....175 E5
  Silverstone NN12 .....214 D4
  Stamford PE9 ....241 D5
  Stanwick NN9 ....113 F3
  Stoke Albany LE16 ....34 B4
  Thrapston NN14 ....76 F4
  Towcester NN12 ....203 A5
  Weston by W LE16 .....18 C6
Green Oaks Lower School

  NN2 ....141 D4
Green Rd NN1 ....161 E2
Green St

  Milton Malsor NN7 ...174 E4
  Northampton NN5 .....159 B5
  Wollaston NN29 ......146 E2
Green The

  Abthorpe NN12 ....201 F2
  Adderbury OX17 ......230 A4
  Barby CV23 ....99 C1
  Blakesley NN12 ....187 B1
  Braunston NN11 ......118 C1
  Byfield NN11 ....183 D7
  Caldecott LE16 ....21 B8

Green The continued
Chelveston NN9 ....133 C8
Church Stowe NN7 ....171 D7
Clipston LE16 ....67 A8
Cosgrove MK19 ....218 F2
Cranford NN14 ....93 A6
Culworth OX17 ....198 C3
Deanshanger MK19 ....228 E4
Everdon NN11 ....178 A8
Flore NN7 ....155 F5
Great Bowden LE16 ....32 B6
Great Brington NN7 ....133 C2
Great Houghton NN4 ....160 E2
Hanslope MK19 ....207 A2
Helidon NN11 ....151 C1
Helmdon NN13 ....211 F4
Hollowell NN6 ....104 B4
Husbands Bosworth LE17 ....45 E5
Kislingbury NN7 ....157 D3
Lilbourne CV23 ....81 A6
Little Addington NN14 ......113 B8
Lubenham LE16 ....30 C3
Lyddington LE15 ....9 D7
Marston St Lawrence
OX17 ....210 B1
Mawsley Village NN14 ....89 B4
Nether Heyford NN7 ....156 B1
Newnham NN11 ....153 D4
 10 Northampton NN1 ....159 C5
 11 Northampton NN4 ....175 F3
Northampton,Hardingstone
NN4 ....175 F8
Orlingbury NN14 ....110 A5
Paulerspury NN12 ....216 B7
Priors Marston CV47 ....166 D7
Roade NN7 ....191 D4
Staverton NN11 ....152 B7
Titchmarsh NN14 ....77 C4
Twywell NN14 ....75 A1
Upper Harlestone NN7 ......139 D4
Wadenhoe PE8 ....58 A4
Weedon Lois NN12 ....200 C3
West Haddon NN6 ....102 B4
Weston by W LE16 ....18 B3
Woodford NN14 ....76 D1
Greenacre Dr NN10 ....148 B8
Greenacres Cvn Pk LE16 .31 C6
Greenaway Cl NN7 ....190 E7
Greenbank Ave NN15 .....72 D1
Greenbank Terr NN14 .....95 B3
Greendale Sq ▌ NN3 ....143 C2
Greenfield Ave
Kettering NN15 ....71 F1
Northampton NN3 ....142 B3
Greenfield Rd NN3 ....142 A2
Greenfield Way NN10 ....132 A1
Greenfields Sch NN2 ....141 B5
Greenfinch Dr NN3 ......142 C6
Greenglades NN14 ....158 E1
Greenhill Cres NN11 .....135 B3
Greenhill Ct
Banbury OX16 ....240 D6
Long Buckby NN6 ....121 A4
Greenhill Rd Elton PE7 ...29 B6
Elton PE8 ....28 F8
Kettering NN16 ....91 A8
Long Buckby NN6 ....121 A4
Rugby CV22 ....241 B6
Greenhills Cl NN2 ....141 B6
Greenhills Rd NN2 ....141 B6
Greening Rd NN4 ....70 C7
Greenland Wlk NN18 ....36 A2
Greens Norton CE Prim Sch
NN12 ....202 E8
Greenside Blisworth NN7 .190 D7
Northampton NN3 ....142 B3
Wappenham NN12 ....213 B8
Greenslade Cl NN15 ......91 A8
Greensward The OX17 ...196 E1
Greenview Dr
Northampton NN3 ....141 E6
Towcester NN12 ....203 B6
Greenway
Braunston NN11 ....118 B1
Eastcote NN12 ....173 A1
Northampton NN3 ....160 C8
Greenway Ave NN3 ....142 D4
Greenway The NN11 .....153 C6
Greenway Wlk MK18 .....240 F7
Greenwood Cl
Byfield NN11 ....183 C7
Moulton NN3 ....126 C2
Greenwood Rd NN5 ......159 A6
Greenyard The NN7 ......179 B7
Greeve Cl NN18 ....36 C1
Grenadier Rd NN11 ......135 B3
Grendon Ave NN7 ....86 B7
Grendon CE Prim Sch
NN7 ....163 D8
Grendon Lakes Watersports
Ctr* NN7 ....145 C1
Grendon Rd NN6 ....144 E1
Grendon Wlk NN3 ....141 F5
Grenville Cl Corby NN17 ..36 A8
Daventry NN11 ....135 E1
Rothwell NN14 ....70 E6
Grenville Comb Sch
MK18 ....240 D3
Grenville Gdns LE16 ......31 D1

Grenville Rd MK18 ....240 C4
Gresham Dr NN4 ....158 E2
Gresley Cl NN11 ....135 A4
Gresley Dr PE9 ....241 D2

Gretton Brook Rd
Corby NN17 ....21 E3
Corby NN17 ....22 C4
Gretton Ct NN8 ....129 D7
Gretton Prim Sch NN17 ..22 C8
Gretton Rd Corby NN17 ...22 F7
Harringworth NN17 ....10 E7
Lyddington LE15 ....9 D5
Rockingham LE16 ....21 B5
Weldon NN17 ....38 A8
Greville Ave NN3 ....142 A4
Greville Cl NN11 ....141 C8
Greyfriars NN1 ....159 C6
Greyfriars Rd NN1 ....153 B8
Greys The NN7 ....159 C6
Grieg Wlk NN18 ....36 A2
Griffin Rd LE16 ....49 E4
Griffith St NN10 ....132 B1
Grimmer Wlk NN10 ......131 D8
Grimsbury Dr OX16 ......240 E9
Grimsbury Grn OX16 .....240 E9
Grimsby Cl NN18 ....36 C4
Grindleford Cl NN14 .....50 E3
Grizedale Cl NN16 ....72 A6
Grombold Ave NN9 ......114 C6
Grooms La NN6 ....105 A4
Grosvenor Cl NN15 ......92 A5
Grosvenor Ctr NN1 ......159 D6
Grosvenor Gn NN2 ......141 D4
Grosvenor Ho NN2 ......141 D4
Grosvenor Pl NN13 ......233 E7
Grosvenor Rd
Banbury OX16 ....240 D7
Kettering NN15 ....92 A5
Rugby CV21 ....241 E8
Wellingborough NN9 ....91 F5
Groundwell Ct ▌ NN3 ...142 F1
Grove Farm Cl NN6 ......121 D4
Grove Farm La NN13 ....242 C2
Grove Pl NN9 ....199 F3
Grove Pl NN9 ....114 D5
Grove Rd
Brafield-on-t-G NN7 ....161 D3
Northampton NN1 ....159 E7
Rushden NN10 ....132 C2
Thrapston NN14 ....76 D1
Grove St Banbury OX16 ...240 D7
Higham Ferrers NN10 ......132 C6
Raunds NN9 ....114 D5
Wellingborough NN8 ....129 E4
Grove The Corby NN18 ....37 C6
Kettering NN15 ....72 B1
Moulton NN3 ....126 C2
Ringstead NN14 ....95 A6
Roade NN7 ....191 E3
Wollaston NN29 ....146 D1
Grove Way NN9 ....111 E3
Grovebury Dell NN2 ......141 A4
Grovelands NN11 ....153 A8
Guardian Ct OX16 ....240 E8
Guildhall Rd NN1 ....159 D5
Guillemot La NN18 ......130 A7
Guilsborough CE Prim Sch
NN6 ....103 E7
Guilsborough Hill NN6 ...104 B5
Guilsborough Rd
Ravensthorpe NN6 ....103 D1
West Haddon NN6 ....102 C5
Guilsborough Sch NN6 .....103 D8
Guinea Orch MK46 ....195 E4
Gullet La LE16 ....18 F2
Gumley Rd LE16 ....30 C7
Gunnell Cl NN15 ....90 F8
Gunnsbrook Cl LE16 .....32 A6
Gunthorpe Pl NN18 ......36 B6
Gurston Rise NN3 ....143 C4
Gynwell NN6 ....85 B8

H

H E Bates Way NN10 .....132 A2
Hachenburg Pl NN10 .....132 C5
Hackleton Prim Sch
NN7 ....177 A3
Hackwood Rd NN14 .....153 E8
Haddon Cl
Rushden NN10 ....132 A1
Wellingborough NN8 ......129 D8
Haddon Ct NN6 ....122 A1
Haddon Rd PE9 ....241 B4
Hadfield Cl CV23 ....80 A5
Hadrian's Gate NN3 .....238 A7
Hafod Cl NN18 ....36 C2
Hagley Cl LE16 ....31 D3
Haigh Dr NN15 ....72 E1
Hailsham Ct OX17 ....220 B8
Haines Rd NN4 ....159 C3
Hale Ave MK11 ....229 E5
Halford St NN14 ....76 C2
Halford Way NN11 ......135 E8
Halfway Thorn NN6 .....124 C1
Halifax Rd NN18 ....36 B5
Hall Acre NN10 ....132 A1
Hall Cl Arthingworth LE16 .67 A8
Harpole NN7 ....157 B6
Kettering NN15 ....90 F8
Kilsby CV23 ....100 A3
Kislingbury NN7 ....157 D4
Naseby NN6 ....66 B1
Old Stratford MK19 ....229 B6
Weston by W LE16 ....18 B4

Hall Dr Finedon NN9 .....111 E4
Long Buckby NN6 ....121 C4
Hall Farm Cl NN6 ....106 B3
Hall Gdns
East Haddon NN6 ....122 D5
Loddington NN14 ....70 C2
Piddcrook PE8 ....43 A3
Hall Hill NN14 ....55 F7
Hall La Ashley LE16 ......18 E2
Drayton LE16 ....20 A5
Kettering NN15 ....90 F8
South Luffenham LE15 .....3 E8
Welford NN6 ....64 D6
Wittering PE8 ....7 C8
Hall Mead Ct NN7 ....172 E6
Hall Meadow Prim Sch
NN9 ....90 F7
Hall Piece Cl NN3 ....143 C3
Hall Rd Collyweston PE9 ..1 C2
King's Cliffe PE8 ....13 F7
Hall's Cl Geddington NN14 .54 B3
Weldon NN17 ....38 A8
Hall's La NN13 ....233 E6
Hallam Cl NN3 ....142 B7
Hallaton Rd LE16 ....18 F7
Hallwood Rd NN16 ......72 C5
Halse Rd NN13 ....222 F1
Halswell Cl NN3 ....142 D4
Ham La NN14 ....95 A4
Ham Meadow Dr NN3 ...143 C4
Hambledon Rise NN4 ....158 E3
Hambleton Rd PE9 ......241 A1
Hamblin Cl NN10 ....132 B2
Hamilton Cl OX16 ....240 E9
Hamilton Ho Corby NN17 .36 E5
Northampton NN3 ....141 C5
Hamilton La NN7 ....138 D6
Hamlet Gn NN6 ....105 A8
Hammas Leys NN6 ......121 C4
Hammerstone La NN3 ...158 F3
Hammond Way LE16 ....31 E4
Hampden Cres NN16 ....72 D3
Hampton Court Ct NN12 .203 B5
Hampton Cl LE16 ....31 F3
Hampton Dr OX17 ....230 F6
Hampton Rd NN10 ......132 B2
Hampton St NN1 ....159 B7
Hamsterly Pk NN3 ......143 A6
Handcross Ct NN18 .....36 B4
Handley Cl NN5 ....140 A1
Hanemill Ct NN18 ....143 C1
Hangerfield Ct NN3 .....142 F4
Hanover Cl NN15 ....92 A7
Hanover Ct
Northampton NN3 ....143 B4
Stamford PE9 ....241 E3
Hanover Dr NN13 ....233 E7
Hans Apel Dr NN13 .....233 D7
Hansbury Ironstone Rly
Mus* NN8 ....158 E2
Hanslope Comb Sch
NN9 ....207 A3
Hanslope Rd MK19 .....218 F7
Harbidges La NN6 ......121 A4
Harborough Rd
Braybrooke LE16 ....49 D7
Brixworth NN6 ....106 C3
Clipston LE16 ....46 A2
Desborough NN14 ....50 D7
Dingley LE16 ....32 D5
Dingley LE16 ....32 E1
Dingley LE16 ....33 A3
East Farndon LE16 ....48 D8
Great Oxendon LE16 ......48 F4
Kelmarsh NN6 ....67 F5
Lubenham LE16 ....31 A3
Maidwell NN6 ....87 B4
Market Harborough LE16 ..31 C7
Northampton NN6 ....140 C4
Rushden NN10 ....132 C1
Stoke Albany LE16 ....34 B4
Theddingworth LE17 ......30 A1
Theddingworth LE17 ......30 B2
Harborough Rd N NN2 ..141 B6
Harborough Way NN10 ..132 C1
Harcourt Sq NN6 ....144 E4
Harcourt St
 9 Kettering NN16 ....72 C2
Market Harborough LE16 ..31 D3
Raunds NN9 ....114 D6
Harcourt Way NN4 ......158 E3
Hardays La NN6 ....102 B4
Harden Cl NN18 ....53 A8
Harding Cl NN6 ....72 F1
Harding Terr NN1 ....159 C7
Hardingstone La NN4 ...175 D8
Hardingstone Prim Sch
NN4 ....175 E7
Hardlands Rd NN6 ......158 C8
Hardwater Rd NN29 .....145 D4
Hardwick Cl NN3 ....142 B7
Hardwick Jun & Inf Sch
NN8 ....129 E5
Hardwick Rd
Gretton NN17 ....10 B1
Little Harrowden NN9 .....110 B3
Northampton NN5 ....175 C8
Priors Marston CV47 ......166 D7
Wellingborough NN8 .....129 D6
Wellingborough, Hatton Park
NN8 ....129 D6
Hardy Dr NN4 ....175 F7
Hare Cl MK18 ....240 E2
Harebell Sq ▌ NN11 ....143 D2
Harefield Rd NN3 ....143 B5

Harefoot Cl NN5 ....158 B8
Haresmoor Dr NN12 ....203 C4
Harksome Hill NN4 ......158 E2
Harlech Cl
Burton Latimer NN15 .....92 C2
Daventry NN11 ....135 C6
Harlestone Ct NN5 ......158 F7
Harlestone Ho NN5 .....159 A7
Harlestone Prim Sch
NN7 ....139 E5
Harlestone Rd
Church Brampton NN6 ....124 D1
Lower Harlestone NN7 ....139 F6
Northampton NN5 ....140 B2
Harley Way
Boughton NN14 ....96 D3
Lower Benefield PE8 ......40 D3
Northampton NN3 ....142 A1
Harnett Dr NN12 ....229 F6
Harold St 10 NN1 ......159 C7
Harpers Cl NN18 ....53 B8
Harpers Prim Sch NN7 ..157 D6
Harrier Pk NN4 ....175 B8
Harriers View OX16 .....240 C6
Harrington Rd
Desborough NN14 ....50 C3
Loddington NN14 ....70 C6
Old NN6 ....107 D7
Rothwell NN14 ....70 C6
Harringworth Rd NN17 ..10 C2
Harris Cl Brackley NN13 ..233 D8
Harris Dr NN10 ....132 C2
Harris St NN8 ....158 D8
Hayes Rd MK19 ....228 F5
Hayes Wlk PE8 ....16 D1
Hayeswood Rd NN3 .....142 F4
Hayman Rd NN13 ....233 C2
Haynes La NN6 ....105 B1
Haynes Rd NN16 ....72 D2
Hayrie The NN4 ....175 A7
Haystack The NN11 .....135 D6

Hayway
Irthlingborough NN9 ......112 C1
Rushden NN10 ....132 A4
Hayway Inf Sch NN10 ...132 B3
Hazel Cl Brackley NN13 ..222 F1
Hartwell NN7 ....192 E2
Hazel Cres NN12 ....203 B5
Hazel Croft NN11 ....118 C1
Hazel Leys Prim Sch
NN11 ....36 C4
Hazel Rd NN15 ....72 C1
Hazeland Ho NN14 ......51 A3
Hazelden Cl NN29 ......146 D1
Hazeldene Rd NN2 ......141 F3
Hazelwood Ct ▌ NN16 ..72 B1
Hazelwood La NN16 ....72 B1
Hazelwood Rd
Corby NN17 ....36 E7
Northampton NN1 ....159 D5
Hazley Wlk MK18 ....240 F4
Headingley Rd NN10 ....132 D2
Headlands
Desborough NN14 ....51 C3
Kettering NN15 ....91 B8
Headlands Lower Sch
NN3 ....142 C2
Headlands The
Market Harborough LE16 ..31 F4
Northampton NN3 ....142 C2
Wellingborough NN8 ......129 F6
Headway NN18 ....53 A8
Healey Cl NN3 ....143 D4
Heart Of The Shires
Village NN7 ....136 F2
Hearth St NN1 ....31 D3
Heath Gn NN5 ....140 D1
Heath Rise NN6 ....129 D6
Heath Terr NN12 ....203 C6
Heath Way
Burton Latimer NN15 .....92 C3
Rugby CV22 ....98 D8
Heathcote Gr NN14 .....50 E4
Heather Cl
Buckingham MK18 ....240 C2
Rugby CV22 ....241 A6
Heather Ct NN5 ....159 A2
Rushden NN10 ....132 A2
Heather La NN11 ....142 E4
Heather Rd NN16 ....72 C2
Heatherbreea Gdns
NN11 ....131 F3
Heatherdale Way NN12 .141 E3
Heathers The NN29 ....146 E2
Heathfield Way NN5 ....141 A1
Heathfield Wlk NN18 ...36 B4
Heathville NN5 ....140 F1
Hecham Way NN10 .....132 B7
Hedge End NN4 ....159 A2
Hedgely Ct NN14 ....159 A2
Hedgerow Way NN11 ...135 C6
Hedges The NN10 ......132 A4
Hedgeway NN4 ....175 C6
Helidon Cl NN2 ....141 E4
Helidon Rd CV47 ....166 D2
Helmdon NN11 ....211 F4
Helmdon Cres NN2 .....141 C4
Helmdon Prim Sch
NN13 ....36 E7
Helmdon Rd
Greatworth OX17 ....210 E2
Northampton NN2 ....141 E4
Sulgrave OX17 ....210 F7
Wappenham NN12 ....213 A8
Weston NN12 ....199 F2
Helmsley Way NN18 ....36 B5

Hemans Rd NN11 . . . . . . .135 B3
Hembury Pl NN4 . . . . .158 F3
Hemery Way NN15 . . . . . . .90 F8
Hemington Rd PE8 . . . . . . .42 F2
Hemmingwell Rd NN8 .130 A7
Hempland Cl NN18 . . . . . . .53 B8
Hemplow Dr NN6 . . . . .64 B2
Henders MK11 . . . . .2 C8
Henley Ct Kettering NN15 . .91 F5
Wellingborough NN8 . . . . .129 C6
Henley Ct NN6 . . . . .120 C6
Henley Ho NN17 . . . . .36 E6
Henry Bird Cl NN4 . . . . . .159 C4
Henry Bird Way NN4 . . . .159 C4
Henry Gotch Inf Sch
NN15 . . . . .72 C1
Henry Smith Ho [2]
NN1 . . . . .135 B3
Henry St
Northampton NN1 . . . . . .159 E7
Rugby CV21 . . . . .241 C8
Henshaw Rd NN8 . . . . . . .129 E3
Hensmans La NN29 . . . . . .54 D3
Henson Cl NN15 . . . . .71 F5
Henson Way NN16 . . . . . . .71 E4
Herbert St NN1 . . . . .159 C6
Hereford Cl NN14 . . . . . . .51 C4
Hereward Rd NN4 . . . . . .159 B2
Herford Cl NN16 . . . . .36 A2
Heritage Way Corby NN17 .32 B7
Raunds NN9 . . . . .114 E7
Hermitage Rd LE16 . . . . . .33 E3
Hermitage The PE9 . . . . .241 B3
Hermitage Way NN4 . . . .175 D7
Herne Hill Ct NN4 . . . . . .158 E2
Herne Rd PE8 . . . . .42 B4
Heron Ave NN4 . . . . .76 E3
Heron Cl
Burton Latimer NN15 . . . . .92 A2
Hinton NN11 . . . . .184 B6
Towcester NN12 . . . . .203 C3
Wellingborough NN8 . . . .130 A7
Heron Ct NN11 . . . . .135 C3
Heron Dr NN13 . . . . .222 D1
Heronsford NN4 . . . . . . .174 E8
Herrieffs Farm Rd NN13 .233 F6
Herriotts La NN8 . . . . . . .130 A5
Hertford Cl
Daventry NN11 . . . . .153 C7
Northampton NN3 . . . . . .143 A1
Hertford Rd NN15 . . . . . .91 C6
Hervey Cl NN3 . . . . .142 D2
Hervey St NN1 . . . . .159 E7
Hesketh Cres NN12 . . . . .203 C4
Hesketh Rd NN12 . . . . . .217 E6
Hesperus NN8 . . . . .129 B4
Hester St NN12 . . . . .159 C8
Hever Cl Rushden NN10 . .148 C8
Thrapston NN14 . . . . .76 E2
Hewlett's Cl NN29 . . . . . .34 F1
Hexham Ct NN4 . . . . . . .159 A2
Heygate St LE16 . . . . .31 E4
Hiawatha NN8 . . . . .129 B4
Hibbert Cl CV22 . . . . . . .241 C6
Hibiscus Cl NN3 . . . . . . .160 C6
Hickmire NN29 . . . . .146 D3
Hicks Ct NN12 . . . . .203 D4
Hicks Rd NN12 . . . . .203 C3
Hidcote Cl
Northampton NN4 . . . . . .175 C7
Wellingborough NN8 . . . .129 D2
Hield Cl NN18 . . . . .36 C1
Higgins Sq NN4 . . . . .158 F2
High Acres OX16 . . . . . . .240 E6
High Barns NN7 . . . . .175 E2
High Barns Ct NN4 . . . . . .141 B3
High Greeve NN4 . . . . . . .176 A6
High Hill Ave NN4 . . . . . . .70 C7
High Leys The NN6 . . . . . .100 F4
High March NN11 . . . . . .153 E8
High March Cl NN11 . . . .153 E8
High Slade NN6 . . . . .125 C8
High St Adderbury OX17 .230 A4
Astcote NN12 . . . . .188 F7
Banbury OX16 . . . . .240 D7
Blakesley NN12 . . . . .187 A1
Blisworth NN7 . . . . .190 D7
Bozeat NN29 . . . . .164 D2
Brackley NN13 . . . . .233 F7
Braunston NN11 . . . . .90 A4
Brigstock NN14 . . . . .55 F8
Brixworth NN6 . . . . .106 B3
Broughton NN14 . . . . .90 A4
Buckingham MK18 . . . . . .240 D4
Bugbrooke NN7 . . . . .172 F7
Burton Latimer NN15 . . . . .92 C2
Byfield NN11 . . . . .183 D7
Charwelton NN11 . . . . . .168 A4
Chelveston NN9 . . . . .133 C8
Clipston LE16 . . . . .67 A8
Collyweston PE9 . . . . .37 A6
Corby NN17 . . . . .37 A6
Cottingham LE16 . . . . .20 C1
Cranford NN14 . . . . .93 A6
Creaton NN6 . . . . .104 F4
Crick NN6 . . . . .100 F5
Croughton NN13 . . . . . . .238 C8
Culworth OX17 . . . . .198 C3
Daventry NN11 . . . . .135 C2
Deanshanger MK19 . . . . .228 E4
Denford NN14 . . . . .95 C6
Desborough NN14 . . . . . . .51 A3
Duddington PE9 . . . . .5 B6
Earls Barton NN6 . . . . . . .144 E4
Easton o t H PE9 . . . . .2 A5
Ecton NN6 . . . . .143 F3
Everdon NN11 . . . . .170 A8
Eydon NN11 . . . . .184 C1

High St continued
Finedon NN9 . . . . .111 F5
Flore NN7 . . . . .155 E5
Gayton NN7 . . . . .173 E2
Great Doddington NN7 . . .145 E6
Great Easton LE16 . . . . . . .20 D7
Great Houghton NN4 . . . .160 E2
Greens Norton NN12 . . . .202 D8
Gretton NN17 . . . . .10 B1
Guilsborough NN6 . . . . . .103 F6
Hanslope MK19 . . . . .207 A2
Harpole NN7 . . . . .157 C6
Harrington NN6 . . . . .69 A5
Higham Ferrers NN10 . . . .132 B5
Husbands Bosworth LE17 . .45 E5
Irchester NN29 . . . . .147 B8
Irthlingborough NN9 . . . .112 C2
Islip NN14 . . . . .76 B2
Kettering NN16 . . . . .72 B2
Ketton PE9 . . . . .1 A6
Kislingbury NN7 . . . . .157 D4
Lamport NN6 . . . . .87 D2
Little Addington NN14 . . . .113 B8
Long Buckby NN6 . . . . . .121 C4
Market Harborough LE16 . .31 E4
Middleton Cheney OX17 . .219 F8
Milton Malsor NN7 . . . . . .174 E4
Morcott LE15 . . . . .3 A2
Moulton NN3 . . . . .126 C1
Naseby NN6 . . . . .85 B8

Highbrook NN18 . . . . .36 A4
Highbury Rd NN16 . . . . . .36 A4
Highclere Gr NN4 . . . . . . .76 E3
Highcroft LE17 . . . . .45 E6
Highcroft Cl NN4 . . . . . . .217 E6
Highcross St LE16 . . . . . . .31 C3

Highdown Cl NN4 . . . . . .158 E3
Highfield Duddington PE9 . . .5 B7
Woodford NN14 . . . . .94 C7
Highfield Cotts LE15 . . . . . .3 E8
Highfield Court Mews
NN13 . . . . .233 E6
Highfield Cres NN15 . . . . .91 E6
Highfield Ct NN13 . . . . . .233 E6
Highfield Gr NN17 . . . . . .36 F7
Highfield Pk NN6 . . . . . . .104 D4
Highfield Rd
Daventry NN11 . . . . .135 B3
Irthlingborough NN9 . . . .112 F2
Kettering NN15 . . . . .91 B7
Mears Ashby NN6 . . . . . .128 C4
Northampton NN1 . . . . . .142 A1
Rushden NN10 . . . . .131 F1
Thrapston NN14 . . . . .76 E2
Wellingborough NN8 . . . .130 B5
Highfield St Finedon NN9 .112 B5
Market Harborough LE16 . .31 D3
Highfield Way NN7 . . . . . .179 B6
Highfields Polebrook PE8 . .42 F3
Towcester NN12 . . . . .203 C3
Highfields Prim Sch
NN15 . . . . .91 B7
Highgate Gn PE8 . . . . . . .28 D8
Highgrove Ct NN10 . . . . .132 B2
Highgrove Gdns PE9 . . . .241 A3
Highlands Ave NN13 . . . .222 E4
Highlands Dr NN11 . . . . .135 B5
Highlands Rd MK18 . . . . .240 D5
Highlands Way NN7 . . . . .176 C4
Highpoint NN13 . . . . .233 F5
Hightown Rd OX16 . . . . .240 E6
Hilda Pl NN16 . . . . .72 E4
Hill Cl NN5 . . . . .140 C2
Hill Crest NN7 . . . . .174 C1
Hill Farm Est NN14 . . . . .113 C7
Hill Farm Rise NN4 . . . . .175 A8
Hill Gdns LE16 . . . . .31 C3
Hill House Cl NN12 . . . . .172 D1
Hill House Gdns NN9 . . . .113 A8
Hill Rd NN11 . . . . .182 C5
Hill Row NN11 . . . . .134 C8
Hill St Brackley NN13 . . . .233 F7
Kettering NN16 . . . . .72 A3
Raunds NN9 . . . . .113 A8
Rugby CV21 . . . . .241 C9
Wellingborough NN8 . . . .129 F4
Hill The Aynho OX17 . . . .237 C7
Great Houghton NN4 . . . .160 E2
Middleton LE16 . . . . .35 B8
Pury End NN12 . . . . .215 F7
Syresham NN13 . . . . .224 B8
Hill Top NN12 . . . . .141 D4
Hill Top Rd NN9 . . . . . . .110 D4
Hill View NN11 . . . . .184 C1
Hill View Cres OX16 . . . .240 E6
Hill View Cty Prim Sch
OX16 . . . . .240 A9
Hillary Cl Daventry NN11 .135 B3
Stamford PE9 . . . . .241 F4
Hillary Rd NN10 . . . . . . .131 F1
Hillberry Rise NN13 . . . . .143 D4
Hillcrest Ave
Burton Latimer NN15 . . . . .92 B1
Kettering NN15 . . . . .72 D1
Market Harborough LE16 . .31 D4
Northampton NN3 . . . . . .142 A3
Hillcrest Cl NN14 . . . . . . .76 E3
Hillcrest La LE17 . . . . .45 E5
Hillcrest Rd NN14 . . . . . .173 E1
Hillcroft View NN12 . . . . .187 B2
Hilldrop Rd NN4 . . . . . . .175 B7
Hillesden Way NN18 . . . .240 E4
Hillfield Rd PE8 . . . . .41 E6
Hillmorton La
Clifton u D CV23 . . . . .80 A4
Lilbourne CV23 . . . . .80 F5
Yelvertoft NN6 . . . . .82 A4
Hillmorton Prim Sch
CV21 . . . . .99 B8
Hillmorton Rd CV22 . . . .241 E7
Hillside Chelveston NN9 . .133 B8
Daventry NN11 . . . . .135 E2
Great Harrowden NN9 . . .110 C4
Hartwell NN7 . . . . .192 D2
West Haddon NN6 . . . . . .102 B4
Hillside Ave
Kettering NN15 . . . . .91 C8
Silverstone NN12 . . . . . . .214 E5
Hillside Cl NN29 . . . . . . .164 D2
Hillside Cotts PE28 . . . . . .97 A4
Hillside Cres
Nether Heyford NN7 . . . .156 C1
Weldon NN17 . . . . .38 A7
Hillside Rd Flore NN7 . . . .155 D6
Market Harborough LE16 . .31 F4
Nether Heyford NN7 . . . .156 C1
Piddington NN7 . . . . .177 B1
Wellingborough NN8 . . . .130 C7
Hillside Terr NN16 . . . . . . .72 A2
Hillside Way NN11 . . . . . .160 C8
Hillside Cl NN9 . . . . .113 F3
Hilltop Blisworth NN7 . . . .174 C1
Dodford NN7 . . . . .154 E5
Great Harrowden NN9 . . .110 C5
Hilltop Ave
Buckingham MK18 . . . . . .240 E5
Desborough NN14 . . . . . . .50 F4
Kettering NN15 . . . . .91 F5
Hilltop Cl Brixworth NN6 .106 B1
Desborough NN14 . . . . . . .50 F4
Hilmorton Rd CV22 . . . . .241 E7
Hilton Rd OX16 . . . . .240 B8
Hind Stile NN10 . . . . .132 A3
Hinton Ave NN18 . . . . . . .36 A4

Hinton Cl NN4 . . . . .158 E3
Northampton NN4 . . . . . .141 C5
Hinton Manor Ct NN11 . .184 B6
Hinton Rd Brackley NN13 .233 E6
Hinton NN11 . . . . .184 B5
Hinton's Cl NN13 . . . . . . .211 F3
Hinwick Cl NN15 . . . . . . .91 D5
Hinwick Hall Coll of F Ed
NN29 . . . . .147 C1
Hinwick Rd
Podington NN29 . . . . . . .147 D1
Wollaston NN29 . . . . . . .146 E1
Hipwell Ct MK46 . . . . . . .195 F3
Hirondelle Cl NN8 . . . . . .175 F5
Historical Transport Mus *
NN10 . . . . .132 B3
History of Stamford Mus *
PE9 . . . . .241 E3
Hobbs Hill NN14 . . . . .70 C6
Hobby Cl NN4 . . . . .175 B8
Hocknell Cl NN4 . . . . . . .175 F6
Hockney Ave NN15 . . . . . .92 A7
Hodge Cl NN12 . . . . .188 F6
Hodge Way NN14 . . . . . . .70 D2
Hodges La NN7 . . . . .157 C6
Hodnet Cl NN4 . . . . .175 D7
Hoe Way NN7 . . . . .191 C4
Hogarth Cl NN8 . . . . .129 F7
Hogarth Dr NN15 . . . . . . .92 A7
Hogarth Wlk NN18 . . . . . .36 E5
Hogg End OX17 . . . . .196 F6
Hogg La OX17 . . . . .231 F5
Holback La MK18 . . . . . . .226 A5
Holbein Gdns NN4 . . . . . .174 E8
Holbein Wlk NN18 . . . . . .36 D5
Holbrook Ave CV21 . . . . .241 C9
Holbush Way NN9 . . . . . .112 E3
Holcot Cl NN8 . . . . .129 F7
Holcot Leys CV22 . . . . . . .98 A7
Holcot Rd Brixworth NN6 .106 D2
Moulton NN3 . . . . .126 C5
Walgrave NN6 . . . . .107 F4
Holcutt Cl NN4 . . . . .175 F7
Holden Gr NN11 . . . . . . .135 B2
Holdenby Rd NN5 . . . . . .140 C2
Holdenby House Gdns &
Falconry Ctr * NN6 . . .123 C4
Holdenby Rd
East Haddon NN6 . . . . . .122 E5
Northampton NN4 . . . . . .141 E4
Spratton NN6 . . . . .124 B8
Holdgate Cl NN13 . . . . . .222 E1
Holes La MK46 . . . . .195 F2
Holiday La MK19 . . . . . . .206 F4
Holland Rd PE9 . . . . .241 E4
Holland Rise OX17 . . . . . .230 F4
Hollands Dr NN15 . . . . . . .92 C2
Hollies The Moulton NN3 .126 B2
Wellingborough NN8 . . . .129 E5
Hollingside Dr NN7 . . . . .141 F3
Hollington Rd NN9 . . . . .114 D6
Hollow Bank NN12 . . . . .142 C6
Hollow The NN6 . . . . .142 C2
Hollow Way Aynho OX17 .237 C7
Eydon NN11 . . . . .184 B1
Hollow Wood NN14 . . . . .184 C1
Holloway Dr NN18 . . . . . .240 E5
Holloway The CV47 . . . . .166 D7
Holloway Rd NN6 . . . . . .106 F4
Hollowell Rd NN6 . . . . . .104 E4
Holly Bush La CV47 . . . . .166 D7
Holly Cl Brackley NN13 . . .222 F1
Market Harborough LE16 . .31 E4
Rushden NN10 . . . . .131 E3
Holly Lodge Dr NN2 . . . . .141 D6
Holly Rd Kettering NN16 . .72 C4
Northampton NN5 . . . . . .159 F8
Rushden NN10 . . . . .131 E3
Holly Wlk NN9 . . . . .111 B4
Hollyhill NN11 . . . . .203 B4
Holm Cl NN7 . . . . .155 A2
Holman Cl NN12 . . . . . . .142 D2
Holme Cl
Wellingborough NN9 . . . .110 E1
Wilbarston NN14 . . . . . . .34 D5
Holme Way CV23 . . . . . . .99 D1
Holmecross Rd NN4 . . . . .114 A6
Holmes Ave NN14 . . . . . .114 C5
Holmes Dr NN9 . . . . .111 A5
Holmfield Dr NN4 . . . . . .114 E6
Holmfield Terr NN6 . . . . .121 A4
Holmfield Way NN6 . . . . .160 C8
Holmfirth Wlk NN18 . . . . .36 C4
Holmleigh Cl NN5 . . . . . .158 C7
Holmwood Cl NN5 . . . . . .140 B1
Holt Rd LE16 . . . . .19 C8
Holt The MK18 . . . . .240 E2
Holton Rd MK18 . . . . . . .240 D5
Holyoake Rd NN29 . . . . .146 D2
Holyoake Terr NN6 . . . . .121 C4
Holyrood Ct NN5 . . . . . . .158 F7
Holyrood Rd NN5 . . . . . .158 F7
Holyrood Wlk NN18 . . . . .36 C3
Home Acre NN7 . . . . .161 B4
Home Cl Blisworth NN7 . .190 D7
Corby NN18 . . . . .36 B1
Dingley LE16 . . . . .33 A3
Eastcote NN12 . . . . .188 F8
Greens Norton NN12 . . . .202 D8
Holcot NN6 . . . . .108 F3
Irthlingborough NN9 . . . .112 F7
Middleton Cheney OX17 . .220 B8
Northampton NN4 . . . . . .175 C2
Silverstone NN12 . . . . . . .214 D4

Home Cl continued
Staverton NN11 . . . . .152 C8
Towcester NN12 . . . . .203 C5
Home Farm Cl
Corby NN18 . . . . .53 B8
Creaton NN6 . . . . .104 F5
Northampton NN3 . . . . . .161 B8
Weedon NN7 . . . . .154 F2
Home Farm Ct
Adderbury OX17 . . . . . . .230 B4
Norton NN11 . . . . .136 C4
Home Farm Gr LE16 . . . . .68 C7
Home Farm La NN16 . . . . .72 E3
Home Farm Rd NN14 . . . .37 E2
Homefield NN11 . . . . .153 C8
Homestead Cl NN3 . . . . .126 D1
Homestead Ct NN12 . . . .141 E1
Homestead Dr NN7 . . . . .173 A7
Homestead Rd NN9 . . . . .111 B4
Homestead Rise NN4 . . . .175 F6
Homestead The NN14 . . . .74 F1
Homestead Way
Northampton NN2 . . . . . .141 E1
Pottersbury NN12 . . . . . .217 E3
Honewelland Ho LE16 . . . .31 D3
Honey Hill Dr NN14 . . . . .228 E5
Honey Holme NN6 . . . . . .106 A1
Honeypot La LE17 . . . . . . .45 E5
Honeystones NN3 . . . . . .126 C1
Honeysuckle Way NN3 . .160 C6
Honiton Gdns NN18 . . . . .36 E4
Hood Cl NN17 . . . . .36 B8
Hood Rd NN11 . . . . .135 E1
Hood St NN1 . . . . .159 E7
Hood Wlk NN15 . . . . .91 D8
Hookhams Path NN9 . . . .146 E2
Hope St NN29 . . . . .164 C4
Hopes Pl NN2 . . . . .141 B3
Hopmeadow Ct [2] NN3 .143 B4
Hoppet Cl NN18 . . . . .53 A8
Hopping Hill Gdns NN5 . .140 D1
Hopping Hill Lower Sch
NN5 . . . . .158 C8
Hopton Cl NN11 . . . . . . .135 D6
Hopton Fields LE16 . . . . . .48 D8
Hora La MK11 . . . . .229 D5
Hornbeam Cl
Banbury OX16 . . . . .240 B7
Podington NN29 . . . . . . .147 E2
Wellingborough NN8 . . . .129 E5
Hornbeam Ct
Desborough NN14 . . . . . . .51 D3
Northampton NN3 . . . . . .142 D3
Hornby Rd NN6 . . . . .144 E5
Horncastle Cl NN11 . . . . .135 C6
Horne Cl CV21 . . . . .99 B8
Horrell Cl NN12 . . . . .132 A2
Horrock's Way NN15 . . . . .72 F1
Horse Fair OX16 . . . . .240 C7
Horse Cres
Northampton NN16 . . . . . .72 B2
Northampton NN3 . . . . . .159 C6
Horse Shoe La LE16 . . . . .32 B6
Horse Well Ct NN3 . . . . . .142 C7
Horsefair Cl LE16 . . . . . . .31 D4
Horsefair Gn NN13 . . . . . .229 D5
Horseleaze Cl NN18 . . . . .53 A8
Horsemoor Sq [2] NN3 . .143 C2
Horsepool Cl CV23 . . . . . .81 A7
Horseshoe Cl
Brixworth NN6 . . . . .106 C2
Creaton NN6 . . . . .104 F4
Horseshoe St NN1 . . . . . .159 C5
Horsham Wlk NN18 . . . . .36 B5
Horsley Rd NN2 . . . . .141 C1
Horton Cl NN11 . . . . .220 A7
Horton Cres
Middleton Cheney OX17 . .220 A8
Rugby CV22 . . . . .241 D7
Horton Dr OX17 . . . . .220 A8
Horton Rd OX17 . . . . .220 A8
Horton Pk NN7 . . . . .177 E2
Horton Rd
Brafield-on-t-G NN7 . . . .177 D7
Hackleton NN7 . . . . .177 A4
Middleton Cheney OX17 . .220 A7
Hortons' La NN14 . . . . . . .76 D2
Hortonsfield Rd NN12 . . .217 F5
Hoskyn Cl CV21 . . . . .98 F8
Hospital Hill NN14 . . . . . . .70 D7
Hospital of St Cross
CV22 . . . . .241 D6
Hothorpe Rd LE17 . . . . . . .46 D8
Houghton Hill NN4 . . . . .160 A1
Hove Rd NN10 . . . . .132 C2
Hove St NN18 . . . . .36 B4
Howard Ave NN11 . . . . . . .34 B7
Howard Bryd Gdns
NN3 . . . . .142 C3
Howard Cl NN15 . . . . .92 A7
Howard Cl [3] NN8 . . . . .130 B5
Howard La NN11 . . . . . . .141 C8
Howard Rd
Banbury OX16 . . . . .240 F8
Wollaston NN29 . . . . . . .146 F2
Howard St NN16 . . . . .72 A2
Howard Way LE16 . . . . . . .31 D1
Howard's Cl NN29 . . . . . .146 D2
Howards Mdw PE8 . . . . . .13 F7
Howcut La NN7 . . . . .178 E3
Howden Gn NN14 . . . . . . .50 E4
Howe Cres Corby NN17 . . .36 A7
Daventry NN11 . . . . .135 E1
Hoy Wlk NN17 . . . . .21 C1
Hoylake NN8 . . . . .129 C7
Hoylake Dr NN4 . . . . .141 F3

Hubbard Cl MK18 ....240 F4
Hubble Rd NN17 ....21 F1
Hudson Cl Corby NN18 ...36 C3
Daventry NN11 ....135 C5
Hudson Dr NN4 ....158 E1
Hudson Rd CV22 ....241 A6
Hulcote NN12 ....203 F8
Hulme Way NN8 ....129 E7
Humber Cl
Daventry NN11 ....134 F4
Northampton NN5 ......140 F2
Humber Gdns NN8 ....129 C6
Humber Wlk NN11 ....21 D2
Humfrey La NN2 ....141 C8
Humphries Dr NN13 .....233 D8
Hunsbarrow Rd NN4 ....158 E4
Hunsbury Cl NN4 ....158 F1
Hunsbury Gn NN4 ....158 D2
Hunsbury Hill Ave NN4 .158 E3
Hunsbury Hill Country Pk*
NN4 ....158 F1
Hunsbury Hill Rd NN4 ..158 F2
Hunsbury Park Lower Sch
NN4 ....158 F2
Hunslet La NN4 ....158 E2
Hunt Cl Brixworth NN6 ..106 C3
Towcester NN12 ....203 C2
Hunt St NN18 ....36 D5
Hunter St
Buckingham MK18 ......240 C3
Northampton NN1 ......159 D7
Rugby CV21 ....241 E9
Hunters Cl
Husbands Bosworth LE17 .45 E6
Northampton NN2 ......141 D6
Hunters Rd NN17 ....22 E1
Hunters' Way NN6 ......106 E2
Hunting Way PE8 ....14 C4
Huntingdon Gdns LE16 ..31 E1
Huntingdon Rd NN14 ....76 E2
Huntsham Cl NN3 ....160 D7
Huntsmead NN3 ....143 D4
Hurst Cl NN15 ....92 C4
Husbands Bosworth CE Prim
Sch LE17 ....45 E5
Hussar Cl NN11 ....135 B1
Hutchinson Ave NN14 ...90 B3
Hutts Cl NN11 ....183 D7
Huxley Cl NN8 ....129 C6
Huxloe Pl ⓘ NN16 ....72 B2
Huxloe Rise NN1 ....142 E6
Huxlow Sch NN9 ....112 E3
Hyacinth Way NN10 ....148 B3
Hyde Cl NN7 ....191 C4
Hyde Dr NN9 ....112 A5
Hyde Rd NN7 ....191 C4

Ibsen Wlk NN18 ....36 C1
Ibstock Cl NN3 ....143 A6
Icknield Dr NN4 ....158 C3
Ideal Bldgs ⓘ NN1 .....159 C7
Ilex Cl NN4 ....159 F1
Ilemvor Way NN6 ....106 C3
Imperial Cl NN10 ....132 A2
Independent St CV23 ...100 A3
Indmere Cl NN4 ....106 C3
Ingleborough Way NN5 .158 D8
Inglewood Ct NN3 ......143 C1
Inham Cl NN18 ....36 C2
Inkerman Way PE8 ....41 F5
Inlands Cl NN11 ....135 D1
Inlands Rise NN11 ......135 D1
Inn Yard Ct LE16 ....68 C7
Insignia Cl ⓘ NN4 .....175 E7
Inwood Cl NN18 ....36 C2
Iona Rd NN17 ....36 C8
Irchester Country Pk Trail*
NN8 ....130 D1
Irchester Country Pk Visitor
Ctr* NN29 ....130 D1
Irchester Ctry Pk*
NN29 ....130 F1
Irchester Narrow Gauge Rly
Mus* NN8 ....130 D1
Irchester Prim Sch
NN29 ....147 A8
Irchester Rd
Podington NN10 ....147 B4
Rushden NN10 ....131 F2
Wollaston NN29 ....146 F3
Irchester Turn NN29 ...131 A2
Ireton Rd LE16 ....31 D2
Irnham Rd PE9 ....261 E5
Iron Cross NN11 ....167 B2
Iron Duke Cl NN11 .....135 B4
Iron Pikes NN6 ....104 F4
Irondale Cl NN4 ....158 E3
Ironmonger St PE9 ....214 F1
Ironstone Ct NN9 ......111 F4
Ironstone La NN4 .....106 C3
Ironstone Way NN6 ....106 C3
Irthlingborough Cty Inf Sch
NN9 ....112 E2
Irthlingborough Cty Jun Sch
NN9 ....112 E2
Irthlingborough Rd
Finedon NN9 ....112 B4
Little Addington NN14 ..113 A7
Wellingborough NN8 ..130 E4
Irvine Dr NN12 ....203 D8
Irving Gr NN17 ....36 E8

Ise Com Coll NN15 ....72 D1
Ise Rd NN15 ....72 D1
Ise Vale Ave NN14 ....51 B3
Ise View Rd NN14 ....51 C3
Isebrook Hospl NN8 .....92 A2
Isebrook Hospl NN8 ....130 B3
Isebrook Sch NN15 .....51 C2
Isham CE Prim Sch NN14 .91 C1
Isham Cl NN2 ....141 D5
Isham Rd
Orlingbury NN14 ......110 A5
Pytchley NN14 ....91 B3
Isley Walley Ind Est NN8 .130 D7
Isley Wlk NN17 ....36 C8
Islington Cl NN12 ......203 D5
Islington Rd NN12 .....203 D5
Ivatt Wlk OX16 ....240 E10
Ivens La NN12 ....171 C1
Ivy Ct NN11 ....135 B1
Ivy La NN9 ....111 F4
Ivy Rd Kettering NN16 ..72 D4
Northampton NN5 ......159 F8
Ivydene Terr NN14 .....90 A4
Ixworth Cl NN3 ....142 F5

Jackdaw Cl NN3 ....161 C8
Jacklin Cl NN8 ....129 C6
Jackson Cl
Market Harborough LE16 ..48 E8
Northampton NN2 .....141 E6
Jackson Rd CV21 ....80 A1
Jackson Way NN15 .....90 F8
Jackson's La NN8 ......129 F5
Jackson's Lane Flats
NN8 ....129 F5
Jacorrin Cl NN2 ....141 E6
Jamb The NN17 ....37 A6
James Lewis Ct NN3 ...142 C2
James Rd NN8 ....130 A4
James St Irchester NN29 .147 B7
Rugby CV21 ....241 D8
James Watt Ave NN17 ...37 A8
James Watt Rd NN11 ...135 A4
Jardine Cl NN3 ....142 D1
Jarman Cl NN18 ....240 F3
Jarretts Yd NN4 ......175 E6
Jarvis Cl NN11 ....233 F8
Jasmine Cl NN16 ......72 D5
Jasmine Gdns NN10 ...148 B7
Jasmine Rd
Kettering NN16 ....72 D4
Northampton NN3 ....143 C5
Javelin Cl NN5 ....158 C8
JBJ Bsns Pk NN7 .....174 D2
Jean Rd NN16 ....72 E3
Jellicoe Cl NN11 ......135 E1
Jenkins Rd CV21 ......80 A1
Jenkinson Cl NN12 ...203 D4
Jenner Cres NN12 ....141 B5
Jennings Cl
Daventry NN11 ....135 C1
Higham Ferrers NN10 .132 B5
Jersey Cl NN3 ....130 B6
Jersey Ct NN3 ....142 F1
Jervis Cl NN11 ....135 E1
Jervoise Way NN16 ...31 F2
Jetty The Creaton NN6 ..104 F4
Hackleton NN7 ....177 B3
Wappenham NN12 ....213 B8
Wardington OX17 ....196 C1
Jeyes Cl NN3 ....126 B1
Jibwood NN14 ....89 B5
Jitty The NN14 ....89 B4
Job's Yd NN16 ....72 B2
John Beverly Mews
NN14 ....70 C6
John Clare Cl NN13 ...222 F1
John Clare Ct NN16 ...72 C6
John Clare Way NN17 .36 D8
John Eagle Cl NN9 ....113 F4
John Gdge Rd NN9 ...145 D6
John Hellins Prim Sch
NN12 ....217 D3
John Pyel Rd NN9 ....112 E1
John Smith Ave NN14 .70 E7
John St Rushden NN10 ..132 B2
Thrapston NN14 ......76 E2
John Thwaites Cl CV22 .241 C7
John White Cl The NN9 .
NN10 ....132 C6
Johns Rd NN7 ....157 A1
Johnson Ave
Brackley NN13 ....233 C8
Rugby CV22 ....241 A7
Johnson Cl NN11 .....183 D8
Johnson's Field MK46 .195 E4
Jones Cl NN11 ....233 D8
Jordan Cl LE16 ....32 A3
Joseph Priestle y Ct ⓘ
NN11 ....159 D7
Joshua Sq NN8 ....158 F2
Jowett Cl NN15 ......92 A8
Jubilee Ave NN18 ....36 D5
Jubilee Cl Byfield NN11 .183 D7
Islip NN14 ....76 B3
Long Buckby NN6 .....121 A4
Northampton NN4 ....158 F3
Jubilee Cres NN8 ....129 F2
Jubilee Ct OX16 .....240 D7
Jubilee Dr NN6 ....108 B5
Jubilee Gdns LE16 ...31 F4
Jubilee Rd NN11 .....135 B2
Jubilee St
Irthlingborough NN9 ..112 E1

Jubilee St continued
Rothwell NN14 ....70 D6
Rugby CV21 ....241 A8
Jubilee Terr Isham NN14 .110 F8
Stony Stratford MK11 .229 E5
Judges Ct NN6 ....104 F4
Judith Rd NN14 ....72 E4
Julian Way NN14 .....141 A3
Junction Rd
Banbury OX16 ....240 E8
Northampton NN2 ....141 E1
Juniper Cl NN12 ......203 B4
Juniper Ct NN12 .....143 D3
Juniper Thorn NN6 ...106 C1
Jura Cl NN17 ....36 B8
Justin Pk LE16 ....48 F7
Jutland Way NN16 ...72 A2

Kane Wlk NN17 ....36 E8
Kangaroo Spinney NN8 .130 E3
Karlstad Cl NN18 .....36 A2
Kathleen Dr NN12 ...141 B5
Katrine Cl NN17 ......21 B1
Kealdale Rd NN3 ....142 A4
Keating Cl NN15 .....92 A8
Keats Cl Earls Barton NN6 .144 F4
Great Houghton NN4 .160 F1
Keats Dr Kettering NN16 ..72 C1
Towcester NN12 .....203 B5
Keats Gr PE9 ....214 B5
Keats Rd Daventry NN11 .135 A5
Higham Ferrers NN10 .132 C6
Keats Way Corby NN17 .36 D8
Higham Ferrers NN10 .132 C6
Keble Cl Daventry NN11 .153 B8
Keble Rd NN13 ....233 D8
Kedleston Cl ⓘ NN4 .175 C8
Keebles Cl NN14 ....37 E2
Keepers Cl NN4 ......129 F1
Kelburn Cl NN4 ......175 B7
Keld Cl NN18 ....36 D2
Kelmarsh Hall* NN6 .67 F4
Kelmarsh Rd
Arthingworth LE16 ..68 C7
Clipston LE16 ....67 A7
Corby NN17 ....67 A7
Kelmscott Cl NN3 ...143 A5
Kelsale Cl NN8 ......158 B8
Kelthorpe Cl PE9 ....1 A4
Kelvin Gr NN17 .....37 A7
Kemp Ho NN17 .....142 A1
Kemps Rd OX17 ....230 A5
Kendal Cl
Northampton NN3 ...142 D4
Rushden NN10 ......132 D1
Wellingborough NN8 .129 D6
Kendalls Cl LE16 ....34 D5
Kenilworth NN8 ......36 D2
Kenilworth Cl
Daventry NN11 .....135 B1
Northampton NN5 ..158 B8
Rushden NN10 .....132 C1
Kenilworth Dr NN15 ..91 F8
Kenilworth Gdns NN14 .76 F2
Kenmore Dr NN14 ..51 B2
Kenmuir Ave NN2 ..141 F2
Kenmuir Cres NN2 .141 F2
Kenmuir Gdns NN2 .141 F2
Kenmuir Rd NN9 ...111 F4
Kennedy Cl NN11 ..135 E1
Kennedy Ho OX16 ..240 B8
Kennel Hill NN14 ...55 F7
Kennel Rd NN12 ...215 C3
Kennel Terr NN6 ...106 B2
Kennels Dr NN12 ..216 E3
Kennels The NN12 .216 D3
Kennet Cl NN8 .....129 C6
Kennet Gn NN5 ....140 F2
Kensington Cl
Kings Sutton OX17 .230 F6
Rushden NN10 .....131 E3
Towcester NN12 ...203 B4
Kensington Gdns NN15 ..91 B8
Kensington Pl MK46 .195 F5
Kensington Wlk NN18 .36 C3
Kent Cl Corby NN17 .36 C7
Kent Pl NN15 ......91 D6
Kent Rd
Northampton NN5 ..158 C6
Rushden NN10 ....132 C3
Wellingborough NN8 .129 F1
Kent The CV21 ....80 A2
Kentford Cl NN14 ..175 B8
Kenton Ct NN15 ...92 A8
Kentstone Cl NN2 ..140 F4
Kerley Cl NN14 ....90 A3
Kerrfield Est NN15 ..158 C2
Kesteven Rd PE9 ..241 E5
Kestian Cl LE16 ...31 D5
Keston Way NN9 ..114 B5
Kestrel Cl NN3 ....142 A4
Kestrel Cres NN3 .222 E1
Kestrel La NN8 ...130 A7
Kestrel Way NN18 ..240 F3
Keswick NN8 .....129 B7
Keswick Dr
Northampton NN3 .142 C4
Rushden NN10 ...132 D3
Keswick Rd NN9 .207 B2
Ketco Ave PE9 ....1 B7
Kettering Gdns ⓘ NN1 .159 E6

Kettering General Hospl
NN16 ....71 F2
Kettering Parkway NN15 .91 E8
Kettering Rd
Broughton NN14 ....90 B5
Burton Latimer NN15 .92 B3
Geddington NN14 ...54 A1
Great Harrowden NN9 ..110 E4
Isham NN14 ....91 E1
Islip NN14 ....75 E1
Market Harborough LE16 .32 B2
Moulton NN3 ....126 F2
Northampton NN1 ...159 E8
Northampton,Spinney Hill
NN3 ....142 A3
Pytchley NN14 .....90 F2
Rothwell NN14,NN16 ..70 E5
Stamford PE9 .....241 D2
Stanion NN14 .....37 E2
Walgrave NN6 ....108 C6
Weldon NN14 .....38 B7
Woodford NN14 ..94 B8
Wothorpe PE9 ....2 C8
Kettering Rd N NN3 .142 C5
Kettering Sta NN15 .72 A1
Kettering Town FC NN16 .72 B5
Kettle End NN12 ..200 C3
Ketton CE Prim Sch PE9 ..1 A5
Ketton Rd PE9 ......1 C3
Kettonby Gdns NN15 .91 B8
Kew Rd CV21 ......241 D9
Keyes Way MK18 ..240 E5
Keyham Ct NN3 ...143 A5
Keys Cl NN11 .....135 D1
Keys La CV47 ....166 E8
Keyston Rd PE18 .116 D2
Keyte's Cl OX17 ..230 A4
KG House Bsns Ctr ⓘ
NN5 ....140 F1
Kiel Wlk NN18 ....36 A2
Kielder Ct NN15 ..92 A4
Kieldsen Cl OX17 .210 B1
Kilbale Cres CV16 .240 D6
Kilborn Cl NN8 ...129 E7
Kilborn Rd NN8 ..129 E6
Kilburn Pl NN10 .132 B4
Kilby Cl NN8 ....129 E3
Kiln La
Litchborough NN12 .171 C1
Welton NN11 ....135 E8
Kiln Way NN8 ..129 C6
Kilsby CE Prim Sch
CV23 ....100 A3
Kilsby Cl NN11 ..99 C7
Kilsby Rd Barby CV23 .99 C1
Crick NN6 ....100 F2
Watford NN6 ...120 B7
Kilvey Rd NN4 ..160 B2
Kilworth Rd
Husbands Bosworth LE17 ..45 D4
Rugby CV21 .....99 B7
Swinford LE17 ..62 C4
Kimberley Rd CV21 .241 D9
Kimble Cl NN4 ..175 B8
Kimbolton Cl NN14 .76 E2
Kimbolton Rd
Chelveston NN9 ..133 D8
Higham Ferrers NN10 .132 C6
Kinewell Cl NN14 ..95 A3
Kinewell Lake Nature Trail*
NN14 ....95 A3
King Charles Cl MK18 .240 E5
King Cup Cl NN10 ..147 E4
King Edward Rd
Northampton NN1 .160 A7
Rugby CV21 ....241 D9
King George Cres MK11 .229 E6
King John Sch The NN6 ..76 D1
King Richard Ct NN4 .175 C6
King St Desborough NN14 ..51 B3
Earls Barton NN6 ..144 E5
Kettering NN16 ...72 C3
Long Buckby NN6 .121 B4
Maidford NN12 ...186 D5
Northampton NN1 .159 C6
Rugby CV21 .....241 C9
Stony Stratford MK11 .229 E5
King Sytle Cl NN6 ...106 B4
King's Cliffe Endowed Prim
Sch PE8 ....13 F7
King's Ct LE16 ...31 E4
King's Forest PE8 .12 E3
King's Head Pl LE16 ..31 E3
King's Heath Lower Sch
NN5 ....140 F2
King's La Flore NN7 ..155 F5
Little Harrowden NN9 ..110 B3
King's Rd Banbury OX16 ..240 B8
Market Harborough LE16 ..31 E3
King's Sutton Sta OX17 .230 E5
King's Way NN12 ..203 B4
Kingfisher Cl
Hinton NN11 ......184 B6
Northampton NN4 .175 A7
Kingfisher Cl NN6 .143 D8
Kingfisher Rd
Brackley NN13 ....233 C8
Buckingham MK18 .240 F2
Kingfisher Way NN15 .92 A2
Kingmaker Way NN4 .159 A2
Kings Arms La NN8 .42 F3
Kings Ave NN10 ..132 C7
Kings Cl NN4 ....175 F3
Kings Cliffe Rd PE8 .14 C4
Kings Ct NN3 ...51 B3
Kings Gn NN11 ..153 C7
Kings La Barrowden LE15 ..3 F5
Pury End NN12 ..215 F7

Kings La continued
Yelvertoft NN6 ....82 B4
Kings Meadow La NN10 .132 B7
Kings Meadow Sch
NN3 ....142 C2
Kings Mill La PE9 ....241 D2
Kings Park Rd NN3 ..141 F6
Kings Pk NN7 ....155 A3
Kings Pl NN10 .....132 C2
Kings Rd Oundle PE8 ..42 A6
Rushden NN10 ....132 C2
Stamford PE9 ....241 D4
Kings St NN8 ....130 A5
Kings Stile OX17 ..208 F1
Kings Sutton Prim Sch
OX17 ....231 A5
Kingsbrook NN18 .36 B3
Kingsbrook Sch MK19 .228 F4
Kingscroft Ct NN3 .143 C1
Kingsfield Cl NN5 ..141 A1
Kingsfield Piece NN12 .215 C4
Kingsfield Way NN5 .141 A1
Kingshill Dr MK19 .228 E5
Kingsland Ave NN2 .141 D3
Kingsland Cl NN2 .141 C3
Kingsland Gdns NN2 .141 C3
Kingsley Ave
Daventry NN11 ...135 B1
Kettering NN16 ..72 B5
Rugby CV21 .....98 F8
Kingsley Dr NN17 .36 D8
Kingsley Grn ⓘ NN2 .141 E1
Kingsley Lower Sch
NN2 ....141 E2
Kingsley Park Mid Sch
NN2 ....141 D1
Kingsley Park Terr NN2 .141 F1
Kingsley Rd
Northampton NN2 ..141 E1
Rothwell NN14 ....70 C2
Silverstone NN12 .214 E5
Kingsley Sch NN15 .141 C2
Kingsmead
King's Cliffe PE8 ..13 F8
Northampton NN2 ..141 A5
Kingsmith Dr NN9 .114 E6
Kingsthorpe Distribution Pk
NN16 ....71 E4
Kingsthorpe Ave NN17 .36 B7
Kingsthorpe CE Lower Sch
NN2 ....141 B3
Kingsthorpe Com Coll
NN2 ....141 B3
Kingsthorpe Gr NN2 .141 C2
Kingsthorpe Grove Lower
Sch NN2 ....141 C2
Kingsthorpe Mid Sch
NN2 ....141 B3
Kingsthorpe Rd NN2 .141 C1
Kingsthorpe Sh Ctr ⓘ
NN2 ....141 C3
Kingston Ave MK11 .229 E5
Kingston La
Blakesley NN12 ..187 B3
Daventry NN11 ..135 B3
Long Buckby NN6 .121 C4
Middleton Cheney OX17 .220 A7
Kingston Way LE16 .32 A5
Kingswell Rd NN2 .141 B3
Kingswell St NN1 .159 C5
Kingswood Comp Sch
NN3 ....36 A3
Kingswood Jun & Inf Sch
NN18 ....36 A3
Kingswood La NN3 .36 A3
Kinross Cl NN3 ..142 A4
Kipling Cl PE9 ..241 A3
Kipling Dr NN12 .203 B5
Kipling Rd Corby NN17 .36 D8
Kettering NN16 ..72 C5
Kippell Hill MK46 .195 F5
Kipton Field NN14 .70 E7
Kirby Cl Corby NN18 .36 A3
Northampton NN4 .175 F7
Kirby Ct NN15 ...91 C5
Kirby Hall* NN17 .23 B6
Kirby La NN17 ...23 C5
Kirby Rd NN17 ..10 C1
Kirkby Rd CV21 ..99 B8
Kirkhams Cl NN6 .82 C3
Kirkstone Wlk ⓘ NN3 .142 C4
Kirkwall NN17 ..21 C1
Kirton Cl NN3 ..143 B5
Kirton End NN9 ..133 C1
Kislingbury Prim Sch
NN7 ....157 D4
Kislingbury Rd
Bugbrooke NN7 ..173 A8
Rothersthorpe NN7 .174 F8
Kitchen Gdns NN14 .89 F6
Kitchener Cl NN11 .135 B4
Kitelee Cl MK19 .207 A3
Kites Cl NN12 ..175 A8
Kits Cl NN7 .....192 D2
Knapshill Cres NN4 .158 F4
Knibb Pl NN15 ..91 F6
Knibb St NN10 ..72 E6
Knight's End Rd LE16 .32 B6
Knight's La NN2 ..141 B3
Knightlands Rd NN9 .112 F3
Knightley Cl NN11 .183 D7
Knightley Rd NN5 ..141 C1
Knighton Cl NN5 ..140 A3

Knightons Way NN6 ......106 C1
Knights Cl Bozeat NN29 ..164 D2
 Corby NN16 ....36 A5
 Earls Barton NN6 ....144 E4
Knights Ct
 Northampton NN1 .....159 F8
 Northampton,Little Billing
 NN3 ....143 B1
 Wellingborough NN8 ..129 F5
Knights Hill NN6 ......85 B8
Knightscliffe Way NN5 ..140 D1
Knob The OX17 ....231 A5
Knoll St LE16 ....71 D4
Knoll The Brixworth NN6 ..106 C2
 Grendon NN7 ....163 D5
Knowle Cl NN3 ......160 C6
Knowles Cl NN10 ....132 D3
Knox Ct NN8 ....130 B4
Knox Rd NN8 ....130 B5
Knuston Dr NN10 ....131 F2
Knuston Spinney NN10 ..131 E1
Knutsford La NN6 ....121 C4
Krohn Cl NN16 ......240 F3
Kylesku Cres NN15 ....91 E8
Kynnesworth Gdns
 NN10 ....132 C6
Kyoto Cl NN3 ....142 A6

L

Laburnhum Cl NN6 ....129 E5
Laburnum Cl NN11 ....184 B6
Laburnum Cres
 Kettering NN16 ....72 D4
 Northampton NN3 ....142 A3
Lace Mews MK46 .....195 F4
Laceby Wlk NN3 .....143 B1
Laddermakers Yd NN7 .172 E7
Lady Cl NN11 ....153 D2
Lady Croft NN11 ....135 B1
Lady Hollows Dr NN4 ..176 A6
Lady Smock Cl NN4 ..175 F2
Lady Winefride's Wlk
 NN3 ....143 B2
Lady's La
 Mears Ashby NN6 ....128 B2
 Northampton NN1 ...159 C6
Ladybower Cl NN16 ....71 E3
Ladybridge Dr NN4 ....144 C6
Lahnstein Ct 12 NN16 ..72 B2
Lake Ave NN15 ......90 F8
Lake Cres NN11 .....135 A2
Lake Wlk
 Adderbury OX17 ....230 B4
 Northampton NN4 ...175 C4
Lakeside
 Irthlingborough NN9 ..131 D7
 Northampton NN3 ....143 A7
Lakeside Bglws NN15 ..91 E6
Lakeside Cl NN14 ....76 D3
Lakeside Dr NN3 ....143 D3
Lakeside Lodges NN3 .143 A7
Lakeview Gn NN3 ....142 C4
Lamb's Cres OX16 ....240 E6
Lambert Way OX17 ....241 C2
Lambert's Cl LE15 ......3 A6
Lambeth Wlk PE9 ....241 C4
Lambourne Way OX7 .230 B4
Lambrook Dr NN4 ....175 C6
Lammas Cl
 Husbands Bosworth LE17 .45 E5
 Orlingbury NN1 .....110 A5
Lammas Clyd NN17 ....23 A1
Lammas Rd NN17 ....135 A5
Lamport Dr NN11 ....135 A5
Lamport Hall* NN6 ....87 E2
Lamport Rd NN6 ......87 E6
Lancaster Ct MK11 ....229 F5
Lancaster Ct NN29 ...146 C3
Lancaster Dr
 Brackley NN13 ......233 E8
 Thrapston NN14 ......76 F2
Lancaster Rd
 Kettering NN16 ....72 C3
 Rothwell NN14 ....70 E7
 Rugby CV21 ....241 C9
 Stamford PE9 ....241 D4
Lancaster St NN10 ...132 C7
Lancaster Way
 Northampton NN4 ...159 A1
 Rushden NN10 ......132 C3
Lancers Way NN7 ....155 B4
Lanchester Way NN11 .134 F3
Lancum Ho NN8 ......129 C5
Landcross Dr NN10 ....160 C7
Landor NN8 ....129 C4
Landor Cl NN17 ......21 D1
Landsdown Dr NN4 ...142 E2
Landsdowne Pl CV21 .241 F7
Landseer Cl CV21 ....80 B1
Landseer Ct NN16 ...36 D5
Lane The Ashby St LV23 .119 B5
 Denton NN7 ....178 B8
 Eastcote NN12 .....173 A1
 Easton o t H PE9 ......2 A5
 Grafton Regis NN12 ..205 D2
 Rothersthorpe NN7 ..174 B6
 Weston by W LE16 ...18 B4
Lanercost Wlk
 Northampton NN3 ...142 C4
 8 Northampton NN3 ...142 C4
Laneside Hollow NN4 .175 C6
Langdale NN14 ....50 F3
Langdale Gr NN17 ...36 D8
Langdale Rd NN11 ...141 D3
Langdale Wlk LE16 ....31 E1

Langdon Cl NN11 ....135 B5
Langford Dr NN4 ....175 D5
Langham Cl NN6 ....104 F5
Langham Pl
 Northampton NN2 ...159 C8
 Walgrave NN6 ......108 A5
Langham Rd NN9 ....114 D7
Langley Cl NN4 .....158 E3
Langley Cres NN9 ...113 B5
Langley Ct NN15 ......92 B2
Langley Way NN15 ....91 C6
Langley Wlk NN18 ...36 D5
Langport Gn NN18 ...36 B6
Langsett Cl
 Kettering NN16 ......71 E3
 Northampton NN3 ...142 F1
Langton Cl NN18 ....36 B6
Langton Pl NN14 ....91 E1
Langton Rd LE16 ....32 A7
Langton Rise NN11 ..137 C6
Lansdown Cl NN11 ..135 D5
Lanson Ct NN15 ......92 C3
Lapford Rd NN18 ....36 E4
Lapland Wlk NN18 ...36 B2
Lapstone Ho NN5 ...159 A5
Lapwing Cl NN4 ....175 F2
Larch Cl Hinton NN1 .184 A6
 Irchester NN29 .....147 A7
Larch Dr NN11 ......135 C5
Larch La NN5 ....140 B2
Larch Rd Corby NN17 ...27 C5
 Kettering NN15 ......72 C1
Larchwood Cl NN8 ...129 E5
Lark Cl MK18 ....240 E2
Lark La NN4 ....175 F4
Lark Rise Brackley NN13 .233 E8
 Northampton NN3 ...143 B4
Larkhall La NN7 .....157 D6
Larkhall Way NN7 ...157 C7
Larkhill NN10 ....132 A4
Larkin Gdns NN10 ..132 A5
Larkwood Cl NN16 ...72 C5
Larratt Rd NN17 .....38 A8
Larwood Cl NN2 ....141 A5
Lasham Ct NN3 .....143 C1
Latham Rd PE8 ......
Latham St NN14 ......55 F7
Latham's Hospl PE8 ..59 B6
Lathbury Rd NN13 ...233 D8
Lathkill St LE16 .....31 F1
Latimer Ct
 Burton Latimer NN15 ...92 C2
 Gretton NN17 ....10 C1
Latimer Cres LE16 ...31 F2
Latimer Ct NN15 ......92 A6
Latimer Rd NN17 ...36 E8
Lattimore Cl NN6 ...102 C5
Latymer Cl LE16 ....49 E5
Latymer Ct 4 NN4 ..159 C6
Laud's Rd NN6 .....175 A4
Lauda Way NN12 ...203 C8
Lauderdale Ave NN4 ..159 A2
Laughton Rd LE16 ...30 C4
Launcelot Cl NN5 ...158 A7
Launde Gdns PE9 ...241 A2
Launde Pk LE16 ....32 A2
Laundry Rd PE8 .....14 C4
Laureate Ho NN11 ..135 B4
Laurel Ct
 Northampton NN3 ...142 E3
 4 Wellingborough NN8 .130 B5
Laurel Rd NN16 .....72 C4
Laurel Valley NN4 ...175 D4
Laurels The Ecton NN6 .143 F3
 Moulton NN3 ....126 B2
Lavant Wlk NN3 ....141 F5
Lavender Cl NN14 ...76 D2
Lavender La NN7 ...177 D1
Lavender Way NN10 .148 C8
Lavender Ct NN15 ...92 A5
Lavenham Cl NN3 ...141 E5
Lavery Cl NN18 .....36 D5
Law's La PE8 ....13 F7
Lawford Rd CV21,CV22,
 CV23 ....241 A8
Lawns The Corby NN18 ..36 A4
 Kettering NN16 ......72 A1
 Kilsby CV23 ....100 A2
 Northampton NN5 ...158 B3
Lawrence Cl
 Kettering NN15 ......92 A8
 Raunds NN9 ....114 B5
Lawrence Ct Corby NN18 .36 D6
 Long Buckby NN6 ...121 B4
 22 Northampton NN1 ..159 C7
Lawrence Rd CV21 ..241 F8
Lawrence Sheriff St
 CV22 ....241 D7
Laws Croft NN13 ...233 C7
Laws Lawn NN14 ....111 F4
Lawson Cres NN8 ...143 C1
Lawson St Kettering NN16 .72 C3
 Raunds NN9 ....114 D6
Lawton Rd NN10 ...132 C3
Lawyers Cl NN13 ...233 E2
Laxton Cl NN17 .....36 B8
Laxton Ct NN15 .....92 A5
Laxton Jun Sch PE8 ..42 A5
Laxton Sch PE8 .....42 A6
Laywood Cl NN9 ...114 C2
Laywood Way NN6 ...131 E8
Lea Rd NN1 ....159 F8
Lea Way NN8 ....129 D3

Leafields NN3 ....160 F8
Leah Bank NN4 .....159 A2
Leah Cl NN18 ....53 A8
Lealand The LE16 ....48 B8
Leam The NN11 .....134 F1
Leamington Spa NN11 .135 A2
Leatherland Ct 10 NN16 .72 B2
Leben Sq NN3 ......143 C5
Leckhampstead Rd
 MK19 ....228 A3
Ledaig Way NN3 ...142 A4
Ledbury Rd NN15 ...91 F5
Lee Way NN9 ....114 D7
Lee's Way NN14 .....54 A3
Lees Cl NN12 ....215 C4
Lees St NN9 ....112 A3
Leeson Cres NN15 ...91 F6
Leeson Cl NN12 ....203 D4
Leeson Ct NN12 ....203 C4
Legg Rd PE8 ....7 D8
Legion Cres NN16 ...71 F3
Leicester Cl NN14 ...72 A3
Leicester La NN16 ...31 D7
Leicester Par NN2 ...159 C8
Leicester Rd
 Husbands Bosworth LE17 .45 D7
 Market Harborough LE16 .31 D5
Leicester St
 Kettering NN16 ......72 A3
 Northampton NN5 ...159 C7
Leicester Terr 2 NN2 .159 C7
Leigh Gr OX16 .....240 C7
Leighton Cl NN18 ...129 F8
Leighton Pl NN14 ...129 F4
Leighton Rd NN18 ...36 D5
Leith Cl NN4 ....159 B8
Leith Ct NN18 ......36 D5
Lenborough Cl NN18 .240 C2
Lenborough Rd MK18 .240 C2
Lennon Cl CV21 .....99 C8
Lennox Gdns OX16 ..240 A6
Lennox Wlk NN5 ...140 D2
Lenthall Sq LE16 ...31 E1
Lenton Cl NN11 .....90 A3
Leonard La 1 NN3 ..126 C1
Leonardo Ct NN18 ...36 A6
Lerwick Way NN17 ...36 C8
Leslie Rd NN7 ......159 B7
Lesson Rd NN6 .....106 B1
Lester Cl OX17 .....230 A6
Letts Rd NN4 ......159 A1
Leven Way NN17 ...21 B1
Levenot Cl OX16 ...240 F8
Lever Rd CV21 ......80 A1
Levitts Rd NN17 ...173 A8
Levy Cl CV21 ......140 A2
Lewin Cl NN14 ....70 B7
Lewin Rd NN18 .....36 B1
Lewis Ho NN14 .....91 E1
Lewis Rd Kettering NN15 .91 C7
 Northampton NN5 ...175 F7
Lexton Cl NN14 ....175 F7
Lexton Gdns OX17 ..220 B8
Leyland Dr NN2 ....141 A5
Leyland Trad Est NN8 ..130 D4
Leyland View NN8 ...130 D4
Leys Ave Desborough NN14 .70 C3
 Towcester NN12 ...203 C5
 Rothwell NN14 ......70 B7
Leys Cl Denton NN7 ...162 B1
Leys Gdns NN8 .....130 B6
Leys La NN4 ....160 F1
Leys Rd Earls Barton NN6 .144 D4
 Pattishall NN12 .....172 D1
 Rugby CV21 ....99 C7
 Wellingborough NN8 ..130 B6
Leys The Bugbrooke NN7 .172 E6
 Denton NN7 ....162 B1
 Long Buckby NN6 ...121 C4
Lianne Ct NN7 .....141 B2
Libourne Rd CV23 ...80 C5
Lilford Pl NN14 ......72 D3
Lilford Rd NN14 ....77 C8
Lilliput Rd NN4 ....160 C3
Lilley Homes The NN6 .129 F2
Lilley Terr NN9 ....112 A3
Lillington Ct NN18 ...36 B6
Lilly Hill NN6 ......240 D6
Lime Ave Banbury OX16 .240 E6
 Buckingham MK18 ...240 F2
 Eydon NN11 ....184 C1
Lilbourne La LE17 ...62 E3
Lime Cl NN7 ....112 F2
Lime Farm Way NN6 ..160 F2
Lime Gr Bugbrooke NN7 .143 A7

Lime Gr continued
 Wellingborough NN8 ..130 A7
Lime Rd Kettering NN16 ..72 F2
 Yardley Gobion NN12 ..217 E6
Lime St
 Irthlingborough NN9 ..112 F2
 Olney MK46 ....195 F3
 Rushden NN10 .....148 B4
Lime Terr NN15 .....72 F1
Lime Tree Mews NN15 ..72 B1
Lime Trees Gr NN7 ....37 A6
Limefields Way NN4 ..175 D6
Limehurst Cl NN5 ...140 C1
Limehurst Rd NN5 ...158 C8
Limehurst Sq NN5 ...158 C8
Limes The
 9 Daventry NN11 ...135 C1
 11 Irthlingborough NN9 .112 F2
 Stony Stratford MK11 ..229 E5
 Thorpe Langton LE16 ..17 A5
 Thrapston NN14 ......76 E2
Limlow Cl NN4 .....158 E3
Limoges Ct NN5 ...140 A2
Linacre Cl NN5 ....142 F6
Lincoln Cl OX16 ...240 B7
Lincoln Ct Brackley NN13 .233 F5
 Market Harborough LE16 .31 F5
Lincoln Ho NN5 ...159 A5
Lincoln Pk NN13 ...233 F5
Lincoln Rd
 Northampton NN5 ...159 A5
 Stamford PE9 ......241 E5
Lincoln St NN2 ....141 C3
Lincoln Way Corby NN18 ..36 C4
 Daventry NN11 ....153 C8
Lincoln Wlk NN18 ...36 B4
Lindale Cl NN3 .....143 B1
Linden Ave
 Higham Ferrers NN10 ..132 B6
 Kettering NN15,NN16 ..72 D1
Linden Cl NN15 ....72 D1
Linden Rd NN3 ....142 A1
Lindens The NN12 ...203 C6
Lindisfarne Dr NN15 ..91 F8
Lindisfarne Rd NN17 ..21 C1
Lindisfarne Way
 Northampton NN4 ...175 C8
 Thrapston NN14 ......76 F2
Lindrick Cl NN11 ...135 E2
Lindsay Ave NN11 ...142 B2
Lindsay St NN16 .....72 B3
Lindsay Terr NN3 ...142 A2
Lindsey Cl PE8 ......14 F1
Lindsey Gdns LE16 ...48 C8
Lindsey Rd PE9 ....241 E4
Lingfield Terr NN12 ..203 A8
Lingfield Wlk NN18 ...36 C2
Lings Lower Sch NN3 .142 F4
Lings Upper Sch NN3 .142 F2
Lings Way NN3 .....143 A4
Lingswood Pk NN3 ...143 A3
Link La NN14 ....89 B4
Link Rd Northampton NN2 .141 B6
 Rushden NN10 .....148 B7
Link The OX16 .....240 A8
Link Way Bugbrooke NN7 .203 C5
 Towcester NN12 ...203 C5
Links Rd NN6 ......130 C8
Links The NN15 .....91 B8
Linley Dr NN14 ......50 F4
Linley Gn NN5 ....140 A1
Linnell Way NN14 ...71 F4
Linnet Cl NN8 .....130 A7
Linnet Rd NN16 ......92 A6
Linnet Rd NN12 ...203 C3
Linnetts La NN10 ...132 B5
Lipscombe Dr MK18 ..240 E4
Lismore Cl NN3 ....143 C2
Lismore Wlk NN17 ...21 C1
Lister Cl NN17 ......22 A1
Lister Dr NN4 ......158 E1
Lister Rd NN18 ....130 A5
Litchborough Rd
 Farthingstone NN12 ..170 F3
 Grimscote NN12 ...188 A7
Litchfield Cl NN16 ...72 C6
Little Back La NN11 ..153 C3
Little Billing Way NN3 .143 A1
Little Bowden Cty Prim Sch
 LE16 ....31 E5
Little Bowden Manor
 LE16 ....31 F3
Little Casterton Rd PE9 .241 B4
Little Church St CV21 .241 C8
Little Cl Bozeat NN29 ..164 C2
 Chapel Brampton NN6 .124 D1
Little Cross St NN1 ..159 B6
Little Elbow St CV21 .241 C8
Little Field NN14 ....175 F4
Little Field Cl NN12 ..189 A8
Little Greeve Way NN4 .176 A6
Little Gull Cl NN4 ...175 F2
Little Harrowden Com Prim
 Sch NN9 ....110 C4
Little Horton House Dr
 NN7 ....177 E2
Little La Aynho OX17 ..237 C7
Little Lime Kiln NN6 ..160 C2
Little London
 Deanshanger NN19 ...228 E4
 Silverstone NN12 ...214 D5
Little Lime Rd NN18 ...36 B1
Little Park St 6 NN8 ..130 A5

Little Pennington St
 CV21 ....241 B8
Little Priel Rd NN17 ..155 B4
Little St Rushden NN10 .132 C1
 Sulgrave OX17 ....211 A8
 Yardley Hastings NN7 .179 B6
Littledale NN8 ......129 D6
Littlewood Cl NN15 ...159 A8
Littlewood Ct NN14 ...70 F4
Livingstone Cl NN14 ...70 F7
Livingstone Rd NN11 .135 C4
Llewellyn Wlk NN18 ...36 D5
Lloyd Cl NN8 ....130 B8
Lloyd's Rd NN17 .....37 B7
Loach Ct NN3 ......142 A6
Loatland St NN14 ....50 F3
Loatlands Prim Sch
 NN14 ....50 F3
Lobelia Rd NN16 .....72 C4
Lock La NN15 ......218 E2
Lockcroft Sq 6 NN3 ..143 D2
Locks Gn PE8 ......16 A8
Locks The CV21 .....80 B1
Locktons CV11 ....201 E2
Lockwood Cl NN1 ...159 A6
Loddington CE Prim Sch
 NN14 ....70 D1
Loddington Rd NN7 ...89 F7
Loddington Way NN14 ..89 B4
Lodge Ave NN4 ....175 C4
Lodge Cl Banbury OX16 .240 D6
 Little Houghton NN7 ..161 B3
 Rugby CV21 ....241 D9
 Rushden NN10 .....148 A8
Lodge The OX17 ...198 D2
Lodge Way
 Irthlingborough NN9 ..140 C3
 Northampton NN5 ...140 D3
Lodore Gdns NN3 ...142 C3
Logan Cres LE16 ....31 C4
Logan Ct NN15 .....31 D3
Logan St LE16 .....31 D3
Logwell Ct NN3 ....142 F1
Loire Cl NN5 ....140 A2
Lombard Way OX16 ..219 A6
Lombardy Ct NN3 ...142 D3
Lomond Cl NN17 ....21 C1
Lomond Dr NN15 ....91 F8
London End
 Earls Barton NN6 ...144 D4
 Irchester NN29 ....147 B8
 Titchmarsh NN14 ....77 D3
 Upper Boddington NN11 .182 C8
London Rd Bozeat NN29 .164 C3
 Braunston NN11 ...118 A1
 Buckingham MK18 ...240 E1
 Daventry NN11 ....153 D8
 Kettering NN15 ......91 C8
 Little Irchester NN8 ...132 C1
 Northampton,Far Cotton
 NN4 ....159 C2
 Northampton,Wootton
 NN4 ....175 D5
 Old Stratford MK19 ..229 C6
 Raunds NN9 ....114 C6
 Roade NN7 ....191 C4
 Stony Stratford MK11 ..229 E5
 Towcester NN12 ...203 D5
 Wansford PE8 ....3 B2
 Wellingborough NN8 ..130 B3
 Willoughby CV23 ...117 C3
 Wollaston NN29 ...146 D1
Lone Pine Ct NN16 ...106 B2
Long Acre NN7 ....161 D3
Long Acres 8 NN15 ...175 B8
Long Acres Dr NN9 ...112 C3
Long Barrow OX17 ...194 F7
 Chapel Brampton NN6 .124 D1
Long Buckby Inf Sch
 NN6 ....121 B4
Long Buckby Rd NN6 .120 C5
Long Buckby Sta NN6 .121 D3
Long Cl NN13 ....36 B1
Long Croft Rd NN14,NN18 .37 C3
Long Furlong CV22 ...98 A8
Long La Olney MK46 ..195 F4
 Warmington PE8 ......8 B2
Long Mallows Rise 9
 NN3 ....143 C2
Long March NN11 ....
Long March Ind Est
 NN11 ....153 D8
Long Marsh Dr NN18 ..36 B1
Long Marsh Sq NN3 ..143 A6
Long Massey MK46 ...195 F3
Long Mdw NN6 .....176 B6
Long Mynd Dr NN5 ...158 D8

Long Row
Leckhampstead MK18 ... 227 E1
Woodford NN14 ... 94 D7
Long Row Cl NN11 ... 170 A8
Long Street Rd MK19 ... 207 A3
Long Wall NN13 ... 233 E6
Longburges OX17 ... 220 B8
Longcroft La NN12 ... 216 C8
Longdown La CV23 ... 118 B7
Longfellow Dr NN16 ... 72 C6
Longfellow Rd NN8 ... 129 B4
Longford Ave NN3 ... 161 A8
Longland Ct NN3 ... 142 B2
Longland Rd NN3 ... 142 C2
Longleat Cl LE16 ... 32 B3
Longleat Ct 5 NN4 ... 175 C8
Longleat Gr NN15 ... 91 C5
Longmead Ct NN3 ... 143 B4
Longueville Ct NN3 ... 142 E4
Longworth Cl OX16 ... 240 E9
Lonsborough Dr NN15 ... 90 E8
Lonsdale Rd
Kettering NN15 ... 91 B7
Stamford PE9 ... 241 A3
Loop Rd PE28 ... 97 A3
Lord Burghley's Hospl
PE9 ... 241 D2
Lordswood Cl NN4 ... 176 A6
Lorne Ct NN17 ... 36 F6
Lorne Rd NN1 ... 159 C7
Lorraine Cres NN3 ... 142 B5
Lorraine Dr NN3 ... 142 C5
Loseby Cl NN10 ... 148 A8
Lotus Ct NN15 ... 72 B1
Louisa Dr NN16 ... 72 E4
Louisa Lilley Homes The 7
NN9 ... 112 F2
Louisberg Cl 4 NN4 ... 175 E7
Louise Rd NN1 ... 159 D7
Lounts Cres LE16 ... 20 D7
Lovap Way NN18 ... 36 B1
Lovat Dr NN5 ... 158 E7
Lovell Cl NN9 ... 114 A4
Lovell Ct 12 NN9 ... 112 F2
Lovers La PE5 ... 8 F2
Lovett Rd NN11 ... 183 D8
Low Farm Pl NN3 ... 141 F7
Low Greeve NN4 ... 176 A6
Low March NN11 ... 153 D7
Lowbury Ct NN4 ... 158 E3
Lower Adelaide St NN2 ... 159 C7
Lower Bath St NN1 ... 159 B6
Lower Cherwell St
OX16 ... 240 D7
Lower Cross St NN1 ... 159 B6
Lower Ecton La NN3 ... 143 D1
Lower End Bradden NN12 ... 201 F5
Hartwell NN7 ... 192 C1
Pytchley NN14 ... 91 A1
Lower Farm Rd NN3 ... 141 F7
Lower Harding St 11
NN1 ... 159 C6
Lower Hester St NN2 ... 159 C8
Lower Hillmorton Rd
CV21 ... 241 F7
Lower Hilmorton Rd 5
CV21 ... 80 A1
Lower King St NN14 ... 51 B3
Lower Meadow Ct NN3 ... 142 E5
Lower Mounts NN1 ... 159 D6
Lower Pastures NN18 ... 53 A8
Lower Priory St NN1 ... 159 B7
Lower Rd
Milton Malsor NN7 ... 174 E4
Stoke Albany LE16 ... 34 B5
Lower St
Desborough NN14 ... 51 A3
Great Addington NN14 ... 94 B2
Great Doddington NN29 ... 145 E6
Kettering NN16 ... 72 A2
Pury End NN12 ... 216 A7
Rugby CV21 ... 99 C8
Twywell NN14 ... 75 A1
Willoughby CV23 ... 117 D4
Lower Stable Yd NN12 ... 203 D5
Lower Steeping NN14 ... 51 B2
Lower Thrift St NN1 ... 159 F6
Lower Weald MK19 ... 229 E2
Lower Wharf MK18 ... 240 E4
Lowick Cl NN8 ... 129 D7
Lowick Ct NN3 ... 142 C7
Lowick La NN14 ... 76 F7
Lowick Rd Aldwincle NN14 ... 76 E7
Islip NN14 ... 76 B3
Lowlands Cl NN3 ... 143 C5
Lowry Cl NN8 ... 129 E7
Loxton Cl NN5 ... 140 C1
Loyd Rd NN1 ... 160 A6
Lubenham All Saints CE Prim
Sch LE16 ... 30 F3
Lubenham Hill LE16 ... 31 C2
Lubenham Rd
East Farndon LE16 ... 31 B1
Marston Trussell LE16 ... 30 D1
Lucas Cl NN9 ... 131 E8
Lucas Ct CV21 ... 241 D9
Lucas La NN7 ... 177 B3
Lucas Rd NN6 ... 121 A3
Lucky La OX16 ... 240 C7
Luddington Rd PE8,PE17 ... 61 C3
Ludlow Cl NN3 ... 143 A7
Luffenham Cl PE9 ... 241 A3
Luffenham Rd LE15 ... 3 F6
Lukes Cl NN13 ... 212 A5
Lulworth Wlk NN18 ... 36 A6
Lumber La NN12 ... 216 B7
Lumbertubs La NN3 ... 142 D5
Lumbertubs Lower Sch
NN3 ... 142 F3
Lumbertubs Rise NN3 ... 142 D5
Lumbertubs Way NN3 ... 142 E3
Lunchfield Ct NN3 ... 126 C1
Lunchfield Gdns NN3 ... 126 C1
Lunchfield La NN3 ... 126 C1
Lunchfield Wlk 7 NN3 ... 126 C1
Lundie Cl NN9 ... 114 D7
Lundy Ave NN18 ... 36 E4
Lupin Cl NN16 ... 72 D4
Lutterworth Rd
Northampton NN1 ... 160 A6
Swinford LE17 ... 62 B6
Lutton Rd PE8 ... 43 C3
Lyddington Rd
Caldecott LE15, L16 ... 9 D2
Gretton NN17 ... 10 A1
Lydia Ct NN10 ... 132 A2
Lyle Ct NN8 ... 129 C7
Lyncrest Ave NN5 ... 158 E7
Lyncrest Lower Sch
NN5 ... 158 E7
Lyncroft Way NN2 ... 141 B1
Lyndhurst Rd CV21 ... 98 F8
Lyndon Way PE9 ... 241 A3
Lyne Wlk NN7 ... 177 B3
Lyneford Way NN10 ... 147 F8
Lynmore Cl NN4 ... 158 C1
Lynmouth Ave NN3 ... 160 C7
Lynmouth Pl NN18 ... 36 E4
Lynton Ave NN2 ... 141 C6
Lynton Gr NN18 ... 36 F4
Lynwood Cl NN16 ... 72 B5
Lytham Cl NN2 ... 141 E3
Lytham Ct NN8 ... 129 C7
Lytham Rd CV22 ... 241 A6
Lyttleton Rd NN5 ... 159 A7
Lyveden New Bield*
PE8 ... 57 A7
Lyveden Pl NN16 ... 72 D3
Lyveden Rd
Brigstock NN14 ... 55 F7
Northampton NN4 ... 160 A1
Lyveden Way NN18 ... 36 C2

M

Macadam Cl NN11 ... 134 F5
Macadam Rd NN17 ... 22 A1
Mackenzie Rd NN9 ... 114 C5
Mackintosh Ct NN15 ... 92 B1
Mackworth Dr NN9 ... 111 E4
Mackworth Gn NN9 ... 111 F4
Maclean Cl NN3 ... 160 C7
Macmillian Way NN3 ... 142 B4
Macon Cl NN5 ... 139 F2
Madams Gdn NN14 ... 70 D7
Madams Hill NN14 ... 70 D7
Madeline Cl LE16 ... 32 A5
Magdalen Cl
Daventry NN11 ... 153 B8
Stony Stratford MK11 ... 229 D6
Syresham NN13 ... 224 C8
Magdalen Ho MK11 ... 229 D6
Magdalen Mdws NN13 ... 222 E1
Magdalen Rd CV23 ... 117 E3
Magdalene Cl NN14 ... 54 B3
Magee St NN1 ... 159 F7
Magellan Cl
Daventry NN11 ... 135 C5
Rothwell NN14 ... 70 E6
Magnolia Cl NN3 ... 160 D6
Magnolia Dr
Daventry NN11 ... 135 C4
Rushden NN10 ... 148 B7
Magpie La NN13 ... 233 E6
Magpie Rd
Sulgrave OX17 ... 210 E7
Towcester NN12 ... 203 C3
Maida Cl NN4 ... 175 E7
Maiden La PE9 ... 241 E3
Maidencastle NN3 ... 143 B3
Maidford Rd Corby NN17 ... 36 C7
Farthingstone NN12 ... 170 D1
Maidwell Hall (Prep Sch for
Boys) NN6 ... 87 B6
Maidwell Prim Sch NN6 ... 87 B6
Maidwell Rd NN6 ... 87 D7
Main Dr NN12 ... 217 B2
Main Rd Collyweston PE9 ... 1 D2
Crick NN6 ... 100 F5
Dingley LE16 ... 32 F3
Earls Barton NN6 ... 144 D6
Farthinghoe NN13 ... 221 B4
Grendon NN7 ... 163 D6
Kilsby CV23 ... 99 F3
Middleton Cheney OX17 ... 220 A8
New Hackleton NN7 ... 177 B3
Northampton, Duston NN5 ... 158 B7
Northampton,Far cotton
NN4 ... 159 B3
Shutlanger NN12 ... 204 D8
Syresham NN13 ... 224 C7
Upper Heyford NN7 ... 156 D4
Wilby NN8 ... 129 B1
Main St Abthorpe NN12 ... 201 F2
Aldwincle NN14 ... 76 F8
Apethorpe PE8 ... 14 C4
Ashby St L CV23 ... 119 C5
Ashley LE16 ... 18 F2
Aston le W NN11 ... 182 F2
Badby NN11 ... 152 F2
Barnwell PE8 ... 59 B5
Barrowden LE15 ... 3 F5
Main St *continued*
Bradden NN12 ... 201 F5
Bythorn PE28 ... 97 D4
Caldecott LE16 ... 21 B8
Charlton OX17 ... 231 F4
Church Stowe NN7 ... 171 E8
Claydon OX17 ... 181 D1
Clifton u D CV23 ... 80 A5
Cold Ashby NN6 ... 84 B5
Cosgrove MK19 ... 218 E2
Cottesbrooke NN6 ... 105 A8
Denton NN7 ... 162 B1
Drayton LE16 ... 20 A5
East Farndon LE16 ... 48 B7
East Haddon NN6 ... 122 D5
Farthingstone NN12 ... 170 E3
Great Addington NN14 ... 94 B2
Great Bowden LE16 ... 32 A6
Great Brington NN7 ... 138 D7
Great Gidding PE17 ... 61 D3
Great Oxendon LE16 ... 48 E3
Gumley LE16 ... 30 A8
Hannington NN6 ... 108 C3
Hellidon NN11 ... 151 D1
Holcot NN6 ... 126 E8
Little Brington NN7 ... 138 C4
Little Harrowden NN9 ... 110 C4
Loddington NN14 ... 70 C1
Lowick NN14 ... 75 F6
Lubenham LE16 ... 30 F3
Lyddington LE15 ... 9 A7
Lyddington LE15 ... 9 C7
Mawsley Village NN14 ... 89 B4
Medbourne LE16 ... 19 A7
Middleton LE16 ... 35 C8
Orton NN14 ... 70 A3
Polebrook PE8 ... 43 A3
Rockingham LE16 ... 21 B4
Slipton NN14 ... 75 A3
Southwick PE8 ... 26 B5
Sutton Bassett LE16 ... 18 A1
Tansor PE8 ... 27 D2
Theddingworth LE17 ... 46 D8
Thorpe by Water LE15 ... 10 A5
Thurning PE8 ... 60 D3
Turweston NN13 ... 234 C8
Upper Stowe NN7 ... 171 F6
Wadenhoe PE8 ... 58 A4
Wakerley LE15 ... 4 A4
Watford NN6 ... 120 C6
Willoughby CV23 ... 117 E3
Woodend NN12 ... 200 F7
Woodnewton PE8 ... 14 E1
Yarwell PE8 ... 15 F8
Maine Cl MK18 ... 240 D2
Malabar Fields NN11 ... 153 B8
Malborough Way NN12 ... 217 F5
Malcolm Ct NN17 ... 36 F6
Malcolm Dr NN5 ... 158 E7
Malcolm Rd NN2 ... 141 F2
Malcolm Sargent Prim Sch
PE9 ... 241 A3
Malcolm Terr NN2 ... 141 F2
Malham Ct NN8 ... 129 D6
Mall The NN16 ... 72 B2
Mallard Cl
Earls Barton NN6 ... 144 F5
Higham Ferrers NN10 ... 132 C8
Northampton NN4 ... 158 F2
Thrapston NN14 ... 76 D3
Mallard Ct PE9 ... 241 D2
Mallard Dr
Buckingham MK18 ... 240 E3
Burton Latimer NN15 ... 92 A2
Hinton NN11 ... 184 B6
Mallery Cl NN10 ... 132 D3
Malletts Cl MK11 ... 229 E5
Mallory Way NN11 ... 135 C5
Mallory Wlk NN3 ... 141 F5
Mallows Dr NN9 ... 114 C7
Malmo Cl NN18 ... 36 A2
Malpas Dr NN5 ... 158 B8
Malt La NN13 ... 224 C8
Malt Mill Cl CV23 ... 100 A2
Malt Mill Gn CV23 ... 100 A2
Malthouse Cl NN9 ... 112 F2
Malthouse Ct NN12 ... 203 C6
Malting La NN14 ... 54 A3
Malting Way NN7 ... 192 D1
Malting Yd PE9 ... 241 E2
Maltings PE8 ... 42 A6
Maltings Rd NN17 ... 10 B1
Maltings The Ashley LE16 ... 18 F3
Rothwell NN14 ... 70 C7
Wollaston NN29 ... 146 D3
Wothorpe PE9 ... 2 E8
Malton Wlk NN18 ... 36 B5
Malvern Ave CV22 ... 241 F6
Malvern Cl Kettering NN16 ... 72 B7
Wellingborough NN8 ... 129 D1
Malvern Dr MK11 ... 229 F4
Malvern Gr NN5 ... 158 D8
Malzor La NN7 ... 174 E4
Manchester Rd NN29 ... 146 C3
Manfield Health Campus
NN3 ... 142 B4
Manfield Rd NN1 ... 160 A7
Manfield Way NN3 ... 142 B4
Manitoba Cl NN18 ... 36 B3
Manitoba Pl NN11 ... 184 C1
Manitoba Way NN11 ... 184 C1
Manning Ct NN3 ... 142 C7
Manning Rd NN3 ... 142 C7
Manning St NN10 ... 132 C1
Manning Wlk CV21 ... 241 C8
Manningham Rd NN9 ... 114 A4
Mannings Rise NN10 ... 132 C1
Mannington Gdns NN4 ... 175 C7
Mannock Rd NN8 ... 129 E3
Manor Cl Bozeat NN29 ... 164 D3
Charwelton NN11 ... 168 A4
Cosgrove MK19 ... 218 E2
Great Addington NN14 ... 94 B2
Great Harrowden NN9 ... 110 D2
Hanslope MK19 ... 207 A2
Harpole NN7 ... 157 C6
Hinton NN11 ... 184 B7
Irchester NN29 ... 147 B8
Isham NN14 ... 110 F8
Middleton Cheney OX17 ... 220 B7
Roade NN7 ... 191 E4
Sulgrave OX17 ... 210 F8
Thrapston NN14 ... 76 D2
Manor Ct Banbury OX16 ... 240 E9
Brackley NN13 ... 233 F8
Cottingham LE16 ... 20 C1
Grendon NN7 ... 163 D5
Little Harrowden NN9 ... 110 C4
Northampton NN2 ... 141 B3
Rushden NN10 ... 148 C8
2 Wellingborough NN8 ... 130 B5
Manor Dr Corby NN18 ... 36 A4
Irthlingborough NN9 ... 113 A2
Manor Farm PE8 ... 14 C4
Manor Farm Cl
Barby CV23 ... 99 C2
Broughton NN14 ... 90 B4
Walgrave NN6 ... 108 A5
Manor Farm Cotts
NN13 ... 238 C8
Manor Farm Ct
Cogenhoe NN7 ... 162 A6
Titchmarsh NN14 ... 77 C4
Manor Farm Rd
Northampton NN3 ... 143 B2
Raunds NN9 ... 114 E6
Manor Gdns
Farthingstone NN12 ... 170 F3
Norton NN11 ... 136 C4
Pytchley NN14 ... 90 F2
Stanwick NN9 ... 114 A3
Manor Ho The NN14 ... 76 D2
Manor House Cl NN6 ... 144 E5
Manor House Gdns
NN9 ... 114 D6
Manor House Mus*
NN16 ... 72 B1
Manor La Clifton u D CV23 ... 80 A5
Farthinghoe NN13 ... 221 B4
Newnham NN11 ... 153 E4
Whilton NN11 ... 137 D6
Wymington NN10 ... 148 A5
Manor Pk Claydon OX17 ... 181 D1
Nether Heyford NN7 ... 156 C2
Manor Pl NN15 ... 91 B8
Manor Rd Banbury OX16 ... 240 E9
Brackley NN13 ... 233 E7
Daventry NN11 ... 135 D1
Earls Barton NN6 ... 144 E5
Great Bowden LE16 ... 32 A6
Grendon NN7 ... 163 D5
Grimscote NN12 ... 188 A8
Hanging Houghton NN6 ... 106 C8
Hinton NN11 ... 184 B6
Kilsby CV23 ... 100 A3
Mears Ashby NN6 ... 128 B2
Medbourne LE16 ... 19 A7
Moulton NN3 ... 142 C8
Northampton NN2 ... 141 B3
Pitsford NN6 ... 125 D5
Rothwell NN14 ... 70 B7
Rugby CV21 ... 241 D9
Rushden NN10 ... 148 B8
Rushton NN14 ... 52 C2
Spratton NN6 ... 105 B1
Stanion NN14 ... 37 E2
Staverton NN11 ... 152 B7
Sulgrave OX17 ... 210 F8
Sutton PE5 ... 8 F2
Weedon NN7 ... 155 B3
Manor St
Buckingham MK18 ... 240 C3
Raunds NN9 ... 114 D6
Manor The NN11 ... 199 C7
Manor View PE9 ... 1 A6
Manor Way
Higham Ferrers NN10 ... 132 C5
Yardley Gobion NN12 ... 217 E6
Manor Wlk
Hanging Houghton NN6 ... 106 C8
Market Harborough LE16 ... 31 E3
Nether Heyford NN7 ... 156 C2
Manorfield Cl NN3 ... 161 B8
Manorfield Rd NN3 ... 161 B8
Manorfields Rd MK19 ... 229 B6
Mansard Cl NN5 ... 158 E6
Manse Cl MK11 ... 229 D6
Mansefield Cl NN14 ... 51 A3
Mansel Cl MK19 ... 218 D2
Mansell Cl NN12 ... 203 C8
Mansfield Ct NN12 ... 202 D8
Mansfield St NN9 ... 113 F4
Manshead Ct MK11 ... 229 F5
Mansion Cl NN3 ... 142 A6
Mansion Hill OX17 ... 219 F8
Mantlefield Rd NN18 ... 36 B6
Manton Ct NN10 ... 132 C2
Manton Rd Corby NN17 ... 22 A2
Irthlingborough NN9 ... 112 E2
Rushden NN10 ... 132 C1
Manton Spinney NN10 ... 131 E2
Maple Cl Brackley NN13 ... 222 F1
Braunston NN11 ... 118 D1
Bugbrooke NN7 ... 172 F7
Hinton NN11 ... 184 A6
Towcester NN12 ... 203 B4
Maple Ct NN17 ... 21 E1
Maple Dr NN8 ... 129 E5
Maple Fields Sch NN18 ... 36 D5
Maple Gr CV21 ... 241 C9
Maple Rd Kettering NN16 ... 72 D4
Rushden NN10 ... 132 C2
Maple Wood NN10 ... 148 B7
Maples The NN11 ... 135 D1
Mapletoft St NN9 ... 114 C5
Mapperley Dr NN3 ... 160 F8
March Edge MK18 ... 240 E4
Marchwood Cl NN3 ... 142 F6
Marconi Ctyd NN17 ... 22 B1
Mare Fair NN1 ... 159 C5
Mare Leys MK18 ... 240 F3
Marecroft LE16 ... 66 F7
Margaret Ave NN8 ... 129 E2
Margaret Cl OX16 ... 240 A7
Margaret Rd
Kettering NN16 ... 72 E3
Twyford OX17 ... 230 B5
Margaret St NN1 ... 159 D7
Marion Sq NN16 ... 72 E3
Maritime Way NN11 ... 135 E1
Marjoram Cl 6 NN4 ... 175 D6
Market Cross NN9 ... 112 F2
Market Harborough CE Prim
Sch LE16 ... 31 D3
Market Harborough District
Hospl LE16 ... 31 D3
Market Harborough Mus*
LE16 ... 31 E3
Market Harborough Sta
LE16 ... 32 A3
Market Hill
Buckingham MK18 ... 240 D4
Rothwell NN14 ... 70 D7
Market Mall CV21 ... 241 C8
Market Pl Banbury OX16 ... 240 D8
Brackley NN13 ... 233 E6
Kettering NN16 ... 72 B1
Long Buckby NN6 ... 121 B4
Olney MK46 ... 195 F3
Oundle PE8 ... 42 A5
Rugby CV21 ... 241 C8
Market Rd NN14 ... 76 D2
Market Sq
Buckingham MK18 ... 240 D4
3 Daventry NN11 ... 135 C2
Hanslope MK19 ... 207 A2
Higham Ferrers NN10 ... 132 C6
Northampton NN1 ... 159 C6
Stony Stratford MK11 ... 229 D5
3 Wellingborough NN8 ... 130 A4
Market St Kettering NN16 ... 72 B2
Northampton NN1 ... 159 E7
Rugby CV21 ... 241 D9
Wellingborough NN8 ... 130 A4
Market Street Mews 10
NN16 ... 72 B2
Market Wlk NN1 ... 159 E7
Markham Cl NN5 ... 140 C1
Markham Ret Pk PE9 ... 241 F5
Markham Wlk NN18 ... 36 B5
Markhams Cl MK18 ... 240 D3
Marks Cl NN9 ... 114 A3
Marlborough Ave NN8 ... 129 D7
Marlborough Cl
Kettering NN15 ... 72 F1
Kings Sutton OX17 ... 230 F6
Marlborough Croft
NN13 ... 233 F6
Marlborough Pl OX16 ... 240 C7
Marlborough Rd
Banbury OX16 ... 240 D7
Northampton NN5 ... 159 A6
Marlborough Way LE16 ... 31 E5
Marley Ind Est OX16 ... 240 D9
Marley Way OX16 ... 240 C9
Marlow Cl NN11 ... 135 B1
Marlow Ct Corby NN18 ... 36 B5
Medbourne LE16 ... 19 A8
Marlow Rd NN12 ... 203 D5
Marlowe Cl NN4 ... 175 B7
Marlstones NN4 ... 158 D2
Marnock Sq 3 NN4 ... 158 F2
Marquee Dr NN3 ... 160 F7
Marriots Rd NN6 ... 121 C3
Marriott Cl NN9 ... 131 E8
Marriott St NN2 ... 159 C8
Marseilles Cl NN5 ... 139 F1
Marsh Cl NN6 ... 101 A5
Marsh La NN9 ... 113 A2
Marsh The NN6 ... 101 A5
Marshall Ct 2 LE16 ... 31 F2
Marshall's Rd NN9 ... 114 C6
Marshleys Ct NN3 ... 143 B5
Marshwell Ct 5 NN3 ... 161 A8
Marsons Dr NN6 ... 100 F5
Marston Hill
Marston St Lawrence
OX17 ... 210 B3
Priors Marston CV47 ... 166 E7
Marston Rd
Greatworth OX17 ... 210 E2
Lubenham LE16 ... 30 D2
Marston Trussell Rd
LE16 ... 47 F7
Marston Way NN11 ... 135 D6
Martel Cl NN5 ... 157 F8
Martha Wallis Ct 1
NN16 ... 72 B2
Martial Daire Bvd NN13 ... 233 E8
Martin Cl
Buckingham MK18 ... 240 F2
Rushden NN10 ... 132 B4
Martin Rd NN15 ... 91 C7
Martindale NN2 ... 140 F5

Martins La NN4 ....175 E8
Martins Rd NN7 ....177 A1
Martins Yd NN15 ....159 B7
Martlet CI NN4 ....175 E5
Marwood CI NN4 ....160 C7
Mary Macmanus Dr
MK18 ....240 D4
Mascord CI OX16 ....240 A7
Mascord Rd OX16 ....240 A7
Masefield CI NN8 ....129 C4
Masefield Dr NN10 ....131 E3
Masefield Rd NN16 ....72 C5
Masefield Way
Corby NN11 ....36 D8
Northampton NN2 ....141 E2
Mason CI Oundle PE8 ......42 A5
Thrapston NN14 ....76 D1
Massey CI NN4 ....175 E8
Masterton CI PE9 ....241 E5
Masterton Rd PE2 ....241 E5
Matchless CI NN5 ....140 A1
Matlock Way NN14 ....50 E4
Matson CI NN14 ....70 B6
Matson CI NN9 ....114 E7
Matthews CI NN14 ....53 C3
Mauduit CI MK19 ....207 A3
Maunsell Rise NN14 ....70 B6
Mauntley Ave NN14 ....55 F7
Maurice Rd LE16 ....48 D8
Mawsley La NN14 ....89 C8
Maxwell Wlk NN18 ....36 E5
May CI NN10 ....148 C7
Maybank NN11 ....153 B8
Maybush Wlk MK46 ....195 E5
Mayfield Rd
Daventry NN11 ....135 C3
Desborough NN14 ....51 C3
Northampton NN3 ....142 B3
Maylan Rd NN17 ....21 F3
Mays Way NN12 ....217 D3
Mazewood Gate PE8 ....13 F7
McGibbon Wlk NN9 ....131 D8
McInnes Way NN9 ....114 D7
Mckeevor PI OX16 ....240 E8
McKenzie CI MK18 ....240 D3
Mdw The NN3 ....142 C1
Meacham CI NN14 ....90 A3
Mead Rd NN15 ....90 F8
Meadow CI
Daventry NN11 ....135 D6
Higham Ferrers NN10 ......132 B6
Market Harborough LE16 ...31 F4
Northampton NN5 ....140 B2
Ringstead NN9 ....95 A3
Wellingborough NN8 ......130 D8
Meadow Ct
Kettering NN16 ....72 B2
Ravenstone MK46 ....194 D2
Towcester NN12 ....203 C5
Meadow Dr NN10 ....132 B6
Meadow Farm CI NN7 .....155 F5
Meadow Gate PE8 ....14 E2
Meadow Gdns MK18 ......240 E1
Meadow La Denford NN14 .95 C6
Little Houghton NN7 ....161 A4
Raunds NN9 ....114 A6
Thornhaugh PE8 ....7 F5
Meadow Rd
Kettering NN16 ....72 A2
Rothwell NN14 ....70 C6
Meadow Rise NN12 ....189 D4
Meadow Row NN18 ....240 D4
Meadow St LE16 ....31 E4
Meadow Sweet Rd
NN10 ....148 C7
Meadow View
Adderbury OX17 ....230 A4
Banbury OX16 ....240 E6
Great Addington NN14 ....94 C3
Higham Ferrers NN10 .....132 A6
Pottersbury NN12 ....217 D3
Meadow Way NN10 ....112 F1
Meadow Wlk
Buckingham MK18 ....240 D4
Higham Ferrers NN10 .....132 B6
Irthlingborough NN9 ....112 F2
Meadowdale Prim Sch
LE16 ....32 B4
Meadowlands NN9 ....110 B3
Meadows The
Northampton NN4 ....175 F2
Wellingborough NN8 ......110 E1
Meadowside Inf Sch
NN15 ....92 B2
Meadowside Jun Sch
NN15 ....92 B2
Meadowswett Wlk NN4 ...175 F2
Meadowvale NN9 ....112 E1
Meads CI NN15 ....92 B1
Meadslade NN7 ....192 D2
Meadway
Buckingham MK18 ....240 D1
Bugbrooke NN7 ....172 F2
Northampton NN10 ....160 D8
Meadway CI NN15 ....91 D8
Mears Ashby Prim Sch
NN6 ....128 B2
Mears Ashby Rd
Earls Barton NN6 ....144 C6
Wilby NN8 ....129 C1
Medbourne CI NN3 ....142 B7
Medbourne Rd
Ashley LE16 ....31 F8
Drayton LE16 ....19 E4
Medbourne LE16 ....31 D6
Medelin Hill NN3 ....142 F6
Medina Rd NN17 ....21 C1
Medinah NN4 ....175 D5

Medlicott CI NN18 ....53 A8
Medway CI
Market Harborough LE16 ..32 A3
Northampton NN5 ....140 A2
Medway Ho PE8 ....42 A6
Medway The NN11 ....135 A1
Medwin NN8 ....129 C4
Meeting La
Burton Latimer NN15 ......92 C2
Corby NN17 ....37 B7
Irthlingborough NN9 ....112 F2
 Kettering NN16 ....72 B2
Northampton NN5 ....158 C7
Rothwell NN14 ....70 C6
Towcester NN12 ....203 C6
Meissen Ave NN14 ....50 F3
Melbourne Ho
Corby NN12 ....22 F1
 Northampton NN5 ....159 A6
Melbourne Rd NN4 ....149 F7
Melchester CI NN4 ....175 E7
Meldon CI NN4 ....175 C8
Mellish CI CV22 ....241 A6
Mellish Rd CV22 ....241 A6
Mellor Rd CV21 ....99 B8
Melloway Rd NN10 ....131 E2
Melrose Ave NN5 ....158 C7
Melrose Ct Kettering NN15 .91 F8
Stamford PE9 ....241 A4
Meltham CI NN13 ....142 F1
Melton Rd NN8 ....130 C5
Melton Rd N NN8 ....130 B5
Melton St NN16 ....72 B3
Melville CI CV22 ....241 A6
Melville St NN1 ....159 F7
Membris Way NN11 ....184 A6
Memorial Gn NN7 ....191 E4
Mendip CI NN16 ....72 B5
Mendip Ct NN11 ....135 B5
Mendip Rd NN5 ....158 D7
Meon CI NN4 ....21 C1
Meon Way NN5 ....158 D8
Mercer CI CV22 ....98 F8
Mercer's Row NN1 ....159 C5
Mercia Gdns NN3 ....142 C1
Mercury Cl NN11 ....135 A4
Mercury Dr NN4 ....160 A2
Mere CI
Brafield-on-t-G NN7 ....160 F2
 Northampton NN4 ....175 B8
Mere Farm Bsns Units
Mere Way NN4 ....175 C8
Merefields NN7 ....175 B8
Merestone Hos OX17 ......210 B1
Merestone Rd NN18 ......36 D3
Mereway Lower Sch
NN4 ....159 C1
Mereway Mid Sch NN4 ...175 C8
Mereway Upper Sch
NN4 ....159 B1
Merlin Gr NN4 ....175 B8
Merrivale CI NN15 ....90 F7
Merry Tom La NN6 ....124 D4
Merrycot La NN6 ....82 B4
Merryfield Sq NN13 ....143 A6
Merryhill NN4 ....158 E2
Mersey CI NN4 ....159 A2
Mersey Gn NN17 ....21 C1
Mershe CI NN4 ....175 F7
Merthyr Rd NN5 ....159 A8
Merton CI NN13 ....233 D8
Merton Rd NN11 ....153 B7
Merton St NN16 ....240 E8
Mertens Dr CV22 ....241 B7
Mescalero NN2 ....141 C4
Meshaw Cres NN3 ....160 B7
Methodist Homestead
NN2 ....141 E1
Mewburn Rd OX16 ....240 B7
Mews Cotts LE16 ....48 E3
Mews The Brixworth NN6 .106 B2
Brockhall NN13 ....137 C2
Great Bowden LE16 ....31 E7
Long Buckby NN6 ....121 B4
Northampton NN3 ....160 D8
 Rugby CV21 ....80 A1
Mickle Hill PE18 ....116 D7
Mickleborough CI LE16 ...18 B3
Micklewell La NN3 ....142 F6
Middle Grass NN9 ....112 E3
Middle Greeve NN4 ....176 A6
Middle La LE16 ....34 B4
Middle March NN11 ....153 D8
Middle St Elton PE8 ....28 D8
Foxton LE16 ....30 E8
Isham NN14 ....110 F8
Kilsby CV23 ....100 A3
Nether Heyford NN7 ......156 C4
Middle Weald MK19 ......229 E1
Middledale Rd LE16 ....34 B4
Middlefield CI NN18 ......240 F4
Middlemarch NN13 .....143 B4
Middlemead Ct NN3 ......143 A1
Middlemore NN3 ....142 F6
Middlethorpe NN12 ......200 B2

Middleton Cheney Com Prim
Sch OX17 ....219 F8
Middleton CI
Banbury OX16 ....219 A7
Northampton NN2 ....141 C5
Middleton Rd Ashley LE16 ..19 B3
Banbury OX16 ....219 A7
Banbury OX16, OX17 .....240 F9
Bringhurst LE16 ....20 C4
Chacombe OX17 ....208 E4
Middlewell Ct NN2 ....142 F1
Middlewich CI NN11 ......135 C6
Midfield Ct NN3 ....142 E5
Midland Cotts CV NN10 ..132 C6
Midland Bsns Units
NN8 ....130 C6
Midland Cotts NN14 ......52 C3
Midland Rd
Higham Ferrers NN10 .....132 C6
Olney MK46 ....195 F5
Raunds NN9 ....114 E7
Rushden NN10 ....132 A3
Thrapston NN14 ....76 C1
Wellingborough NN8 ......130 B4
Midland Works Bsns Ctr
Midland Rd NN8 ....
Midway OX17 ....209 A1
Milbury NN6 ....144 F3
Milby La NN14 ....54 A2
Mildmay CI PE8 ....41 E5
Mile St NN29 ....164 D3
Miles CI NN9 ....114 B5
Miles La NN6 ....121 C4
Miles Well Ct NN3 ....142 D3
Milford Ave MK11 ....229 E4
Military Rd NN1 ....159 D7
Military Road Lower Sch
NN1 ....
Militia CI NN4 ....175 E7
Milking Slade Rd PE17 ...61 F3
Mill CI Braunston NN11 ..118 B1
Corby NN18 ....36 B1
Raunds NN9 ....114 C6
Mill Dale Rd NN15 ....91 D8
Mill End NN10 ....148 B7
Mill Fields NN10 ....132 B7
Mill Hill Corby NN18 ......53 B7
Rushden NN10 ....148 B7
Mill Hill Rd LE16 ....31 F3
Mill Ho Brackley NN13 ...223 E5
Buckingham MK18 ....240 C3
 Northampton NN2 ......159 C7
Mill La Adderbury OX17 ..230 A3
Barrowden LE15 ....4 A5
Brackley NN13 ....234 A6
Brigstock NN14 ....55 F7
Buckingham MK18 ....240 C3
Caldecott LE16 ....44 E5
Chipping Warden OX17 ...196 F6
Cogenhoe NN7 ....162 A7
Croughton NN13 ....238 C7
Greens Norton NN12 .....202 E7
Grimscote NN12 ....172 B1
Isham NN14 ....91 F1
Islip NN14 ....76 C3
Ketton PE9 ....1 A5
Kings Sutton OX17 ....230 F4
Kislingbury NN7 ....157 D3
Lowick NN14 ....76 C4
Northampton NN2 ....159 C7
Northampton,Kingsthorpe
NN5 ....141 B2
Old NN6 ....88 E3
Oundle PE8 ....27 B1
Stoke Bruerne NN12 .....191 A1
Stony Stratford MK11 ....229 D5
Wadenhoe PE8 ....58 A3
Westbury NN13 ....234 F4
Mill Mdw NN2 ....141 D5
Mill Park Reserve*
NN6 ....121 A4
Mill Rd Bozeat NN29 .....164 C2
Cottingham LE16 ....20 C2
Great Gidding PE17 ......61 E3
Gretton LE15, NN17 ......9 F2
Irthlingborough NN9 ......131 B7
Islip NN14 ....76 B3
Kettering NN16 ....72 C2
Kislingbury NN7 ....157 D3
Northampton NN2 ....159 C7
Oundle PE8 ....41 F4
Rugby CV21 ....241 E9
Ryhall PE9 ....230 B5
Whitfield NN13 ....223 E4
Woodford NN14 ....94 C7
Yarwell PE8 ....16 A7
Mill Road Pas NN16 ....72 C2
Mill St PE9 ....5 B6
Millais Rd NN18 ....36 E5
Millbank NN3 ....143 D2
Millbrook Jun & Inf Schs
NN15 ....91 F8
Milldale Gdns NN15 ......91 F8
Millenium CI NN15 ....91 A7
Millennium Way NN11 ...135 C2
Thrapston NN14 ....76 E1
Miller Hill NN4 ....158 E2
Miller Rd Banbury OX16 ..240 A8
Burton Latimer NN15 .....92 B1
Miller St NN9 ....114 D7
Millers CI Finedon NN9 ..112 A5
Kislingbury NN7 ....157 D3
Miller's Yd LE16 ....31 E3
Millers CI
Lower Boddington NN11 ..182 C5

Millers CI continued
Rushden NN10 ....131 F2
Millers Gdns LE16 ....31 B2
Millers La NN8 ....145 F8
Millers Pk NN8 ....130 A1
Millers Way NN4 ....175 F3
Millfield Ave LE16 ....20 D1
Millfields Ave CV21 ....98 F8
Millgate The NN14 ....91 F1
Millholm Rd NN14 ....51 B2
Mills CI NN6 ....144 F4
Millside CI NN2 ....141 D5
Millstone CI NN4 ....158 D2
Millway NN5 ....158 C6
Millway St Sch NN5 ......158 D6
Millwood Way PE8 ....13 F7
Millwright CI OX16 ....240 B8
Milner Rd NN9 ....111 F4
Milngate The NN14 ....200 B2
Milton Ave NN8 ....129 C3
Milton Bridge NN4 ....176 A6
Milton CI Kettering NN16 .72 C5
Milton Malsor NN7 ....174 E3
Milton Parochial Prim Sch
NN7 ....174 E4
Milton CI Corby NN17 .....36 C8
Daventry NN11 ....135 B2
Gayton NN7 ....173 F2
Little Irchester NN8 ......130 C1
Oundle PE8 ....41 F5
Milton St Banbury OX16 ..240 C7
Higham Ferrers NN10 ....132 B5
Northampton NN2 ....141 F1
Milton St N NN2 ....141 E1
Milton Terr PE8 ....44 C4
Milverton Cres NN3 ......160 D7
Mimosa CI NN3 ....160 C6
Minden CI NN18 ....35 F2
Minehead CI NN18 ....36 A2
Minerva Way NN8 ....130 A4
Minshull CI MK18 ....240 D4
Minster Ho NN1 ......159 D6
Minton CI NN14 ....50 F3
Mirfield CI NN18 ....36 B1
Mistletoe PI NN3 ....142 C1
Mitchell CI NN5 ....140 D2
Mitchell Rd NN17 ....22 B2
Mitchell St NN16 ....72 C5
Mitchison CI CV23 ....118 C8
Mitre CI MK18 ....240 C2
Mitre Ct MK18 ....240 C2
Mitre Way NN18 ....233 F2
Moat Farm Dr CV21 ......99 A7
Moat La NN12 ....203 C6
Moat PI NN1 ....159 B6
Moat Yd NN12 ....203 C6
Mobbs Millen Ho NN1 ...160 A7
Moffatt Terr NN8 ....130 A5
Mold Cres OX16 ....240 A8
Molesworth Bglws PE9 ...1 A6
Monarch Rd NN2 ....141 C1
Monarch Terr NN2 ....159 C8
Monk's Hall NN1 ....159 F7
Monks Cres NN5 ....140 D3
Monks Pond St NN1 ......159 B6
Monks Rd NN29 ....146 D3
Monks Way Corby NN18 ..36 A4
Crick NN6 ....101 A6
Wellingborough NN8 .....130 A3
Monkswood NN12 ....214 C4
Monmouth CI NN14 .....76 F2
Monmouth Rd NN5 ....159 A7
Monroe CI LE16 ....31 C5
Monson Way PE8 ....41 E7
Montabaur Rd NN13 .....234 A7
Montagu CI NN15 ....91 D5
Montagu St NN16 ....72 C2
Montagu Terr NN8 ....130 A6
Montague Cres NN5 .....140 D2
Montague Ct NN14 ....76 D2
Montague Dr CV23 ....103 A3
Montague St NN10 ......132 A2
Montcalm CI NN15 ....72 F1
Montfort CI NN5 ....140 B2
Montrose CI
Market Harborough LE16 ..31 D1
Stamford PE9 ....241 A4
Montrose CI CV22 ....241 C6
Montsaye Com Coll
NN14 ....70 B7
Monument St OX16 ......240 C7
Moonshine Gap NN6 .....128 D6
Moor End PE8 ....60 D3
Moor Field NN12 ....203 B8
Moor La CV23 ....117 D3
Moor Rd NN10 ....132 A2
Moore CI Corby NN17 ....36 C6
Kettering NN15 ....92 A7
Moore St NN2 ....141 F1
Moorend Rd NN12 ....217 C6
Moores CI NN7 ....172 F7
Moores Hill MK46 ....195 F5
Moorfield Gn NN14 ....70 B6
Moorfield Rd NN14 ....70 B6
Moorhen Rd MK18 ....240 E3
Moorhouse Way NN15 ...90 E8
Moorings The
Buckingham MK18 ....240 C3
Mawsley NN14 ....94 E6
Moorland CI NN13 ....142 E2
Moorlands NN8 ....129 D7
Moors CI NN15 ....228 E4

Moors Dr The OX17 ......219 F8
Moors La CV21,CV23 .....99 D8
Morby Ct NN15 ....92 B1
Morcott Rd LE15 ....3 C5
Mordaunt CI NN14 ....75 E6
Mordaunt La NN5 ....140 D1
More Rd NN11 ....135 B4
Morehay La
King's Cliffe PE8 ....13 E6
King's Cliffe PE8 ....13 F7
Moreton Ave NN3 ....129 D2
Moreton Rd
Buckingham MK18 ....240 D5
Eydon NN11 ....184 C1
Moreton Way NN2 ....141 C5
Morgan CI NN3 ....143 C4
Morgan Dr NN6 ....106 C3
Morgans CI PE8 ....43 A3
Moriston CI NN17 ....21 C1
Morland Rd NN18 ....36 E5
Morley St Kettering NN16 .72 C4
Market Harborough LE16 ..31 D3
Morley Wlk NN17 ....36 C8
Morris Ave NN10 ....131 F1
Morris CI NN8 ....129 A6
Morris Rd Daventry NN11 .134 F3
Northampton NN2 ....141 D3
Morrison Park Rd NN6 ...102 C5
Mortar Pit Rd NN3 ....143 C5
Mortimer CI NN4 ....159 A2
Morton CI CV22 ....98 F8
Morton CI NN3 ....160 D7
Mortons Bush NN4 ......176 A6
Moss CI Rugby CV22 ....241 A6
Towcester NN12 ....203 C8
Moss Wlk NN18 ....36 A2
Motala CI NN18 ....36 A2
Motherwell Ho NN17 ....37 A8
Motspur Dr NN2 ....141 B1
Motts The NN7 ....157 B6
Moulton Coll NN3 ....126 C1
Moulton Crossing NN3 ...142 E8
Moulton La NN2,NN3 .....141 C8
Moulton Park Bsns Ctr
NN3 ....142 A6
Moulton Prim Sch NN3 ..126 C1
Moulton Rd Holcot NN6 ..126 D7
Pitsford NN6 ....125 D3
Moulton Sch NN3 ....126 B1
Moulton Way N NN3 ....142 C6
Moulton Way S NN3 ....142 C6
Moultrie Rd CV21,CV22 ..241 D7
Mount Pleasant
Earls Barton NN6 ....144 F4
Harpole NN7 ....157 C7
Wardington OX17 ....196 E1
Woodford Halse NN11 ...184 D6
Yardley Gobion NN12 ....217 F6
Mount Pleasant CI
MK18 ....240 C2
Mount Pleasant Rd LE15 ..3 A6
Mountbatten Ave PE9 ...241 C4
Mountbatten Dr NN14 ...95 C3
Mountbatten Way NN9 ..114 A6
Mountbatten Way NN9 ..153 E8
Mountbatten Way NN9 ..114 A6
Mountclair CI NN3 ....160 E8
Mountfield Rd
Irthlingborough NN9 ......112 F3
Northampton NN3 ....142 A3
Mounthill Ave MK19 .....229 B7
Mounts Bsns Ctr NN1 ...159 D7
Mounts CI NN1 ....142 E3
Mounts La NN11 ....153 E4
Mounts The NN1 ....121 B3
Mow Mead MK46 ....195 F5
Mowsley Ct LE17 ....45 E6
Mowsley Rd
Husbands Bosworth LE17 ..45 E6
Theddingworth LE16 .....46 C8
Moyeady Ave CV22 ......98 E8
Muirfield Dr NN11 ....135 E2
Muirfield Rd NN8 ....129 C7
Mulberry CI
Northampton NN4 ....158 F2
Wellingborough NN8 .....129 E6
Mulberry Ct LE16 ....20 A5
Mull Dr NN17 ....36 C8
Mullions The NN4 ....175 E5
Mulso Rd NN14 ....112 A4
Mumford Dr NN2 ....141 A4
Muncaster Gdns NN4 ...175 D7
Muncaster Way NN6 ....102 C5
Murcott NN6 ....121 A4
Murcott CI NN6 ....121 A4
Murray Ave NN2 ....141 D1
Murray Ho NN1 ....160 A8
Murray Wlk NN18 ....36 E5
Murray Way NN12 ......241 D8
Murrayfield Rd CV23 ....103 A3
Mursley CI NN11 ....229 F5
Murswell La NN12 ....214 D4
Murswell La NN12 ....214 D4
Muscott La NN5 ....158 C6
Muscott La NN5 ....158 C6
Musgrave CI NN4 ....160 A6
Musgrave CI NN4 ....175 F7
Mushroom Field Rd
NN3 ....143 D2
Musk CI LE16 ....20 D7
Musson CI NN9 ....112 E2
Mussott CI NN7 ....155 E6
Myers CI OX17 ....231 F5
Myers Rd CV21 ....99 C8

Myers Way OX17 ....231 F5
Myrtle Rd NN16 ....72 C4

N

Nags Head La NN9 ....115 F2
Nairn Rd PE9 ....241 A3
Nansen Cl
Daventry NN11 ....135 C5
Rothwell NN14 ....70 E6
Nansen Wlk NN18 ....36 B2
Nantwich Dr NN11 ....135 D6
Naomi Cl NN3 ....142 F1
Napier Ct Daventry NN11 .153 D8
Wellingborough NN8 ....129 A4
Nares Cl CV22 ....241 E6
Narvik Rd NN18 ....36 A2
Naseby Battle & Farm Mus*
NN6 ....85 B7
Naseby CE Prim Sch NN6 .66 B1
Naseby Cl
Market Harborough LE16 ...31 E2
Wellingborough NN8 ....129 D7
Naseby Ct NN18 ....240 E5
Naseby Dr NN11 ....135 C6
Naseby Rd Clipston LE16 ..66 F8
Corby NN17 ....36 C7
Kettering NN16 ....72 E3
Rugby CV22 ....241 E6
Sibbertoft LE16 ....46 F2
Thornby NN6 ....84 E4
Welford NN6 ....65 D5
Naseby Sq LE16 ....31 E2
Naseby St NN2 ....159 C8
Nash Ct NN15 ....92 A8
Nasmith Ave NN17 ....37 A8
Nasmyth Rd NN11 ....134 F5
Nassington Prim Sch
PE8 ....15 F5
Nassington Rd
Woodnewton PE8 ....14 F1
Yarwell PE8 ....15 F7
Navigation Row NN1 ...159 C4
Navisford Cl NN14 ....54 E2
Neale Ave NN16 ....72 B5
Neale Cl
Northampton NN3 ....160 E8
Wollaston NN29 ....146 C3
Needham Rd NN4 ....113 F4
Neithrop Ave OX16 ....240 B9
Neithrop Cl OX16 ....240 B9
Neithrop Cty Inf Sch
OX16 ....240 A8
Neithrop Cty Jun Sch
OX16 ....240 A8
Nelson Ave NN1 ....184 B6
Nelson Cl NN11 ....135 E2
Nelson Ct NN18 ....240 C3
Nelson Dr NN14 ....70 E7
Nelson Rd NN8 ....36 B8
Nelson St
Buckingham MK18 ....240 C3
Kettering NN16 ....72 C3
Market Harborough LE16 .131 D3
2 Northampton NN1 ...159 C7
Nene Ct Kettering NN15 ...92 A5
Raunds NN9 ....114 D7
Wansford PE8 ....8 A3
Wellingborough NN8 ....129 C6
Nene Cres NN17 ....21 C1
Nene Ct Thrapston NN14 ...24 C7
Wellingborough NN8 .....130 C3
Nene Dr NN5 ....140 F2
Nene Ent Ctr NN2 ....159 C8
Nene La NN12 ....205 A5
Nene Park (Billing &
Diamonds FC) NN9 ...113 A2
Nene PI NN5 ....141 C2
Nene Rise
Burton Latimer NN15 .....92 A2
Higham Ferrers NN10 ...132 B5
Nene Rise NN2 ....161 F6
Nene Side Cl NN11 ....133 D1
Nene Univ Coll Northampton
NN2 ....141 E5
Nene Valley Bsns Pk PE8 .42 B5
Nene Valley Ret Pk
NN1 ....159 B4
Nene Valley Way NN3 ...160 D5
Nene View
Irthlingborough NN14 ...112 F2
Islip NN14 ....114 C8
Oundle PE8 ....41 F6
Nene Way
Kislingbury NN7 ....157 C3
Northampton NN5 ....141 A2
Oundle PE8 ....41 F6
Sutton PE5 ....8 F2
Nene Whitewater Ctr*
NN1 ....160 B3
Nene Wlk Daventry NN11 .135 A1
Northampton NN5 ....140 F2
Neneside Cl NN4 ....155 B3
Nepcote Cl NN15 ....91 D8
Nesbitt Cl NN1 ....160 E8
Nest Farm Cres NN8 ...130 A8
Nest Farm Rd NN8 ....130 A7
Nest La NN8 ....130 B7
Nether Jackson Ct 3
NN3 ....234 A4
Nether La NN7 ....155 F4
Netherfield Gr NN17 ....36 F8
Netherfield NN15 ....91 C7

Nethermead Ct NN3 .....142 F4
Netherton NN14 ....89 B4
Nettle Gap Cl NN1 ....175 F6
Neuville Way NN14 ....50 F3
Nevill Cl MK19 ....207 B2
Nevill Holt Rd LE16 ....19 F6
Nevill Holt Sch LE16 ....19 D8
Neville Day Cl PE9 ....1 F5
Neville Ho NN17 ....36 E6
Nevis Cl NN17 ....21 C1
New Bldgs NN16 ....72 B2
New Cotts NN17 ....24 B5
New Croft NN7 ....155 B3
New Cross Rd PE9 ....241 D4
New Forest Way NN11 ...135 B4
New Hall NN1 ....114 E5
New La PE8 ....8 C1
New Post Office Sq
NN17 ....36 E6
New Rd Banbury OX16 ...240 D7
Brackley NN13 ....233 E6
Castlethorpe MK19 ....218 F5
Collyweston PE9 ....1 C2
Easton o t H PE9 ....2 A5
Farthingstone NN12 ....221 A4
Geddington NN14 ....54 A2
Greens Norton NN12 ...202 D8
Maidford NN12 ....186 D6
Northampton NN4 ....175 E6
Oundle PE8 ....42 A6
New South Bridge Rd
NN4 ....159 C4
New St Brixworth NN6 ...106 D2
Daventry NN11 ....135 C1
Desborough NN14 ....51 A3
Earls Barton NN6 ....147 B8
Irchester NN29 ....147 F2
Irthlingborough NN9 ...112 F2
Oundle PE8 ....42 A5
Rothwell NN14 ....70 D7
Rugby CV22 ....241 A8
Stamford PE9 ....241 D4
Stony Stratford MK11 ...229 D5
Weedon NN7 ....155 C3
Wellingborough NN8 ...130 A5
New Street Cl NN6 ....147 B8
New Terr NN11 ....183 D7
New Town PE9 ....2 A5
New Town Rd 2 NN1 ...159 F6
Newark Dr NN18 ....36 C6
Newbery Dr NN13 ....233 D8
Newbold Cl
Banbury OX16 ....240 E6
Oundle PE8 ....41 E6
Newbold Rd CV21 ....241 C9
Newbolt Ct NN12 ....216 B8
Newbottle & Charlton CE
Prim Sch OX17 ....231 F5
Newboults La PE9 ....241 C3
Newbridge NN6 ....136 D8
Newbridge La NN6 ....114 A3
Newbury Ct NN10 ....132 D3
Newbury St NN11 ....135 C6
Newby Ct NN3 ....142 C3
Newcomb Ct PE9 ....241 C3
Newcombe Rd NN5 ....159 A7
Newcombe St LE16 ....31 E2
Newcomen Rd NN8 ....130 B5
Newell Rd NN14 ....95 B3
Newham Ct NN14 ....70 C7
Newham Rd PE9 ....241 C5
Newington Rd NN2 ....141 C4
Newland NN1 ....159 C6
Newland PI OX16 ....240 D7
Newland Rd
Banbury OX16 ....240 D7
Walgrave NN6 ....108 A5
Newland Sq NN2 ....141 C4
Newland St
Braybrooke LE16 ....49 E5
Kettering NN16 ....72 B2
Rugby CV22 ....241 A8
Newland Wlk 3 NN1 ...159 D6
Newlands Brixworth NN6 .106 B2
King's Sutton OX17 .....231 A6
Naseby NN6 ....66 C1
Newlands Ctr NN16 ....72 B2
Newlands Rd NN16 ....64 E5
Newman St
Burton Latimer NN15 .....92 B2
Higham Ferrers NN10 ...132 C7
2 Kettering NN16 ....72 B2
Newnham Dr NN11 ....135 A5
Newnham Prim Sch
NN11 ....153 D7
Newnham Rd NN2 ....141 D3
Newnham Windmill*
NN11 ....153 D7
Newport Pagnell Rd
Horton NN7 ....177 D1
Northampton NN4,NN7 ...176 A7
Newport Pagnell Rd W
NN4 ....175 D8
Newport Rd
Hanslope MK19 ....207 B2
Northampton NN5 ....159 A7
Newstead Cl NN13 ....143 D3
Newstead Ct NN15 ....91 C5
Newstone Cres NN4 ....158 C4
Newton Cl
Daventry NN11 ....135 A4
Rushden NN10 ....132 D1
Newton Gr NN17 ....22 A1
Newton Rd
Clifton u D CV23 ....80 A7

Newton Rd continued
Geddington NN14 ....54 A3
Higham Ferrers NN10 ...132 E5
Kettering NN15 ....91 F5
Northampton NN5 ....158 D8
Rushden NN10 ....132 E1
Wollaston NN29 ....146 D2
Newton Road Com Prim Sch
NN10 ....132 C2
Newton Way LE16 ....49 F6
Newton Way LE16 ....114 E5
Newtown Brigstock NN14 ...55 E8
Woodford NN14 ....94 D7
Newtown Rd
Little Irchester NN8 ...130 C1
Raunds NN9 ....114 E5
Newtown St NN14 ....94 D7
Nibbits La NN11 ....153 D6
Nicholas Hawksmoor Prim
Sch NN12 ....203 B5
Nicholas La NN9 ....112 E1
Nicholas Rd NN9 ....112 E1
Nicholas Way NN10 ....131 F3
Nicholls Ct NN3 ....142 E5
Nicholls Ho 1 NN4 ...159 A3
Nicholls La NN3 ....51 A4
Nichols Way NN7 ....114 C7
Nielson Rd NN8 ....130 C8
Nigel Ct NN13 ....234 A5
Nightingale Cl
Brackley NN13 ....222 E2
Daventry NN11 ....135 D6
Nightingale Dr NN12 ...203 C3
Nightingale La NN8 ....130 B7
Nightingale PI MK18 ...240 E4
Niort Way NN8 ....129 C8
Nippendale NN12 ....132 C2
Nithsdale Ave LE16 ....31 F2
Nithsdale Cres LE16 ....31 F2
Nithsdale Rd NN7 ....36 D7
Noble Ave NN9 ....113 A5
Nobold Ct LE16 ....66 F8
Nook The Corby NN17 ...37 B6
Cottingham LE16 ....20 D1
Easton o t H PE9 ....2 A5
Norbury Ct LE16 ....31 D3
Norbury Rd NN8 ....129 D8
Norfolk Cl NN13 ....36 C7
Norfolk Sq NN7 ....241 D4
Norfolk St NN2 ....159 C8
Norfolk Terr NN8 ....159 C8
Norman Rd NN3 ....142 B1
Norman Way
Irchester NN29 ....147 C8
Wellingborough NN8 ...129 D2
Norman-D-Gate NN1 ...159 D5
Normandy Lodge NN13 .233 E8
Normead Sq 4 MK18 ...240 D4
Norris Acre NN13 ....222 F6
Norris Rd NN10 ....98 C5
Norris Way NN10 ....131 E3
Norris Way Ind Est
NN10 ....131 E3
Norse Wlk NN18 ....36 A2
North Ave NN15 ....92 B3
North Bar PI OX16 ....240 C8
North Bar St OX16 ....240 C8
North Cape Wlk NN18 ...36 A2
North Cl NN11 ....118 C6
North End NN10 ....132 B7
North Field Cl NN16 ...72 A4
North Folds Rd NN18 ...35 F1
North Hayes Ct NN3 ...142 F5
North Hill NN18 ....225 F0
North Holme Ct NN3 ...142 D5
North La LE16 ....30 D8
North Lea LE16 ....18 B3
North Leys Ct NN3 ...142 C7
North Lodge Rd NN LE15 .3 B8
North Oval NN3 ....140 F2
North Oxfordshire Coll
OX16 ....240 B7
North Paddock Ct NN3 .142 C7
North Park Dr NN16 ...72 C5
North Portway Cl NN3 .142 F7
North Priors Ct NN3 ...143 A4
North Rd Clifton u D CV23 .80 A6
Earls Barton NN6 ....144 E5
Northampton NN1 ....141 F6
South Kilworth LE17 ....63 D8
North St Banbury OX16 ...240 E9
Castlethorpe MK19 ....218 F5
Daventry NN11 ....135 C2
Kilsby CV23 ....99 F3
Mears Ashby NN6 ....128 B2
Oundle PE8 ....42 A5
Raunds NN9 ....114 E7
Rothersthorpe NN7 ....174 B6
Rugby CV21 ....241 C8
Rushden NN10 ....132 B3
Swinford LE17 ....62 B4
Titchmarsh NN14 ....77 C4
Wellingborough NN8 ...129 F5
North Way
Deanshanger MK19 ...228 E5
Pottersbury NN12 ....217 E2
North Western Ave
NN2 ....159 B5
Northall NN6 ....108 A5
Northall Mews NN16 ...72 A2
Northall St NN16 ....72 B3
Northam Ct NN16 ....72 B4
Northampton (Sywell)
Airport NN6 ....127 C5
Northampton Christian Sch
NN1 ....160 A8
Northampton Coll NN3 .142 D3

Northampton General Hospl
NN1 ....159 E5
Northampton High Sch
NN4 ....176 F1
Northampton La N NN3 .142 C8
Northampton La S NN3 .142 C7
Northampton Prep Sch
NN4 ....160 E3
Northampton Rd
Blisworth NN7 ....174 D1
Brackley NN13 ....223 A1
Brixworth NN6 ....106 B1
Broughton NN14 ....90 A3
Chapel Brampton NN6 .124 C1
Cosgrove MK19 ....217 F7
Denton NN7 ....178 B8
Earls Barton NN6 ....144 D5
Ecton NN6 ....143 F4
Harpole NN7 ....157 C5
Kettering NN15 ....71 F1
Litchborough NN12 ...171 E2
Market Harborough LE16 .31 F3
Orlingbury NN14 ....109 F5
Roade NN7 ....191 D5
Towcester NN12 ....203 C7
Welford NN6 ....64 E4
Wellingborough NN8 ...129 D3
West Haddon NN6 ....102 C4
Yardley Hastings NN7 ...177 F6
Northampton Sch for Boys
NN4 ....160 A6
Northampton Sch For Girls
NN3 ....142 A4
Northampton Sta NN1 ...159 B6
Northampton Town FC
NN5 ....158 E5
Northamptonshire Gram Sch
NN6 ....125 D4
Northamptonshire
Reg Nursery Training
NN6 ....124 F1
Northants County Cricket
Club* NN1 ....160 A8
Northants Ent Pk NN2 ...141 E6
Northbank LE16 ....31 E3
Northbrook NN18 ....36 B4
Northcot La OX16 ....240 B9
Northcote Rd CV22 ....241 B8
Northcote St NN1 ....159 C7
Northen Way NN8 ....129 F8
Northend NN11 ....99 F6
Northend Sq MK18 ....240 D4
Northern Cl NN17 ....22 B8
Northern Way NN11 ...135 D4
Northfield Ave
Kettering NN15 ....72 A3
Ringstead NN14 ....95 B3
Northfield Gn NN6 ....122 D5
Northfield La PE8 ....15 E5
Northfield Rd
Broughton NN14 ....71 C1
Northampton NN5 ....140 B1
Northfield Way NN2 ...141 B4
Northfields Ct NN16 ...241 E4
Northgate NN12 ....203 C7
Northgate Sch NN2 ....141 C2
Northleigh Gr NN13 ....31 C4
Northumberland Ave
PE9 ....241 C4
Northumberland Cl
NN15 ....91 D6
Northumberland Rd
OX16 ....240 E8
Northumberland Rd
NN15 ....91 D6
Northumbria Gdns NN3 .142 E1
Northway CV21 ....241 C8
Northwood Rd NN3 ....142 B2
Nortoft NN6 ....103 F7
Norton Cl NN11 ....71 F1
Norton Cres NN12 ....203 B6
Norton Leys CV22 ....98 A6
Norton Rd Corby NN17 ...36 F7
Daventry NN11 ....135 D2
Northampton NN2 ....141 C3
Norton St NN14 ....76 D7
Norton's PI NN8 ....240 C3
Norway Cl NN18 ....36 A3
Notre Dame Mews 3
NN1 ....159 D6
Nuffield Cl NN13 ....233 D8
Nuffield Dr OX16 ....240 A10
Nunn Mills Rd NN1 ....159 E4
Nunneley Way LE16 ....31 F5
Nunnery Ave NN14 ....70 C7
Nunns La NN6 ....121 B4
Nursery La
Banbury OX16 ....240 C9
Wellingborough NN8 ...130 B7
Nursery End LE16 ....31 C2
Nursery Gdns NN10 ...112 E2
Nursery La
Banbury OX16 ....240 C9
Northampton NN5 ....141 C3
Nutcote NN6 ....85 B8
Nuthall Cl NN11 ....160 F8

O

Oak Ave NN7 ....174 B1
Oak Cl Broughton NN14 ...90 B4
Hartwell NN7 ....192 E2
Irchester NN29 ....147 A7
Market Harborough LE16 .31 F4
Towcester NN12 ....203 C4
Oak Dr NN11 ....184 B6
Oak Gr NN11 ....135 C5
Oak La NN6 ....100 F6
Oak Rd Brackley NN13 ...222 F1
Kettering NN15 ....72 D1
Oak St
2 Northampton NN1 ...159 C7
Rugby CV22 ....241 C7
Rushden NN10 ....132 B4
Weedon NN7 ....155 A2
Oak Terr NN9 ....112 F2
Oak Tree Cl NN14 ....50 F3
Oak View NN10 ....110 F1
Oak Way NN9 ....112 F2
Oakdown Cres MK46 ...195 F3
Oakfield NN10 ....132 A4
Oakfield Prim Sch CV22 .241 A6
Oakfield Rd CV22 ....241 B7
Oakgrove Rd NN4 ....175 D6
Oakham Cl
Desborough NN14 ....50 F4
Rushden NN3 ....142 B7
Oakham La NN11 ....152 B7
Oaklands Bugbrooke NN7 .173 A7
Northampton NN4 ....155 A2
Oaklands Dr NN12 ....142 E1
Oaklands Pk 4 LE16 ...31 F2
Oakleas Rise NN14 ....76 D1
Oakleigh Cl NN9 ....114 C7
Oakleigh Dr NN5 ....140 C1
Oakley Cl NN18 ....36 A1
Oakley Dr Moulton NN3 .126 D1
Wellingborough NN8 ...129 D3
Oakley Hay Ind Est NN18 .36 A1
Oakley Mews LE16 ....31 D3
Oakley Pond NN18 ....53 B8
Oakley Rd Corby NN13 ...37 A6
Corby NN17 ....36 C3
Corby,Pipewell NN14 ...52 D8
Rushden NN10 ....73 B4
Rushden NN14 ....52 E5
Oakley St Kettering NN16 .72 B4
Northampton NN1 ....159 D7
Oakmont Cl NN4 ....175 C5
Oakpark Cl NN3 ....143 A6
Oakpits Way NN10 ....132 C1
Oaks Dr NN10 ....132 B6
Oaks The NN4 ....175 F3
Oaktree Ct Aldwincle NN14 .76 F8
2 Kettering NN16 ....72 B1
Oakway NN8 ....129 F7
Oakway Jun & Inf Sch
NN8 ....130 A7
Oakwood Cl PE8 ....27 D2
Oakwood Rd NN1 ....142 A1
Oat Hill Dr NN3 ....143 D2
Oat Hill Rd NN12 ....203 C4
Oathill Cl NN6 ....106 B1
Oathill Rise NN15 ....92 C2
Oban Cl Kettering NN15 ...91 E8
Stamford PE9 ....241 A4
Obelisk Cl NN2 ....141 C8
Obelisk Rd NN2 ....112 A5
Obelisk Rise NN2 ....141 C6
Occupation Rd
Corby NN17 ....36 F7
Middleton LE16 ....20 B2
Oundle PE8 ....42 A7
Octagon The NN7 ....37 A8
Octagon Way NN3 ....142 F2
Octavian Way NN13 ...234 A7
Odeon Bldgs NN17 ....37 A7
Ode A43 NN14 ....89 F2
Old Barn Ct NN3 ....142 F3
Old Brewery Wlk NN11 .233 F6
Old Brickyard The NN6 .102 C4
Old Carpenters Cl NN3 .143 C2
Old Cl NN4 ....175 E2
Old Dairy Farm* NN7 .171 E6
Old Dry La NN14 ....55 F8
Old End NN7 ....177 A1
Old Farm La NN14 ....76 B3
Old Forge Dr NN6 ....102 C4
Old Forge La NN11 ....169 C2
Old Gaol Mus* MK18 ...240 D4
Old Gn LE16 ....18 F6
Old Gorse Way NN14 ...89 A4
Old Gram School The
NN6 ....103 F6
Old Great North Rd
Stamford PE9 ....241 D2
Stibbington PE8 ....8 C2
Wansford PE8 ....2 F7
Old Greens Norton Rd
NN12 ....203 B7
Old Grimsbury Rd OX16 .240 E9
Old Hall La LE16 ....30 F3
Old Holt Rd LE16 ....19 A7
Old La NN13 ....221 A4
Old Leicester Rd PE8 ...8 A3
Old Manor Ct NN11 ....135 E8
Old North Rd PE8 ....8 A4
Old Oundle Rd PE8 ....7 D6
Old Parr Cl OX16 ....240 E9
Old Parr Rd OX16 ....240 D7
Old Quarry Ct NN3 ....142 E4
Old Rd Braunston NN11 .134 C8
Scaldwell NN6 ....107 A7

Old Rd continued
Stanion NN14 . . . . .37 E2
Walgrave NN6 . . . . .107 F5
Old Rectory Dr PE8 . . . . .8 A6
Old Rectory Rd PE8 . . . . .8 A4
Old Rickyard The NN11 . .199 D7
Old School Cotts NN6 . . . .105 A8
Old School Ct MK18 . . . . . .240 C3
Old School La NN17 . . . . . .187 A1
Old School Mews LE16 . . . .31 E3
Old School Pl DX16 . . . . . .229 C8
Old Stable Yd MK19 . . . . . .229 E7
Old Stratford Prim Sch
MK19 . . . . .229 B6
Old Tiffield Rd NN12 . . . . .203 C8
Old Towcester Rd NN4 . . .159 C4
Old Town NN13 . . . . .234 A7
Old Vineyard The NN10 . .132 B6
Old Yew Ct NN2 . . . . .141 B3
Olde Forde Cl NN6 . . . . . . .106 B1
Olde Hall Ct NN6 . . . . .105 B1
Olden Rd NN3 . . . . .143 C5
Oldenburg Rd NN18 . . . . . . .35 F3
Oldenmead Ct NN3 . . . . . . .142 F3
Oldland Rd NN18 . . . . .35 F3
Oleander Cres NN3 . . . . . .143 C4
Oliver Cl NN10 . . . . .132 C2
Oliver St
Northampton NN1 . . . . .141 E1
Rugby CV21 . . . . .241 B8
Ollerton Wlk NN14 . . . . . . .36 C5
Ollis Cl NN17 . . . . .36 E8
Olney Fst Sch MK46 . . . . . .195 E3
Olney Mid Sch MK46 . . . . .195 F5
Olney Rd MK46 . . . . .195 F5
Olympia Cl NN4 . . . . .175 B8
Olympic Way
Kettering NN15 . . . . .91 A7
Wellingborough NN8 . . . . . .129 C5
Omega Pl CV21 . . . . .241 D9
Onley La CV22 . . . . .98 D6
Onley Pk CV23 . . . . .117 C8
Oransay Cl NN3 . . . . .143 C2
Orchard Cl Badby NN11 . .152 F3
Banbury OX16 . . . . .240 B8
East Haddon NN6 . . . . .122 D5
Finedon NN9 . . . . .111 F5
Hannington NN6 . . . . .108 C3
Hollowell NN6 . . . . .104 B5
Milton Malsor NN7 . . . . .174 E4
Northampton NN4 . . . . .175 E6
Orlingbury NN14 . . . . .110 A5
Ringstead NN14 . . . . .95 C3
Rushden NN10 . . . . .131 F3
Spratton NN6 . . . . .124 B8
Towcester NN12 . . . . .203 C4
Warmington PE8 . . . . .28 B3
Weedon NN7 . . . . .155 C3
Weldon NN17 . . . . .38 B8
Wilbarston LE16 . . . . .34 C5
Wollaston NN29 . . . . .146 D3
Yardley Gobion NN12 . . . . . .217 F6
Yelvertoft NN6 . . . . .82 B4
Orchard Cotts NN6 . . . . . .125 C5
Orchard Cres
Kettering NN16 . . . . .72 C4
Woodnewton PE8 . . . . .14 E2
Orchard Ct
Pattishall NN12 . . . . .172 D1
Woodford NN14 . . . . .94 C7
Orchard Dene MK18 . . . . .240 D4
Orchard Est NN14 . . . . .90 F2
Orchard Field NN14 . . . . . .93 A6
Orchard Gn NN3 . . . . .142 C2
Orchard Hill NN3 . . . . .143 A1
Orchard Ho NN17 . . . . .38 B8
Orchard La Denton NN7 . .162 B1
Gretton NN17 . . . . .10 C1
King's Cliffe PE8 . . . . .15 F2
Woodnewton PE8 . . . . .14 E2
Orchard Pl NN29 . . . . .147 A8
Orchard Rd Finedon NN9 .111 F5
Raunds NN9 . . . . .114 B5
Stamford PE9 . . . . .241 D3
Orchard Rise
Long Buckby NN6 . . . . .121 D4
Olney MK46 . . . . .195 F3
Orchard Sch The NN16 . . . . .72 B1
Orchard St
Daventry NN11 . . . . .135 B2
Market Harborough LE16 . . .31 E4
❸ Northampton NN5 . . . . .159 A6
Orchard Terr
Finedon NN9 . . . . .111 F5
Welford NN6 . . . . .64 E6
Wellingborough NN8 . . . . . .129 F5
Orchard The
Apethorpe PE8 . . . . .14 C4
Bozeat NN29 . . . . .164 D3
Flore NN7 . . . . .155 F5
Kislingbury NN7 . . . . .157 D3
Potterspury NN12 . . . . .217 C3
Sibbertoft LE16 . . . . .47 A2
Theddingworth LE17 . . . . . . .32 B7
Upper Boddington NN11 . .182 C7
Orchard Way
Banbury OX16 . . . . .240 B8
Cogenhoe NN7 . . . . .161 F6
Easton o t H PE9 . . . . .1 F6
Harpole NN7 . . . . .157 C6
King's Sutton OX17 . . . . . . .231 A5
Northampton NN5 . . . . .158 C6
Roade NN7 . . . . .191 D4
Orchards The NN6 . . . . . . .103 D1
Ordnance Rd NN7 . . . . . . .154 F3
Oriel Rd NN11 . . . . .153 C7
Oriel St NN11 . . . . .233 D8

Orient Way NN8 . . . . .130 A4
Orion Way NN15 . . . . .91 C5
Orkney Wlk NN17 . . . . .36 B8
Orlingbury Rd
Great Harrowden NN9 . . . .110 D2
Isham NN14 . . . . .110 D7
Little Harrowden NN9 . . . . .110 B4
Pytchley NN14 . . . . .90 F1
Ormond Pl NN14 . . . . .110 E8
Orson Leys CV22 . . . . .98 A7
Orton Pl NN8 . . . . .129 D7
Orton Rd Kettering NN15 . .91 F5
Loddington NN14 . . . . .70 D2
Orwell Cl Clifton u D CV23 .80 A5
Raunds NN9 . . . . .114 D7
Wellingborough NN8 . . . . . .129 C6
Osborn Cl NN15 . . . . .129 E3
Osborn's Ct NN46 . . . . .195 C1
Osborne Rd NN10 . . . . .132 D4
Osborne St NN2 . . . . .141 C2
Osier Bed La NN17 . . . . . . .24 B5
Osiers The NN11 . . . . .51 D2
Osler Cl NN2 . . . . .141 B5
Oslo Gdns NN18 . . . . .36 A3
Osmund Dr NN3 . . . . .143 A5
Osprey Dr NN11 . . . . .135 C3
Osprey La NN8 . . . . .130 B7
Osprey Rise NN4 . . . . .175 B8
Osprey View ❻ NN4 . . . . .175 B8
Osters La MK18 . . . . .240 F2
Ostlers Way NN15 . . . . .91 B7
Oswald Rd NN10 . . . . .132 C2
Osyth Cl NN4 . . . . .160 B2
Otters Brook NN8 . . . . . . .240 E3
Oulton Rise NN1 . . . . .141 F8
Oundle & Kings Cliffe Mid
Sch PE8 . . . . .41 E7
Oundle CE Prim Sch PE8 . .41 F5
Oundle Mus* PE8 . . . . .41 F5
Oundle Rd Elton PE8 . . . . . .16 F1
Thrapston NN14 . . . . .76 E2
Weldon NN17 . . . . .38 E7
Woodnewton PE8 . . . . .14 F1
Our Lady & Pope John RC
Sch NN18 . . . . .36 C4
Our Lady's Convent Prep Sch
NN15 . . . . .71 F1
Our Lady's Jun & Inf Sch
NN12 . . . . .129 D3
Our Lady's RC Jun & Inf Sch
NN8 . . . . .129 D3
Ouse Cl NN8 . . . . .129 C6
Ouse La NN11 . . . . .129 C6
Ousebank Way MK11 . . . . .229 D5
Outlaw La NN8 . . . . .129 C6
Oval Cres NN10 . . . . .132 D2
Oval Rd Rugby CV22 . . . . . . .98 D8
Rushden NN10 . . . . .132 D2
Oval The Kettering NN15 . . .91 B8
Market Harborough LE16 . . .31 E4
Overdale Cl LE16 . . . . .32 A3
Overfield Ave LE16 . . . . . . .31 F5
Overhills MK46 . . . . .195 E4
Overleys Ct NN15 . . . . .143 B5
Overmead Rd NN8 . . . . . . .143 D2
Overn Ave MK18 . . . . .240 C4
Overn Cl MK18 . . . . .240 D4
Overn Cres MK18 . . . . .240 D4
Overslade Cl NN4 . . . . .175 A8
Overslade Jun Sch CV22 . .98 A7
Overstone Cl NN3 . . . . .126 C1
Overstone Cres NN6 . . . . .127 B1
Overstone Cty Prim Sch
NN6 .127 B1
Overstone La NN6 . . . . . . .126 F1
Overstone Park Prep & High
Sch NN6 . . . . .143 B8
Overstone Rd
Moulton NN3 . . . . .126 D1
Northampton NN3 . . . . .127 A1
Sywell NN6 . . . . .127 D3
Overthorpe Prep Sch
OX17 . . . . .219 C8
Overthorpe Rd
Banbury OX16 . . . . .219 B6
Banbury, Grimsbury OX16 . .240 F8
Ovett Cl NN15 . . . . .90 F8
Owen Cl NN8 . . . . .129 D8
Owen Mews NN8 . . . . .129 B5
Owen Way NN10 . . . . .132 A5
Owl Cl NN3 . . . . .141 F7
Owl End La NN11 . . . . .182 C5
Owl End Way NN11 . . . . . .182 C5
Oxburgh Ct ❼ NN4 . . . . . .175 C8
Oxendon Hall LE16 . . . . . . .48 E3
Oxendon Rd
Braybrooke LE16 . . . . .49 A1
Clipston LE16 . . . . .48 B1
East Farndon LE16 . . . . .48 B5
Oxfield Park Dr MK19 . . . .229 C2
Oxford Cl Daventry NN11 . .135 A5
Earls Barton NN6 . . . . .144 F3
Oxford Ct NN13 . . . . .233 F5
Oxford Rd
Adderbury OX17 . . . . .230 A3
Banbury OX15,OX16 . . . . . .240 C6
Corby NN17 . . . . .36 C6
Evenley NN13 . . . . .233 E5
Stamford PE9 . . . . .241 C5
Stratford St Daventry NN13 .135 C1
Finedon NN9 . . . . .112 B5
Kettering NN16 . . . . .72 A3
Northampton NN4 . . . . .159 B3

Oxford St continued
Rothwell NN14 . . . . .70 D2
Rugby CV21 . . . . .241 E8
Stony Stratford MK11 . . . . .229 D5
Wellingborough NN8 . . . . . .129 F4
Woodford NN14 . . . . .148 A7
Oxfordshire Sch of Art &
Design OX16 . . . . .240 B7
Oxleys MK46 . . . . .195 C4
Oxwich Cl NN4 . . . . .160 A1

P

Packer Rd NN15 . . . . .90 E8
Packwood Ave CV21 . . . . . . .99 C8
Paddock Cl NN6 . . . . .103 D1
Paddock Ct LE16 . . . . .31 E3
Paddock End NN14 . . . . . . .89 B4
Paddock La
Desborough NN14 . . . . .51 A3
Medars Ashby NN6 . . . . . . .128 B2
Medbourne LE16 . . . . .19 D8
Paddock Mill Ct ❶ NN3 .143 B4
Paddock The Crick NN6 . .100 F5
Lower Boddington NN11 . .182 C5
Naseby NN6 . . . . .114 C4
Stamford PE9 . . . . .241 C3
Weedon Lois NN12 . . . . . . .200 B2
Welton NN11 . . . . .135 E8
Woodnewton PE8 . . . . .14 E2
Paddocks Cl NN6 . . . . .108 A5
Paddocks Rd NN10 . . . . . .131 F3
Paddocks The
Brixworth NN6 . . . . .106 B3
Bugbrooke NN7 . . . . .172 F7
Moulton NN3 . . . . .126 C1
Orlingbury NN14 . . . . .109 F5
Shutlanger NN12 . . . . .204 D8
Souldern OX27 . . . . .237 E3
Paddocks Way NN3 . . . . . .143 A1
Paddox Cl CV22 . . . . .98 F6
Paddox Dr CV22 . . . . .100 A3
Paddox Prim Sch
Rugby CV22 . . . . .98 D8
Rugby CV22 . . . . .98 E8
Padmans Cl NN14 . . . . .89 D2
Padwell Ct ❷ NN3 . . . . . .161 A8
Page Hill Ave MK18 . . . . . .240 C4
Paget Cl NN14 . . . . .160 E2
Paget Rd LE16 . . . . .30 E3
Pagnell Ct NN4 . . . . .176 A7
Palk Rd NN8 . . . . .129 D4
Palm Rd NN10 . . . . .131 E3
Palmer Ave NN9 . . . . .113 B4
Palmer Cl NN8 . . . . .129 D7
Palmer Ct NN8 . . . . .129 C5
Palmer Sq NN3 . . . . .143 A8
Palmer's Ct CV21 . . . . .99 B8
Palmerston Ct ❺ NN1 . . . .159 E6
Palmerston Rd ❻ NN1 . . . .159 E6
Palmerston St NN16 . . . . . .159 E6
Parade Bank NN6 . . . . .126 C1
Parade The NN1 . . . . .159 C6
Paradise Ave NN15 . . . . . . .91 D6
Paradise Ho NN8 . . . . .129 F5
Paradise La NN15 . . . . .91 D6
Paradise St NN16 . . . . .72 A3
Pargeter Cl OX17 . . . . .210 E2
Park Ave Kettering NN16 . . .72 C4
Northampton NN3 . . . . .140 A1
Northampton, Abington
NN1 .160 A8
Raunds NN9 . . . . .114 E5
Rushden NN10 . . . . .132 A2
Park Ave N NN2 . . . . .140 A1
Park Ave S NN3 . . . . .160 B7
Park Cl Badby NN11 . . . . . .153 A3
Brafield-on-t-G NN7 . . . . . .161 E2
Cosgrove NN12 . . . . .218 F2
Isham NN14 . . . . .110 H8
King's Sutton PE8 . . . . .14 A8
Northampton NN5 . . . . .140 A1
Sywell NN6 . . . . .127 D2
Watford NN6 . . . . .120 C6
Whittlebury NN12 . . . . .215 C4
Park Cres B NN8 . . . . .130 A5
Park Cres E NN5 . . . . .140 F1
Park Cres W NN5 . . . . .140 F1
Park Dr
Market Harborough LE16 . . .31 E4
Northampton NN5 . . . . .140 F1
Park End NN13 . . . . .238 D8
Park End Works NN13 . . . .238 D7
Park Farm Barns NN7 . . . .172 E3
Park Farm Cft NN14 . . . . . . .37 E2
Park Farm Ind Est NN8 . . .129 A5
Park Farm Way NN8 . . . . .129 A5
Park Hill Rd NN3 . . . . .142 D3
Park Ho LE16 . . . . .31 E4
Park La Earls Barton NN6 . .144 D4
Gayton NN7 . . . . .173 E2
Harpole NN7 . . . . .157 D6
Hartwell NN7 . . . . .192 C1
Northampton NN5 . . . . .140 A2
Paulerspury NN12 . . . . .216 B7
Stamford PE9 . . . . .241 E2
Sulgrave OX17 . . . . .210 F7
Watford NN6 . . . . .120 C6
Park Leys NN11 . . . . .135 C1
Park Lodge NN6 . . . . .36 E6

Park Mews
Market Harborough LE16 . . .31 E4
Towcester NN12 . . . . .203 C6
Wellingborough NN8 . . . . . .130 A5
Park Pl NN10 . . . . .132 B2
Park Rd Banbury OX16 . . . .240 B8
Burton Latimer NN15 . . . . . .92 B2
Hanslope MK19 . . . . .207 B1
Hartwell NN7 . . . . .192 C1
Irthlingborough NN9 . . . . . .112 F1
Kettering NN16 . . . . .72 C4
Raunds NN9 . . . . .114 E6
Rugby CV21 . . . . .241 C9
Rushden NN10 . . . . .132 C1
Stony Stratford MK11 . . . . .229 D5
Titchmarsh NN14 . . . . .77 C4
Wellingborough NN8 . . . . . .130 A5
Park Spinney Cl NN6 . . . . .84 A5
Park Sq NN5 . . . . .140 F2
Park View Kettering NN16 . .72 B4
Moulton NN3 . . . . .142 E8
Stamford PE9 . . . . .241 F2
Thrapston NN14 . . . . .76 D2
Wellingborough NN8 . . . . . .130 B4
Park View Cl NN3 . . . . .126 E1
Park View Rd NN12 . . . . . .203 B5
Park Wlk Brigstock NN14 . .55 E7
Easton o t H PE9 . . . . .2 A6
Parker Rd PE8 . . . . .7 D8
Parkers Terr NN9 . . . . .111 F4
Parkfield Ave NN14 . . . . . .159 C1
Parkfield Cres NN14 . . . . .159 C1
Parkfield Rd
Brixworth NN6 . . . . .106 A1
Long Buckby NN6 . . . . .122 A5
Rugby CV22 . . . . .241 A8
Parkham Ind Est NN10 . . .131 D3
Parklands Banbury OX16 . .240 D8
Crick NN6 . . . . .100 C7
Stanwick NN9 . . . . .113 F3
Wellingborough NN8 . . . . . .127 D1
Parklands Ave NN3 . . . . . .142 A5
Parklands Cl NN14 . . . . .70 D1
Parklands Cres NN3 . . . . .142 A5
Parklands Lower Sch
NN3 .142 A5
Parklands Mid Sch NN3 . .142 A5
Parkside NN3 . . . . .143 D2
Parkside NN3 . . . . .159 E5
Parkway Nassington PE8 . . .15 F5
Parkway NN8 . . . . .129 C5
Parkway Cl PE8 . . . . .15 F5
Parkwood St NN5 . . . . .159 A5
Parnell Cl Rugby CV21 . . . .241 E8
West Haddon NN6 . . . . .102 C5
Parracombe Way NN3 . . . .160 C7
Parson's St OX16 . . . . .240 D8
Parsons Cl Ecton NN6 . . . .143 D1
Nether Heyford NN7 . . . . . .156 C2
Parsons Gr NN17 . . . . .22 A1
Parsons Meade NN12 . . . . .158 E2
Parsons Rd
Daventry NN11 . . . . .134 F5
Irchester NN29 . . . . .147 B8
Parsons St
Adderbury OX17 . . . . .230 A4
Woodford Halse NN11 . . . .184 C6
Parsons' Cl NN7 . . . . .163 D5
Partridge Cl
Buckingham MK18 . . . . .240 F2
Charwelton NN11 . . . . .168 A5
Northampton NN2 . . . . .141 A5
Partridge La NN11 . . . . . . .184 C1
Parva Ct NN3 . . . . .142 E3
Pascoe Cres NN11 . . . . .135 A4
Pashler Gdns NN14 . . . . . . .76 D2
Pasteur Cl NN2 . . . . .141 B5
Pasteur Ctyd NN17 . . . . . . .37 B8
Pasture Ter NN11 . . . . .135 C1
Pastures The
Market Harborough LE16 . . .31 C3
Northampton NN2 . . . . .141 A5
Weedon NN7 . . . . .155 D3
Paterson Rd NN8 . . . . .130 B8
Patrick Cl NN15 . . . . .91 C6
Patrick Rd Corby NN14 . . . .36 C4
Kettering NN15 . . . . .91 C6
Patrick St LE16 . . . . .31 F5
Patricks La MK19 . . . . .228 E4
Patterdale Wlk ❶ NN3 . . .142 E8
Patterson Cl NN3 . . . . .142 E1
Pattishall CE Prim Sch
NN12 . . . . .188 F8
Pavilion Dr NN4 . . . . .159 F1
Pavilion Dr PE8 . . . . .41 E6
Pavilions Way NN13 . . . . . .233 F7
Paxford NN18 . . . . .36 C4
Paxmans Pl OX16 . . . . .240 C6
Paxton Cl NN3 . . . . .142 D4
Paxton Rd NN3 . . . . .142 D4
Payne's La LE16 . . . . .31 E7
Paynes Ct NN18 . . . . .240 E5
Peace Cl NN4 . . . . .160 B3
Peace Hill NN7 . . . . .172 E7
Peacock Dr NN14 . . . . .90 E5
Peacock Pl ❶ NN1 . . . . . . .159 D6
Peacock's Cl OX17 . . . . . . .220 A8
Peak The NN7 . . . . .156 C1
Peake Cl LE16 . . . . .35 B8

Pear Tree Cl
Bozeat NN29 . . . . .164 D3
Northampton NN3 . . . . .143 A2
Pear Tree Gdns LE16 . . . . . .31 D2
Pearmain Ave NN8 . . . . . . .129 F7
Pearmain Ct NN3 . . . . .143 A2
Peartree Cl NN11 . . . . .135 C4
Peaselands NN14 . . . . .50 F4
Pear Ct CV22 . . . . .241 A8
Pebble La Brackley NN13 .233 F7
❹ Wellingborough NN8 . . .130 A4
Peckbleford Rd NN15 . . . . .91 D8
Peck Way NN10 . . . . .132 B4
Peel Rd NN5 . . . . .158 C8
Pedley's La Clipston LE16 . .66 F8
Denford NN14 . . . . .95 C6
Pegasus Ct NN12 . . . . .233 F7
Pelham St NN3 . . . . .103 E7
Pell Ct NN3 . . . . .142 E3
Pells Cl NN6 . . . . .103 E7
Pemberton St NN10 . . . . . .132 A3
Pembroke Cl
Rushden NN10 . . . . .132 C1
Thrapston NN14 . . . . .76 D2
Pembroke Cres NN5 . . . . .159 B8
Pembroke Gdns NN5 . . . . .159 A8
Pembroke Ho MK46 . . . . . .195 F3
Pembroke Rd
Northampton NN5 . . . . .159 B8
Stamford PE9 . . . . .241 C5
Pembroke Way NN11 . . . . .153 B7
Pen Ct NN1 . . . . .159 D4
Pen Gn La NN17 . . . . .37 A8
Penarth Rd NN5 . . . . .159 A8
Pendered Rd NN8 . . . . .130 A6
Pendle Ave NN16 . . . . .72 A6
Pendle Rd NN5 . . . . .158 C8
Pendred Rd CV22 . . . . .241 A8
Penfold Ct NN2 . . . . .141 B4
Penfold Dr NN3 . . . . .143 B3
Penfold Gdns NN3 . . . . . . .143 C3
Penfold La NN3 . . . . .143 C3
Peninsular Cl ❶ NN4 . . . .175 E7
Penistone Rd NN3 . . . . .142 E3
Penistone Wlk ❸ NN3 . . . .142 E3
Penn Gdns NN4 . . . . .175 B7
Pennard Cl NN4 . . . . .160 B2
Pennant Rd NN11 . . . . .135 B5
Pennine Way
Kettering NN16 . . . . .72 B6
Northampton NN5 . . . . .158 C8
Pennington Mews CV21 . .241 B8
Pennington St CV21 . . . . . .241 B8
Pennycress Pl NN3 . . . . . . .143 D1
Penrhyn Ct NN14 . . . . .76 E2
Penrith Ct NN3 . . . . .142 E8
Penrith Dr NN8 . . . . .129 C5
Penrose Cl OX16 . . . . .240 A8
Penrose Dr OX16 . . . . .240 A8
Penteiowes The PE18 . . . .116 D2
Penthorne Cl NN14 . . . . . . .188 A8
Pentlands NN11 . . . . .229 F4
Penvale Rd NN4 . . . . .175 B7
Pepper Alley OX15 . . . . . . .236 E4
Peppercorn Way NN4 . . . .175 D6
Perceval Cl NN5 . . . . .140 D1
Perch Cl NN11 . . . . .135 B6
Percival Rd Rugby CV22 . .241 A6
Rugby CV22 . . . . .98 D8
Percy Rd
Northampton NN1 . . . . .159 F7
Woodford Halse NN11 . . . .184 C6
Peregrine Pl NN4 . . . . .175 A8
Perkins Cl LE16 . . . . .31 F4
Perkins Ct ❹ NN14 . . . . . .130 A5
Perkins Rd NN9 . . . . .131 E8
Perkins Way NN11 . . . . . . .153 C4
Perry Cl NN15 . . . . .91 A7
Perry St NN1 . . . . .159 F7
Pershore Ct NN16 . . . . .145 E8
Perth Ho NN17 . . . . .22 F1
Perth Rd NN16 . . . . .241 A4
Peterborough Rd
Morcott LE15 . . . . .3 D6
Wansford PE8 . . . . .8 A3
Warmington PE8 . . . . .28 C4
Petergate PE9 . . . . .241 C2
Peterhouse Ct PE9 . . . . . . .241 D5
Peters La NN6 . . . . .106 F5
Pether Ave NN13 . . . . .233 C8
Petherton Ct NN16 . . . . .72 B3
Pettiver Cres ❷ CV21 . . . .80 A1
Petworth Dr LE16 . . . . .32 B2
Petworth Gdns NN18 . . . . .36 B5
Pevensey Cl NN10 . . . . .132 D1
Pevensey Wlk NN10 . . . . . .132 D1
Peveril's Way NN5 . . . . .158 E6
Peveril Cl NN10 . . . . .132 C6
Peveril Rd
Greatworth OX17 . . . . .210 E2
Northampton NN5 . . . . .158 C7
Pevers La MK46 . . . . .195 A1
PewsI Rd NN14 . . . . .50 E4
Pexley Ct PE8 . . . . .41 E5
Pheasant Way NN7 . . . . . . .141 A5
Pheonix Parkway NN17 . . .29 E1
Philip Way NN10 . . . . .132 A5
Phillips Cl PE9 . . . . .241 E2
Phillips Way NN6 . . . . .121 C4
Phipps Rd NN11 . . . . .184 B6
Phoenix Cl NN8 . . . . .130 B3
Phoenix Parkway NN17 . . .22 B2
Phoenix St ❼ NN1 . . . . . . .159 C6
Piccadilly Bldgs ❹ NN16 .72 B1
Piccadilly Cl NN1 . . . . .159 F7
Pickerings The NN6 . . . . . .106 C1

Picks Cl LE16 . . . . 32 B3
Piddington La NN7 . . . . 177 A2
Pie Cnr NN6 . . . . 127 D3
Piece The Cogenhoe NN7 . .161 F6
Spratton NN6 . . . . .105 B1
Pied Bull Cl PE9 . . . . .1 A6
Pierce Cres PE8 . . . . .28 C3
Pigeon Hill NN12 . . . . .189 D3
Pightle Cres MK18 . . . . . .240 D5
Pightle The MK18 . . . . . .240 D4
Pightles Terr NN10 . . . . . .132 C1
Pightles Wlk NN10 . . . . . .132 C1
Pigott's La NN15 . . . . .92 C2
Pike La NN11 . . . . .159 C6
Pike Rd NN18 . . . . .66 A3
Pikemead Ct NN3 . . . . . . .143 B4
Pilgrim Way NN8 . . . . . . .129 F3
Pilgrims La NN7 . . . . .173 A7
Pilgrims Pl NN14 . . . . .159 C2
Pilot Rd NN17 . . . . .27 C8
Pilton Cl NN3 . . . . .143 C5
Pilton Rd PE8 . . . . .58 A4
Pincet La LE17 . . . . .45 A6
Pindar Rd NN8 . . . . .129 C2
Pindar Rise NN3 . . . . .142 E6
Pinders La CV21 . . . . .241 D9
Pine Ave NN6 . . . . .127 D3
Pine Cl Desborough NN14 . .51 C2
Irchester NN29 . . . . .147 A7
Northampton NN4 . . . . .175 E3
Rushden NN10 . . . . .148 A8
Pine Copse Cl NN5 . . . . . .140 A2
Pine Cres NN3 . . . . .127 D1
Pine Ct NN7 . . . . .138 C4
Pine Gr CV21 . . . . .240 B3
Pine Rd NN15 . . . . .72 D1
Pine Ridge NN3 . . . . .142 F7
Pine Trees NN3 . . . . .142 D1
Pine Wlk NN17 . . . . .21 E1
Pineham Ave NN2 . . . . . . .115 B6
Pines The LE16 . . . . .32 A6
Pinetrees Cl NN7 . . . . . . .177 B3
Pinewood Cl NN16 . . . . . . .72 B6
Pinewood Rd NN3 . . . . . .142 B3
Pinfold Cl LE15 . . . . .3 E8
Pinfold Gn NN11 . . . . .152 F3
Pinfold La Stamford PE9 . .242 E2
Stamford PE9 . . . . .241 F3
Pinfold St CV21 . . . . .241 A8
Pingle La LE15 . . . . .3 B6
Pinhill Rd OX16 . . . . .240 B9
Pioneer Ave
Burton Latimer NN15 . . . . . . .92 B2
Desborough NN14 . . . . .50 F2
Pioneer Cl NN4 . . . . .175 E7
Piper Cl NN8 . . . . .129 F8
Piper's Hill Rd NN15 . . . . .91 C8
Pipers Ct
Irthlingborough NN9 . . . . . . .112 F2
Kettering NN15 . . . . .72 C1
Pipewell Rd
Desborough NN14 . . . . .51 C4
East Carlton LE16 . . . . .35 B3
Pippin Cl Cogenhoe NN7 . .161 E5
Rushden NN10 . . . . .131 E3
Wellingborough NN8 . . . . . . .129 F4
Pippin La NN3 . . . . .143 A2
Pit La PE9 . . . . .1 A7
Pitchers La LE16 . . . . .20 D7
Pitchford Ave MK18 . . . .240 E5
Pitchford Wlk MK18 . . . .240 E5
Pitsford & Brampton Sta*
NN6 . . . . .124 E2
Pitsford Prim Sch NN6 . .125 D5
Pitsford Rd
Chapel Brampton NN6 . . . . .124 E1
Moulton NN3 . . . . .124 E8
Pitstone Rd NN4 . . . . . . .158 E3
Pitt Gn MK18 . . . . .240 F4
Pitt St NN8 . . . . .129 E4
Pittams Cl NN6 . . . . .121 B3
Pittams La NN12 . . . . . . .213 B8
Pittoms La CV23 . . . . .99 C1
Pittoms Rd NN3 . . . . .203 C5
Plank Hos NN12 . . . . .203 C5
Plantagenet Cl NN13 . . . .233 E8
Plantagenet Sq NN4 . . . .158 F2
Playford Cl NN14 . . . . .70 F7
Pleasant Row NN14 . . . . . .94 D7
Plessey Cl NN12 . . . . .203 D5
Pleydell Gdns NN4 . . . . . .159 C2
Pleydell Rd NN4 . . . . .159 C2
Plough Cl Daventry NN11 . .143 E6
Rothwell NN14 . . . . .70 D7
Plough La NN2 . . . . .141 A6
Plough Mews NN4 . . . . . .233 F7
Ploughmans Way NN4 . . .175 F3
Ploughmans Wlk NN4 . . .141 B5
Plover Cl
Buckingham MK18 . . . . .240 E2
Towcester NN12 . . . . .203 C3
Plowden Cl NN11 . . . . . . .182 F2
Plowman St CV21 . . . . . . .241 B8
Plum Park La NN12 . . . . .216 D8
Plumpton Cl NN18 . . . . . . .36 B5
Plumpton La NN11 . . . . . .199 D7
Plumpton Rd
Weston NN12 . . . . .200 A2
Woodend NN12 . . . . .200 F6
Plumtree Ave NN6 . . . . . .130 A7
Poachers Cl NN4 . . . . .175 F3
Poachers Way NN12 . . . . .141 C6
Pochin Dr LE16 . . . . .16 F5
Poddington Rd NN10 . . . .148 A4
Podmore Way NN14 . . . . . .90 A3
Poets Way NN11 . . . . .153 E5

Poitiers Ct NN5 . . . . .139 F1
Pokas Cotts NN9 . . . . . . .133 C8
Polar Star Cl NN11 . . . . . .135 A4
**Polebrook Airfield Nature
Reserve*** PE8 . . . . .43 F3
Polebrook CE Prim Sch
PE8 .43 A3
Polebrook Ct PE8 . . . . .42 F3
Polegate Ct NN18 . . . . .36 B5
Police Flats NN17 . . . . . . .36 E6
Pollard St NN16 . . . . .72 B4
Polquil NN13 . . . . .77 D3
Polwell La NN15 . . . . .92 A4
Pomfret Rd NN12 . . . . . . .203 C6
Pond Bank NN7 . . . . .190 D8
Pond Farm Cl NN5 . . . . . .158 C7
Pond Wood Cl NN3 . . . . .142 B6
Ponder St NN14 . . . . .70 D7
Ponds Cl NN9 . . . . .114 D6
Pool Cl NN12 . . . . .188 D8
Pool St NN11 . . . . .184 B5
Poolside Cl OX16 . . . . . . .240 A8
Pope Rd NN8 . . . . .129 C3
Pope St CV22 . . . . .241 A8
Popham Ct NN9 . . . . .114 C7
Poplar Cl Daventry NN11 . .135 C5
Irchester NN29 . . . . .147 A8
Rushden NN10 . . . . .148 A8
Towcester NN12 . . . . .203 C4
Poplar Ct NN3 . . . . .142 D5
Poplar Gr CV21 . . . . .241 C9
Poplar Pl
Wellingborough NN8 . . . . . .129 F4
Wollaston NN29 . . . . .146 E2
Poplar Rd
Burton Latimer NN15 . . . . . . .92 C4
Corby NN17 . . . . .20 D1
Finedon NN9 . . . . .112 A5
Kettering NN16 . . . . .72 D2
Poplar Rise NN12 . . . . . . .213 B8
Poplar St NN16 . . . . .130 A5
Poplar's Farm Rd NN15 . . .92 B8
Poplars Cl
Blakesley NN12 . . . . .187 B1
Middleton Cheney OX17 . . . .220 A8
Raunds NN9 . . . . .114 C6
Poplars Ct
Market Harborough LE16 . . . .31 D4
Scaldwell NN6 . . . . .106 F6
Poplars La NN6 . . . . .126 E8
Poplars Rd
Buckingham MK18 . . . . .240 D3
Charcombe OX17 . . . . .208 F4
Poplars The
Guilsborough NN6 . . . . .103 C7
Long Buckby NN6 . . . . .121 B3
Northampton NN1 . . . . .159 C7
Poppy Cl NN10 . . . . .148 C8
Poppy Leys NN6 . . . . .125 B8
Poppyfield Ct
Northampton NN3 . . . . .142 F4
Thrapston NN14 . . . . .76 D3
Porlock Cl NN5 . . . . .158 D8
Port Rd NN5 . . . . .140 A2
Portchester Gdns
NN3 . . . . .160 F8
Porter's Cl NN13 . . . . . . .228 E4
Porter's La PE9 . . . . .2 A5
Portfield Cl MK18 . . . . . .240 E3
Portfield Way MK18 . . . .240 E3
Portland Cl NN11 . . . . . . .135 D1
Portland Pl
Irthlingborough NN9 . . . . . .112 F3
Rugby CV21 . . . . .241 F7
Portland Rd
Irthlingborough NN9 . . . . . .112 F3
Rugby CV21 . . . . .241 F7
Portlow La NN6 . . . . .100 F6
Portree Wlk NN17 . . . . . . .36 C8
Portstone Cl NN5 . . . . . . .140 A2
Portway Cl Aynho OX17 . . .237 D7
Portway Dr NN13 . . . . . . .238 D7
Portway Gdns OX17 . . . . .237 D7
Portwey Cl NN6 . . . . .106 C1
Post Office Cl NN17 . . . . . .37 B6
Postle Cl CV23 . . . . .99 F2
Potter Cl NN9 . . . . .114 A4
Potters End NN11 . . . . . .183 A8
Pottersbury Lodge Sch
NN12 . . . . .217 A6
Pound Cl Corby NN18 . . . . .36 B7
Ringstead NN14 . . . . .95 B3
Wicken MK19 . . . . .228 A4
Pound Ct NN3 . . . . .126 B1
Pound La Badby NN11 . . . .152 F3
Bugbrooke NN7 . . . . .173 A7
Eastcote NN12 . . . . .172 F1
Moulton NN3 . . . . .126 C1
Northampton NN3 . . . . .143 C2
Pound PI NN11 . . . . .111 F4
Pound The
Great Brington NN7 . . . . . . .138 D6
Horton NN7 . . . . .177 E1
Nether Heyford NN7 . . . . . .156 B1
Syresham NN13 . . . . .224 B7
Poundfield Rd NN12 . . . . .217 E2
Power Pk OX16 . . . . .240 E7
Poyntz Gdns NN6 . . . . . . .158 E8
Poyntz La NN17 . . . . .158 E8
Pratt Rd NN10 . . . . .132 C2
Premier Way NN9 . . . . . . .113 E8
Prentice Cl NN3 . . . . .143 A5
Prentice Wlk NN17 . . . . . .37 A6
Prescott Ave OX16 . . . . . .240 A8

Prescott Cl
Banbury OX16 . . . . .240 A8
Northampton NN3 . . . . .143 C4
Pressland Dr NN10 . . . . . .132 C6
Prestbury Rd NN5 . . . . . . .140 A1
Prestidge Row NN11 . . . .199 C7
Preston Cт
Burton Latimer NN15 . . . . . . .92 C3
Northampton NN3 . . . . .142 E3
Preston Deanery Rd
NN7 . . . . .176 B1
Preston Dr NN11 . . . . .135 C6
Preston Hedges Prim Sch
NN4 . . . . .175 F6
Preston Rd NN11 . . . . .184 C2
Prestwold Way NN3 . . . . .143 B5
Prices Way NN13 . . . . . . .222 E5
Pride Pl LE16 . . . . .31 D2
Priestgate PE8 . . . . .14 E2
Priestley Ct NN17 . . . . .22 D1
Priestwell Ct NN6 . . . . . . .122 D5
Primrose Cl Corby NN16 . . .36 C2
Kettering NN16 . . . . .72 D4
Primrose Gdns NN9 . . . . .114 D5
Primrose Hill
Daventry NN11 . . . . .135 C2
Northampton NN2 . . . . .159 C7
Raunds NN9 . . . . .114 D6
Primrose Pl NN18 . . . . . . .130 C5
Primrose Way NN8 . . . . . .240 C2
Primrose Wlk
Hinton NN11 . . . . .184 B6
Northampton NN4 . . . . .175 F2
Primula Cl NN14 . . . . .160 C6
Primula Cl NN3 . . . . .159 C8
Prince Cl NN11 . . . . .135 B3
Prince Of Wales Row
NN2 . . . . .141 C4
Prince Rupert Ave NN14 . . .50 F3
Prince St NN6 . . . . .144 D5
Prince William Rd PE8 . . . .41 E5
Prince William Sch PE8 . . .42 B4
Princes Ave NN14 . . . . .51 B3
Princes Cl NN7 . . . . .155 A3
Princes Cl NN16 . . . . .72 B3
Princes Rd PE9 . . . . .241 D4
Princes St Kettering NN16 . .72 C2
Rugby CV21 . . . . .241 C9
Princes Wlk NN8 . . . . .129 E4
Princess Anne Bldg
NN2 . . . . .141 C4
Princess Cl NN3 . . . . .160 B6
Princess Marina Hospl
NN5 . . . . .158 B6
Princess Way NN8 . . . . . .129 E2
Princethorpe Dr
Banbury OX16 . . . . .219 A7
Northampton NN3 . . . . .160 F8
Princewood Rd NN17 . . . . .21 E3
Printers Yd NN11 . . . . .72 B2
Priors Cl NN10 . . . . .147 F8
Priors Ct Corby NN11 . . . . .23 A1
Rushden NN10 . . . . .132 B2
Stony Stratford MK11 . . . . . .229 B4
Priors Haw Rd NN17 . . . . .23 A1
Priors Marston Rd
Byfield NN11 . . . . .167 B8
Hellidon NN11 . . . . .165 A3
Priors Chapel NN11 . . . . . . .135 D1
Priors Ct Daventry NN11 . . .135 D1
Northampton NN3 . . . . .160 B6
Priory Cres NN7 . . . . .191 C4
Priory Ct Geddington NN14 . .54 A2
Weedon NN7 . . . . .155 A2
Priory Gdns PE9 . . . . .241 B5
Priory Ho NN11 . . . . .184 D3
Priory Rd Stamford PE9 . . .241 F3
Wellingborough NN8 . . . . . .129 F3
Wollaston NN29 . . . . .146 D3
Priory Vale Rd OX16 . . . . .240 F9
Pritchard Cl NN3 . . . . .143 C5
Probyn Cl NN3 . . . . .143 A6
Promenade The NN8 . . . .129 E2
Prospect Ave
Irchester NN29 . . . . .147 A7
Rushden NN10 . . . . .132 B4
Prospect Cl NN29 . . . . . . .146 D3
Prospect Cl NN12 . . . . . . .217 F6
Prospect Pl MK19 . . . . . . .218 F5
Prospect Rd
Banbury OX16 . . . . .240 D7
Stony Stratford MK11 . . . . . .229 C5
Prospect Way NN11 . . . . . .134 F3
Provence Cl NN5 . . . . .139 F1
Pudding Bag La NN29 . . . .164 D3
Puddledock NN12 . . . . . . .214 D5
Purbeck Rd NN10 . . . . . . .131 D2
Purse La NN15 . . . . .207 F8
Purser Rd NN1 . . . . .159 F8
Purston Cross Rds
PE9 . . . . .2 C3
Purvis Rd NN10 . . . . .132 A2
Pury Hill Bsns Pk NN12 . .204 E1
Pury Rd NN12 . . . . .205 A3
Puxley Rd NN19 . . . . .228 D5
Pye Cl CV23 . . . . .117 C4
Pyghtle The
Earls Barton NN6 . . . . .144 E5
Olney MK46 . . . . .195 F3
Wellingborough NN8 . . . . . .129 F6
Pyghtle Way NN14 . . . . . .175 A7
Pyghtles The
Daventry NN11 . . . . .135 B1
Wollaston NN29 . . . . .146 D1
Pyke Way NN6 . . . . .101 A6
Pyket Way NN15 . . . . .160 E8
Pyramid Cl NN3 . . . . .142 E2
Pytchley Cl NN6 . . . . .106 B2
Pytchley Ct Corby NN17 . . .36 B8

Pytchley Ct continued
West Haddon NN6 . . . . .102 C4
Pytchley Dr NN6 . . . . .121 B4
**Pytchley Endowed CE Prim
Sch** NN14 . . . . .90 C2
Pytchley La NN15 . . . . .91 C5
Pytchley Lodge Ind Est
NN15 . . . . .91 C5
Pytchley Lodge Rd NN15 . .91 C5
Pytchley Rd
Kettering NN15 . . . . .91 C6
Orlingbury NN14 . . . . .109 F5
Rugby CV22 . . . . .241 E6
Rushden NN10 . . . . .131 F3
Pytchley Rise NN8 . . . . . .129 D3
Pytchley St NN1 . . . . .159 E6
Pytchley View NN15 . . . . .126 D1
Pytchley Way
Brixworth NN6 . . . . .106 B2
Northampton NN5 . . . . .140 B2
Pywell Cl NN17 . . . . .22 E2
Pywell Rd NN17 . . . . .22 E2

Q

Quakers Cl NN7 . . . . .172 F7
Quantock Cl
Daventry NN11 . . . . .135 B5
Kettering NN16 . . . . .92 A5
Quantock Cres NN5 . . . . .158 D8
Quarry Green Cl MK19 . . .228 B3
Quarry Park Cl NN3 . . . . .142 B6
Quarry Rd Brixworth NN6 . .106 C3
Northampton NN5 . . . . .140 B2
Quarterstone NN14 . . . . .158 D1
Quatercroft NN3 . . . . .142 B2
Quebec Cl Corby NN18 . . . .36 C2
Queen Eleanor Comb Sch
MK11 . . . . .229 F4
Queen Eleanor Comp Sch
PE9 . . . . .241 D5
Queen Eleanor Lower Sch
NN4 . . . . .159 B2
Queen Eleanor Rd
Geddington NN14 . . . . .54 A3
Northampton NN4 . . . . .159 C2
Queen Eleanor St MK11 . .229 F4
Queen Eleanor Terr
NN4 . . . . .159 C2
Queen St Bozeat NN29 . . .164 C2
Desborough NN14 . . . . .51 B3
Earls Barton NN6 . . . . .144 F5
Geddington NN14 . . . . .54 A2
Irthlingborough NN9 . . . . . .112 C2
Kettering NN16 . . . . .72 D4
Market Harborough LE16 . . . .32 A2
Middleton Cheney OX17 . . . .219 F5
Rugby CV21 . . . . .241 C8
Thrapston NN14 . . . . .76 E2
Weedon NN7 . . . . .155 A2
Queen Victoria St CV21 . .241 E8
Queen's Park Par NN2 . . .141 C2
Queen's Rd NN1 . . . . .155 A3
Queen's Rd
Banbury OX16 . . . . .240 B8
Northampton NN1 . . . . .159 E2
Towcester NN12 . . . . .203 C6
Queen's Sq NN1 . . . . .36 E5
Queen's Wlk PE9 . . . . .241 E3
Queens Cl LE16 . . . . .34 C5
Queens Cres NN4 . . . . . . .141 D2
Queens Rd
Daventry NN11 . . . . .135 B3
Wollaston LE16 . . . . .34 D5
Wollaston NN29 . . . . .146 D2
Queens St
Culworth OX17 . . . . .198 D2
Farthinghoe NN13 . . . . .221 B4
Stamford PE9 . . . . .241 D4
Wellingborough NN8 . . . . . .130 A5
Queensberry Rd NN15 . . . .72 B1
Queensbury Cl NN15 . . . . .72 B1
Queensland Gdns NN2 . . .141 D2
Queensway
Banbury OX16 . . . . .240 B6
Burton Latimer NN15 . . . . . . .92 B1
Higham Ferrers NN10 . . . . . .132 C5
Wellingborough NN8 . . . . . .129 C4
Queensway Prim Sch
OX16 . . . . .240 A6
Queenswood Ave NN3 . . .142 D5
Quernstone La NN14 . . . . .158 E3
Quinton Green Cotts
NN7 . . . . .192 C7
Quinton House Sch
NN5 . . . . .158 B5
Quinton La NN11 . . . . .184 C6
Quinton Rd NN11 . . . . .153 F5
Quintonside NN4 . . . . .175 E3
Quorn Cl Kettering NN15 . . .92 A5
Wellingborough NN8 . . . . . .129 F2
Quorn Rd NN10 . . . . .132 A3
Quorn Way NN1 . . . . .159 B7

R

Racecourse Rd PE9 . . . . . . .2 D5
Racedown NN8 . . . . .129 D3
Radcliffe Cl NN9 . . . . .132 B3
Radcliffe Rd PE9 . . . . .241 D3
Radleigh Cl NN4 . . . . .159 A2

Radnor Way NN15 . . . . . . .92 A5
Radstone NN13 . . . . .222 F6
Radstone Rd NN13 . . . . . .222 F2
Radstone Way NN2 . . . . . .141 C5
Raeburn Rd NN2 . . . . .141 F2
Raeburn Sch NN2 . . . . . . .141 F2
Raglan Cl NN10 . . . . .132 D1
Raglan St NN1 . . . . .159 E6
Ragsdale Cl NN14 . . . . .70 E7
Ragsdale St NN14 . . . . .70 E7
Ragsdale Wlk NN3 . . . . . .142 E6
Ragworth Way NN17 . . . . .100 B6
Railway Cotts
Church Brampton NN6 . . . . .140 A7
Kilsby CV23 . . . . .100 A6
Nether Heyford NN7 . . . . . .172 A8
Railway Terr CV21 . . . . . . .241 D9
Railway View NN16 . . . . . . .72 A2
Raincliffe Cl OX17 . . . . . . .237 C2
Rainsborough Cres NN4 . .158 F4
Rainsborough Gdns LE16 . .48 D8
Rainsbrook Ave NN13 . . . .160 F8
Rainsbrook Valley Rly*
CV22 . . . . .98 C6
Raisins Field Cl NN3 . . . . .143 C3
Rakestone Cl NN4 . . . . . . .175 D6
Raleigh Cl Corby NN17 . . . .36 A8
Rothwell NN14 . . . . .70 E7
Raleigh Ct NN11 . . . . .135 B5
Ramsay Cl NN9 . . . . .114 C7
Randall Ho NN1 . . . . .159 F7
Randall Rd NN2 . . . . .141 E1
Rands Way NN3 . . . . .114 E5
Ranelagh Rd NN8 . . . . . . .130 B4
Rankine Ho NN17 . . . . .36 D8
Rannoch Cl NN15 . . . . .91 E8
Rannoch Way NN17 . . . . . .21 C1
Ransome Rd NN4 . . . . . . .159 D3
Rathbone Cl CV21 . . . . .99 A8
Rathlin Cl NN17 . . . . .36 C8
Raunds Manor Sch The
NN9 . . . . .114 C6
Raunds Rd
Chelveston NN9 . . . . .133 C8
Stanwick NN9 . . . . .114 A4
Raven Dr NN15 . . . . .92 A6
Ravens Croft NN4 . . . . . . .175 A7
Ravens Way NN3 . . . . .161 C8
Ravensbank NN12 . . . . . . .132 B4
Ravenscourt NN17 . . . . . . .36 F8
Ravensthorpe Rd NN6 . . . .122 D5
Rawley Cres NN5 . . . . .140 A1
Rawlings Cl NN11 . . . . . . .135 D1
Rawlins Cl CV22 . . . . .230 A5
Ray Cl PE8 . . . . .41 F7
Raymond Cl NN29 . . . . . . .146 E1
Raymond Rd NN5 . . . . . . .159 A7
Raynsford Rd NN5 . . . . . . .158 F8
Rea Cl NN4 . . . . .175 C7
Recreation Ground Rd
PE9 . . . . .241 D3
Rectory Cl Barby CV23 . . . .99 F1
Crick NN6 . . . . .100 F5
Stanwick NN9 . . . . .113 D4
Rectory Cm LE16 . . . . .48 B8
Rectory Farm Ct PE8 . . . . .28 D8
Rectory Farm Lower Sch
NN3 . . . . .143 C5
Rectory Farm Mews PE8 . .28 D8
Rectory Farm Rd NN3 . . . .143 D4
Rectory Hill NN14 . . . . .93 A7
Rectory La Barby CV23 . . . .99 F1
Holcot NN6 . . . . .126 E8
Market Harborough LE16 . . . .32 A2
Medbourne LE16 . . . . .19 A7
Middleton Cheney OX17 . . . .208 F1
Milton Malsor NN7 . . . . .174 E3
Orlingbury NN14 . . . . .110 A5
Walgrave NN6 . . . . .108 A4
Woodford NN14 . . . . .94 D6
Yardley Hastings NN7 . . . . .179 A7
Rectory Rd NN10 . . . . .132 B2
Rectory Way NN12 . . . . . .213 B8
Rectory Wlk NN15 . . . . .91 F7
Red Hill Cres NN3 . . . . . . .146 D3
Red House La NN6 . . . . . . .108 E4
Red House Rd NN3 . . . . . .142 B7
Red House Wharf NN7 . . .155 C4
Red Lion Sq PE9 . . . . .241 D3
Red Lion St
Kings Sutton OX17 . . . . .230 F5
Stamford PE9 . . . . .241 D3
Red Lodge Rd NN17 . . . . . .12 A1
Red Row NN9 . . . . .114 D6
Red Wood Cl NN14 . . . . . . .51 C2
Redbourn Pk NN4 . . . . . . .160 B3
Redbourne Ct NN11 . . . . . .229 F5
Redcot Gdns PE9 . . . . .241 C4
Redding Cl NN10 . . . . .148 A7
Redgrave Cl NN15 . . . . . . .90 F7
Redhill Way NN9 . . . . .110 E1
Redhouse Rd NN14 . . . . . .109 C4
Redland Cl LE15 . . . . .3 B5
Redland Dr NN2 . . . . .141 A4
Redltech Cl LE16 . . . . .32 B3
Redmile's La PE9 . . . . .1 A5
Redmoor NN12 . . . . .203 B4
Redruth Cl NN4 . . . . .159 B1
Redshaw Cl MK18 . . . . . . .240 A8
Redwell Jun & Inf Sch
NN8 . . . . .129 E7
Redwell L Ctr NN8 . . . . . . .129 E7
Redwell Rd NN8 . . . . .129 F6
Redwing Ave NN13 . . . . . .142 C6
Redwood Cl NN27 . . . . . . .142 B2
Reedham Cl NN3 . . . . .140 C1
Reedhill NN11 . . . . .158 E1
Reedway NN3 . . . . .142 A4

St Gilbert's CE Prim Sch
PE9 ....241 C3
St Giles Mews MK11 ......229 D6
St Giles' CI NN15 ....73 A1
St Giles' Sq NN1 ....159 D5
St Giles' Ter NN1 ....159 D6
St Giles's CI NN14 ....51 A3
St Gregory's RC Lower Sch
NN3 ....142 C3
St Gregory's Rd NN3 ......142 D3
St Helens CI NN6 ....84 D4
St Hilda's CI NN17 ....153 C8
St Hughes CI NN11 ....153 C8
St James CI
■ Daventry NN11 ....135 C1
Hanslope MK19 ....207 A2
St James Inf Sch NN11 ....135 C1
St James Mill Rd E NN1 ....159 B4
St James Rd
Brackley NN13 ....233 F5
Corby NN18 ....37 A6
St James Ret Pk NN1 ......159 B5
St James St NN1 ....135 C1
St James' CE Lower Sch
NN5 ....159 A6
St James' CI
Kettering NN15 ....92 A8
Rushden NN10 ....132 C4
St James' Cres NN14 ....76 E2
St James' Lake Nature
Reserve* NN1 ....159 A4
St James' Mill Rd NN5 .....159 A4
St James' Park Rd NN5 ....159 A5
St James' Rd NN5 ....159 A5
St John St CV21 ....241 C9
St John's Ave NN2 ....141 C6
St John's Ho ❸ NN1 ....159 C6
St John's La NN19 ....228 B4
St John's PI NN17 ....37 B6
St John's Rd
Banbury OX16 ....240 C7
Kettering NN15 ....91 F8
St John's Sq NN11 ....135 C2
St John's St
Northampton NN1 ....159 D5
Stamford PE9 ....241 D3
Wellingborough NN8 ......129 F5
St John's Terr NN1 ....159 D5
St John's Way NN7 ....177 A2
St John's Wlk NN1 ....142 D1
St Johns Ave CV22 ....98 E8
St Johns CI
Daventry NN11 ....153 B8
Rothersthorpe NN7 ....174 A6
St Johns Ct NN1 ....159 D5
St Johns Rd NN12 ....189 E4
St Joseph's CI NN15 ....73 A1
St Joseph's RC Prim Sch
LE16 ....217 D3
St Josephs CI MK46 ....195 F4
St Julien CI NN5 ....140 A2
St Katharine's Way
NN29 ....131 B1
St Katherine's Ct ☷
NN1 ....159 C6
St Katherine's Sq ☷
NN1 ....159 C6
St Katherine's St ☷
NN1 ....159 C6
St Lawrence Way NN9 ......113 F4
St Lawrence CE Jun Sch
NN12 ....203 C3
St Lawrence Ct ▣ NN1 ....159 E6
St Lawrence Ho ▣ NN1 ...159 C6
St Lawrence Lower Sch
NN10 ....148 A5
St Lawrence Rd NN12 .....203 C5
St Lawrence Rd S NN12 ...203 A2
St Lawrence Wlk NN10 ...148 B5
St Leonard's CE Lower Sch
OX16 ....240 F8
St Leonard's CI
Banbury OX16 ....240 E8
Kettering NN15 ....92 A8
St Leonard's Rd NN4 ......159 C3
St Leonard's St PE9 ....241 E3
St Leonards CI CV47 ......166 D8
St Leonards Ct NN4 ....159 C3
St Lukes CE Lower Sch
NN5 ....158 C6
St Luke's CI NN11 ....92 A8
St Luke's Ho ⅏ NN1 ....159 C6
St Luke's Hospl LE16 ....31 D5
St Luke's Rd NN18 ....37 A5
St Lukes CI NN6 ....105 B1
St Magdalene's Wlk ..PE7 ..72 F2
St Margaret's Gdns ❸
NN5 ....140 F1
St Margarets Ave NN10 ...132 A1
St Marie's RC Inf Sch
CV22 ....241 C7
St Marie's RC Jun Sch
CV22 ....241 B7
St Mark's CI
Kettering NN15 ....73 A1
Rushden NN10 ....131 E2
St Mark's Cres NN2 ....141 B6
St Mark's Rd NN18 ....37 A5
St Marks Rd ❼ NN1 ....159 C6
St Martin's CI PE9 ....241 E2
St Martins CI NN17 ....22 E3
St Martins Ho ▣ NN1 ......159 C6
St Martins Yd ❸ LE16 ......31 E3
St Martin's Way NN7 ......155 B3

St Mary & St Giles CE Mid
Sch MK11 ....229 E6
St Mary's Ave
Finedon NN9 ....111 F5
Rushden NN10 ....132 B1
Stony Stratford MK11 ......229 E6
St Mary's CE Prim Sch
Banbury OX16 ....240 C8
Burton Latimer NN15 ......92 C2
Kettering NN16 ....72 C2
St Mary's CI
Nassington PE8 ....15 E5
Priors Hardwick CV47 ....166 A5
St Mary's Ct Finedon NN9 ..111 E5
Market Harborough LE16 ..32 A4
❷ Northampton NN1 ....159 D7
St Mary's Hill PE9 ....241 D3
St Mary's Hospl NN1 ......135 A2
St Mary's Paddock NN8 ..130 C4
St Mary's PI
Market Harborough LE16 ..31 F3
Stamford PE9 ....241 E3
St Mary's RC Lower Sch
NN5 ....140 F1
St Mary's RC Mid Sch
NN3 ....142 C3
St Mary's RC Prim Sch
NN11 ....182 F2
St Mary's Rd
Bozeat NN29 ....164 D2
Kettering NN15 ....72 C1
Market Harborough LE16 ..31 F3
St Mary's St
Northampton NN1 ....159 C6
Stamford PE9 ....241 D3
St Mary's Way
Nassington PE8 ....15 E5
Roade NN7 ....191 D5
Weedon NN7 ....155 B3
St Marys CI
Thrapston NN14 ....76 F3
Woodnewton PE8 ....14 E2
St Marys Ct NN7 ....173 F2
St Marys Hill PE8 ....14 E2
St Marys Rd NN29 ....146 E2
St Matthew's Bloxam CE Prim
Sch CV22 ....241 B7
St Matthew's Par NN2 ....141 F5
St Matthew's Rd NN15 ....73 A1
St Matthews St CV21 .....241 C8
St Michael's Ave NN1 .....159 E7
St Michael's CI NN2 ....141 B6
St Michael's La NN9 ....146 D2
St Michael's Mount
NN1 ....159 E7
St Michael's Rd
Kettering NN16 ....91 C8
Northampton NN1 ....159 D6
St Michaels Gdns ..NN1 ....91 C8
St Nicholas CI
Kettering NN15 ....72 F2
Market Harborough LE16 ..145 D6
St Nicholas La NN29 ......145 D6
St Nicholas Rd NN29 .....145 D6
St Nicholas Way
Islip NN14 ....76 B3
Market Harborough LE16 ..145 D6
St Oswald's CI NN15 ....91 F8
St Osyths La PE8 ....42 A5
St Patrick St ❶ NN1 ....159 C7
St Patrick's RC Prim Sch
NN18 ....36 D4
St Paul's CE Lower Sch
NN2 ....159 C8
St Paul's Ct
Kettering NN15 ....72 B1
Stony Stratford MK11 ......229 D6
St Paul's St PE9 ....241 E3
St Paul's Terr NN1 ....159 C8
St Peter's Ave
Kettering NN16 ....72 C1
Rushden NN10 ....131 F2
St Peter's CE Jun Sch
NN9 ....114 E6
St Peter's CI NN14 ....37 F2
St Peter's Gate NN13 .....233 A7
St Peter's Gdns NN3 ......142 D1
St Peter's Hill PE9 ....241 D3
St Peter's Ho ⅏ NN1 ......159 C7
St Peter's Ind Sch NN3 ...143 A3
St Peter's Rd
Brackley NN13 ....233 B8
Rugby CV21 ....241 E8
St Peter's Sch PE9 ....91 B8
St Peter's St
Northampton NN1 ....159 B5
Stamford PE9 ....241 D2
St Peter's Vale PE9 ....241 D2
St Peter's Way
Corby NN17 ....37 A6
Irthlingborough NN9 ......112 F2
Northampton NN1 ....159 C5
Weedon NN7 ....155 B3
St Peters CI NN11 ....153 B8
St Peters Rd PE8 ....41 F7
St Peters Sq ⅏ NN1 ....159 C7
St Peters Way NN1 ....161 F6
St Peters Wlk ▣ NN1 .....159 C5
St Philip's CI NN15 ....73 A1
St Rumbold's La MK18 ...240 C3
St Rumbolds Dr OX17 ....231 A5
St Saviour's Rd NN15 ......73 A1
St Simon's CI NN15 ....73 A1
St Stephen's Rd NN15 .....73 A1
St Stephens Ho ❾ NN1 ..159 C6
St Swithins CE Prim Sch
NN15 ....72 F2

St Theresa's CI NN15 ......72 F1
St Thomas More RC Prim Sch
NN16 ....71 F1
St Thomas Rd NN7 ....161 D3
St Valentine's CI NN15 .....73 A1
St Vincents Ave NN15 .....72 F2
St Wilfrids Rd PE8 ....41 F7
Salcey Ave NN7 ....192 D2
Salcey CI
❷ Daventry NN11 ....135 B4
Hartwell NN7 ....192 E2
Kettering NN15 ....92 A5
Salcey Forest Trail*
NN7 ....192 F4
Salcey Forest Trail(Rose
Copse)* NN7 ....192 C3
Salcey Rise NN7 ....177 B1
Salcey St NN4 ....159 C2
Salcombe Rd NN18 ....36 C4
Salem CI NN6 ....121 A3
Salem La ❷ NN8 ....130 A5
Salem CI NN15 ....92 B5
Salford CI NN6 ....64 E6
Salisbury Rd NN8 ....130 C5
Salisbury St
Kettering NN16 ....72 C4
Northampton NN2 ....159 C8
Sallow Ave NN3 ....143 C3
Sallow Rd NN17 ....22 E1
Salmons La OX17 ....220 B8
Salt Pikes NN6 ....125 B8
Salthouse Rd NN4 ....160 C2
Saltwell Sq ❷ NN3 ....143 C2
Samuel PI NN17 ....37 A8
Samuels CI NN3 ....113 F3
Samwell Way NN4 ....158 C1
Sandby Rd NN16 ....36 E4
Sandell CI OX16 ....240 C7
Sanders CI
Braunston NN11 ....118 B1
Wellingborough NN8 ......111 B1
Sanders La NN12 ....217 D3
Sanders Lodge Ind Est
NN10 ....131 D3
Sanders Rd NN8 ....111 B1
Sanders Terr NN6 ....125 B8
Sanderson CI NN15 ....91 A8
Sandfield CI NN3 ....142 B6
Sandhill Rd ❷ NN5 ....159 A6
Sandhills CI NN2 ....105 A1
Sandhills Rd NN2 ....141 B6
Sandhurst CI NN4 ....175 B8
Sandhurst Dr MK18 ......240 C2
Sandiland Rd NN3 ....142 B2
Sandlands Ave NN4 ....55 F7
Sandlands CI NN14 ....55 F7
Sandover NN4 ....175 D6
Sandown Rd CV21 ....241 E9
Sandpiper CI NN15 ....92 A2
Sandpiper La NN8 ....130 A7
Sandringham CI
Brackley NN13 ....233 E7
Northampton NN1 ....160 B7
Rushden NN10 ....132 A1
Stamford PE9 ....241 D5
Towcester NN12 ....203 C4
Wellingborough NN8 ......126 B8
Sandringham Ct NN15 .....91 D5
Sandringham Way LE16 ...32 B3
Sands CI NN12 ....172 D1
Sandy CI
Buckingham MK18 ....240 F3
Sandy Hill LE16 ....126 C2
Sandy La
Church Brampton NN6 ...140 D8
Harpole NN7 ....157 E7
Northampton NN5 ....139 F2
Rugby CV21 ....241 B8
Sandyhome Rd NN3 ......203 C5
Saneco La NN7 ....106 B3
Sansom Ct NN3 ....142 D4
Sansome CI NN7 ....177 B3
Saplings The NN16 ....72 C6
Sapphire CI NN15 ....72 C1
Sarek Pk NN4 ....174 F7
Sargeants La NN4 ....175 C4
Sargent Rd NN18 ....36 E4
Sargent's Ct PE9 ....241 E4
Sarrington Rd NN7 ....36 F8
Sartoris Rd NN10 ....131 F2
Saruman La NN3 ....143 B6
Sassoon CI NN8 ....129 C6
Sassoon Mews NN8 ......129 B6
Saunders CI NN16 ....72 B1
Saunton Rd CV22 ....241 B6
Savill CI NN4 ....175 C7
Sawyers Cres NN9 ....133 B8
Saxby Cres NN8 ....130 C4
Saxilby CI NN18 ....36 C4
Saxon Acre NN13 ....233 F7
Saxon Ave NN15 ....175 E3
Saxon CI
Desborough NN14 ....55 F7
Market Harborough LE16 ..31 F4
Saxon Dale NN16 ....72 C5
Saxon Ho NN6 ....106 B2
Saxon Rise
Earls Barton NN6 ....144 E3
Irchester NN29 ....147 D8
Northampton NN5 ....158 B7
Saxon St NN3 ....142 B1
Saxon Way NN9 ....149 A8
Saxon Way E NN18 ....53 A8

Saxon Way W NN18 ....52 F8
Saxonlea CI NN10 ....131 E3
Scaldwell Rd
Brixworth NN6 ....106 D4
Old NN6 ....107 C7
Scapa Rd NN17 ....22 E3
Scarborough St NN9 .....112 E2
Scarborough Wlk NN18 ...36 B4
Scarletwell St NN1 ....159 B6
Scarplands The NN5 ......158 C6
Scarpwell NN9 ....112 E3
Scholars CI NN11 ....159 D5
Scholars Row NN14 ....89 B4
School CI
Braunston NN11 ....118 D1
Greens Norton NN12 .....202 D8
Yelvertoft NN6 ....82 A4
School End OX17 ....237 C7
School Farm Yd LE16 ....18 B3
School Gdns CV21 ....80 A1
School Hill
Irchester NN9 ....147 B8
Middleton LE16 ....35 C8
Newnham NN11 ....153 D4
School La Abthorpe NN12 ..202 A2
Badby NN11 ....152 F3
Banbury OX16 ....240 C8
Barrowden LE15 ....3 F5
Braybrooke LE16 ....49 F5
Buckingham MK18 ....240 C3
Bythorn PE28 ....97 C6
Castlethorpe MK19 ....218 F5
Cottingham LE16 ....20 C1
Denford NN14 ....95 C6
Elton PE8 ....28 D8
Evenley NN13 ....233 F2
Everdon NN11 ....170 A8
Eydon NN11 ....184 C1
Greens Norton NN12 .....202 D8
Hannington NN6 ....108 C2
Harpole NN7 ....157 B6
Hartwell NN7 ....192 D2
Husbands Bosworth LE17 ..45 E5
Irchester NN29 ....147 A8
Islip NN14 ....76 B2
Kettering NN16 ....72 B2
Kislingbury NN7 ....157 D4
Little Harrowden NN6 .....110 C4
Lubenham LE16 ....30 F3
Market Harborough LE16 ..31 E3
Morcott LE15 ....3 A4
Moulton NN3 ....126 C1
Naseby NN6 ....85 B8
Priors Marston CV47 ......166 D8
Quinton NN7 ....176 B1
Rothwell NN14 ....70 D7
Scaldwell NN6 ....106 A6
Swinford LE17 ....62 B4
Titchmarsh NN14 ....77 C4
Wappenham NN12 ....213 B8
Warmington PE8 ....28 B3
Welton NN11 ....160 A2
Wilbarston LE16 ....34 C5
Yardley Gobion NN12 .....217 E6
Yelvertoft NN6 ....82 B4
School PI NN18 ....36 D5
School Rd Gretton NN17 ..18 D1
Irchester NN29 ....147 A8
Mawsley Village NN14 ....89 B4
Pattishall NN12 ....188 F8
Spratton NN6 ....105 B1
School St Daventry NN11 ..135 A2
Rugby CV21 ....80 A1
Sulgrave OX17 ....210 F7
Woodford Halse NN11 ....184 C6
School View OX16 ....240 F8
Schoolfield Gr CV21 ....241 A8
Scirocco CI NN4 ....141 C6
Scoborough Rd LE16,
LE17 ....30 A1
Scotgate
Harringworth NN17 ....10 F7
Stamford PE9 ....241 D3
Scotia CI NN4 ....160 C2
Scotland End LE16 ....31 F1
Scotland La NN15 ....32 A2
Scotland St NN16 ....72 C3
Scotney CI ▣ NN4 ....175 C8
Scotney Way NN14 ....18 D1
Scots Mere NN9 ....112 D3
Scott Ave NN14 ....70 E7
Scott CI Daventry NN11 ...135 C4
Market Harborough LE16 ..31 F3
Ravensthorpe NN6 ....103 D1
Scott Rd Corby NN17 ....37 A6
Kettering NN16 ....91 C8
Scotter Wlk NN18 ....36 C4
Scotts CI LE16 ....34 C5
Scriveners La NN12 ....216 A8
Scrivens Hill NN11 ....184 D6
Scully CI ❸ NN4 ....175 C7
Scythe Rd NN11 ....135 B3
Seabrooke Ave CV22 .....241 B8
Seaford Wlk NN18 ....36 B5
Seagrave CI NN3 ....143 B5
Seagrave St NN15 ....91 C8
Sears CI NN7 ....155 E6
Sears Ho NN4 ....88 B6
Seaton Cres NN18 ....36 C5
Seaton Dr NN3 ....142 F1
Seaton Rd Barrowden LE15 ..3 D4
Harringworth NN17 ....10 C8
Stamford PE9 ....241 D2
Second Ave NN8 ....129 D3
Second La NN5 ....158 F6
Second St NN13 ....238 E6
Sedbergh Rd NN18 ....36 C4

Sedgemoor Ct NN11 ......135 C6
Sedgemoor Way NN11 ...135 C6
Sedgwick Ct NN13 ....142 F3
Sedlescombe Pk CV22 ....98 A8
Seefield CI NN13 ....142 E1
Selby CI LE16 ....48 E8
Selby CI NN15 ....91 F8
Selby Gdns NN29 ....164 C2
Selby Rd NN16 ....36 C4
Selsey Rd NN18 ....36 B5
Selston Wlk NN3 ....160 D7
Selwyn CI NN11 ....153 C7
Selwyn Rd PE9 ....241 C5
Semilong Ho ❹ NN2 .....159 C7
Semilong Rd NN2 ....159 B8
Senna Dr NN12 ....203 C8
Sentinel Rd NN4 ....158 E1
Sentry CI ❸ NN4 ....175 E7
Senwick Dr NN8 ....130 C4
Senwick Rd NN8 ....130 C4
Setchells Yd PE8 ....41 F5
Settlersfields NN15 ....1A5
Seven Sisters CI NN11 ...221 B4
Severn CI NN8 ....129 C6
Severn Ct NN15 ....92 B2
Severn Dr NN5 ....140 F2
Severn Ho PE8 ....42 A6
Severn The NN11 ....135 A1
Severn Way NN16 ....72 A5
Severn Wlk NN17 ....21 C1
Sewter Gdns PE8 ....15 E6
Sexton CI NN11 ....135 B3
Seymour PI PE8 ....41 E7
Seymour St NN5 ....159 A6
Shackleton CI NN14 ....70 E7
Shackleton Dr NN11 .....135 C5
Shades The OX16 ....240 C7
Shadowfax Dr NN3 ....143 C5
Shaftesbury Ave NN18 ....36 B6
Shaftesbury St NN16 ......72 C2
Shakespeare Ave NN11 ..135 B2
Shakespeare Dr NN15 ...92 A2
Shakespeare Rd
Kettering NN15 ....72 B5
Northampton NN1 ....159 E7
Rushden NN10 ....131 E2
Shakespeare Way NN17 ..36 D8
Shale End NN5 ....140 A3
Shannon CI NN10 ....132 D3
Shannon Ct NN14 ....36 E4
Shannon Way NN15 ....92 B2
Shap Gn NN3 ....142 C4
Shard CI NN4 ....175 D6
Sharman CI NN11 ....135 C5
Sharman Rd
Northampton NN5 ....159 A5
Wellingborough NN8 .....129 F4
Sharman Way NN14 ....70 F7
Sharmans CI NN7 ....162 A6
Sharpes La NN6 ....121 B4
Sharplands NN7 ....163 D5
Sharrow PY ❸ NN3 ....143 D2
Sharwood Terr NN29 .....147 B8
Shatterstone ❷ NN4 .....175 D6
Shaw CI NN18 ....129 B5
Shawell Rd LE17 ....62 A4
Sheaf CI NN5 ....140 B2
Sheaf St NN11 ....135 C1
Shearwater La NN14 ......130 A7
Shedfield Way NN4 ....175 C6
Sheep Market PE9 ....241 D3
Sheep St Kettering NN16 ..72 B1
Northampton NN1 ....159 C5
Rugby CV21 ....241 C8
Wellingborough NN8 .....130 A4
Sheerwater Dr NN3 ....143 D3
Sheffield Ct NN9 ....114 D3
Sheffield Way NN16 ....144 E3
Sheffield Wlk NN18 ....36 B4
Sheila PI NN15 ....72 E4
Sheldons La NN6 ....108 A5
Shelland CI NN3 ....143 B5
Shelland Ct LE16 ....32 A2
Shelley CI Daventry NN11 ..135 B2
Stamford PE9 ....241 A4
Towcester NN12 ....203 B5
Shelley Dr Corby NN17 ....21 D1
Higham Ferrers NN10 ....132 B5
Shelley Rd Kettering NN16 ..72 C5
Wellingborough NN8 .....129 B4
Shelley St NN2 ....141 F1
Shelleycotes Rd NN6 .....106 A1
Shelmerdine Rise NN9 ...114 D6
Shelsley Dr NN11 ....135 C4
Shelton CI Corby NN17 ....22 E2
Rounds NN9 ....114 E4
Shelton Rd Corby NN17 ...22 E2
Wallaston NN29 ....164 A1
Shepherd CI NN2 ....141 A5
Shepherds Hill NN11 .....146 F1
Shepherds Wlk
Bugbrooke NN7 ....173 A8
Harpole NN7 ....157 C6
Sheppard Way NN7 ....213 B8
Shepperton CI
Castlethorpe MK19 ....218 F5
Northampton NN3 ....143 C2
Sheppey La NN7 ....177 B3
Shepton CI NN18 ....36 A6
Sheraton CI NN3 ....142 C2
Sherborne Way NN14 .....76 F2
Sherborne Wlk NN18 ......36 A6
Sheriff Rd
Northampton NN1 ....159 F7
Rugby CV21 ....241 F8
Sherrard Rd LE16 ....31 E5
Sherwood Ave NN2 ......140 F6

Sherwood Cl Corby NN17 ...36 E8
  Stamford PE9 ....241 B3
Sherwood Dr
  Daventry NN11 ....135 B4
  Kettering NN15 ....91 F5
Shetland Way NN17 ...21 C1
Shieling Ct NN18 ....36 A1
Ship La PE8 ....41 F4
Shipton Way NN10 ...131 C3
Shire Pl NN3 ....143 C5
Shires Rd NN17 ....21 C1
Shires Bsns Pk The
  NN13 ....234 A6
Shires Rd NN13 ....234 A6
Shirley Rd NN10 ....132 B3
Shoal Creek NN4 ....175 C5
Shoe Maker Cl NN12 ..188 F7
Shoemakers Ct NN10 ..132 B3
Shop La NN7 ....179 B6
Shoreham St NN18 ......36 B5
Short Cl PE8 ....28 B3
Short La Cogenhoe NN7 162 A6
  Thorpe Malsor NN14 ....71 B3
  Wellingborough NN8 ...129 F5
Short Massey MK46 ...195 E5
Short Stocks NN10 ....132 D2
Shortlands Cl NN13 ...211 F3
Shortlands The NN9 ...113 B5
Shortwoods Cl NN9 ...114 D5
Shotwell Mill La NN14 ..70 D8
Showsley Rd NN12 ....204 D8
Shrewsbury Ave LE16 ..32 B2
Shropshire Cl LE16 .....31 E4
Shropshire Pl LE16 .....31 E4
Shrubberies The NN14 ..94 D7
Shrubfield Gr NN17 .....36 F8
Shuckburgh Cres CV22 ..9B D8
Shuckburgh Rd CV47 ..166 D8
Shurville Cl NN6 ....144 F3
Shutlanger Rd NN12 ...190 F1
Sibbertoft Rd
  Clipston LE16 ....47 E1
  Husbands Bosworth LE17 ..45 F2
  Marston Trussell LE16 ....47 B6
Sibley Rd NN9 ....112 B4
Siddeley Way NN11 ...134 F3
Siddons Cl PE8 ....41 E7
Siddons Way NN15 ....126 D1
Siderook Ct NN3 ....142 F5
Sidegate La NN8 ....130 F8
Sidings Ind Ctr The
  NN13 ....234 A8
Sidings The
  Irthlingborough NN9 ...131 D8
  Rugby CV21 ....241 D6
Sidlaw Ct MK11 ....229 F4
Sidmouth Wlk NN18 ....36 F4
Sidney Rd Rugby CV22 ..9B D8
  Woodford Halse NN11 ..184 C6
Sillswood MK46 ....195 E4
Silver St Abthorpe NN12 201 F2
  Brixworth NN6 ....106 B3
  Broughton NN14 ....90 A5
  Chacombe OX17 ....208 E4
  Kettering NN16 ....72 B2
  Northampton NN1 .....159 C6
  Stony Stratford MK11 ..229 D5
  Walgrave NN6 ....108 A5
  Wellingborough NN8 ...130 A4
Silver St N OX17 ....208 E4
Silverdale Gr NN10 ...131 E2
Silverdale Rd NN10 ...142 D2
Silverstone CE Jun Sch
  NN12 ....214 D4
Silverstone Cl NN12 ...141 D5
Silverstone Inf Sch
  NN12 ....214 D5
Silverstone Motor Racing
  Circuit* NN12 ....225 E8
Silverwood Ct NN15 ....91 C8
Silverwood Rd NN15 ...91 C8
Simborough Way LE16 ..32 B3
Simon de Senlis Ct
  NN1 ....159 D7
Simon de Senlis Lower Sch
  NN4 ....175 B8
Simon's Wlk
  17 Northampton NN1 ..159 C6
  Pattishall NN12 ....172 D1
Simpson Ave NN10 ....132 C7
Simpson Barracks NN4 175 D6
Sinclair Ave OX16 .....240 A9
Sinclair Dr Banbury OX16 240 A9
  Wellingborough NN8 ...126 B6
Sir Christopher Hatton Sch
  NN8 ....130 A6
Sir Georges La OX17 ..230 A4
Sir John Brown Ct NN16 .72 A2
Sir John Pascoe Way
  NN5 ....158 C8
Sissinghurst Dr NN14 ..76 F2
Siward View NN5 ......140 D2
Six Cotts MK18 ....226 E5
Six Willows NN9 ....110 B3
Sixth St NN13 ....238 E7
Skagerrak Cl NN18 .....36 A2
Skawle Ct NN14 ....142 F3
Skeffington Cl NN14 ...54 A2
Skelton Wlk NN13 .....142 C4
Sketty Cl NN4 ....160 C1
Skiddaw Wlk NN1 .....142 C4
Skin Yard La NN6 .....121 B4
Skinner Ave NN15 .....158 D5
Skinner's Hill NN10 ...132 B2
Skippon Cl LE16 ....31 D2
Skipton Cl Corby NN18 ..36 B4
  Northampton NN4 .....175 B7

Skittle Alley OX17 .....237 C7
Skye Rd NN17 ....36 B8
Slade Cl NN14 ....54 B3
Slade Cres NN15 ....91 B7
Slade Ho NN11 ....153 C8
Slade Lea OX17 ....220 B8
Slade Rd CV21,CV22 ..241 E7
Slade The Daventry NN11 153 C8
  Silverstone NN12 ......214 E5
Slade Valley Ave NN14 ..70 F7
Sladeswell Ct **8** NN3 ..161 A8
Slapton Prep Sch NN12 201 E2
Slate Drift PE9 ....1 E3
Slaters Cl NN14 ....132 D2
Slawston Rd
  Medbourne LE16 ....18 E7
  Welham LE16 ....17 F6
Slim Cl NN15 ....72 F1
Slip The NN6 ....106 C2
Slips The NN9 ....110 E2
Slipton La NN14 ....75 A3
Small Cres MK18 ......240 F3
Smart's Cl NN13 ......233 D8
Smarts Est CV23 ......100 A3
Smith Cl NN7 ....177 A1
Smith Ct NN9 ....114 D5
Smith St NN6 ....105 A1
Smitherway NN7 ......173 A8
Smithfield Pl NN14 ...114 D6
Smithland Ct NN12 ...202 D8
Smiths Orch OX17 ....241 E8
Smiths Way NN9 ......110 B3
Smithy The
  Northampton NN3 .....142 D1
  Rushden NN10 ....132 B1
Smyth Cl LE16 ....31 E5
Smyth Ct NN3 ....142 E3
Snetterton Cl NN3 ....141 F4
Snowball Sq **1** NN3 ...143 C2
Soar Gn NN17 ....21 C1
Solly's Way NN12 .....203 C5
Somerby Cl PE9 ....241 D5
Somerford Rd NN8 ...129 E6
Somerset St NN1 ......159 E7
Somerton Ct NN18 .....36 A6
Somervaille Ct OX17 ..230 D3
Somerville Rd
  Brackley NN13 ....233 D8
  Daventry NN11 ....153 B8
  Stamford PE9 ....241 B4
Sondes Cl PE8 ....41 E7
Sondes Rd NN17 ....22 E2
Sopwith Way NN11 ...135 B5
Sorrel Cl Isham NN14 ..91 F1
Sorrels The NN14 ......91 F1
Sotheby Rose NN9 ....143 D3
Soudan Ave NN13 .....233 E8
Sourton Pl NN11 ......135 D6
South Ave NN15 ....92 B3
South Bank NN13 .....234 B7
South Bar St OX16 ...240 C7
South Bridge Cl PE8 ...41 F4
South Bridge Rd NN4 .159 D4
South Cl Braunston NN11 118 D1
  Greatworth OX17 ......210 D1
  Long Buckby NN6 .....121 B3
  Rushden NN10 ....132 C1
South Copse NN4 .....175 B7
South End Jun & Inf Sch
  NN10 ....148 B8
South Fields Dr NN6 ..101 A5
South Folds Rd NN18 ..35 F1
South Gate NN1 ....148 B5
South Holme Ct NN14 142 E5
South Kilworth CE Prim Sch
  LE17 ....63 C8
South Kilworth Rd NN6 ..64 B5
South March NN11 ....153 D8
South Oval NN5 ....140 F1
South Paddock Ct NN3 142 F4
South Pk NN10 ....132 B1
South Pl NN11 ....135 B3
South Portway Cl NN3 142 F6
South Priors Ct NN3 ..143 A3
South Rd Clifton u D CV23 .80 A5
  Corby NN17 ....37 B6
  Oundle PE8 ....37 B6
South St Banbury OX16 240 E9
  Castlethorpe MK19 ...218 F5
  Isham NN14 ....110 F8
  Northampton NN1 .....159 F6
  Rugby CV21 ....241 D9
  Weedon NN7 ....173 C6
  Wollaston NN29 ......146 D2
  Woodford Halse NN11 184 C6
South Terr
  Greens Norton NN12 ..202 E8
  Kettering NN16 ....91 F6
South Vale NN7 ....179 A5
South View
  Brixworth NN6 ....106 B3
  Harpole NN7 ....139 B6
  Nether Heyford NN7 ..156 B1
  Roade NN7 ....191 D4
  Whilton NN11 ....137 C6
South Way NN11 ......135 D1
Southall Rd NN17 ......37 B6
Southam Rd
  Banbury OX16 ....240 C9
  Priors Marston CV47 ..166 D7
Southampton Rd NN4 159 C3
Southbrook NN18 ......35 F1
Southbrook Jun & Int Schs
  NN11 ....135 E1
Southbrook Rd CV22 ..241 B2
Southcrest NN4 ....158 F1
Southcroft NN3 ....142 C7

Southern Ave NN4 ....159 D3
Southfield Ct NN13 ...233 E6
Southfield Dr NN15 ....91 F4
Southfield Rd
  Gretton NN17 ....10 C1
  Northampton NN5 .....158 B6
  Rugby CV22 ....241 E6
Southfield Sch for Girls
  NN15 ....91 C7
Southfields NN10 .....132 C1
Southgate Dr
  Kettering NN15 ....72 D2
  Towcester NN12 ......203 D5
Southlands NN15 ....72 B1
Southleigh Gr LE16 ....31 D4
Southwick Hall* PE8 ...26 C5
Southwood Hill NN14 .159 A3
Sovereign Ct NN3 ....142 F6
Sovereign Pk LE16 ....31 F1
Sovereigns Ct NN16 ...72 C6
Sower Leys Rd NN18 ..36 C4
Spalding Rd NN18 ......36 C4
Spansiade Rd NN3 ....143 A1
Sparke Cl NN8 ....129 D7
Spectacle La NN3 .....125 F1
Speke Dr NN11 ....135 C5
Spelhoe St NN1 ....142 F6
Spenclayh Cl NN8 ....129 F7
Spencer Bridge Rd NN5 159 A7
Spencer Cl
  Bugbrooke NN7 ....173 A8
  Chapel Brampton NN6 124 D1
  Earls Barton NN6 .....144 E4
  Evenley NN13 ....233 F2
Spencer Ct Corby NN17 ..36 E5
  Rushden NN10 ....102 C4
  West Haddon NN6 ....106 C2
Spencer Gdns NN13 ..233 E6
Spencer Haven NN5 ..159 A7
Spencer Mid Sch NN5 159 A7
Spencer Par
  Northampton NN1 .....159 D6
  Stanwick NN9 ....113 F3
Spencer Rd
  Irthlingborough NN9 ..112 E1
  Long Buckby NN6 .....121 B3
  Northampton NN1 .....159 D6
Spencer St
  Burton Latimer NN15 ..92 B2
  Earls Barton NN6 .....144 E4
  Market Harborough LE16 ..31 D3
  Northampton NN5 .....159 A5
  Raunds NN9 ....114 E6
  Ringstead NN14 ....113 B2
  Wollaston NN29 ......146 D2
Spencer Wlk NN18 .....36 E5
Spendlove Dr NN17 ....10 C1
Spens Ho NN2 ....141 D5
Spey Cl NN8 ....129 C6
Spiceball Park Rd OX16 240 D8
Spiers Dr NN13 ....233 D7
Spilsby Cl NN18 ....36 A4
Spinners Cotts OX17 ..210 F7
Spinney Bank OX17 ..230 F5
Spinney Cl
  Boughton NN2 ....141 C7
  Market Harborough LE16 ..31 D3
  Rushden NN10 ....131 F2
  Thrapston NN14 ....76 D1
  Towcester NN12 ......203 C3
Spinney Dr
  Kettering NN15 ....91 D7
  Northampton NN17 ...175 C4
Spinney Gr NN17 ....36 E7
Spinney Hill NN10 ....131 F1
Spinney Hill Cres NN3 142 A4
Spinney Hill Rd
  Northampton NN3 .....142 A4
  Olney MK46 ....195 E3
Spinney La
  Kettering NN15 ....91 D7
  Wellingborough NN8 ..129 C2
Spinney Rd
  Burton Latimer NN15 ..92 C3
  Irthlingborough NN15 ..112 E7
  Rushden NN10 ....131 F1
  Weldon NN17 ....38 C7
Spinney Rise
  Daventry NN11 ....135 C1
  Denford NN14 ....95 C6
Spinney St NN9 ....114 D6
Spinney Terr **8** NN9 ..112 F2
Spinney Way NN2 ....142 A5
Spinneys The NN3 ....143 A3
Sponne Sch NN12 ....203 B6
Sponnes Rd NN12 ....203 C5
Spratton CE Prim Sch
  NN6 ....105 B1
Spratton Hall Sch NN6 105 B1
Spratton Rd NN6 .....106 A2
Spring Cl Boughton NN2 125 C1
  Daventry NN11 ....153 C8
  Hollowell NN6 ....106 B4
  Irthlingborough NN9 ..112 F2
  Kilsby CV23 ....100 A8
Spring Gdns
  Burton Latimer NN15 ..92 C3
  Earls Barton NN6 .....144 F4
  Higham Ferrers NN10 132 B6
  Northampton NN1 .....159 D5
  Rothwell NN14 ....70 D7

Spring Gdns continued
  Towcester NN12 ......203 D5
  Wellingborough NN8 ..129 F4
Spring Gr NN8 ....129 F4
Spring Ho NN8 ....129 F4
Spring La Alderton NN12 ..260 F2
  Flore NN7 ....155 E5
  Northampton NN1 .....159 B6
  Olney MK46 ....195 F3
  8 Wellingborough NN8 130 A4
Spring Lane Lower Sch
  NN1 ....159 B6
Spring Rise NN15 ......91 C7
Spring St
  4 Irthlingborough NN9 ..112 F2
  Rugby CV21 ....241 D8
Spring Terr
  Irthlingborough NN9 ..112 F2
  Wellingborough NN8 ..129 A6
Springbanks Way **2**
  NN4 ....175 C8
Springer Straight **1**
  NN4 ....158 F3
Springfield Flore NN7 ..155 E5
  Northampton NN14 ...175 E7
  Olney MK46 ....195 F4
Springfield Ave NN14 ..76 E3
Springfield Cl
  LE16 ....31 C2
  Northampton NN3 .....142 F3
Springfield Gdns MK19 228 E4
Springfield Gr NN17 ...36 F8
Springfield Rd
  Kettering NN15 ....91 C7
  Oundle PE8 ....41 F7
  Rushden NN10 ....148 D8
  Walgrave NN6 ....107 F5
  Wilbarston LE16 ....34 C4
Springfield St LE16 ....31 F2
Springfield Way NN13 233 E8
Springfields NN12 ....203 B5
Springhill Gdns LE16 ..31 C2
Springhill Hos CV22 ...98 C8
Springs The
  Northampton NN4 .....159 A3
  Long Buckby NN11 ....62 C4
Springwell Cl NN4 ....175 C5
Springwood Ct NN3 ..142 F5
Spruce Ct
  Northampton NN3 .....159 A3
  Kettering NN15 ....72 C4
Spurlings NN8 ....129 D7
Spy Glass Hill NN4 ...175 B6
Square The Aynho OX17 237 A7
  Earls Barton NN6 .....144 E4
  Greatworth OX17 .....210 E1
  Kings Sutton OX17 ...230 F5
  Market Harborough LE16 ..31 E3
  Moreton Pinkney NN11 199 F7
  Northampton NN1 .....175 F3
  Pitsford NN6 ....125 C4
  Raunds NN9 ....114 D6
  South Luffenham LE15 ..3 D8
  Thorpe Malsor NN14 ...71 B3
  Welford NN6 ....64 D1
  Yardley Hastings NN7 179 A6
Squire Cl NN18 ....36 A4
Squires Wlk NN18 .....142 B3
Squirrel La NN15 ....92 C3
Squirrels Way MK18 ..240 E2
Stable Ct Brackley NN13 233 F7
Stable Rd NN2 ....141 C3
  Pitsford NN6 ....125 D4
Stable Hill NN11 ....55 F7
Stable Yd NN14 ....70 C1
Stablegate Way LE16 ..32 A2
Stables La NN6 ....140 B8
Stables The PE8 ....8 A3
Stadtpenine Cl NN17 ..36 C7
Staff Hos NN16 ....71 F2
Staffa Wlk NN17 ....36 B8
Stafford Cl NN11 .....135 D5
Stafford Pl NN3 ....141 F7
Stafford Rd NN17 ......22 C8
Staffords La NN6 .....102 B4
Stagshaw Cl **2** NN4 ...175 C8
Staines Cl NN5 ....158 E6
Stalbridge Wlk NN18 ..36 A6
Stamford & Rutland Hospl
  PE9 ....241 E3
Stamford Bsns Pk PE9 241 F4
Stamford Cl LE16 ......31 E2
Stamford Coll PE9 ....241 E4
Stamford High Sch PE9 241 E2
Stamford High Sch (Welland
  Ho) PE9 ....241 D2
Stamford High Sch Jun
  PE9 ....241 D2
Stamford La PE8 ....28 B3
Stamford Rd
  Corby NN14,NN18,NN17 ..37 E4
  Duddington PE9 ....5 C7
  Easton o t H PE9 ....23 B5
  Geddington NN14 ......54 C2
  Ketton PE9 ....72 E5
  South Luffenham LE15 ..3 D7
  Weldon NN17 ....23 E2
Stamford Sta PE9 ....241 D2
Stamford Wlk Corby NN14 36 C4
Stanbridge Cl OX16 ..240 A7
Stanbridge Ct MK11 ..229 F5

She – Ste 263

Standens Barn Lower Sch
  NN3 ....160 F8
Standens Barn Rd NN3 142 F1
Standing Stones NN3 ..143 B3
Standside NN5 ....158 F6
Stanfield Rd NN5 .....158 C6
Stanford Cl NN6 ....84 A5
Stanford Hall* LE17 ..62 A3
Stanford Rd
  Cold Ashby NN6 ....84 A5
  Swinford LE17 ....62 D3
Stanford Way NN4 ...175 C8
Stanhill Row NN12 ...201 F1
Stanhope Rd NN2 .....141 D1
Stanier Cl NN16 ....72 A3
Stanier Pl OX16 ....240 E9
Stanier Rd NN17 ....22 E2
Stanion CE Prim Sch
  NN14 ....37 E3
Stanion La Corby NN18 ..37 D5
  Corby NN18 ....37 D5
Stanion Rd NN14 ....37 E3
Stanley Boddington Cl
  NN15 ....91 C8
Stanley Ct MK46 .....195 F3
Stanley Rd
  Northampton NN5 .....159 A6
  Wellingborough NN8 ..130 B5
Stanley St
  Northampton NN2 .....159 C8
  Rothwell NN14 ....70 E7
  Stamford PE9 ....241 E3
Stanley Way NN11 ...135 C5
Stanmead Way NN6 ..106 B2
Stanton Ave NN3 .....142 A4
Stanton Cl NN8 ....111 B1
Stanway Cl LE16 ....32 A3
Stanwell Ct OX17 ....209 A1
Stanwell Dr OX17 ....209 A1
Stanwell Lea OX17 ...209 A2
Stanwell Way NN8 ...129 C3
Stanwick Prim Sch NN9 114 A3
Stanwick Rd
  Higham Ferrers NN10 132 C8
  Raunds NN9 ....114 B4
Star Cnr CV23 ....99 C1
Star La PE9 ....241 E3
Starmer's Yd NN5 ....158 C7
Starmers La NN7 .....157 D4
Starvold Cl NN6 ......105 A1
Station Cl Daventry NN11 135 D3
  Ecton NN3 ....143 C1
  Long Buckby NN6 .....121 B3
Station Cotts NN13 ....53 D7
Station Rd Bletchley NN1 184 C6
Station Mews NN3 ....143 C2
Station Rd
  Aynho OX15,OX17 ...237 A6
  Blisworth NN7 ....174 B2
  Brixworth NN6 ....106 A4
  Buckingham MK18 ...240 C2
  Burton Latimer NN15 ..92 A2
  Castlethorpe MK19 ...218 F5
  Clifton OX17 ....236 F5
  Cogenhoe NN7 ....161 E6
  Corby NN17 ....37 A6
  Cottesbrooke NN6 ...105 A7
  Desborough NN14 ....51 A4
  Earls Barton NN6 .....144 E3
  Earls Barton NN6 .....144 F1
  Finedon NN9 ....111 D6
  Great Bowden LE16 ...32 A6
  Great Easton LE16 ....20 E6
  Gretton NN17 ....10 B1
  Helmdon NN13 ....211 F4
  Husbands Bosworth LE17 ..45 D3
  Irchester MK44 ....147 C8
  Irthlingborough NN9 ..113 A2
  Kettering NN15 ....72 B1
  Ketton PE9 ....72 E5
  King's Cliffe PE8 ....13 F7
  Lilbourne CV23 ....81 A7
  Little Houghton NN7 ..161 C5
  Long Buckby NN6 ....121 A2
  Morcott LE15 ....3 B6
  Nassington PE8 ....15 F5
  North Kilworth LE17 ..45 A4
  Northampton NN1 .....143 C1
  Oundle PE8 ....42 A6
  Raunds NN9 ....115 B7
  Ravensthorpe NN6 ....94 F2
  Rushden NN10 ....132 A3
  Rushton NN14 ....53 C2
  Stamford PE9 ....241 D2
  Stamford PE9 ....241 E2
  Theddingworth LE17 ..46 C8
  Watford NN6 ....120 C5
  Welton NN11 ....119 E1
  Weston NN14 ....102 B4
  Woodford Halse NN11 184 C6
Station Terr MK18 ....240 C2
Station Yard Ind Est
  OX17 ....230 A2
Stavanger Cl NN18 .....36 A2
Staveley Way NN16 ..106 C3
Staverton CE Prim Sch
  NN11 ....152 C7
Staverton Leys CV22 ..98 A7
Staverton Rd NN11 ..135 B1
Steadfold La PE9 ....1 C8
Steam Brewery Mus*
  NN1 ....241 D3
Steane View NN13 ...233 D7
Steel La NN14 ....76 D1
Steel Rd NN17 ....22 E2

Steele Rd NN8 129 D4
Steele St CV22 241 A8
Steene St NN5 159 A6
Stefen Way NN11 153 B7
Stenhouse Cl NN6 121 D4
Stenson St NN5 159 A6
Stephen Bennett Cl
NN5 158 C8
Stephen St CV21 241 B8
Stephenson Cl NN11 134 F4
Stephenson Ct
Kilsby CV23 99 F2
Roade NN7 191 C4
Stephenson Way NN17 37 A8
Sterling Ct NN14 70 C1
Sterndale Cl NN14 50 E4
Stevens Ct NN6 144 F5
Stevens St LE16 31 D3
Stevenson St NN4 159 C2
Stewart Cl NN3 126 B2
Stewart Dr NN12 214 D4
Stewarts Rd NN8 130 B8
Steyning Cl NN18 36 A5
Stile Cl NN11 135 A2
Stilebrook Rd MK46 195 F6
Stimpson Ave NN1 159 F7
Stimpson Avenue Lower Sch
NN1 159 F7
Stinford Leys LE16 32 B3
Stirling Rd PE9 241 B3
Stirling St NN5 158 F6
Stirrup Ho NN5 159 B5
Stitchman Ho 8 NN5 159 A6
Stock's Hill PE9 1 A5
Stock's La NN17 37 B6
Stockbridge Rd NN17 22 A1
Stocken Cl MK46 195 E4
Stockerston La LE16 20 D8
Stockholme Cl NN18 36 A2
Stocking Cl NN7 192 D1
Stocking Green Cl
MK19 207 A3
Stockley St 6 NN1 159 E6
Stockmead Rd NN3 161 A8
Stocks Hill Finedon NN9 111 E4
Silverstone NN12 214 D5
Stocks The MK19 218 E2
Stockwell Ave NN4 175 D5
Stockwell Cl LE16 32 B3
Stockwell La
Hellidon NN11 151 D1
Sulgrave OX17 210 F8
Stockwell Rd NN7 174 F4
Stockwell Way NN7 174 F4
Stockwood Dr NN17 21 F1
Stoke Albany Rd LE16 18 E1
Stoke Bruerne CE Prim Sch
NN12 205 A8
Stoke Doyle PE8 41 C1
Stoke Doyle Rd PE8 41 D4
Stoke Firs Cl NN4 175 F6
Stoke Hill Oundle PE8 41 F5
Stoke Albany LE16 34 A4
Stoke Rd Ashton NN7 205 E8
Blisworth NN7 190 E4
Desborough NN14 51 A7
Lyddington LE15 9 C7
Stokes Rd NN18 36 D4
Stone Circle Rd NN3 142 E7
Stone Cl NN29 146 D2
Stone Hill Ct NN3 142 E4
Stone House Mews NN6 84 E4
Stone Pit Cl MK46 195 E3
Stone Way NN5 158 B7
Stonebridge Ct NN3 142 F3
Stonehill Way NN6 125 B8
Stonehouse Ct CV23 81 A6
Stonehurst Cl NN7 192 C1
Stonelea Rd NN6 127 D3
Stoneleigh Chase NN5 140 D1
Stonepit Dr LE16 20 D1
Stoneway Badby NN11 152 F2
Hartwell NN7 192 E2
Stonewold Cl NN2 141 A4
Stoney Piece Cl NN29 164 C2
Stoneyhurst NN4 158 F3
Stony Hill NN12 216 C8
Stony Stratford Nature
Reserve* MK11 229 D7
Stook The NN11 135 C6
Storefield Cotts NN14 53 A4
Stornoway Rd NN17 21 C1
Stotfold Ct MK11 229 E4
Stour Rd Corby NN17 21 D1
Northampton NN5 158 F6
Stour The NN11 153 A8
Stourhead Dr NN4 175 C7
Stourton Cl NN8 129 D1
Stow Cl NN8 129 D1
Stowe Ave MK18 240 C4
Stowe Cl MK18 240 C4
Stowe Rise MK18 240 C4
Stowe Wlk NN3 141 F5
Stradlers Cl NN4 175 E5
Stratfield Way NN15 91 D5
Stratford Arc MK11 229 D5
Stratford Dr NN4 175 D6
Stratford Rd
Buckingham MK18 240 E4
Cosgrove MK19 218 D1
Deanshanger MK19 228 F4
Roade NN7 191 C3
... Stratford MK12 229 F6
... CV21 99 A7
... Wlk NN17 21 C1

Stratton Cl
Market Harborough LE16 31 D1
Northampton NN3 160 D7
Stratton Dr NN13 233 D7
Strawberry Hill NN3 143 C3
Strawberry Hill Cotts
MK44 149 F2
Straws Cl NN9 112 E1
Stream Bank Cl NN8 129 D4
Streambank Rd NN3 142 E6
Streatfield Rd NN5 159 A8
Streather Ct NN9 114 C5
Streather Dr NN17 36 E7
Street The LE15 3 E8
Streeton Way NN6 144 E5
Strelley Ave NN3 160 F8
Stringer's Hill NN14 90 F2
Strode Rd NN8 130 B5
Stronglands Ct PE8 41 F6
Stuart Cl Kettering NN16 72 C2
Northampton NN4 174 F7
Stuart Cres LE16 30 F7
Stuart Rd Brackley NN13 233 E8
Corby NN17 36 F6
Market Harborough LE16 31 E2
Stubbing End NN18 53 B8
Stubble Cl NN2 141 A6
Stubbs Cl NN8 129 F7
Stubbs La NN15 92 A8
Stubbs Rd NN11 170 B7
Stud Farm Cl OX17 196 E1
Studfall Ave NN17 36 E8
Studfall Ct NN17 36 E7
Studfall Inf Sch NN17 36 E8
Studfall Jun Sch NN17 36 D8
Studland Rd NN2 141 B1
Sturdee Cl NN11 135 D1
Sturgess Ct NN15 92 C2
Sturminster Way NN18 36 A6
Sturton Wlk NN18 36 C4
Styles Pl NN6 82 B3
Sudborough Rd
Brigstock NN14 56 A4
Slipton NN14 75 A6
Suffolk Pl NN15 91 D6
Sulby Hall Old Dr NN6 46 B1
Sulby Rd
Northampton NN3 142 E6
Welford NN6 65 A8
Sulehay Rd PE8 7 C1
Sulgrave Dr NN17 36 C7
Sulgrave Manor* OX17 211 A8
Sulgrave Rd
Culworth OX17 198 D1
Northampton NN5 158 F7
Summer Leys Nature Res*
NN29 145 F4
Summerfield Rd NN15 91 C8
Summerfields NN4 158 E2
Summerhouse Rd NN3 142 A6
Summerlee Mews NN9 111 F4
Summerlee Rd NN9 111 F4
Summers Cl OX17 230 A5
Summers Way LE16 31 D2
Summit Rise NN4 175 D7
Sun Hill NN14 70 C7
Sun St CV21 241 E8
Sun Yd NN12 203 D5
Sunbeam Cl CV21 241 E8
Sunderland St NN5 159 A6
Sundew Ct NN4 158 D1
Sunley Ct NN15 91 C8
Sunningdale Cl NN2 141 E2
Sunningdale Dr
Daventry NN11 135 E3
Rushden NN10 148 D8
Sunny Bank NN6 126 E8
Sunny Side NN6 144 D4
Sunny View NN7 179 B6
Sunnyside Ecton NN6 143 F4
Northampton NN4 175 E6
Woodford NN14 94 D7
Sunnyside Lower Sch
NN2 141 D6
Sunset Ct NN3 143 A2
Surfleet Cl NN18 36 C4
Surrey Cl NN17 36 C6
Surrey Rd NN15 91 D6
Surtees Way NN12 203 C7
Sussex Cl NN5 158 C6
Sussex Ct 6 NN1 159 C6
Sussex Rd Kettering NN15 91 C6
Stamford PE9 241 D4
Sutcliffe Rd PE8 7 D8
Sutherland Rd NN18 36 D4
Sutherland Way PE9 241 B3
Sutton Acre NN7 155 E5
Sutton Cl
Aston le W NN11 182 F3
Northampton NN2 141 D6
Sutton Ct LE16 31 E1
Sutton Rd
Great Bowden LE16 32 B6
Great Bowden LE16 32 E7
Oundle PE8 42 B4
Weston by W LE16 18 B3
Sutton St NN7 155 F5
Sutton's Wlk NN12 188 F7
Swain Ct NN3 142 E3
Swale Cl Corby NN17 21 D1
Roade NN7 191 C3
Swale Dr
Northampton NN5 140 F3
Wellingborough NN8 129 C6
Swallow Cl
Brackley NN13 222 E1
Buckingham MK18 240 E2
Kettering NN15 92 B6

Swallow Cl *continued*
Northampton NN4 175 A7
Swallow Dr NN10 132 B5
Swan Ave NN14 55 E8
Swan Cl Brackley NN13 222 D2
Buckingham MK18 240 E2
Burton Latimer NN15 92 A2
Hinton NN11 184 B6
Middleton Cheney OX17 219 F8
Thrapston NN14 76 D3
Swan Close Rd OX16 240 D7
Swan Ind Est OX16 240 D7
Swan St NN1 159 D5
Swan Terr MK11 229 D5
Swan Valley Way NN4 174 C8
Swanage Ct NN18 36 A6
Swanhill PE8 8 A4
Swann Dale NN11 135 D1
Swann Dale Cl NN11 135 D1
Swans La 6 NN8 130 A4
Swans Way NN10 132 C8
Swansea Cres NN5 159 A7
Swansea Rd NN5 159 A8
Swansgate Ctr The 9
NN8 130 A4
Swanson Ho PE9 241 F4
Swanspool Ct NN8 130 A4
Swanspool Par NN8 130 A3
Swedish Hos NN7 139 D4
Sweetacre Cl NN7 163 D4
Swift Cl NN4 175 F3
Swift Way NN13 222 E1
Swinburne Cl NN16 72 C6
Swinburne Rd NN8 129 B4
Swinfen's Yd MK11 229 D5
Swinford CE Prim Sch
LE17 62 B4
Swinford Cnr LE17 62 A8
Swinford Hollow NN3 161 A8
Swinford Rd LE17 62 A8
Swingbridge St LE16 30 E8
Swinnertons La NN6 82 B4
Swinneyford Rd NN12 203 C5
Swyncombe Gn NN7 192 C1
Sycamore Ave NN11 184 B6
Sycamore Cl
Buckingham MK18 240 F2
Corby NN17 21 E1
Daventry NN11 135 C5
Kettering NN16 72 D4
Rushden NN10 132 C2
Towcester NN12 203 C4
Sycamore Dr
Desborough NN14 51 D2
Sywell NN6 143 D8
Sycamore Gr CV21 241 C9
Sycamore Rd
Greens Norton NN12 202 E8
Northampton NN5 158 C7
Sycamore Yd NN12 187 B1
Sycamores The LE17 63 D8
Sydney St NN16 72 D2
Syers Green Cl NN6 121 A4
Syers Green La NN6 121 A4
Syke The NN14 55 F7
Sykes Ct NN17 37 A8
Syles Cl NN6 102 B5
Sylmond Gdns NN10 148 A7
Sylvanus Ho NN8 129 D5
Symington St NN5 159 A7
Symington Way LE16 31 E3
Syresham St James CE Prim
Sch NN13 224 C7
Syresham Way NN2 141 C5
Sywell Airport Bsns Pk
NN6 127 F4
Sywell Ave NN8 129 D6
Sywell CE Prim Sch
NN6 127 D3
Sywell Rd Holcot NN6 126 F8
Mears Ashby NN6 128 A1
Overstone NN6 127 B1
Wellingborough NN8 129 C6
Sywell Resr Ctry Pk*
NN6 144 A7
Sywell Way NN8 129 D6

T

Taborley Cl NN3 142 E1
Tadcaster Cl NN11 135 C6
Taggies Yd NN14 109 F5
Tainty Cl NN9 111 E5
Talan Rise NN3 143 C5
Talavera Cl NN11 135 B1
Talavera Way NN3 142 D6
Talbot Rd
Northampton NN1 159 E7
Rushden NN10 131 F1
Wellingborough NN8 130 C5
Talbot Rd N NN8 130 C5
Talbot Yd LE16 31 E3
Talbots Hyde MK46 195 E4
Tall Trees Cl NN4 174 F8
Tallyfield End NN4 158 E3
Tamar Cl NN5 140 E2
Tamar Gn NN17 21 D1
Tamar Sq NN11 135 A1
Tamarisk Dr NN3 142 C6
Tancred Cl 1 NN4 175 E7
Taney Ct PE8 42 A5
Tanfield La NN1 160 C5
Tanfields Gr NN17 36 E8
Tanglewood NN4 175 D4
Tann Rd NN9 111 F5
Tanner St NN1 159 C5
Tanner's La NN16 72 B2

Tannery The LE15 4 A5
Tansor Cl NN17 36 B8
Tansy Cl NN4 158 D1
Tantree Way NN6 106 C2
Tapeley Gdns NN4 175 D7
Taper Way NN11 135 B3
Tarn Croft NN3 142 B3
Tarragon Way NN4 175 D6
Tarrant Cl NN3 126 D1
Tarrant Way NN3 126 D1
Tarrys End NN6 82 B4
Tasman Way NN14 70 E6
Tate Gr NN4 175 F7
Tattersall Cl NN3 142 A5
Taunton Ave Corby NN18 36 B6
Northampton NN3 160 C7
Tavern La 1 NN11 135 C1
Tavern Wlk NN18 36 A4
Tavistock Cl 3 NN3 143 D2
Tavistock Rd NN15 92 A5
Tavistock Sq NN18 36 F4
Tay Cl NN17 21 D1
Taylor Ave NN3 142 C1
Taylor Cl NN8 129 C7
Taylors Gn PE8 28 B2
Teal Cl
Burton Latimer NN15 91 F2
Daventry NN11 135 C4
Higham Ferrers NN10 132 C8
Northampton NN4 174 E8
Teal La NN8 130 B7
Teasel Cl NN10 148 C7
Tebbitt Cl NN6 121 B4
Tebbutt Cl NN14 70 F7
Tebbutt's Yd NN6 144 E4
Tees Cl NN8 129 C6
Teesdale NN3 142 F6
Teesdale Rd NN17 36 D7
Teeton La NN6 104 E3
Teeton Rd
Guilsborough NN6 103 F5
Ravensthorpe NN6 103 E1
Telford Way
Kettering NN16 71 F4
Northampton NN5 158 D4
Telfords La NN17 37 A8
Temperance Terr MK11 229 C6
Templar Dr NN2 141 A4
Templar Rd NN15 72 F1
Temple Bar 21 NN1 159 C7
Temple St CV21,CV22 241 E7
Ten Pines NN3 142 F7
Tenbury Way NN14 70 F7
Tenby Rd NN5 159 A8
Tenlands OX17 219 F8
Tennyson Cl
3 Northampton NN5 158 F8
Towcester NN12 203 B5
Tennyson Dr NN17 36 D8
Tennyson Rd
Daventry NN11 135 B3
Kettering NN16 72 B2
Rothwell NN14 70 C7
Rushden NN10 131 F2
Wellingborough NN8 129 D3
Tennyson Road Inf Sch
NN10 131 F2
Tennyson Way PE9 241 A4
Tenter Cl NN10 132 B5
Tenter Ct PE9 241 E2
Tenter La Finedon NN9 111 F5
Stamford PE9 241 E3
Tenter Rd NN3 141 F7
Tentsmuir Cl NN16 72 A6
Terrace The NN13 224 C5
Terrington Cl NN13 233 E7
Test Gn NN17 21 D1
Tettenhall Cl NN18 36 A1
Teviot Cl Corby NN17 21 D1
Northampton NN5 140 E2
Tewkesbury Cl
Northampton NN4 159 A1
Wellingborough NN8 129 D6
Tewkesbury Dr NN10 148 D8
Tews End La NN12 216 C8
Thackers Cl PE8 8 A4
Thames Ct NN15 92 B2
Thames Rd
Daventry NN11 135 A1
Northampton NN4 175 C7
Wellingborough NN8 129 C6
Thames Rise NN16 72 A4
Thames Wlk NN17 21 D1
Thatch Meadow Dr LE16 32 B3
Thatchwell Ct NN3 160 F8
Thebwell Rd 3 NN3 142 F1
Theddingworth Rd
Husbands Bosworth LE17 46 A6
Lubenham LE16 30 C2
Marston Trussell LE16 47 B8
Thenford Rd OX17 209 C1
Thenford St NN1 159 E6
Thetford Cl NN18 36 B1
Third Ave NN8 129 D3
Third St NN13 238 E6
Thirlestane Cres NN4 159 B3
Thirlestane Rd NN4 159 B3
Thirlmere NN8 129 C5
Thirlmere Ave NN3 142 C3
Thirlmere Cl
Daventry NN11 135 A2
Kettering NN16 71 E3
Thirlmere Flats NN16 71 E3
Thirsk Rd NN18 36 C5
Thistle Ct 3 NN4 159 A3
Thistleholme Cl NN2 141 E3
Thoday Cl NN14 90 A3

Thomas Becket RC Upper
Sch NN3 142 B5
Thomas Chapman Gr
NN4 159 C4
Thomas Cl Byfield NN11 183 D6
Corby NN18 36 D4
Crick NN6 101 A6
Thomas Crewe Cl NN13 233 F7
Thomas Flawn Rd NN9 131 D8
Thomas Rd NN15 91 C7
Thomas Rippin Cl NN14 54 A2
Thomas St
Northampton NN1 159 D7
Wellingborough NN8 130 B5
Thompson Way NN15 90 F8
Thor Wlk NN18 36 A2
Thorburn Rd NN3 160 E8
Thoresby Ct NN18 36 C5
Thorn Cl NN16 72 B6
Thorn Hill NN4 159 A3
Thornapple Cl NN3 143 C4
Thornborough Cl LE16 32 A2
Thornbridge Cl NN10 132 A1
Thornby Dr NN2 141 B3
Thornby Rd NN6 84 B5
Thorne Ct NN18 36 C5
Thornfield NN3 143 C4
Thorngate St NN16 72 C2
Thornhill OX17 208 F4
Thornlea Croft MK46 195 F3
Thornton Cl Crick NN6 101 A6
Flore NN7 155 F5
Newnham NN11 153 D3
Thornton Coll MK17 235 C5
Thornton Rd
Northampton NN2 141 B1
Thornton MK17 235 F2
Thoroughsale Rd NN17 36 E7
Thorpe Cl Banbury OX16 219 A6
Banbury OX16 240 F8
Wellingborough NN8 129 C5
Thorpe Ct NN14 77 C7
Thorpe Dr Banbury OX16 219 A6
Banbury OX16 240 F8
Thorpe La OX16 240 F8
Thorpe Langton Rd LE16 17 D6
Thorpe Mead OX16 240 F7
Thorpe Pl OX16 240 F8
Thorpe Rd
Chacombe OX17 208 E4
Earls Barton NN6 144 E2
Lyddington LE15 9 D6
Northampton NN4 159 C3
Thorpe Waterville NN14 77 A8
Wardington OX17 208 F8
Thorpe St NN9 114 D5
Thorpe Way OX16 240 F8
Thorpeville NN3 142 D7
Thorplands Lower Sch
NN3 142 E5
Thrapston Prim Sch
NN14 76 D1
Thrapston Rd
Finedon NN9 112 B7
Woodford NN14 94 D8
Three Shires Hospl NN1 159 F5
Thrift St
Higham Ferrers NN10 132 B5
Irchester NN29 147 A7
Wollaston NN29 146 D2
Thrupp Bridge NN4 176 A6
Thrush La NN8 130 B6
Thruxton Dr NN3 141 F4
Thurburn Cl NN14 90 B5
Thurning Rd PE8,PE28 79 F7
Thursby Rd NN1 160 B7
Thurso Wlk NN17 21 D1
Thurspit Pl 8 NN3 143 D2
Thurston Dr NN15 91 A8
Thyme Ct NN3 142 E3
Tibbs Way NN7 173 A6
Tideswell Cl
Desborough NN14 50 E4
Northampton NN4 174 F8
Tiffany Gdns NN4 175 C6
Tiffield CE Prim Sch
NN12 189 D3
Tiffield Rd NN7 189 E8
Tilbury Rd NN6 122 C5
Tilbury Rise NN6 122 C5
Tilley Hill Cl PE8 41 E7
Timber Ct CV22 241 E7
Timken Way NN11 135 A4
Timor Ct MK11 229 D6
Timpson Cl NN16 72 C5
Timson Cl LE16 31 D5
Tingdene Rd NN9 111 F5
Tingewick Rd MK18 240 B3
Tingewick Road Ind Est
MK18 240 B3
Tinkers Cres NN6 128 B2
Tinsley Cl NN3 143 B3
Tintagel Cl NN10 132 D1
Tintern Ave NN5 159 A7
Tintern Ct NN15 91 F8
Tinwell Rd PE9 241 B2
Tinwell Road La PE9 241 B2
Tippings La LE15 3 F5
Tiptoe Cl NN3 143 C3
Titchmarsh CE Prim Sch
NN14 77 C4
Tithe Barn Cl NN9 114 E7
Tithe Barn Rd NN8 130 A4
Tithe Barn Way NN4 174 B8
Tithe Cl Holcot NN6 126 E8
Ringstead NN14 95 A3
Tithe Ct OX16 240 A7
Tithe La OX15,OX17 236 C6

Tithe Rd NN7 ....155 A2
Tithe Way NN7 ....191 D5
Titley Bawk Ave NN6 .....144 F6
Titty Ho NN9 ....114 C5
Tiverton Ave NN13 ....141 C7
Tixover Grange PE9 ....4 F8
Todd's Hill PE9 ....5 B6
Todmorden Cl NN18 ....36 C5
Tofts Cl NN14 ....77 D4
Tolethorpe Sq PE9 ....241 E4
Toll Bar La PE28 ....97 B4
Toll Bar Rd NN14 ....76 B2
Toll Gate Pl NN18 ....37 B6
Tollbar NN10 ....132 B5
Toller Pl NN15 ....91 F6
Toller St NN10 ....72 C3
Tollgate Cl NN2 ....141 B2
Tollgate Way NN15 ....91 F6
Tom Brown St CV21 ....241 E8
Tompson Cl NN11 ....118 C1
Toms Cl
  Northampton NN4 ....175 C3
  Theddingworth LE17 .....46 D8
Tonmead Rd NN3 ....142 E3
Top Farm Cl NN14 ....76 F3
Top Farm La NN29 ....145 E7
Top Lodge NN17 ....5 A1
Top Station Rd NN13 .....234 A8
Top Dysons NN14 ....92 F7
Top End
  Little Addington NN14 ..113 B7
  Pytchley NN14 ....90 F2
Top Farm Ct NN11 ....184 B6
Top Station Road Ind Est
  NN13 ....234 A8
Top Yard Barn LE16 ....31 F6
Topwell Ct NN3 ....143 A1
Tordoff Pl NN16 ....72 B2
Torkington Gdns PE9 .....241 D3
Torkington St PE9 ....241 B3
Torrance Rd CV21 ....241 B8
Torridge Cl NN16 ....71 F4
Torridon Cl NN17 ....21 C1
Torrington Cres NN8 ....129 D6
Torrington Gn NN4 ......129 C6
Torrington Rd NN8 ......129 C6
Torrington Way NN8 .....129 C6
Torville Cres NN15 ....91 A8
Totnes Cl NN18 ....54 E7
Toulouse Cl 11 NN4 .....175 E7
Touraine Cl NN5 ....139 F2
Tove La NN12 ....203 A6
Tovey Dr NN11 ....135 D1
Towcester Br NN11 ......217 B3
Towcester Inf Sch
  NN12 ....203 C5
Towcester Rd
  Blisworth NN7 ....190 B6
  Greens Norton NN12 ...188 E1
  Litchborough NN12 .....171 C1
  Milton Malsor NN7 .....174 E5
  Northampton NN4 ......159 B2
  Old Stratford MK19 ....229 B7
  Silverstone NN12 ......214 E4
  Towcester NN12 ....203 A8
  Whittlebury NN12 .....215 C5
Tower Cl NN9 ....112 A4
Tower Field Sq NN3 .....143 A6
Tower Hill Cl NN4 ......158 E1
Tower Hill Rd NN18 ......36 A4
Tower Rd CV22 ....241 E6
Tower St NN1 ....159 C6
Town Cl NN9 ....110 C3
Town End NN5 ....126 F6
Townley Way NN6 ....144 E5
Towns End NN6 ....121 C4
Townsend Banbury OX16 .240 B8
  Hinton NN11 ....184 B6
Townsend Cl
  Hanging Houghton NN6 .106 C8
  Wellingborough NN8 ...129 E7
Townsend Ct PE8 ....39 E7
Townsend La
  Thorpe Mandeville OX17 .209 F6
  Upper Boddington NN11 182 B8
Townsend Leys NN10 ....132 B8
Townsend Rd
  Rugby CV21 ....241 F8
  Walgrave NN6 ....107 F5
Townson Cl NN6 ....107 D7
Townwell La NN29 ......147 B8
Towrise OX17 ....210 F8
Towton Cl NN4 ....159 A1
Trafalgar Rd NN16 ....72 A2
Trafalgar Way NN11 .....135 D1
Trafford Rd NN10 ....132 D2
Trailli La NN14 ....94 D6
Tramway Ind Est The
  OX16 ....240 E7
Tramway Rd OX16 ......240 E7
Treefields MK18 ....240 E3
Treen Cl NN14 ....76 F2
Treetops NN3 ....143 A5
Trefoil Cl NN10 ....148 C7
Trelawney NN8 ....129 E6
Trengothal Ct NN13 .....223 D4
Trent Cl
  Northampton NN5 .....140 F2
  Wellingborough NN8 ...129 C6
Trent Cres NN15 ....92 B7
Trent Ct NN11 ....153 A8
Trent Rd Corby NN17 ....21 D1
  Kettering NN15 ....72 A5
  Wittering PE8 ....7 D8
Trent Wlk NN11 ....135 A1
Trentham Cl NN14 ......175 C7

Tresham Gn NN5 ....140 D1
Tresham Inst Corby NN11 .36 E6
  Kettering NN15 ....72 C1
  Kettering NN16 ....91 D8
  Wellingborough NN8 ...130 A6
Tresham St
  Kettering NN16 ....72 C3
  Rothwell NN14 ....78 E1
Trevithick Rd NN17 ......37 C8
Trevor Cl NN5 ....158 E7
Trevor Dr CV22 ....241 D6
Trevor White Dr CV22 ..241 D6
Trimley Cl NN3 ....160 D6
Trinity Ave NN2 ....141 D1
Trinity CE Lower Sch
  NN8 ....76 F8
Trinity Cl Daventry NN11 153 B8
  Old Stratford MK19 ...229 E7
Trinity Cl NN14 ....70 C6
Trinity Ctr NN8 ....129 A7
Trinity Rd Rothwell NN14 .70 C6
  Stamford PE9 ....241 C4
Trinity Sch NN11 ....141 D1
Trinity Way NN11 ......141 D1
Trinity Way OX17 ......230 D3
Triumph Gdns NN5 .....139 F1
Trojan Ctr NN8 ....130 B8
Tromso Cl NN18 ....36 A2
Troon Cres NN8 ....129 C7
Truedick Wlk NN3 ......142 C4
Trussell Rd NN13 ......143 C1
Tudely Cl NN14 ....72 F3
Tudor Cl 4 NN16 ......72 C2
Tudor Gdns MK11 ......229 E4
Tudor Rd NN1,NN2 .....142 A2
Tudor Way
  Brackley NN13 ....233 E8
  Wellingborough NN8 ..129 E7
Tudor Wlk NN10 ....132 C3
Tulbrook Stones OX17 ..220 B7
Tulip Dr NN10 ....148 B7
Tunnel Hill Cotts NN4 ..159 A2
Tunwell La NN17 ....37 B7
Turn Furlong NN2 .....141 A5
Turnberry Ct NN8 .....129 C7
Turnberry La NN4 .....175 C5
Turnbrook Cl NN9 .....112 E3
Turnells Mill La NN8 ..130 A1
Turner Cl Kettering NN15 .92 A8
  Rugby CV22 ....99 B8
Turner Rd Corby NN18 ..36 E5
  Wellingborough NN8 ..129 F7
Turners Mus* NN4 ....175 D7
Turners Yd PE8 ....41 F5
Turnpike Cl LE16 ....31 D5
Turvins Mdw CV47 ....166 D8
Turweston Manor NN13 234 D6
Turweston Rd NN13 ...223 A1
Tweed Cl
  Burton Latimer NN15 ..92 B7
  Daventry NN11 ....153 A8
Tweed Rd NN5 ....158 E6
Twickenham Ct 5 NN18 .36 E5
Twigden Rd NN7 ......157 D3
Twistle The NN11 ......183 C7
Twitch Hill NN14 ......204 D8
Twyford Ave
  Raunds NN9 ....114 C7
  Twyford OX17 ....230 A6
Twyford Dr NN7 ....161 A8
Twyford Gr 7 NN7 ....161 A8
Twyford St OX17 ....230 A6
Twyford St NN7 ....161 A8
Twywell Hills & Dales Nature
  Res* NN14 ....93 F8
Tyebeck Ct NN14 ......141 B3
Tyler Way NN14 ....76 C1
Tyne Ave NN17 ....21 D1
Tymecrosse Gdns LE16 .31 D5
Tynan Cl NN15 ....92 A8
Tyne Cl NN8 ....129 C6
Tyne Rd Corby NN17 ...21 D1
  Daventry NN11 ....153 A8
  Northampton NN5 ....158 E6
Tyrell Cl MK18 ....240 C2
Tyringham Cl NN3 .....142 D1
Tyrrell Way NN12 .....203 C8
Tyson Ctyd NN18 ....37 E7

Uffington Rd PE9 ......241 F3
Uist Wlk NN17 ....21 C1
Ullswater Cl
  Higham Ferrers NN10 .132 B8
  Wellingborough NN8 ..129 C5
Ullswater Rd NN11 .....71 E2
Underbank La NN1 ....142 C6
Underwood Rd NN14 ...70 C7
Union St Banbury OX16 240 B8
  Desborough NN14 .....51 B3
  Kettering NN16 ....112 A5
  Kettering NN16 ....72 A3
  Rugby CV22 ....241 C7
Unity Cl NN29 ....146 C3
Unity St NN14 ....70 C6
Univ Coll Northampton
  NN2 ....141 D1
Univ of Buckingham
  Buckingham MK18 ...240 C2
  Buckingham MK18 ...240 E2
Univ of Leicester (Annexe)
  NN2 ....159 C8
Upland Rd NN3 ....143 B5
Upper Astrop Rd OX17 231 A5
Upper Bath St NN1 ....159 C6
Upper Cross St 10 NN1 159 C6

Upper Dane NN14 ....50 E3
Upper George St NN10 132 C7
Upper Glen Ave NN7 ..174 B2
Upper Gn NN11 ....199 D7
Upper Green Pl LE16 ...32 A6
Upper Havelock St 7
  NN8 ....130 A5
Upper High St NN7 ...157 C7
Upper Kings Ave NN10 132 C7
Upper Mounts NN1 ....159 C6
Upper Park Ave NN10 .131 F1
Upper Priory St 7 NN1 159 C7
Upper Queen St NN10 .132 C3
Upper St NN16 ....72 A2
Upper Steeping NN14 ..51 B2
Upper Thrift St NN1 ...159 F6
Upper Windsor St OX16 240 D7
Upperfield Gr NN17 .....36 E8
Uppingham Rd
  Caldecott LE16 ....9 B2
  Corby NN17 ....36 A7
  Medbourne LE16 ....16 D2
Upton Cl NN2 ....141 D6
Upton Way NN4,NN5 ..158 C3
Usher Ho NN1 ....141 C5

Vale Cl CV21 ....99 A8
Vale Mead Lower Sch
  NN3 ....143 A5
Vale St NN13 ....72 A3
Vale The NN1 ....141 F1
Valentine Way NN3 ...143 C3
Valley Cl NN13 ....234 A8
Valley Cres
  Brackley NN13 ....234 A8
  Northampton NN3 ...143 B1
Valley End NN12 ......172 D1
Valley Rd Banbury OX16 240 D6
  Brackley NN13 ....234 A8
  Buckingham MK18 ...240 F3
  Northampton NN3 ...143 B1
  Weston by W LE16 ...118 B3
Valley Rise
  Brackley NN13 ....233 F8
  Desborough NN14 .....51 B2
Valley St LE16 ....31 D5
Valley Way LE16 ....32 B4
Valley Wlk NN16 ......72 C3
Vancouver Cl NN18 ....36 A2
Vantage Mdw NN3 ....143 D3
Vara Cl NN18 ....36 A2
Varden Cl NN8 ....129 C7
Varley Cl NN8 ....129 E8
Vaughan Cl LE16 ......48 E8
Vaux Rd NN11 ....111 A1
Velbert Ho NN17 ......21 E1
Velocette Way NN11 ..140 A1
Vence Cl PE9 ....241 C3
Venture Cl NN17 ......22 F1
Verdant Vale 11 NN4 ..175 D6
Verney Cl NN18 ......240 D4
Vernier Cl NN11 ......135 A3
Vernon Ave CV22 ......98 A8
Vernon Cl NN11 ......153 A8
Vernon Ct Kettering NN16 71 F5
  10 Northampton NN1 .159 F6
Vernon Rd NN11 ......203 D5
Vernon St NN1 ....159 F6
Vernon Terr NN1 .....159 F6
Vernon Terrace Lower Sch
  NN1 ....159 F6
Verona Cl NN13 ......234 A8
Vicarage Cl
  Harlestone NN7 .....177 A3
  Northampton NN2 ...141 A3
  Weedon Bec NN7 ....129 D6
  Whittlebury NN12 ...215 C5
  Yardley Gobion NN12 217 E6
Vicarage Hill NN11 ...153 C8
Vicarage La Denton NN7 178 B8
  East Haddon NN6 ....122 D5
  Mears Ashby NN6 ...128 B2
  Northampton NN3 ...141 B3
  Priors Marston CV47 .146 B8
Vicarage Rd
  Northampton NN5 ...159 A7
  Rushden NN10 ....132 B3
  Stony Stratford MK11 229 D6
Vicarage Rise NN12 ..200 C3
Vicarage Wlk MK11 ..229 D6
Viceroy Cl NN9 ....114 C6
Vickers Cl NN14 ......70 F7
Victoria Ave
  Market Harborough LE16 32 A5
  Rugby CV21 ....241 C7
Victoria Bsns Pk NN5 .159 B6
Victoria Cl
  Earls Barton NN6 ...108 A5
  Rushden NN10 ......132 B3
  West Haddon NN6 ..102 C5
Victoria Ct Rothwell NN14 70 D7
  Rushden NN10 ......132 B3
  Woodford NN14 ......79 A3
Victoria Gdns NN1 ...159 D5
Victoria Ho NN1 .....159 C6
Victoria Inf Sch NN8 .130 B6
Victoria Jun Sch NN8 130 B6
Victoria Pk NN8 .....130 B2

Victoria Pl OX16 .....240 E8
Victoria Prom NN1 ..159 D5
Victoria Rd
  Cogenhoe NN7 ......161 E5
  Finedon NN9 ....111 F5
  Northampton NN6 ...159 E6
  Oundle PE8 ....42 A6
  Rushden NN10 ......132 B3
  Stamford PE9 ....241 B4
  Wellingborough NN8 .130 B4
Victoria Rose NN14 ..240 C3
Victoria St
  Burton Latimer NN15 92 B2
  Desborough NN14 ...51 A3
  Earls Barton NN6 ...144 F6
  Irthlingborough NN9 .112 E1
  Kettering NN16 ......72 B2
  Northampton NN1 ...159 D6
  Rugby CV21 ....241 B8
Vienne Cl NN5 ....157 F8
Viking Cl NN16 ....72 C6
Viking Way NN18 .....36 B1
Villa Gdns NN15 ......92 B1
Villa La NN9 ....113 F3
Villa Way NN4 ....175 F5
Villagers Cl NN4 ....175 E5
Vincent Cl NN5 ......157 F8
Vinco Terr PE8 ....28 D8
Vine Cl PE8 ....42 A5
Vine Hill Cl NN10 ...132 A6
Vine Hill Dr NN10 ...132 B6
Vine St PE9 ....241 E3
Vineyard Cl NN14 ...240 C9
Violet Cl OX16 ....36 D2
Violet La Creaton NN6 104 F4
  Rothwell NN14,NN16 .71 C6
Viscount Rd NN4 ....143 C6
Vivian Rd NN8 ....130 B5
Vokes Cl NN3 ....143 A1
Volunteer Cl NN4 ...175 E6
Vulcan Cl NN11 .....135 A3
Vyse Rd NN7 ....141 C8

Wadcroft 3 NN16 ....72 B2
Wadd Close La NN11 137 D6
Wade Meadow Ct NN3 142 F4
Wadenhoe La PE8 ....57 F4
Wade's Cl PE8 ....114 F1
Wadham Ct NN11 ...153 C7
Waggoners Way NN7 173 A4
Wagtail Cl NN11 ....142 C7
Waingrove NN3 .....143 B4
Wainwright Ave NN14 76 D1
Wake Way NN4 ......175 F3
Wakefield Cl NN10 ..148 A4
Wakefield Dr NN6 ....64 D5
Wakefield Rd NN2 ..141 D4
Wakefield Way NN7 .154 C4
Wakehurst Dr NN4 ..175 C7
Wakerley Great Wood Forest
  Trail* LE15 ....41 A3
Wakerley Great Wood
  Orienteering Course*
  LE15 ....41 A3
Wakerley Rd
  Barrowden LE15 ....4 A4
  Harringworth NN17 ..10 F7
Walcot Cl PE8 ....41 E7
Walcot La NN6 ......127 A8
Walcot Way PE9 ....241 A4
Walcote Rd LE17 ....63 C8
Wales St
  Kings Sutton OX17 .230 F5
  Rothwell NN14 ......70 C7
Walford Pl CV22 ....98 F8
Walgrave NN6 ....108 A5
Walgrave Prim Sch
  NN6 ....108 A5
Walgrave Rd Holcot NN6 107 E1
  Old NN6 ....108 A5
  Walgrave NN6 ....108 B4
Walk The NN6 ......124 B8
Walker Dr NN12 ....203 C8
Walker Rd NN2 .....141 C3
Walker's La 11 NN16 .72 A2
Walker's Way NN9 ..111 F4
Walkers Acre NN6 ..108 A5
Walkers Field PE8 ....72 C3
Walkers La NN6 ....140 B8
Walkers Way NN8 ..175 F5
Walks The PE9 ....1 D2
Wallace Gdns NN14 .76 E3
Wallace Rd NN2 ....141 F2
Walled Cl NN11 ....241 C4
Walledwell Ct 4 NN3 142 F1
Wallingford End 6
  NN3 ....161 A8
Wallis Cl NN8 ....129 A4
Wallis Cres NN15 ...91 C8
Wallis Rd NN15 .....91 C8
Wallwin Cl NN7 ....191 C4
Walmer Cl NN10 ...132 D1
Walnut Cl Brackley NN13 222 F1
  Braunston NN11 ....118 D2
  Clifton CV13 ....236 E4
  Culworth OX17 ....198 D2
  Silverstone NN12 ..214 D4
  Weldon NN17 ....38 B8
Walnut Cres NN10 ..72 D4
Walnut Dr OX17 ...181 D1
Walnut Gr NN3 ....143 A1
Walsingham Ave NN15 91 F8
Waltham Cl NN17 ...21 F1
Waltham Gdns OX16 219 A6

Walton Ave OX17 ...230 B5
Walton Heath Way NN2 141 E3
Walton Pl NN18 .....36 B6
Wansell Rd NN17 ...37 F8
Wansford Pl NN17 ..36 B8
Wansford Rd Elton PE8 16 E3
  Yarwell PE8 ....7 F2
Wansford Sta* PE8 ..16 E8
Wansford Wlk NN3 142 E6
Wantage Cl
  Hackleton NN7 ....177 B3
  Moulton NN3 ....126 E1
  Northampton NN2 147 B8
Wantage Rd
  Irchester NN29 ....147 B8
  Northampton NN1 160 A8
Wappenham Rd
  Abthorpe NN12 ....201 F1
  Helmdon NN13 ....212 A5
  Syresham NN13 ...213 C2
Ward Rd NN13 .....234 A5
Wardens Lodge 2
  NN11 ....135 C2
Wardington Rd OX17 208 D6
Wardle Cl NN1 ......72 B3
Wardle's Cl NN7 ...138 C7
Wardlow Cl NN4 ...174 F8
Wards La NN6 ....82 C3
Ware Orch CV23 ....99 C2
Ware Rd CV23 ....99 C2
Wareham Gn NN3 ..36 B6
Warehouse The LE16 31 D4
Wareing La NN7 ...178 B8
Warkton La NN15 ...73 B1
Warkton Way NN17 36 B8
Warkworth Rd OX17 219 E7
Warmington Sch PE8 28 B3
Warminster Cl NN14 .36 A7
Warmonds Hill NN10 132 B5
Warners Hill NN29 .164 D2
Warnham NN8 ......129 B5
Warren Bridge PE8 ..41 E5
Warren Cl
  Buckingham MK18 240 E2
  Irchester NN29 ....147 C7
Warren End
  Desborough NN14 ..51 B4
  Mawsley Village NN14 89 A4
Warren Hill NN6 ....71 E3
Warren La Bythorn PE28 97 D4
  Clopton NN14 ....78 F1
Warren Rd
  Northampton NN5 158 F7
  Stanion NN14 ....37 E3
  Wothorpe PE9 ....2 E7
  Yardley Gobion NN12 217 F6
Warren The
  Northampton NN4 175 F8
  Thorpe Mandeville OX17 210 A6
Warren St MK12 ....229 B1
Warrenne Keep PE9 241 D2
Warrens Cl NN9 ....112 F2
Warrington Rd MK46 159 F5
Warth Park Way NN4 114 B7
Wartnaby St LE16 ..31 D3
Warwick Ave NN14 .37 E3
Warwick Cl
  Daventry NN11 ....135 B1
  Kettering NN15 .....91 F8
Warwick Gdns NN14 76 F2
Warwick Prim Sch NN8 129 F7
Warwick Rd
  Banbury OX16 .....240 C8
  Banbury, Ruscote OX16 240 A9
  Hanslope MK12 ....207 A3
  Upper Boddington NN11 182 C7
  Wellingborough NN8 129 F7
Warwick St
  Daventry NN11 ....135 B1
  Rugby CV21,CV22 241 C7
Warwick Way NN11 135 C1
Warwickshire Coll CV21 241 C7
Washbrook Cl NN13 143 B1
Washbrook La NN6 143 F5
Washbrook Rd NN10 132 A3
Washingley La PE7 ..44 F6
Washington La NN14 76 E3
Washington Sq NN16 72 C3
Washington St NN2 141 C3
Washta Dr OX17 ...220 B7
Water Cl NN13 .....229 B7
Water La
  Adderbury OX17 ..230 A3
  Bradden NN12 .....201 F5
  Chacombe OX17 ..133 B8
  Cottingham LE16 ...35 D8
  Northampton NN4 159 C2
  Shutlanger NN12 ..204 D8
  Towcester NN12 ...203 C5
  Weldon NN17 ....38 A8
Water Meadow Cl NN18 36 B1
Water St Kettering NN16 72 C3
  Stamford PE9 ......241 E2
Waterfall Way LE16 ..18 F6
Waterford Rd PE18 ..31 E5
Waterloo NN11 .....135 B1
Watergate PE7 ......44 F5
Waterhouse Gdns NN15 92 A7
Watering La NN4 ...175 C3
Waterlee Furlong NN6 106 C1

Waterloo NN11 ...135 C1
Waterloo Dr CO16 ...240 E8
Waterloo Way NN11 ...131 D8
Waterlow Bridge NN9 ...111 F5
Watermeadow Dr NN3 ...142 F6
Watermill Cl NN14 ...51 D3
Waterperry Ct OX16 ...240 E8
Waterpike NN6 ...106 C2
Waterpump Ct NN3 ...142 F5
Waters La OX17 ...209 B1
Watersmeet NN1 ...160 C6
Waterworks La NN8 ...129 C7
Waterworks Way LE17 ...45 F5
Watery La Brackley NN13 ...234 A7
  Nether Heyford NN7 ...156 C2
Watford Rd Crick NN6 ...101 A2
  West Haddon NN6 ...102 B3
Watkin Cl NN11 ...123 A8
Watkin Terr NN1 ...159 D7
Watling St Kilsby CV23 ...100 A3
  Potterspury NN12 ...217 D3
Watling St E NN12 ...203 C6
Watling St W NN12 ...203 C6
Watson Ave LE16 ...48 D8
Watson Cl Oundle PE8 ...41 E7
  Wellingborough NN8 ...129 C7
Watson Rd NN6 ...121 B2
Watts Cl NN13 ...207 A3
Watts La CV21 ...99 B8
Watts Way NN6 ...121 C3
Wavell Cl NN15 ...72 E1
Waveney Cl NN11 ...153 A8
Waveney Way NN5 ...140 F1
Waver Cl NN18 ...36 D3
Waverley Ave NN17 ...37 A6
Waverley Gdns PE9 ...241 B4
Waverley Pl PE9 ...241 B4
Waverley Rd
  Kettering NN15 ...91 D8
  Northampton NN2 ...141 E1
  Rugby CV21 ...80 A1
Waynflete Ave NN13 ...233 E7
Waynflete Cl NN13 ...233 E7
Waypost Ct NN3 ...142 F3
Wayside Acres 3 NN4 ...175 B8
Weares Cl LE15 ...3 B5
Weaver Cl NN16 ...72 B6
Weavers End MK19 ...207 B2
Weavers Rd NN8 ...129 D4
Weavers Sch NN8 ...129 D4
Weavers The NN4 ...175 C6
Webb Cl Banbury OX16 ...240 E9
  Oundle PE8 ...42 B5
Webb Ellis Bsns Pk
  CV21 ...241 D9
Webb Ellis Rd CV22 ...241 A7
Webb Rd NN9 ...114 C2
Webbs Factory NN11 ...141 D1
Webbs La NN6 ...127 D3
Webster Cl NN7 ...114 D7
Weddell Way NN4 ...160 C2
Wedmore Cl NN5 ...158 D7
Wedmore Ct NN18 ...36 B6
Weedon Bec Prim Sch
  NN7 ...155 B3
Weedon La NN11 ...136 C4
Weedon Lois CE Prim Sch
  NN12 ...200 B2
Weedon Rd
  Farthingstone NN12 ...170 F3
  Kislingbury NN7 ...157 D5
  Nether Heyford NN7 ...156 B2
  Newnham NN11 ...153 C6
  Northampton NN5 ...158 D5
Weekley Glebe Rd NN16 ...72 D5
Weekley Wood La NN16 ...72 E6
Weggs Farm Rd NN5 ...139 F1
Weinaher Cl LE16 ...34 C5
Weir Cl NN8 ...129 F7
Welbeck Ct Corby NN18 ...36 C5
  Kettering NN15 ...91 F8
Welbourne Cl NN9 ...114 C6
Weldon CE Prim Sch
  NN17 ...38 A8
Weldon Cl NN8 ...129 D7
Weldon North Ind Est
  NN17 ...22 F1
Weldon Rd NN17 ...37 C7
Weldon St NN16 ...72 C3
Welford Ave NN9 ...113 B5
Welford Cl NN9 ...113 B5
Welford Gr NN17 ...36 C7
Welford Rd
  Husbands Bosworth LE17 ...45 E3
  Northampton NN4 ...141 B4
  Rugby CV21 ...241 E9
  Sibbertoft LE16 ...46 D2
  South Kilworth LE17 ...63 D7
  Spratton NN6 ...124 A8
  Thornby NN6 ...84 D4
  Welford NN6 ...64 F2
Welford Sibbertoft & Sulby
  Endowed Sch NN6 ...64 E5
Welham La LE16 ...17 E8
Welham Rd
  Great Bowden LE16 ...32 B8
  Thorpe Langton LE16 ...17 B5
  Welham LE16 ...18 A8
  Weston by W LE16 ...18 A4
Well Hill Cl NN6 ...100 F5
Well La Barnwell PE8 ...59 B7
  ...gh NN6 ...170 A8
  ...gh NN6 ...103 F6
  ...N14 ...70 D7

Well La continued
  Staverton NN11 ...152 B7
  Welton NN11 ...119 E1
Well St Buckingham MK18 ...240 D3
  Finedon NN9 ...111 F5
Well Yd NN2 ...141 B3
Welland Ave LE16 ...30 E7
Welland Cl Caldecott LE16 ...21 C8
  Daventry NN11 ...152 F8
  Gretton NN17 ...22 B8
  Raunds NN9 ...114 C7
Welland Ct
  Burton Latimer NN15 ...92 B2
  Desborough NN14 ...51 A3
  3 Market Harborough
  LE16 ...31 F2
Welland Gn NN5 ...140 F2
Welland Ind Est LE16 ...32 B4
Welland Mews PE9 ...241 E2
Welland Park Coll LE16 ...31 E2
Welland Park Rd LE16 ...31 E2
Welland Rd NN15 ...72 A5
Welland Rise ...46 F2
Welland Vale Rd LE16 ...21 E1
Welland View Rd LE16 ...20 D1
Welland Way NN14 ...141 A2
Welland Wlk NN5 ...140 F2
Wellesley Cl OX16 ...240 E8
Wellingborough Jun Sch
  NN8 ...130 B3
Wellingborough Park Jun
  Sch NN8 ...130 A5
Wellingborough Rd
  Broughton NN14 ...90 B3
  Earls Barton NN6 ...144 F6
  Finedon NN9 ...110 F4
  Great Harrowden NN9 ...110 E1
  Irthlingborough NN9 ...131 C8
  Isham NN14 ...110 F8
  Little Harrowden NN9 ...110 B3
  Mears Ashby NN6 ...128 D2
  Northampton NN3 ...142 E1
  Olney MK46 ...195 F5
  Rushden NN10 ...131 F3
  Sywell NN6 ...127 F4
  Wellingborough NN8 ...111 E1
Wellingborough Sch
  NN8 ...130 B3
Wellingborough Sta
  NN8 ...130 C5
Wellington Ave OX16 ...240 E9
Wellington Pl 10 NN1 ...159 C7
Wellington Sq NN11 ...153 C8
Wellington St
  Kettering NN16 ...72 C3
  Northampton NN1 ...159 D6
Wellington Terr NN14 ...76 B2
Wellington Wks NN16 ...72 C3
Wells Cl
  Husbands Bosworth LE17 ...45 E5
  Kettering NN15 ...90 F8
Wells Ct NN3 ...142 C8
Wells Gn NN18 ...36 B6
Wells St CV21 ...241 D8
Wells The NN9 ...111 F5
Wellspring NN7 ...190 D7
Welsh Rd
  Aston le W NN11 ...182 C8
  Chipping Warden OX17 ...197 C6
Welton CE Prim Sch
  NN11 ...119 E1
Welton La NN11 ...119 D6
Welton Pk NN11 ...119 E1
Welton Pl CV22 ...179 D8
Welton Rd
  Braunston NN11 ...118 D1
  Daventry NN11 ...135 C3
Wenlock Way NN5 ...140 D1
Wensleydale NN2 ...140 F5
Wensleydale Pk NN17 ...36 D8
Wentin Cl NN11 ...36 C1
Wentworth Ave NN9 ...129 C7
Wentworth Cl NN11 ...135 E2
Wentworth Cotts MK18 ...227 A5
Wentworth Dr PE8 ...41 E7
Wentworth Rd
  Finedon NN9 ...112 A5
  Rugby CV22 ...241 B6
  Rushden NN10 ...132 A2
Wentworth Way
  Northampton NN2 ...141 E3
  Stoke Bruerne NN12 ...204 F8
Weskers Cl LE16 ...17 E4
Wesley Ct NN9 ...114 C6
Wesley Dr OX16 ...240 B6
Wesley Pl OX17 ...208 E4
Wesley Rd CV21 ...99 A8
Wessex Cl NN16 ...72 B4
Wessex Way NN14 ...142 B1
West Ave NN15 ...92 B3
West Bank NN15 ...142 E6
West Bar St OX16 ...240 C7
West Brook
  Blisworth NN7 ...190 D8
  Newnham NN11 ...153 D4
West Cres NN10 ...131 E2
West Ct NN11 ...135 C1
West End Bugbrooke NN7 ...172 E7
  Scaldwell NN6 ...108 E5
  Silverstone NN12 ...214 C4
  Welford NN6 ...64 D4
  West Haddon NN6 ...102 B4
West Farm Cl NN6 ...108 C3
West Farm Ct NN6 ...108 C3
West Furlong NN6 ...73 F1
West Glebe Rd NN17 ...36 F7
West Haddon Prim Sch
  NN6 ...102 B4

West Haddon Rd
  Cold Ashby NN6 ...84 A5
  Crick NN6 ...101 B6
  Guilsborough NN6 ...103 D7
  Ravensthorpe NN6 ...103 D7
  Watford NN6 ...120 D7
West Leyes CV21 ...241 C8
West Leys Ct NN3 ...142 C7
West Lodge Farm Rural Ctr*
  NN14 ...51 C6
West March NN11 ...153 D7
West Mill PE9 ...1 F4
West Oval NN15 ...140 F1
West Paddock Ct NN3 ...142 F4
West Priors Ct NN3 ...143 A4
West Ridge NN2 ...141 D3
West Rising NN4 ...175 D7
West Side Rise MK46 ...195 F4
West St Banbury OX16 ...240 E9
  Broughton NN14 ...90 A5
  Buckingham MK18 ...240 E4
  Earls Barton NN6 ...144 E4
  Easton o t H PE9 ...2 A5
  Ecton NN6 ...143 F4
  Geddington NN14 ...54 A3
  Kettering NN16 ...72 B1
  King's Cliffe PE8 ...13 E7
  Long Buckby NN6 ...121 A4
  Moulton NN3 ...126 C1
  Northampton NN6 ...159 F6
  Olney MK46 ...195 F4
  Oundle PE8 ...41 F5
  Raunds NN9 ...114 D6
  Rushden NN10 ...132 B2
  Stamford PE9 ...241 C3
  Stanwick NN9 ...113 A3
  Weedon NN7 ...155 B3
  Welford NN6 ...64 E6
  Wellingborough NN8 ...129 F4
West Street Gdns PE9 ...241 C3
West View Corby NN17 ...37 B7
  Daventry NN11 ...135 B1
West View Rd CV22 ...241 A7
West Villa Rd NN8 ...129 F4
West Way
  Earls Barton NN6 ...144 D5
  Weedon NN7 ...155 B3
Westbeech Ct OX16 ...240 C7
Westbourne Gr CV22 ...241 B6
Westbrook NN8 ...129 B4
Westburgh Sq NN11 ...153 C8
Westbury Cl NN5 ...158 D7
Westbury Wlk NN8 ...36 B6
Westcott Way Corby NN18 ...36 D5
  Northampton NN5 ...160 E7
Westerdale NN2 ...140 F5
Western Ave
  Buckingham MK18 ...240 C4
  Daventry NN11 ...153 B8
  Easton o t H PE9 ...1 F5
  Nether Harborough LE16 ...31 D1
Western Cl NN11 ...135 B2
Western Cres LE16 ...240 E6
Western Dr MK19 ...207 A3
Western Terr NN11 ...135 B2
Western Way NN10 ...132 D3
Westfield Ave
  Deanshanger MK19 ...228 D5
  Raunds NN9 ...114 B4
Westfield Barns CV47 ...166 D7
Westfield Cl LE16 ...31 C3
Westfield Cres NN6 ...64 E6
Westfield Ctr NN13 ...233 E8
Westfield Dr NN9 ...114 B4
Westfield Fst Sch OX12 ...82 B2
Westfield Pl NN10 ...131 F2
Westfield Rd
  Northampton NN5 ...158 F6
  Northampton, Duston NN5 ...158 B8
  Rugby CV22 ...241 B7
  Wellingborough NN8 ...129 E4
Westfields
  Buckingham MK18 ...240 C3
  Easton o t H PE9 ...1 F5
  Little Harrowden NN9 ...110 B3
  Wellingborough NN8 ...130 D3
Westfields Ave NN10 ...132 B5
Westfields Rd NN17 ...36 E8
Westfields Terr NN10 ...132 B5
Westgate La NN11 ...183 C7
Westgate St NN6 ...30 E3
Westgate Rd NN5 ...158 D6
Westhaven PE9 ...2 A5
Westhill Ave NN13 ...233 E7
Westhill Cl
  Brackley NN13 ...233 E7
  Kettering NN15 ...71 F1
Westhill Dr NN15 ...71 F1
Westhill Gdns NN13 ...233 D7
Westhorp OX17 ...210 D2
Westhorpe Ashley LE16 ...18 E2
  Sibbertoft LE16 ...46 F2
Westhorpe La NN11 ...183 C7
Westhorpe Mews NN13 ...183 C6
Westland Cl LE16 ...30 E3
Westleigh Cl NN11 ...159 F8
Westleigh Pk NN3 ...141 E6
Westleigh Rd NN15 ...92 B8
Westmead Cl NN3 ...142 F1
Westminster Cl NN13 ...234 A7
Westminster Cres NN13 ...234 A7
Westminster Croft
  NN13 ...233 F7

Westminster Dr NN15 ...91 F7
Westminster Rd
  Brackley NN13 ...233 F6
  Wellingborough NN8 ...129 E7
Westminster Way CV22 ...241 A7
Westminster Wlk NN18 ...36 C4
Westmoreland Cl PE8 ...15 E5
Westmorland Terr NN1 ...51 C4
Weston Favell CE Lower Sch
  NN3 ...160 D8
Weston Favell Ctr NN3 ...142 F2
Weston Favell Upper Sch
  NN3 ...142 D3
Weston Mill La NN3 ...160 E6
Weston Rd Ashley LE16 ...18 D3
  Olney MK46 ...195 D5
  Ravenstone NN6 ...194 E2
  Sulgrave OX17 ...211 A8
  Sutton Bassett LE16 ...18 A2
  Welham LE16 ...17 F5
Weston Way NN3 ...160 C8
Weston Wlk NN18 ...36 C6
Westone Ave NN3 ...142 E1
Westonville PE9 ...1 D2
Westover Rd NN15 ...71 F1
Westvilla Cotts NN8 ...129 F4
Westway Kettering NN15 ...71 F1
  Rugby CV22 ...241 C8
Westway The NN11 ...153 D8
Westwood Rd CV22 ...98 F7
Westwood Wlk NN18 ...36 C5
Wetenhall Rd NN9 ...114 A4
Wetheral Cl NN3 ...142 C4
Weymouth Cl NN18 ...36 B6
Whaddon Cl NN14 ...158 E1
Whaddon Field NN6 ...108 C8
Whalley Gr NN7 ...161 F6
Wharf Cl MK19 ...229 B7
Wharf La
  Old Stratford MK19 ...229 C7
  Souldern OX27 ...237 B4
Wharf Rd
  Higham Ferrers NN10 ...132 B6
  Stamford PE9 ...241 E3
Wharf View NN8 ...240 E4
Wharfe Gn NN5 ...140 F2
Wharfedale Rd NN17 ...21 E1
Wharfside NN8 ...240 D4
Wharton Cl NN8 ...129 F5
Wheat Cl NN11 ...135 C6
Wheatcroft Gdns NN10 ...132 C2
Wheatens Cl NN6 ...125 E5
Wheatfield Dr NN15 ...92 C2
Wheatfield Rd NN3 ...142 B1
Wheatfield Rd N NN3 ...142 B2
Wheatfield Rd S NN3 ...142 B1
Wheatfield Terr NN3 ...142 B1
Wheatley Ave NN7 ...36 F6
Wheel La NN15 ...3 F5
Wheeler's Rise NN13 ...238 C8
Wheelwright Cl NN9 ...114 E7
Wheelwright Ho NN47 ...70 D7
Wheelwrights Way
  MK19 ...229 C7
Wheelwrights Yd NN29 ...164 D2
Wherside Way NN5 ...158 C8
Whilton Rd
  Great Brington NN7 ...138 C7
  Northampton NN7 ...141 D4
Whistlefield Cotts NN6 ...143 A7
Whistlers Cl NN14 ...158 D1
Whiston Rd
  Cogenhoe NN7 ...162 C6
  Denton NN7 ...162 B2
  Northampton NN7 ...141 D4
Whitby Cl NN15 ...91 F6
White Cotts MK18 ...226 D4
White Delves NN8 ...129 E7
White Doe Dr NN3 ...142 C7
White Hills Cres NN2 ...141 B6
White Hills Way NN2 ...141 B6
White House Cl NN10 ...132 B5
White House Ind Est
  NN6 ...144 D6
White Lion Wlk OX16 ...240 C8
White Post Ct NN17 ...21 F1
White Way NN6 ...144 E5
Whitecroft Gdns NN11 ...184 B7
Whitefield Rd NN5 ...140 C1
Whitefield Way NN6 ...124 C7
Whiteford Dr NN15 ...91 C7
Whitefield Way NN12 ...41 A2
Whitemees Cl MK46 ...195 E4
Whitmore Cl NN12 ...214 D5
Whitney Rd NN15 ...92 B1
Whitsundale Cl NN9 ...111 F8
Whittall St OX17 ...230 F5
Whittam Cl NN4 ...114 C7
Whittemore Rd NN10 ...132 D3
Whittle Cl Daventry NN11 ...135 A5

Whittle Cl continued
  Wellingborough NN8 ...129 B6
Whittle Rd NN17 ...37 B8
Whittlebury CE Prim Sch
  NN12 ...215 C4
Whittlebury Cl NN2 ...141 D5
Whittlebury Ct NN11 ...215 C5
Whittlebury Rd NN12 ...214 E5
Whittles Cross NN4 ...176 A6
Whittlesea Terr NN14 ...94 D6
Whitton Cl NN17 ...91 D2
Whittons La NN12 ...203 C6
Whitwell Cl PE8 ...41 E5
Whitworth Ave NN17 ...37 A8
Whitworth Cres NN6 ...144 E5
Whitworth Rd
  Northampton NN1 ...159 F7
  Wellingborough NN8 ...130 C5
Whitworth Way
  Irthlingborough NN9 ...131 E8
  Northampton NN9 ...130 B2
Whytewell Rd NN8 ...129 F6
Wick Cl NN18 ...36 C3
Wicken Park Rd MK19 ...228 B1
Wicken Rd MK18 ...227 E1
Wickery Dene NN4 ...176 A6
Wicksteed Cl NN15 ...91 C6
Wicksteed L Pk* NN15 ...91 C6
Wigston Rd 3 CV21 ...80 A1
Wilbarston CE Prim Sch
  LE16 ...34 C5
Wilbarston Rd LE16 ...34 B4
Wilberforce St 3 NN1 ...159 E6
Wilby CE Prim Sch NN8 ...129 B1
Wilby Cl NN17 ...36 B8
Wilby La NN29 ...145 D6
Wilby Rd NN6 ...128 D2
Wilby St NN1 ...159 F6
Wilby Way NN8 ...129 D1
Wilbye Grange NN8 ...129 D2
Wild Cherry Cl NN11 ...184 B6
Wildacre Rd NN10 ...132 C3
Wildern La NN4 ...175 C5
Wilford Ave NN3 ...160 F8
Wilkie Cl NN15 ...90 F8
Willetts Cl NN17 ...36 E8
Willey Cl MK11 ...229 F4
William Rd NN6 ...121 B3
William St
  Burton Latimer NN15 ...92 B2
  Finedon NN9 ...112 A4
  Kettering NN16 ...72 B4
  Northampton NN1 ...159 D7
  Rugby CV21 ...241 D8
William Steele Way
  NN10 ...132 C5
William Trigg Cl NN9 ...131 C8
William's Way NN29 ...146 E1
Williams Cl NN13 ...206 F3
Williams Terr NN11 ...135 B2
Williams Way NN10 ...132 B5
Williamscot Hill OX17 ...208 B6
Willis Way NN12 ...203 C5
Williton Cl NN3 ...160 D7
Willoughby Cl NN11 ...135 B3
Willoughby Pl CV22 ...98 D7
Willow Brook Rd NN17 ...36 C8
Willow Brook Sq NN3 ...143 D2
Willow Cl
  Desborough NN14 ...51 C3
  Hinton NN11 ...184 A6
  Spratton NN6 ...124 A8
  Towcester NN12 ...203 C3
Willow Cres
  Great Houghton NN4 ...160 F2
  Market Harborough LE16 ...31 C2
Willow Ct NN4 ...160 A7
Willow Dr MK18 ...240 F2
Willow Gr MK19 ...229 B6
Willow Herb Cl NN14 ...148 C7
Willow La
  Great Houghton NN4 ...160 E2
  King's Cliffe PE8 ...13 F7
  Stanion NN14 ...37 D7
  Stony Stratford MK11 ...229 C5
Willow Rd Brackley NN13 ...234 A6
  Kettering NN15 ...72 C1
Willow Rise NN11 ...161 B8
Willow Tree Gdns NN12 ...99 A8
Willow View NN7 ...157 E2
Willowbrook East Ind Est
  NN17 ...22 C2
Willows Hill NN12 ...201 F5
Willows The
  Daventry NN11 ...135 C3
  King's Sutton OX17 ...231 A6
  Little Harrowden NN9 ...110 B3
  Silverstone NN12 ...214 C5
Wills Cl NN6 ...103 E7
Wilson Cl LE14 ...52 A8
Wilmington Wlk 1 NN18 ...36 B5
Wilson Cl NN11 ...135 A4
Wilson Cres NN9 ...112 C1
Wilson Ct NN9 ...132 A2
Wilson Way NN6 ...144 E3
Wilson Cl NN14 ...51 A2
Wilton Cl NN15 ...91 F8
Wimbledon St NN5 ...159 A6
Wimborne Ave OX16 ...240 B8
Wimborne Cl NN15 ...143 D3
Wimborne Pl NN11 ...135 C6
Wimborne Wlk NN18 ...36 A7
Wimpole Cl NN8 ...129 C4

Any feature in this atlas can be given a unique reference to help you find the same feature on other Ordnance Survey maps of the area, or to help someone else locate you if they do not have a Street Atlas.

The grid squares in this atlas match the Ordnance Survey National Grid and are at 500 metre intervals. The small figures at the bottom and sides of every other grid line are the National Grid kilometre values (**00** to **99** km) and are repeated across the country every 100 km (see left).

To give a unique National Grid reference you need to locate where in the country you are. The country is divided into 100 km squares with each square given a unique two-letter reference. Use the administrative map to determine in which 100 km square a particular page of this atlas falls.

The bold letters and numbers between each grid line (**A** to **F**, **1** to **8**) are for use within a specific Street Atlas only, and when used with the page number, are a convenient way of referencing these grid squares.

Example   The railway bridge over DARLEY GREEN RD in grid square B1

Step 1: Identify the two-letter reference, in this example the page is in **SP**

Step 2: Identify the 1 km square in which the railway bridge falls. Use the figures in the southwest corner of this square: Eastings **17**, Northings **74**. This gives a unique reference: **SP 17 74**, accurate to 1 km.

Step 3: To give a more precise reference accurate to 100 m you need to estimate how many tenths along and how many tenths up this 1 km square the feature is (to help with this the 1 km square is divided into four 500 m squares). This makes the bridge about **8** tenths along and about **1** tenth up from the southwest corner.

This gives a unique reference: **SP 178 741**, accurate to 100 m.

Eastings (read from left to right along the bottom) come before Northings (read from bottom to top). If you have trouble remembering say to yourself "Along the hall, THEN up the stairs"!

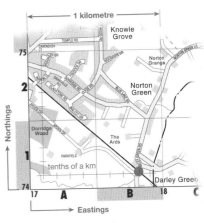

Addresses

Name and Address	Telephone	Page	Grid reference

Name and Address	Telephone	Page	Grid reference